Learn iPhone and iPad cocos2d Game Development

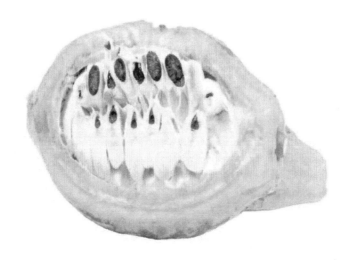

Steffen Itterheim

Apress®

Learn iPhone and iPad cocos2d Game Development

ISBN-13 (pbk): 978-1-4302-3303-9

ISBN-13 (electronic): 978-1-4302-3304-6

Trademarked names, logos, and images may appear in this book. Rather than use a trademark symbol with every occurrence of a trademarked name, logo, or image we use the names, logos, and images only in an editorial fashion and to the benefit of the trademark owner, with no intention of infringement of the trademark.

The use in this publication of trade names, trademarks, service marks, and similar terms, even if they are not identified as such, is not to be taken as an expression of opinion as to whether or not they are subject to proprietary rights.

President and Publisher: Paul Manning
Lead Editor: Clay Andres
Development Editor: Brian MacDonald
Technical Reviewer: Boon Chew
Editorial Board: Steve Anglin, Mark Beckner, Ewan Buckingham, Gary Cornell, Jonathan Gennick, Jonathan Hassell, Michelle Lowman, Matthew Moodie, Duncan Parkes, Jeffrey Pepper, Frank Pohlmann, Douglas Pundick, Ben Renow-Clarke, Dominic Shakeshaft, Matt Wade, Tom Welsh
Coordinating Editor: Kelly Moritz
Copy Editors: Sharon Terdeman and Damon Larson
Compositor: MacPS, LLC
Indexer: John Collin
Artist: April Milne
Cover Designer: Anna Ishchenko

Distributed to the book trade worldwide by Springer Science+Business Media, LLC., 233 Spring Street, 6th Floor, New York, NY 10013. Phone 1-800-SPRINGER, fax (201) 348-4505, e-mail orders-ny@springer-sbm.com, or visit www.springeronline.com.

For information on translations, please e-mail rights@apress.com, or visit www.apress.com.

Apress and friends of ED books may be purchased in bulk for academic, corporate, or promotional use. eBook versions and licenses are also available for most titles. For more information, reference our Special Bulk Sales–eBook Licensing web page at www.apress.com/info/bulksales.

The information in this book is distributed on an "as is" basis, without warranty. Although every precaution has been taken in the preparation of this work, neither the author(s) nor Apress shall have any liability to any person or entity with respect to any loss or damage caused or alleged to be caused directly or indirectly by the information contained in this work.

The source code for this book is available to readers at www.apress.com.

To Gabi, the one and only space ant.
Sometimes alien, often antsy, always loved.

Contents at a Glance

Contents

Chapter 4: Your First Game 65

Chapter 5: Game Building Blocks 93

Chapter 6: Sprites In-Depth 117

About the Author

Steffen Itterheim has been a game development enthusiast since the early 1990s. His work in the Doom and Duke Nukem 3D communities landed him his first freelance job as beta tester for 3D Realms. He has been a professional game developer for well over ten years, having worked most of his career as a game play and tools programmer for Electronic Arts Phenomic. His first contact with cocos2d was in 2009, when he cofounded an aspiring iOS games startup company called Fun Armada. He loves to teach and enable other game developers so that they can work smarter, not harder. Occasionally you'll find him strolling around in the lush vineyards near his domicile at daytime, and the desert of Nevada at night, collecting bottle caps.

About the Technical Reviewer

 **Boon Chew** is the managing director for Nanaimo Studio, a game studio based out of Seattle and Shanghai that specializes in web and mobile games. He has extensive experience with game development and interactive media, having previously worked for companies such as Vivendi Universal, Amazon, Microsoft, and various game studios and advertising agencies. His passion is in building things and working with great people. You can reach Boon at boon@nanaimostudio.com.

Acknowledgments

This is the part of the book that make me a little anxious. I don't want to forget anyone who has been instrumental and helpful in creating this book, yet I know I can't mention each and every one of you. If you're not mentioned here, that doesn't mean I'm not thankful for your contribution! Give me a pen and I'll scribble your name right here in your copy of the book, and I'll sincerely apologize for not having mentioned you here in the first place.

My first thanks go to you, dear reader. Without you, this book wouldn't make any sense. Without knowing that you might read and enjoy this book, and hopefully learn from it, I probably wouldn't even have considered writing it in the first place. I've received valuable insights and requests from my blog readers and other people I've met or mailed during the course of this book. Thank you all!

Now follow the people who helped get this book written, in the order I met them.

My first thanks go to Jack Nutting, who put the idea of writing a book on cocos2d in my head in the first place. I'm grateful that he did not sugarcoat how much work goes into writing a book, so I wasn't unprepared.

Clay Andres I have to thank for being such a kind person, whose input on my chapter proposals were invaluable and to the point. He helped me form the idea of what the book was to become, and he's generally a delightful person to talk to. Clay, I hope that storm did not flood your house.

Many thanks to Kelly Moritz, the coordinating editor, who though incredibly busy always found the time and patience to answer my questions and follow up on my requests. When chaos ensued, she was the one to put everything back in order and made it happen.

Lots and lots of feedback and suggestions I received from Brian MacDonald, the development editor for the book, and Boon Chew, the technical reviewer. They made me go to even greater lengths. Brian helped me understand many of the intricacies of writing a book while Boon pointed out a lot of technical inaccuracies and additional explanations needed. Many thanks to both of you.

Many thanks go to the copy editors, Sharon Terdeman and Damon Larson. Without you, the book's text would be rife with syntax errors and compiler warnings, to put it in programmer's terms. Sharon, when you said that my chapters are always easy work, I actually didn't believe you even though I know you're the expert. And Damon, thanks for putting on the reader's hat and suggesting all those confusing paragraphs to be rephrased.

I also wish to thank Bernie Watkins, who managed the Alpha Book feedback and my contracts. Thanks also to Chris Guillebeau for being an outstanding inspirational blogger and role model.

Of course my friends and family all took some part in writing this book, through both feedback and plain-and-simple patience with putting up with my writing spree. Thank you!

Preface

In May 2009 I made first contact. For the first time in my life, I was subjected to the Mac OS platform and started learning Xcode, Objective-C, and cocos2d. Even for an experienced developer, it was a struggle. It was at that time that I realized that cocos2d was good, but it lacked documentation, tutorials, and how-to articles—especially when compared with the other technologies I was learning at the time.

Fast forward a year to May 2010. I had completed four cocos2d projects. My Objective-C and cocos2d had become fluent. It pained me to see how other developers were still struggling with the same basic issues and were falling victim to the same misconceptions that I did about a year earlier. The cocos2d documentation was still severely lacking.

I knew that other developers using cocos2d were having great success attracting readers to their blogs by writing tutorials and sharing what they know about cocos2d. To date, most of the cocos2d documentation is actively being created in a decentralized fashion by other developers. I saw a need for a web site to channel all of the information that's spread over so many different web sites.

I created the `www.learn-cocos2d.com` web site to share what I knew about cocos2d and game development, to write tutorials and FAQs, and to redirect readers interested in cocos2d to all the important sources of information. In turn, I would be selling cocos2d-related products, hoping it might one day bring me close to the ultimate goal of becoming financially independent. The business model has been proven to work by many shining examples. And I enjoy helping others, having been the go-to guy in all companies I've worked for. I knew I could make the web site a win for everyone. I was excited.

From day one, the web site was a success—beyond my wildest imaginations. Then, within 24 hours of taking the web site live, Jack Nutting asked me if I had considered writing a cocos2d book. The rest is history, and the result is the book you're reading right now.

I took everything I had in mind for the web site and put it in the book. But that alone would have amounted to maybe a quarter of the book, at most. I hope the four months I spent writing the book full-time paid off by being able to provide an unprecedented level of detail on how cocos2d works, and how to work with cocos2d.

I learned a lot in the process, including a lot of things I didn't even expect not to know, weird as that may sound. And I wish nothing more than for you to learn a great deal about cocos2d and game development from this book.

Chapter 1

Introduction

Did you ever imagine yourself writing a computer game and being able to make money selling it? With Apple's iTunes App Store and the accompanying mobile devices iPhone, iPod Touch, and iPad, it's now easier than ever. Of course, that doesn't mean that it's easy—there's still a lot to learn about game development and programming games. But you are reading this book, so I believe you've already made up your mind to take this journey. And you've chosen one of the most interesting game engines to work with: cocos2d for iPhone.

Developers using cocos2d have a huge variety of backgrounds. Some, like me, have been professional game developers for years and even decades. Others are just starting to learn programming for iOS devices or are freshly venturing into the exciting field of game development. Whatever your background might be, I'm sure you'll get something out of this book.

There's one thing that unites all cocos2d developers: we love games, and we love creating and programming them. This book will pay homage to that, yet won't forget about the tools that will help ease the development process. Most of all, you'll be making games that matter along the way, and you'll see how this knowledge is applied in real game development.

You see, I get bored by books that spend all their pages teaching me how to make yet another dull Asteroids clone using some specific game-programming API. What's more important, I think, are game programming concepts and tools, the things you take with you even as APIs or your personal programming preferences change. I've literally amassed hundreds of programming and game development books over 20 years. The books I value the most to this day are those who went beyond the technology and taught me why certain things are designed and programmed the way they are. This book will focus not just on working game code but also why it works and which tradeoffs to consider.

I would like you to learn how to write games that matter, games that are popular on the App Store and relevant to players. I'll walk you through the ideas and technical concepts behind these games in this book, and, of course, how cocos2d and Objective-C make these games tick. You'll find that the source code that comes with the book is enriched with a lot of comments, which should help you navigate and understand all the nooks and crannies of the code.

Learning from someone else's source code with a guide to help focus on what's important is what works best for me whenever I'm learning something new—and I like to think it will work great for you too. And since you can base your own games on the book's source code, I'm looking forward to playing your games in the near future! Don't forget to let me know about them! You can reach me at steffen@learn-cocos2d.com or visit my website dedicated to learning cocos2d at www.learn-cocos2d.com.

Why Use cocos2d for iPhone?

When game developers look for a game engine, they first evaluate their options. I think cocos2d is a great choice for a lot of developers, for many reasons.

It's Free

First of all, it is free. It doesn't cost you a dime to work with it. You are allowed to create both free and commercial iPhone, iPod, and iPad Apps. You don't have to pay royalties either. Seriously, no strings attached.

Since cocos2d is basically a one-man product created by Ricardo Quesada you might want to consider making a donation to help further development of cocos2d, or consider buying one of his commercial source code projects. Both donations and projects are available on the cocos2d Store web site: http://www.cocos2d-iphone.org/store.

It's Open Source

The next good reason to use cocos2d is that it's open source. This means there's no black box preventing you from learning from the game engine code, or making changes to it where necessary. You can download cocos2d from www.cocos2d-iphone.org/download.

It's Objective, See?

Furthermore, the code is written in Objective-C, Apple's native programming language for writing iPhone Apps. It's the same language used by the iPhone SDK, which makes it easier to understand Apple's documentation and implement iPhone SDK functionality.

A lot of other useful APIs like Facebook Connect and OpenFeint are also written in Objective-C, so it makes it easier to integrate those, too.

NOTE: Learning Objective-C is advised, even if you prefer some other language. I have a strong C++ and C# background and the Objective-C syntax looked very odd at first glance. I wasn't happy at the prospect of learning a new programming language that was said to be old and outdated. Not surprisingly, I struggled for a while to get the hang of writing code in a programming language that required me to let go of old habits and expectations.

Don't let the thought of programming with Objective-C distract you, though. It does require some getting used to, but it pays off soon enough, if only for the sheer amount of documentation available. I promise you won't look back!

It's 2D

Of course, cocos2d carries the 2D in its name for a reason. It focuses on helping you create 2D games. It's a specialization few other iOS game engines are currently offering. It does not prevent you from loading and displaying 3D objects, but you do need to write your own 3D rendering code or refer to other solutions to load and display 3D models. But I'm going to say that the iOS devices are an ideal platform for great 2D games. They're generally easier to develop and easier to understand, too. And in many cases, they are less demanding on the hardware, allowing you to create more vibrant, more detailed graphics.

It's Got Physics

There are also two physics engines you can choose from that are already integrated with cocos2d. On one hand there's Chipmunk and on the other there's Box2d. Both physics engines superficially differ only in the language they're written in: Chipmunk is written in C, Box2d is written in C++. The feature set is almost the same. If you're looking for differences, you'll find some, but it requires a good understanding of how physics engines work to base your choice on the differences. In general, you should simply choose the physics engine you think is easier to understand and better documented, and for most developers that tends to be Box2d. Plus, its object-oriented nature makes it a little easier to use with Objective-C.

It's Less Technical

What game developers enjoy most about cocos2d is how it hides the low-level OpenGL ES code. Most of the graphics are drawn using simple Sprite classes that are created from image files. In other words, a Sprite is a texture that can have scaling, rotation, and color applied to it by simply changing the appropriate Objective-C properties of the CCSprite class. You don't have to be concerned about how this is implemented using OpenGL ES code, which is a good thing.

At the same time, cocos2d gives you the flexibility to add your own OpenGL ES code at any time for any game object that needs it. And if you're thinking about adding some Cocoa Touch user interface elements, you'll appreciate knowing that these can be mixed in as well.

And cocos2d doesn't just shield you from the Open GL ES intricacies; it also provides high-level abstraction of commonly performed tasks, some of which may require extensive knowledge of the iPhone SDK. But if you need more low-level access, cocos2d won't hold you back.

It's Still Programming

In general, you could say that cocos2d makes programming iOS games simpler while still truly requiring excellent programming skills first and foremost. Other iOS game engines like Unity, iTorque, and Shiva focus their efforts on providing toolsets and workflows to reduce the amount of programming knowledge required. In turn, you give away some technical freedom—and cash too. With cocos2d, you have to put in a little extra effort but you're as close to the core of game programming as possible, without having to actually deal with the core.

It's Got a Great Community

The cocos2d community always has someone quick to answer a question, and developers are generally open to sharing knowledge and information.

New tutorials and sample source code are released on an almost daily basis, most of it for free. And you'll find scattered over the Internet plenty of resources to learn from and get inspired by.

Once your game is complete and released on the App Store, you can even promote it on the cocos2d web site. At the very least, you'll get the attention of fellow developers, and hopefully valuable feedback.

> **NOTE:** To stay up to date with what's happening in the cocos2d community, I recommend following cocos2d on Twitter: `http://twitter.com/cocos2d`.
>
> While you're at it, you might want to follow me as well: `http://twitter.com/ gaminghorror`.
>
> Next, enter "cocos2d" in Twitter's search box and then click the "Save this search" link. That way you can regularly check for new posts about cocos2d with a single click. More often than not, you'll come across useful cocos2d-related information that would otherwise have passed you by. And you'll definitely get to know your fellow developers who are also working with cocos2d.

Important cocos2d Tidbits

There are two things I feel are important to cocos2d developers so I'd like to mention them here right away.

Section 3.3.1

While it may sound like a certain secret government organization in the Star Trek Universe, Section 3.3.1 actually is a section of Apple's Developer License Agreement. It has become synonymous with a certain change in policy with the release of the iPhone SDK 4. The policy more or less restricts iOS developers to the use of the Objective-C, C, C++, and JavaScript programming languages. This change to limit iOS development to specific programming languages has generated a great amount of discussion and worry among iOS developers.

Since cocos2d is written entirely in Objective-C, and external libraries like the physics engines Chipmunk and Box2d are written in C and C++ respectively, while targeting the iPhone SDK directly and not making use of any private APIs, it's fair to say that cocos2d developers should not need to worry at all. Games and apps made with cocos2d will not be rejected by Apple on the basis of Section 3.3.1.

The general consensus is that the change in Apple's policy regarding use of languages and disallowing "intermediate layers" is primarily to prevent applications and games written in Adobe Flash from gaining a foothold in the iOS market.

Porting to Other Platforms

You may have noticed that cocos2d ports exist for various platforms, including Windows and Android. They share the same name and development philosophy, but are written in different languages by different authors and have no affiliation with cocos2d for iPhone. For example, the Android cocos2d port is written in Java, which is the native language when developing for Android devices.

If you're interested in porting your games to other platforms, you should know that the various cocos2d game engines differ a lot. Porting your game to, for example, Android isn't an easy task. First there's the language barrier—all your Objective-C code must be rewritten in Java. When that's done, you still need to make a lot of modifications to cope with numerous changes in the cocos2d API or possibly unsupported features of the port or the target platform. Finally, every port can have its own kind of bugs, and every platform has its own technical limitations and challenges.

Overall, porting iOS games written with cocos2d to other platforms that also have a cocos2d game engine entails almost the same effort as rewriting the game for the target platform using some other game engine. This means there's no switch you can flip and it'll work. The similarity of the cocos2d engines across various platforms is in name and philosophy only.

This Book Is for You

I'd like to imagine you picked this book because its title caught your interest. I suppose you want to make 2D games for the iPhone and iPad, and the game engine of your choice is cocos2d for iPhone. Or maybe you don't care so much about the game engine but you do want to make 2D games for the iOS devices in general. Maybe you're looking for some in-depth discussion on cocos2d, since you've been using it for a while already. Whatever your reasons for choosing this book, I'm sure you'll get a lot out it.

Prerequisites

As with every programming book, there are some prerequisites that are nice to have, and some that are almost mandatory.

Programming Experience

The only thing that's mandatory for this book is some degree of programming experience, so let's get that out of the way first. You should have an understanding of programming concepts like loops, functions, classes, and so forth. If you have written a computer program before, preferably using an object-oriented programming language, you should be fine.

Still with me? Good.

Objective-C

So you do have programming experience, but maybe you've never written anything in that obscure language called Objective-C.

You don't need to know Objective-C for this book, but it definitely helps to know the language basics. If you are already familiar with at least one other object-oriented programming language, such as C++, C#, or Java, you may be able to pick it up as you go. But to be honest, I found it hard to do that myself even after roughly 15 years of programming experience with C++, C#, and various scripting languages. There are always those small, bothersome questions about tiny things you just don't get right away, and they tend to steal your attention away. In that case, it's handy to have a resource you can refer to whenever there's something you need to understand about Objective-C.

I had one invaluable Objective-C book to learn from, and I recommend it wholeheartedly as companion book in case you want to learn more about Objective-C and Xcode. It's called *Learn Objective-C on the Mac* by Mark Dalrymple and Scott Knaster, published by Apress.

There is also Apple's "Introduction to the Objective-C Programming Language," which proved valuable as an online reference. It's available here:

```
http://developer.apple.com/mac/library/DOCUMENTATION/Cocoa/Conceptual/Objective
C/Introduction/introObjectiveC.html
```

Objective-C may seem scary with its square brackets, and you may have picked up some horror stories about its memory management and how there's no garbage collection on the iPhone. Worry not.

First of all, Objective-C is just a different set of clothes. It looks unfamiliar but the underlying programming concepts like loops, classes, inheritance, and function calls still work in the same way as in other programming languages. The terminology might be different, for example: what Objective-C developers call sending messages is in essence the same as calling a method. As for memory management, let's just say cocos2d makes it as easy for you as possible, and I'll help you understand the very simple and basic rules you can follow.

What You Will Learn

I will provide you with a fair share of my game development experiences to show how interactive games are made. I believe that learning to program is not at all about memorizing API methods, yet a lot of game development books I've read over the past two decades follow that "reference handbook" approach. But that's what the API documentation is for. When I started programming some 20 years ago, I thought I'd never learn to program just by looking at a huge stack of compiler reference handbooks and manuals. Back at that time, compiler manuals were still printed and, obviously, didn't come with online versions. The World Wide Web was still in its infancy. So all that information was stacked some 15 inches high on my desk and it seemed very daunting to try to learn all of this.

Today, I still don't recall most methods and APIs from memory, and I keep forgetting about those I used to know. I look them up time and time again. After 20 years of programming, I do know what's really important to learn: the concepts. Good programming concepts and best practices stick around for a long time, and they help with programming in any language. Learning concepts is done best by understanding the rationale behind the choices that were made in designing, structuring, and writing the source code. That's what I'll focus on the most.

What Beginning iOS Game Developers Will Learn

But don't worry—I'll also ease you into the most important aspects of cocos2d. I'll focus on the kind of classes, methods, and concepts that you should be able to recall from memory just because they are so fundamental to programming with cocos2d.

You'll also learn about the essential tools supporting or being supported by cocos2d. Without these tools, you'd be only half the cocos2d programmer you can be. You'll use tools like Zwoptex and ParticleDesigner to create games that will be increasingly complex and challenging to develop. Due to the scope of this book, these games will not be complete and polished games, nor will we be able to discuss every line of code.

Instead, I'll annotate the code with many helpful comments so that it's easy to follow and understand.

I leave it up to you to improve on these skeleton game projects, and I'm excited to see your results. I think giving you multiple starting points to base your own work on works better than walking you through the typical Asteroids games over the course of the whole book.

I chose the game projects for this book based on popularity on the App Store and relevance for game developers, who often inquire about how to solve the specific problems that these games present. For example, the line-drawing game genre is a huge favorite among cocos2d game developers, yet line-drawing games require you to overcome deceivingly complex challenges.

I've also seen a fair bit of other developers' cocos2d code and followed the discussions on code design, structure, and style. I'll base my code samples on a framework that relies on composition over inheritance, and will explain why this is preferable. One other frequent question that has to do with code design is how different objects should communicate with each other. There are interesting pros and cons for each approach to code design and structure, and I want to convey these concepts as they help you write more stable code with fewer bugs and better performance.

What iPhone App Developers Will Learn

So you are an iPhone app developer and you've worked with the iPhone SDK before? Perfect. Then you'll be most interested in how making games works in a world without Interface Builder. In fact, there are other tools you'll be using. They may not be as shiny as Apple's tools but they'll be useful nonetheless.

The programming considerations will change, too. You don't normally send and receive a lot of events in game programming, and you let a larger number of objects decide what to do with an event. For performance reasons and to reduce user input latency, game engine systems often work more closely connected with each other. A lot of work is done in loops and update methods, which are called at every frame or at specific points in time. While a user interface-driven application spends most of the time waiting for a user's input, a game keeps pushing a lot of data and pixels behind the scenes, even when the player is not doing anything. So there's a lot more going on and game code tends to be more streamlined and efficient because of concerns for performance.

What Cocos2d Developers Will Learn

You're already familiar with cocos2d? You may be wondering if you can learn anything new from this book. I say you will. Maybe you need to skip the first chapters ahead, but you'll definitely get hooked by the games' sample source code supplied with the book. You'll learn how I structure my code and the rationale behind it. You'll probably find inspiration reading about the various games and how I implemented them. There's also a good amount of tips you'll benefit from.

Most importantly, this book isn't written by some geek you've never heard of and never will hear from again, with no e-mail address or web site to post your follow-up questions to. Instead, it's written by a geek you may not have heard of but who will definitely be around. I'm actively engaged with the cocos2d community at my `www.learn-cocos2d.com` blog, where I'll basically keep on writing this book.

What's in This Book

Here's a brief overview of the chapters in this book.

Chapter 2 – Getting Started

We'll cover setting up cocos2d for development, installing project templates, and creating the first "Hello World" project. You'll learn about cocos2d basics, like scenes and nodes.

Chapter 3 – Essentials

I'll explain the essential cocos2d classes that you'll need most often, such as Sprites, Transitions, and Actions. And how to use them, of course.

Chapter 4 – Your First Game

Enemies drop from the top and you have to avoid them by tilting your device. This will be our first simple game using accelerometer controls.

Chapter 5 – Game Building Blocks

Now prepare yourself for a bigger game, one that requires a better code structure. You'll learn how scenes and nodes are layered and the various ways that game objects can exchange information.

Chapter 6 – Sprites In-Depth

You'll learn what a Texture Atlas is and why we'll be using it for our next game, and how to create a Texture Atlas with the Zwoptex tool.

Chapter 7 – Scrolling with Joy

With the Texture Atlas ready, you'll learn how to implement a parallax scrolling shooter game, controlled by touch input.

Chapter 8 – Shoot 'em Up

Without enemies, our shooter wouldn't have much to shoot at, right? So I'll show you how to add gameplay code to spawn, move, hit, and animate the enemy hordes.

Chapter 9 – Particle Effects

By using the ParticleDesigner tool, you'll add some particle effects to the side-scrolling game.

Chapter 10 – Working with Tilemaps

Infinitely jumping upwards, you'll apply what you've learned from the side-scrolling game in portrait mode to create another popular iOS game genre.

Chapter 11 – Isometric Tilemaps

Since cocos2d supports the TMX file format, we'll take a look at how to create tile-based games using the Tiled editor.

Chapter 12 – Physics Engines

Directing where things go with the move of your fingertips—you'll learn here how that's done.

Chapter 13 – Pinball Game

This is a primer on using the Chipmunk and Box2d physics engines—and the crazy things you can do with them.

Chapter 14 – Game Center

This time, you'll use real physics for a gravity-defying, planet-bouncing, ball-shooter in space. It's not going to be realistic, but it's going to have real physics. A conundrum, maybe, but fun in any case.

Chapter 15 – Conclusion

This is where the book ends. Worry not, your journey won't. You'll get inspiration on where to go from here.

Questions & Feedback

I do hope I get the right mixture of easing you into cocos2d and iOS game development while challenging you with advanced game-programming concepts.

If at any time I fail and leave you wondering, please feel free to contact me at steffen@learn-cocos2d.com with any questions you might have. I'll continue to fill any gaps I might leave in this book on my www.learn-cocos2d.com website. Your feedback is always welcome!

Chapter **2**

Getting Started

I want to get you up to speed and developing cocos2d games as quickly as possible. By the end of this chapter, you'll be able to create new cocos2d projects based on the supplied Xcode project templates. I'll also introduce you to the important bits of knowledge you need to keep in mind during game development. And since it's always been a big source of confusion, I'll explain how memory management works in the context of cocos2d, hopefully helping you avoid some of the common pitfalls. At the end of this chapter, you'll have a first cocos2d project based on a project template up and running.

What You Need to Get Started

In this section, I'll quickly walk you through the requirements and necessary steps to get started. Getting registered as an iOS developer and creating the necessary provisioning profiles is excellently documented by Apple, so I won't recreate that detailed information here.

System Requirements

These are the minimum hardware and software requirements for developing iOS applications.

- Intel-based Mac computer with 1 GB RAM
- Mac OS X 10.6 (Snow Leopard) or higher
- Any iOS Device

For development, any Intel-based Mac computer suffices. Even the Mac mini is perfectly fine for developing iPhone applications and games. I do recommend you have 2 GB of RAM (Random Access Memory) or more installed, so if you have that option, please take it. It'll make using your computer so much smoother, especially since game development tools often require much more memory than most other software. You'll be handling a lot of images, audio files, and program code, and you'll probably be running all these tools in parallel.

Note that Mac OS X 10.6 is mandatory for iOS development since the release of the iPhone SDK 4 in June 2010. If you are running an older version of Mac OS X, please consult the Max OS X Technical Specifications web site (www.apple.com/macosx/specs.html) to learn if your Mac meets the system requirements and how to purchase Mac OS X 10.6 .

Register as iOS Developer

If you haven't done so yet, the very first step is to register at Apple as an iPhone developer. Access to the iPhone Developer Program costs $99 per year. It grants you access to the iPhone SDK and the iPhone Developer Portal where you set up your development devices and profiles. You also get access to iTunes Connect where you manage your contracts and publish apps.

You can register as an iOS developer on the iPhone Dev Center at http://developer.apple.com/iphone.

Certificates & Provisioning Profiles

Eventually you'll want to deploy the games you're building onto your iOS device. To do so, you must create an iPhone Development Certificate, register your iOS device, and enable it for development. Finally, you'll create Development or Distribution Provisioning Profiles, download them to your computer and set up each Xcode project to use them.

Once more, all of these steps are explained on the iPhone Provisioning Portal. Apple has done an excellent job at documenting these steps on the **How To** tabs of each section of the Provisioning Portal. The iPhone Provisioning Portal is accessible for registered iOS Developers and located at https://developer.apple.com/iphone/manage/overview/index.action.

Download & Install the iPhone SDK

As a registered iPhone developer, you can download the latest iPhone SDK from the iPhone Dev Center. The download is a whopping 2 GB and will take several minutes to install. So be prepared and have some coffee, or as I prefer, some hot chocolate around.

After installation of the iPhone SDK is complete, you are set with everything you need to develop iOS applications, including the Xcode IDE (integrated development environment). If you've never worked with Xcode before, I suggest you familiarize yourself with it. I recommend *Learn Xcode Tools for Mac OS X and iPhone Development* by Ian Piper (Apress, 2010).

NOTE: It may be tempting to be at the bleeding edge of iPhone SDK development. From time to time, beta versions of the iPhone SDK are made available. I recommend *not* using iPhone SDK beta versions unless you have a very, very good reason to do so!

Beta versions can contain bugs, they may be incompatible with the current cocos2d version, and they are under NDA. This means it's hard to find solutions if any issue related to the beta version arises, since no one is allowed to discuss the beta SDK in public.

Moreover, you have to install a beta version of the iOS to your device and you can't revert back to a previous iOS version. Installed apps on your device may be incompatible with the new iOS beta and they usually aren't updated until the new iPhone SDK is officially released. If you rely on any apps to do your work, don't upgrade.

Download & Install cocos2d

The next step is to get cocos2d. You can download it from `www.cocos2d-iphone.org/download`.

I recommend downloading the stable version. The unstable version doesn't mean it's going to crash all the time; consider it to be a beta version. It'll work just fine in general but it may have some rough edges and untested features. Before you consider the unstable version, please review the Release Notes to see if it contains anything of particular use to you. If not, just go with the stable version.

Double-click the downloaded file to extract the archive anywhere on your Mac. It'll create a subfolder named *cocos2d-iphone-0.99.3* or similar, depending on the exact version number of cocos2d you downloaded.

Install cocos2d Xcode Project Templates

Now open the Terminal App, which you'll find in the *Utilities* folder of your *Applications* folder on your Mac. Or just enter *Terminal.app* in Spotlight to locate it. The cocos2d Xcode Project Templates installation procedure is driven by a shell script, but it's really simple to do.

First, in the Terminal window, enter `sudo` followed by a space. In a Finder window, locate the file *install-templates.sh* in the cocos2d folder and drag and drop it onto the Terminal window. This will add the full path and file name right after the `sudo` command, so it should look like this:

```
sudo /book/cocos2d-iphone-0.99.3/install-templates.sh
```

Press Return and Terminal will ask you to enter your system password. The script requires root access to proceed with installation. If everything goes fine you should see a number of lines printed on the Terminal window. Most of them will start with "...copying". If that's the case, the templates should now be installed.

If you get any kind of error, verify that there is a space between sudo and the path, and that the path to the *install-templates.sh* script is correct. If the script complains that the templates have already been installed, add the -f parameter at the end of the command as suggested by the script. This will overwrite previous, possibly outdated, Xcode project templates. It will not affect any of your existing projects based on any of the cocos2d templates.

Create a cocos2d Application

Now open Xcode and select **File ➤ New Project**. Under User Templates you should see the cocos2d Project Templates as shown in Figure 2–1.

NOTE: The Box2d and Chipmunk application templates will be discussed in Chapter 13. Feel free to try them out if you want to have some fun with physics right now.

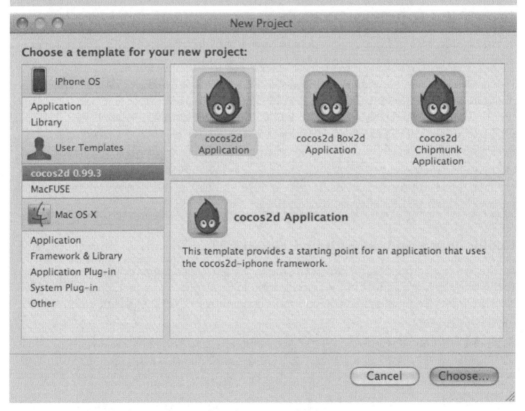

Figure 2–1. *The cocos2d Xcode project templates*

Choose the cocos2d Application Template and name it "HelloWorld".

NOTE: It is good practice *not* to use space characters in project names. Xcode doesn't mind, but some tools you might use do. It's just a matter of defensively avoiding any potential hiccups.

For a very, very long time, programmers who built operating systems and applications could rely on file names not containing spaces. Even today, after modern operating systems have allowed spaces in file names for at least the last 10 years, there are occasional problems related to spaces and special characters in file names. I always avoid naming anything code-related, whether projects, source files, or resources with spaces or other special characters. Only numbers, digits, and the minus sign and underscore are always safe for developers to use in file names.

Xcode will create the project based on the template. An Xcode project window like the one in Figure 2–2 will open up.

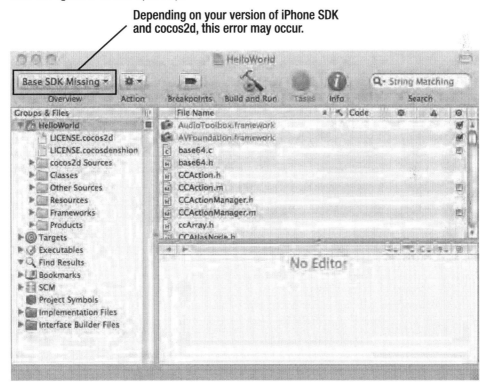

Figure 2–2. *The new HelloWorld Xcode may show a "Base SDK Missing" error.*

The Base SDK Missing error as shown in Figure 2–2 may occur, depending on the iPhone SDK version and the version of cocos2d. It's nothing serious. In my case, the iPhone SDK 4 was just released while the cocos2d stable version from the web site was still using the iPhone SDK 3, which is no longer part of the iPhone SDK distribution. Hence it says "Base SDK Missing" since the project template still refers to iPhone SDK 3.

To solve this issue, open the **Project** menu in Xcode and select **Edit Project Settings**. A dialog titled *Project "HelloWorld" Info* opens, as shown in Figure 2–3. At the bottom of this dialog, look for the dropdown labeled *Base SDK for All Configurations*. It will read something like *iPhone Device 3.0 (missing)*. Change this to the most current iPhone SDK version that's available.

> **NOTE:** Setting the Base SDK to a specific SDK version doesn't mean that your app will work only on devices running this particular version of the iOS. Instead, this is defined by a Build Setting named iPhone OS Deployment Target, which you can find on the Build tab of the Get Info dialog. There you can select which iOS version your app will run with, from iOS 2.0 through iOS 4.0.

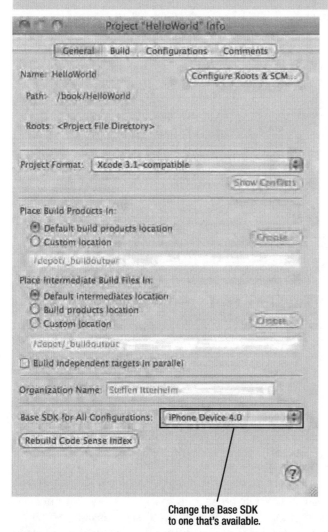

Change the Base SDK
to one that's available.

Figure 2–3. *To fix the "Base SDK Missing" error, change the Base SDK setting to the SDK version available on your system.*

Now you'll be able to **Build and Run** the project. By default, the iPhone Simulator will start up and the result should look like Figure 2–4.

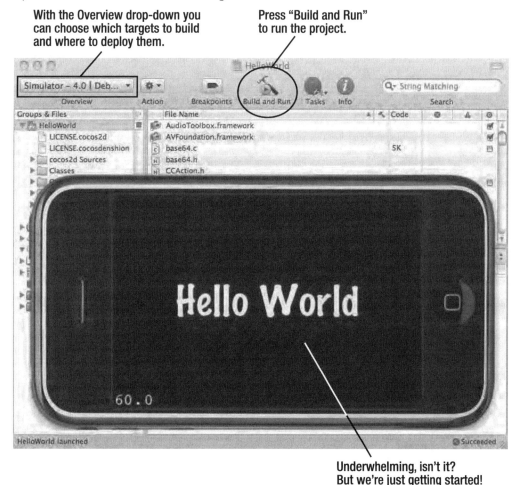

With the Overview drop-down you can choose which targets to build and where to deploy them.

Press "Build and Run" to run the project.

Underwhelming, isn't it? But we're just getting started!

Figure 2–4. *Success! The template project works and displays a "Hello World" label running in the iPhone Simulator.*

The HelloWorld Application

So here we are—with minimal fuss you created a running cocos2d application. Perfect. Say no more. Say no more.

But now you want to know how it works, right? Well, I didn't expect you'd let me off the hook so easily. And something tells me that, however deep I go into the details over the course of the book, you'll want to know more. That's the spirit!

Let's check what's in the Hello World Xcode project and see how it all works so you get a rough overview of how things are connected.

Locating the HelloWorld files

First, a quick primer in case you've never worked with Xcode before. By default, you'll see a pane called Groups & Files on the left side of the Xcode project window, like the one in Figure 2–5. That's where Xcode keeps all file references, among plenty of other things like Targets and Executables. Just focus on the Groups & Files for now that are below the HelloWorld project.

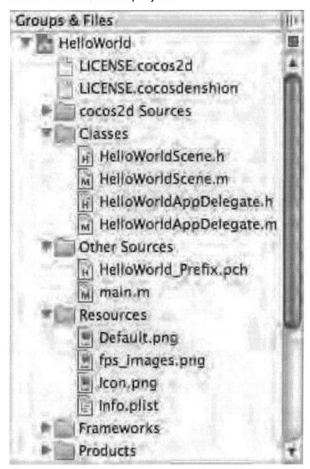

Figure 2–5. *Xcode's Groups & Files pane. The expanded groups contain the project files we'll be looking at.*

In the group named *cocos2d Sources* you'll find all the files the cocos2d game engine consists of. Feel free to explore these files. You don't need to know the details of the cocos2d game engine, but it's good to have the source files sitting there, especially when it comes to debugging, or in case you get curious and want to know how things work under the hood.

> **NOTE:** Xcode's Groups & Files pane looks a lot like folders and files Finder. Don't mistake what Xcode calls groups for Finder's folders. You can have your files in Xcode arranged in many groups, but in Finder they can still all be in the same folder. This is why they are called groups. They allow you to rearrange files freely, regardless of where they are stored on the Mac's hard drive.

Resources

Let's work from the bottom up. In the Resources group you'll find (and later add) all the additional files that aren't source code, such as images and audio files.

The *Default.png* file is the image that's displayed when iOS is loading your app and *Icon.png* is, of course, the app's icon. The *fps_images.png* file is used by cocos2d to display the framerate; you should not remove or modify it.

Inside the *Info.plist* file, you'll find a number of settings for your application. You'll only need to make changes here when you get close to publishing your app.

Other Sources

If you're familiar with programming in C or similar languages, you may recognize *main.m* in the *Other Sources* group as the starting point of the application.

Main.m

Everything that happens between the `main` function and the `HelloWorldAppDelegate` class is behind the scenes magic of the iPhone SDK, over which you have no control. Since you'll hardly ever need to change *main.m,* you can safely ignore its contents. Still, it never hurts to peek inside.

To quickly sum up, the `main` function creates an `NSAutoreleasePool` and then calls `UIApplicationMain` to start the application using `HelloWorldAppDelegate` as the class that implements the `UIApplicationDelegate` protocol.

```
int main(int argc, char *argv[]) {
        NSAutoreleasePool *pool = [NSAutoreleasePool new];
        int retVal = UIApplicationMain(argc, argv, nil, @"HelloWorldAppDelegate");
        [pool release];
        return retVal;
}
```

Really, the only interesting point to take away from this is that every iOS application uses an NSAutoreleasePool to help you manage memory. In short, by using the autorelease message on objects, you don't have to worry about sending them a release message. The autorelease pool ensures that the memory of autorelease objects is eventually released.

Don't worry if you don't know what the heck I'm talking about here. I'll introduce you to memory management with cocos2d later in this chapter and it'll become clearer why every iOS application is wrapped inside an NSAutoreleasePool.

Precompiled Prefix Header

Just in case you're wondering what the *HelloWorld_prefix.pch* header file is for, it's a tool used to speed up compilation. You are supposed to add the header files of frameworks that never or only rarely change to the prefix header. This causes the framework's code to be compiled in advance and made available to all your classes. Unfortunately, it also has the disadvantage that, if a header added to the prefix header changes, all your code will recompile, which is why you should only add header files that rarely or never change.

For example, the *cocos2d.h* header file is a good candidate to add to the prefix header, as I've done in Listing 2–1. To create a noticeable increase in compilation time, your project would need to be reasonably complex, however, so don't get your stopwatch out just yet. But it's good practice to add the *cocos2d.h* as a prefix header right away, if only to never have to write #import "cocos2d.h" in any of your source files again.

Listing 2–1. *Adding the cocos2d.h Header File to the Prefix Header*

```
#ifdef __OBJC__
        #import <Foundation/Foundation.h>
        #import <UIKit/UIKit.h>
        #import "cocos2d.h"
#endif
```

Once again, you can refer to Apple's developer documentation if you want to learn more about reducing build times with prefix headers: http://developer.apple.com/mac/library/documentation/DeveloperTools/Conceptual/XcodeBuildSystem/800-Reducing_Build_Times/bs_speed_up_build.html.

Classes

There are two classes that make up the core of the HelloWorld project. The HelloWorldAppDelegate class handles the application's global events and state changes, while the HelloWorldScene class contains all the code that displays the Hello World label.

HelloWorldAppDelegate

Every iOS application has one AppDelegate class that implements the UIApplicationDelegate protocol. In our HelloWorld project, it's called HelloWorldAppDelegate, and that naming scheme is the same for every new project you're going to create: project name plus AppDelegate. I'm going to refer to it simply as the AppDelegate from now on because it's a global concept you'll find in every iOS application.

The AppDelegate is used to track state changes of the application, and to do this it receives messages from the iOS at certain points in time. For example, it allows you to determine when the user gets an incoming phone call or when the application is low on memory. The very first message your application will receive is the applicationDidFinishLaunching method. That's where all the startup code goes and where cocos2d is initialized.

If you want to learn more about the AppDelegate's various methods, what they do and when these messages are sent by the iPhone SDK, you can look it up in Apple's reference documentation on the UIApplicationDelegate protocol at http://developer.apple.com/iphone/library/documentation/uikit/reference/UIApplicationDelegate_Protocol.

> **NOTE:** Since I'm talking about application startup, I might as well talk about application shutdown. You may eventually notice an oddity with the AppDelegate's dealloc method. It never gets called! Any breakpoint set in the AppDelegate dealloc method will never be hit!
>
> This is normal behavior. When iOS terminates an application, it simply wipes the memory clean to speed up the shutdown process. That's why any code inside the dealloc method of the AppDelegate class is never run. Also, it's bad practice to call dealloc manually so don't try to "fix" this issue by doing so. If you ever need to run code in your AppDelegate just before the application terminates, do it inside the applicationWillTerminate method. If you target iOS 4 or higher, you should use applicationDidEnterBackground instead.

In most cases, there are only three things you might want to change during the cocos2d initialization process:

```
[[CCDirector sharedDirector] setDeviceOrientation:CCDeviceOrientationLandscapeLeft];
[[CCDirector sharedDirector] setAnimationInterval:1.0/60];
[[CCDirector sharedDirector] setDisplayFPS:YES];
```

I'll provide a few details on each of these in the following sections.

Device Orientation

The most important one is setting the device orientation. The HelloWorld application uses a landscape orientation, which means you'll be holding your iOS device sideways. If you change this option from CCDeviceOrientationLandscapeLeft to CCDeviceOrientationLandscapeRight, you'll find that the message "Hello World" is now displayed upside down compared to what it was before.

Here's a list of supported device orientations. Try each of them to see how they change the Hello World text label orientation.

- CCDeviceOrientationPortrait
- CCDeviceOrientationPortraitUpsideDown
- CCDeviceOrientationLandscapeLeft
- CCDeviceOrientationLandscapeRight

NOTE: You can change the device orientation at a later point in time, even during gameplay. For example, you can make this a game setting the user can choose. As long as you change from one landscape mode to another or one portrait mode to another, you don't need to modify your code. Allowing the user to choose to play the game in any of the two landscape or portrait directions is very straightforward to implement. Since everyone has a very subjective opinion on that matter, it's a good idea to let the user choose between the regular and the upside-down orientation.

Animation Interval

The animation interval determines how often cocos2d updates the screen. Effectively, this affects the maximum framerate your game can achieve. The animation interval is not given in frames per second, however. It's the inverse because it determines how frequently cocos2d should update the screen. That's why the parameter is 1.0/60—because 1 divided by 60 results in 0.0167, which is the time in seconds between each call to update the screen. Of course, if your game is complex, it might take the CPU or GPU longer than 0.0167 seconds to display a frame, so there's no guarantee that 60 fps will be achieved throughout. As a matter of fact, it's your responsibility to keep the game running at a high framerate. I'll explain techniques to improve performance throughout the book.

In some cases, it may be preferable to lock the framerate to 30 frames per second. This may be helpful in very complex games where you can't achieve 60 fps consistently and the framerate fluctuates a lot between 30 and 60 fps. In such a case, it's often better to lock the framerate to the lowest common denominator because a lower but steady framerate is perceived as smoother by players than a framerate that tends to fluctuate abruptly, even when the actual average framerate may be higher. Human perception is a tricky thing.

NOTE: You can't render more than 60 frames per second on iOS devices. The device's display is locked to update at 60 frames per second (Hz), and forcing cocos2d to render more frames than 60 per second is, at best, not doing anything. At worst, it can actually slow down your framerate. Stick with the `animationInterval` of 1.0/60 if you want to run cocos2d at the fastest possible rate.

Display FPS

Enabling the FPS display will show a small number at the lower left corner of the screen. This is your framerate, or the frames per second the screen is updated. Ideally your game should be running at 60 fps at all times, especially if it's an action or twitch-based game. Some games, such as most puzzle games, can go with a constant 30 fps just fine. The FPS display helps you keep track of the framerate and any hiccups or stutters your game is experiencing.

> **NOTE:** If you need to tweak the responsiveness of the FPS display, you can do so by modifying the CC_DIRECTOR_FPS_INTERVAL line in *ccConfig.h*. You'll find this file in the *cocos2d Sources/cocos2d* group. By default it is set to 0.1, which means the framerate display will be updated ten times per second. If you increase the value, the FPS display will average out over a longer period of time. However, you won't be able to see any sudden, short drops in framerate, which can still be noticeable to. Keep that in mind.

HelloWorldScene

The HelloWorldScene class is where pure cocos2d code does its magic to display the Hello World Label. Before I get into that, you should understand that cocos2d uses a hierarchy of CCNode objects to determine what is displayed where.

The base class of all nodes is the CCNode class, which contains a position but has no visual representation. It's the parent class for all other node classes, including the two most fundamental ones: CCScene and CCLayer.

CCScene is an abstract concept and does nothing more than to allow proper placement of objects in the scene according to their pixel coordinates. A CCScene node is thus always used as the parent object for every cocos2d scene hierarchy.

The CCLayer class does very little by itself other than allowing touch and accelerometer input. You'll normally use it as the first class added to the CCScene, simply because most games use at least simple touch input.

If you open the *HelloWorldScene.h* header file, you'll see that the HelloWorld class is derived from CCLayer.

Since CCScene is merely an abstract concept, the default way of setting up a scene has always been to use a static initializer +(id) scene in your class. This method creates a regular CCScene object and then adds an instance of your class to the scene. In almost all cases that's the only place where a CCScene is created and used. The following is a generic example of the +(id) scene method:

```
+(id) scene
{
        CCScene *scene = [CCScene node];
        id node = [HelloWorld node];
        [scene addChild:node];

        return scene;
}
```

First, a CCScene object is created using the static initializer +(id) node of the CCScene class. Next, our HelloWorld class is created using the same +(id) node method and then added to the scene. The scene is then returned to the caller.

Moving on to the -(id) init method in Listing 2–2, you'll notice something that might seem odd: self is assigned the return value from the init message sent to the super object in the call to self = [super init]. If you come from a C++ background, you'll shudder in pain looking at this. Don't get too upset, it's alright. It simply means that in Objective-C we have to manually call the super class's init method. There is no automatic call to the parent class. And we do have to assign self the return value of the [super init] message because it might return nil:

Listing 2–2. *The init Method Creates and Adds the Hello World Label*

```
-(id) init
{
        if ((self = [super init])) {
                // create and initialize a label
                CCLabel* label = [CCLabel labelWithString:@"Hello World"
                                                fontName:@"Marker Felt" fontSize:64];

                // get the window (screen) size from CCDirector
                CGSize size = [[CCDirector sharedDirector] winSize];

                // position the label at the center of the screen
                label.position = CGPointMake(size.width / 2, size.height / 2);

                // add the label as a child to this Layer
                [self addChild: label];
        }
        return self;
}
```

If you're deeply concerned by the way Objective-C programmers write the call to [super init], here's an alternative that might ease your mind. It's fundamentally the same, just not what tradition dictates:

```
-(id) init
{
        self = [super init];
        if (self != nil) {
                // do init stuff here …
        }
        return self;
}
```

Now let me explain how the label is added to the scene. If you look again at the init method in Listing 2–2, you'll see that a CCLabel object is created using one of init's static initializer methods. It'll return a new instance of the CCLabel class as an autoreleased object. To not have its memory freed after control leaves the init method, you have to add the label to self as child using the [self addChild:label] message. In between, the label is assigned a position at the center of the screen. Note that whether you assign the position before or after the call to addChild doesn't matter.

Memory Management with cocos2d

At this point I need to talk a bit about memory management and the autorelease message.

Normally, when you create an object in Objective-C, you do so by calling `alloc`. By doing this, you become responsible to release the object when you don't need it anymore. The following is a typical `alloc`/`init` and `release` cycle:

```
// allocate a new instance of NSObject
NSObject* myObject = [[NSObject alloc] init];

// do something with myObject here …

// release the memory used by myObject
// if you don't release it, the object is leaked and the memory used by it is never freed.
[myObject release];
```

Now, with the `autorelease` message and the fact that iOS applications always use an autorelease pool, you can avoid sending the `release` message. Here's the same example rewritten using autorelease:

```
// allocate a new instance of NSObject
NSObject* myObject = [[[NSObject alloc] init] autorelease];

// do something with myObject here …

// no need to call release, in fact you should not send release as it would crash.
```

As you can see, this simplifies memory management somewhat in that you no longer have to remember to send the `release` message. The autorelease pool takes care of that for you by sending the object a `release` message at a later time. Creating the object gets just a little bit more complex because the `autorelease` message was added.

Now consider the following code, which illustrates how you'd allocate a CCNode object if you followed the traditional release style:

```
// allocate a new instance of CCNode
CCNode* myNode = [[CCNode alloc] init]];

// do something with myNode …

[myNode release];
```

This is *not* the preferred way to create cocos2d objects. It's much easier to use the static initializer methods, which return an `autorelease` object. Contrary to what Apple recommends, the use of `autorelease` is consistently built into the cocos2d engine's design by moving calls like `[[[NSObject alloc] init] autorelease]` to a static method in the class itself. And that's a good thing—do not fight it! It will make your life easier since you don't have to remember which objects need to be released, which is often cause for either crashes due to over-releasing certain objects or memory leaks due to not releasing all objects.

In the case of the CCNode class, the static initializer is +(id) node. The following code sends the alloc message to self, which is equivalent to using [CCNode alloc] if the code is placed in the CCNode implementation.

```
+(id) node
{
        return [[[self alloc] init] autorelease];
}
```

It's just a little more generic to use self in this case, and perfectly legal in case you happen to be a C++ programmer now scratching your head.

Seeing this, we can rewrite the CCNode allocation to use the static initializer and, quite unsurprisingly, the code is now very short, concise, and tidy. Just the way I like it:

```
// allocate a new instance of CCNode
CCNode* myNode = [CCNode node];

// do something with myNode …
```

That's the beauty of using autorelease objects. You don't need to remember to send them a release message. Each time cocos2d advances to the next frame, the autorelease objects that are no longer in use are released automatically. But there's also one caveat. If you use this code and at least one frame later you want to access the myNode object, it'll be gone. Sending any messages to it will cause an EXC_BAD_ACCESS crash.

Simply adding the CCNode* myNode variable as a member to your class doesn't mean that the memory used by the object is automatically retained. If you want an autorelease object to stick around into the next and future frames, you do need to retain it and subsequently release it if you don't explicitly add it as a child node.

There's an even better way to use autorelease objects and keep them around without explicitly calling retain. Usually you'll create CCNode objects and add them to the scene hierarchy by adding the nodes as children to another CCNode derived object. You can even get rid of the member variable if you want to, by relying on cocos2d to store the object for you.

```
// creating an autorelease instance of CCNode
-(void) init
{
        myNode = [CCNode node];
        myNode.tag = 123;

        // adding the node as children to self (assuming self is derived from CCNode)
        [self addChild:myNode];
}

-(void) update:(ccTime)delta
{
        // later access and use the myNode object again
        CCNode* myNode = [self getChildByTag:123];

        // do something with myNode
}
```

The magic is that addChild adds the object to a collection, in this case a CCArray that's similar to the NSMutableArray of the iPhone SDK, but faster. The CCArray and the NSMutableArray and any other iPhone SDK collection automatically send a retain message to any object added to them, and send a release message to any object removed from the collection. Thus the object stays around and remains valid and can be accessed at a later time, yet it will automatically be released after it has been removed from the collection.

What you should keep in mind is that managing memory for cocos2d objects is best done as I described here. You may run into other developers who say that autorelease is bad or slow and shouldn't be used. Don't give in to them.

> **NOTE:** The Apple developer documentation recommends reducing the number of autorelease objects. Most cocos2d objects, however, are created as autorelease objects. It makes memory management much easier, as I've shown.
>
> If you start using alloc/init and release for every cocos2d object, you'll get yourself into a lot of pain for little to no benefit. That isn't to say that you'll never use alloc/init; it does have its uses and is sometimes even required. But for cocos2d objects, you should rely on using the static autorelease initializers.
>
> Autorelease objects have only one caveat, and that's that their memory is in use until the game advances by one frame. This means if you create a lot of throw-away autorelease objects every frame, you might be wasting memory. But that's actually a rare occurrence.

This concludes my quick primer on cocos2d memory management. Memory management in the Objective-C world is governed by simple rules:

- If you own (alloc, copy, or retain) an object, you must release it later
- If you send autorelease to an object, you must not release it

For a more in-depth discussion of memory management, refer to Apple's Memory Management Programming Guide (http://developer.apple.com/iphone/library/documentation/Cocoa/Conceptual/MemoryMgmt/MemoryMgmt.html).

Changing the World

What good is a template project like HelloWorld if I don't have you tinker with it at least a little? I'll have you change the world by touching it! How's that for a start?

First you'll make two changes to the init method to enable touch input and to use a tag value to retrieve the label at a later point. The changes are highlighted in Listing 2–3.

Listing 2–3. *Enabling Touch and Gaining Access to the Label Object*

```
-(id) init
{
        if ((self = [super init])) {
                // create and initialize a label
                CCLabel* label = [CCLabel labelWithString:@"Hello World"
                                            fontName:@"Marker Felt" fontSize:64];

                // get the window (screen) size from CCDirector
                CGSize size = [[CCDirector sharedDirector] winSize];

                // position the label at the center of the screen
                label.position = CGPointMake(size.width / 2, size.height / 2);

                // add the label as a child to this Layer
                [self addChild: label];

                // our label needs a tag so we can find it later on
                // you can pick any arbitrary number
                label.tag = 13;

                // must be enabled if you want to receive touch events!
                self.isTouchEnabled = YES;
        }
        return self;
}
```

The `label` object gets 13 assigned to its tag property. Now why did you do that? I know, I told you to but I must have had a reason, right? In the previous section, I explained that's how you can later access a child object of your class—you can refer to it by its tag. The tag number is completely arbitrary, other than that it must be a positive number and every object should have its own tag number, so there aren't two with the same number or you couldn't tell which you'd be retrieving.

> **TIP:** Instead of using magic numbers like 13 as tag values, you should get in the habit of defining constants to use with tags. You'll have a hard time remembering what tag number 13 stands for, compared to writing a meaningful variable name like kTagForLabel. I'll get to this in Chapter 5.

Secondly, `self.isTouchEnabled` is set to YES. This is a property of the `CCLayer` class and tells it that you want to receive touch messages. Only then will the method ccTouchesBegan be called:

```
-(void) ccTouchesBegan:(NSSet*)touches withEvent:(UIEvent*)event;
{
        CCLabel* label = (CCLabel*)[self getChildByTag:13];
        label.scale = CCRANDOM_0_1();
}
```

By using `[self getChildByTag:13]`, you can access the `CCLabel` object by its tag property, which you assigned in the init method. You can then use the label as usual. In this case, we use cocos2d's handy CCRANDOM_0_1() macro to change the label's scale property to a value between 0 and 1. This will change the label's size every time you touch the screen.

Since getChildByTag will always return the label, we can safely cast it to a (CCLabel*) object. However, you should be aware that doing so will crash your game if the retrieved object is not derived from the CCLabel class for some reason. This could easily happen if you accidentally give another object the same tag number 13. For that reason, it is good practice to use a defensive programming style and verify that what you're working with is exactly what you expect. Defensive programming uses assertions to verify that assumptions made are true. For this, you should use the NSAssert method:

```
-(void) ccTouchesBegan:(NSSet*)touches withEvent:(UIEvent*)event;
{
        CCNode* node = [self getChildByTag:13];

        // defensive programming: verify the returned node is a CCLabel class object
        NSAssert([node isKindOfClass:[CCLabel class]], @"node is not a CCLabel!");

        CCLabel* label = (CCLabel*)node;
        label.scale = CCRANDOM_0_1();
}
```

In this case, we expect the node returned by getChildByTag to be an object derived from CCLabel, but we can never be sure, which is why adding an NSAssert to verify the fact is helpful in finding errors before they lead to a crash.

Note that this adds two more lines of code, but in terms of performance things remain the same. The call to NSAssert is completely removed in Release builds, and the cast CCLabel* label = (CCLabel*)node; is what we've done already, just on the same line. Essentially, both versions perform exactly the same but in the second case you get the benefit of being notified when you didn't get the expected CCLabel object, instead of crashing with an EXC_BAD_ACCESS error.

What Else You Should Know

Since this is the Getting Started chapter, I think it's important to take the opportunity to introduce you to some vital but often overlooked aspects of iOS game development. I want you to be aware of the subtle differences among various iOS devices. In particular, available memory is often incorrectly considered because you can only use a fraction of each device's memory safely.

I also want you to know that the iPhone Simulator is a great tool for testing your game, but it can't be used to assess performance, memory usage, and other features. The simulator experience can differ greatly from running your game on an actual iOS device. Don't fall into the trap of making assessments based on your game's behavior in the iPhone Simulator. It's only the device that counts.

The iOS Devices

When you develop for iOS devices, you need to take into account their differences. Most independent and hobby game developers can't afford to purchase each slightly different iOS device, of which there are eight at the time of this writing, with roughly two more to be released each year. At the very least, you need to understand that there are important differences.

You might want to refer to Apple's spec sheets to familiarize yourself with the iOS device technical specifications. The following links list the iPhone, iPod Touch, and iPad device specifications, respectively.

http://support.apple.com/specs/#iphone

http://support.apple.com/specs/#ipodtouch

http://support.apple.com/specs/#ipad

Table 2–1 gives a quick summary of the most important hardware differences that concern game developers. The table lists iPod Touch devices by generation since Apple didn't use suffixes like "3G" for its iPod Touch models. This table serves to show that the iOS devices are not as homogenous as you might expect. Note that the iPhone 4 graphics chip is still unknown because for the first time it forms a single chip with the CPU.

Table 2–1. *iOS Hardware Differences*

Device	Processor	Graphics	Resolution	Memory (RAM)
First generation devices	412 MHz	PowerVR MBX	480x320	128 MB
iPhone 3G (second generation.)	412 MHz	PowerVR MBX	480x320	128 MB
iPod Touch (second generation)	532 MHz	PowerVR MBX	480x320	128 MB
Third generation devices	600 MHz	PowerVR SGX535	480x320	256 MB
iPad	1000 MHz	PowerVR SGX535	1024x768	256 MB
iPhone 4	1000 MHz	Unknown	960x640	512 MB

As you can see, with every new generation iOS devices usually have a faster CPU, a more powerful graphics chip, and increased memory and screen resolution. This trend will continue, with newer devices getting more and more powerful. If you plan to make money from iOS games, keep in mind that the older models still have significant market share, and this changes only very slowly, much slower than the rate at which new devices are released. Even today, if you do not design your game to run on second-generation devices, you are giving up a significant portion of the market!

Usually when game developers look at hardware features, they tend to focus on the CPU speed and graphics chip to assess what's technically possible. However, being mobile devices, the iOS devices until the most recent iPhone 4 are limited mostly by the amount of available RAM.

> **NOTE:** RAM is not to be confused with the flash storage memory where MP3s, videos, apps, and photos are stored, of which even the smallest iOS device has 8 GBs. Flash storage memory is equivalent to the hard drive on your desktop computer. RAM is the memory your application uses to store code, data, and textures while it's running.

About Memory Usage

Current iOS devices have 128, 256, or 512 MB of RAM installed. However, that's not the amount of memory available to apps. iOS uses a big chunk of memory all the time, and this is compounded by iOS 4 multitasking. Each device running iOS 4 may be running various background tasks that use up an undefined additional amount of memory.

Over time, iOS developers have been able to close in on the theoretical maximum amount of RAM an app can use before it's forcibly closed by the OS. Table 2–2 shows what you can expect to work with. Ideally, you want to keep your memory usage below the number in the Memory Warning Threshold column at all times. This is especially challenging on devices with only 128 MB of RAM because there is only 20-25 MB of RAM more or less guaranteed to be available for an app. Around that point your app might start receiving Memory Warning notifications. You can ignore Memory Warning Level 1 notifications, but if the app continues to use more memory you may get a Memory Warning Level 2 message, at which point the OS basically threatens to close your app if you don't free some memory right now. It's like your mom threatening not to buy your new computer if you don't clean up your room right now! Please oblige.

Table 2–2. *Installed Memory Is Not Free Memory.*

Installed Memory	Available Memory	Memory Warning Threshold
128 MB	35-40 MB	20-25 MB
256 MB	120-150 MB	80-90 MB
512 MB	340-370 MB	260-300 MB (estimated)

Cocos2d can help you a little with freeing memory by calling the purge methods. By adding the purgeCachedData method to the AppDelegate's applicationDidReceiveMemoryWarning method, you can have cocos2d try to free up some more unused memory:

```
- (void)applicationDidReceiveMemoryWarning:(UIApplication *)application {
        [[CCTextureCache sharedTextureCache] removeUnusedTextures];
        [[CCDirector sharedDirector] purgeCachedData];
}
```

But when your games get more complex, you may need to implement your own scheme of handling Memory Warnings. The problem inherent with Memory Warnings is that they can cause performance glitches as your app frees big chunks of memory. If you rely on the cocos2d mechanisms to do this, it may remove a sprite's texture from memory, but if within a few frames that sprite is needed again, the texture will be reloaded during gameplay, which is slow. This can create noticeable stutters, so having your own memory management scheme implemented is preferable. You should be able to differentiate between textures that may be needed again soon and those that aren't needed at all right now. Unfortunately, there's no one size fits all solution— or I'd provide you with one.

If you are developing on a device with 256 or 512 MB of memory, keep in mind that the majority of iOS devices only have 128 MB. Unless you plan to limit your game to third- and fourth- generation iOS devices, you would do well to buy a cheap, used first- or second-generation device and test your game primarily with that device in order to catch issues of excessive memory consumption early. That's when they are still easy and cheap to fix, especially if they require a change in the game's design. In general, it's advisable to use the device for development that's the weakest one available to you in terms of hardware capabilities. This helps you catch any performance or low-memory issues as early as possible.

> **NOTE:** It's also recommended that you test your app on a device running iOS 4, which has a good number of background tasks running, to test for a worst-case scenario of background tasks using up additional memory. Multitasking is only available for third-generation and newer devices, which means only devices with 256 MB of RAM are allowed to run apps in the background. That's good news, since the 128 MB of the first- and second-generation devices would simply be too little. If you design for those devices, and I think you should, you don't have to worry too much about background tasks eating away your app's precious memory.

On devices with 128 MB of RAM, you can at most allocate around 35 to 40 MB memory. Keep in mind that this is only a theoretical maximum; the number varies on each device and may even depend on which apps the user had previously used. This is the reason app developers recommend rebooting a device if you are experiencing crashes. It can free up some more memory. The number one cause for apps to quit unexpectedly is that the device ran out of memory. So be sure to be wary of your app's memory usage, and to frequently reboot your devices when you get weird behavior.

You can measure memory usage using the Instruments application, which is explained in Apple's Instruments User Guide (http://developer.apple.com/iphone/library/ documentation/DeveloperTools/Conceptual/InstrumentsUserGuide/Introduction/Intro duction.html).

The Simulator

Apple's iPhone SDK allows you to run and test iPhone and iPad applications on your Mac with the iPhone Simulator and the iPad Simulator. The primary purpose of the simulator is to let you more rapidly test your application because deployment to an iOS device takes longer and longer as your game gets bigger and bigger. Games in particular use a lot of images and other assets that need to be transferred, slowing down deployment.

However, there are several caveats to using the simulator. The following sections reveal what the simulator does not allow you to do. For all these reasons, it is recommended that you test your game early and often on a device. At least after every major change or near the end of the day, you should run a test on your iOS device to verify that the game behaves exactly as intended.

Can't Assess Performance

The performance of your game running in the simulator depends entirely on your computer's CPU. The graphics rendering process does not even use the hardware acceleration capabilities of your Mac's graphics chip. That's why the framerate of your game running in the simulator has no meaning at all. You can't even be sure that comparing the framerate before and after a change will reveal the same results on the device. In extreme cases, the framerate in the simulator may go up even as it goes down on the device. Always do your performance testing on the device, using the Release build configuration.

Can't Assess Memory Usage

The simulator is able to use all the memory available on your computer, so there's a lot more memory available on the simulator than on the device. This means you won't get Memory Warnings and your game will run fine on the simulator but you may be in for a shock (a crash) when you try the game for the first time on an iOS device.

You can, however, assess how much memory is currently used by your game using the simulator.

Can't Use All iOS Device Features

Some features, like device orientation, can be simulated using menu items or keyboard shortcuts, but this comes nowhere close to the experience of a real device. And certain hardware features, like multitouch input, accelerometer, vibration, or obtaining location information can't be tested at all on the simulator because your computer's hardware can't simulate these features. No, it doesn't help to shake your Mac or touch its screen. Try it if you don't believe me.

Runtime Behavior Can Differ

From time to time you may encounter nasty cases where a game runs just fine on the simulator but crashes on the device, or the game slows down for no apparent reason. There may also be graphical glitches that appear only on the Simulator or only on the device. If in doubt, and before delving into a prolonged quest to figure out what's wrong, always try running your game on the device if you're having trouble on the simulator, or vice versa. Sometimes, the problem may just go away but if not, you may get a hint about what's going on.

About Logging

By default, your cocos2d projects will have two build configurations named Debug and Release. The main difference between the two is that only in debug builds are certain functions like CCLOG compiled and used by the game code. That's the single most important factor when it comes to performance variations between debug and release builds.

> **NOTE:** The CCLOG macro wraps Apple's NSLog method so that CCLOG is only compiled in debug builds, but omitted in release builds. I recommend using CCLOG in place of NSLog because logging is for your eyes only. NSLog can slow down your published game because it will be run even in release builds!

One NSLog or CCLOG in the wrong place can spam the Debugger Console window with logging messages, causing slowdowns and lag. Logging is very slow, and a continuous stream of log messages printed to the Debugger Console can drag your game's performance down to a crawl. If you suspect your game's performance to be particularly slow in debug builds, always check the Debugger Console for excessive logging activities. From the **Run** Menu in Xcode, select **Console** to show the Debugger Console window.

Logging is also the main reason you should only use Release builds to test your game's performance.

Conclusion

Wow, that was a lot for a Getting Started chapter! In the first part of this chapter you learned to download and set up all the necessary tools up to the point where you had your first cocos2d template project running.

I then walked you through the workings of the template project to get you up to speed with how an iOS cocos2d application works in principle, and somewhat in detail as well. I do have a pet peeve about proper memory management, which is why I also included those details. I think it's important because it's easy to misunderstand or even completely ignore memory management, and then you might be building your game on a very crumbly foundation.

I did manage to sneak in a short "do it yourself" section to at least show you how touch input is done in cocos2d and how cocos2d objects are stored and retrieved.

Finally, I thought it important to give you the details about the various iOS devices and what you can expect in terms of available memory. I also discussed the simulator and how it differs for testing your game compared with testing it on a device.

In the next chapter you'll learn all the essential features of cocos2d, which will bring you closer to making a complete cocos2d game.

Chapter 3

Essentials

This chapter will introduce you to the essential building blocks of the cocos2d game engine. You'll be using most of these classes in every game you create, and understanding what's available and how these classes work together will help you write better games. Armed with this knowledge, you'll find it a lot easier to start working with cocos2d.

Accompanying this chapter is an Xcode project named *Essentials* that includes everything I discuss here plus additional examples. The source code is full of comments so you can read it as if it were an appendix to the book.

We'll start with a high-level overview of the cocos2d game engine architecture. Every game engine is different in the way game objects are managed and presented on the screen. It's best to begin with an understanding of what the individual elements are and how they fit together.

Singletons in cocos2d

Cocos2d makes good use of the Singleton design pattern, which I believe deserves mention because it's regularly and hotly debated. In principle, a *singleton* is a regular class that is instantiated only once during the lifetime of the application. To ensure that this is the case, a static method is used to both create and access the instance of the object. So instead of using `alloc/init` or a static autorelease initializer, you gain access to a singleton object via methods that begin with `shared`. Here are some of cocos2d's most-used singleton classes and how you access them:

```
CCActionManager* sharedManager = [CCActionManager sharedManager];
CCDirector* sharedDirector = [CCDirector sharedDirector];
CCSpriteFrameCache* sharedCache = [CCSpriteFrameCache sharedSpriteFrameCache];
CCTextureCache* sharedTexCache = [CCTextureCache sharedTextureCache];
CCTouchDispatcher* sharedDispatcher = [CCTouchDispatcher sharedDispatcher];
CDAudioManager* sharedManager = [CDAudioManager sharedManager];
SimpleAudioEngine* sharedEngine = [SimpleAudioEngine sharedEngine];
```

The upside of a singleton is that it can be used anywhere by any class at any time. It acts almost like a global class, much like global variables. Singletons are very useful if you have a combination of data and methods you need to use in many different places. Audio is a good example of this, because any of your classes—whether the player, an enemy, a menu button, or a cutscene—might want to play a sound effect or change the background music. So it makes a lot of sense to use a singleton for playing audio. Likewise, if you have global game stats, perhaps the size of the player's army and each platoon's number of troops, you might want to store that information in a singleton so you can carry it over from one level to another. Implementing a singleton is straightforward, as Listing 3–1 shows. This code implements the class MyManager as a singleton with minimal code. The sharedManager static method grants access to the single instance of MyManager. If the instance doesn't exist, a MyManager instance will be allocated and initialized; otherwise, the existing instance is returned.

Listing 3–1. *Implementing the Exemplary Class MyManager as a Singleton*

```
static MyManager *sharedManager = nil;

+(MyManager*) sharedManager
{
        if (sharedManager == nil)
        {
                sharedManager = [[MyManager alloc] init];
        }
        return sharedManager;
}
```

However, singletons also have an ugly side. Because they're simple to use and implement and can be accessed from any other class, there's a tendency to use them in places they shouldn't be used.

For example, you might think you have only one player object, so why not make the player class a singleton? Everything seems to be fine—until you realize that whenever the player advances from one level to another, the singleton not only keeps the player's score but also his last animation frame, his health, and all the items he has picked up, and the he might even begin the new level in Berserk mode because that mode was active when he left the previous level.

To fix that, you go in and add another method to reset certain variables when changing levels. So far so good, but as you add more features to the game, you'll end up having to add and maintain more and more variables when switching a level. What's worse, suppose one day a friend suggests you give the iPad version a two-player mode. But, oh wait, your player is a singleton; you can have only one player at any time! This gives you a major headache: refactor a lot of code or miss out on the cool two-player mode?

The more you rely on singletons, the more such issues will surface. Before creating a singleton class, always consider whether you really need only one instance of this class and its data and whether this might change at a later time.

The Director

The CCDirector class, or simply Director for short, is the heart of the cocos2d game engine. If you recall the HelloWorld application from Chapter 2, you'll remember that a lot of the cocos2d initialization procedure involved calls to [CCDirector sharedDirector]. The Director is a singleton and for good reason: it stores global configuration settings for cocos2d and also manages the cocos2d scenes.

The major uses of the Director include:

- Access to and changing scenes
- Access to cocos2d configuration details
- Access to views (OpenGL, UIView, UIWindow)
- Pausing, resuming, and ending the game
- Converting UIKit and OpenGL coordinates

There are actually four different types of Directors you can choose from, but they differ only in details. The most common Director is the CCDisplayLinkDirector, which uses Apple's CADisplayLink class internally. It's the preferred choice but available only on iOS versions 3.1 or higher; the alternative is to use the CCFastDirector. If you plan on using Cocoa Touch views alongside cocos2d, you may have to switch over to the CCThreadedFastDirector because it's the only one that fully supports them. The downside is that the CCThreadedFastDirector puts a greater strain on the device's battery. If that's very important to you, you can fall back to using the CCTimerDirector, but this should really be a last resort because it's the slowest director type.

The Scene Graph

Sometimes called a scene hierarchy, the scene graph is a hierarchy of every cocos2d node that's currently active. Every node has exactly one parent node, except the scene itself, and can have any number of child nodes.

When you add nodes to other nodes, you're building a scene graph of nodes. Figure 3–1 depicts an excerpt from an imaginary game's scene graph. At the top level, you always have the scene node, usually followed by a layer node, which in cocos2d is responsible for receiving touch and accelerometer input.

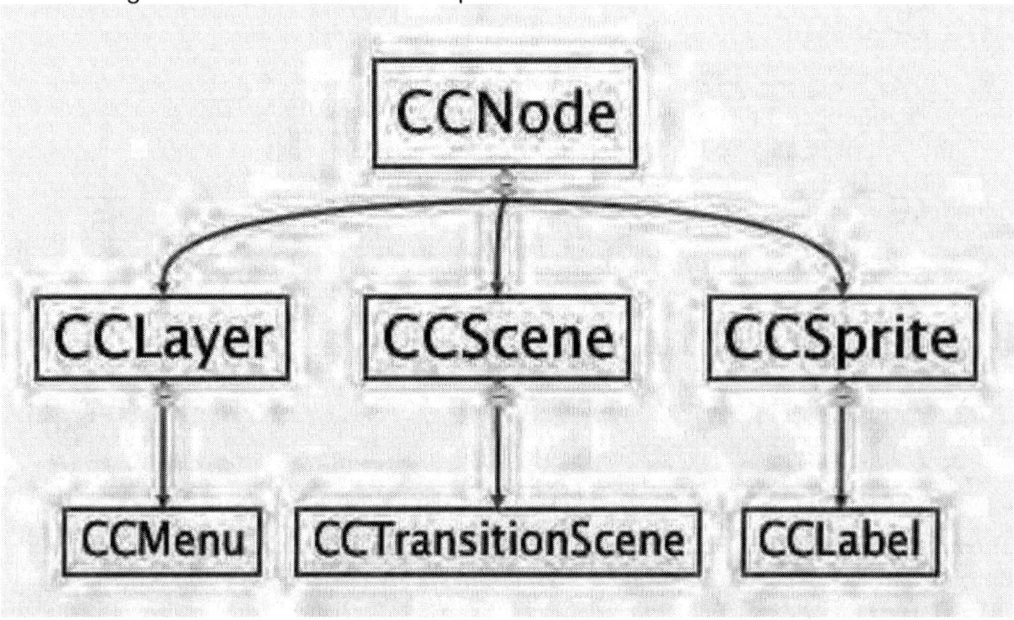

Figure 3–1. *A very simplified cocos2d scene graph using a variety of different nodes to display a player and his weapon, the game's score, and an in-game menu to pause the game or access game options.*

Building on top of the CCLayer object are the constituents of your game, most of them some form of sprite nodes, including the occasional label node displaying the game's score. Menu and menu item nodes are used to display the in-game menu in this example, allowing the player to pause the game or return to the main menu.

You'll notice in Figure 3–1 that the PlayerSprite node has another node added to it named PlayerWeaponSprite. In other words, the PlayerWeaponSprite is attached to the PlayerSprite. If the PlayerSprite moves, rotates, or scales, the PlayerWeaponSprite will do the same without any additional code. This is what makes the scene graph so powerful: most changes you make to a node affect all of its child nodes. But it's also what makes it confusing at times because suddenly things like position and rotation become relative to the parent node.

I wrote a small sample Xcode project called *NodeHierarchy,* which comes with the book's source code and shows an example of how nodes in a hierarchy affect one another. It's much more easily understood if you see it on screen than if I tried to explain it with text and images.

The CCNode Class Hierarchy

All nodes have a common parent class, CCNode, which defines a lot of the common properties and methods, except how to display the node. Figure 3–2 shows the most important classes derived from CCNode. These are the ones you'll work with most often and you can actually make quite impressive games with just these classes.

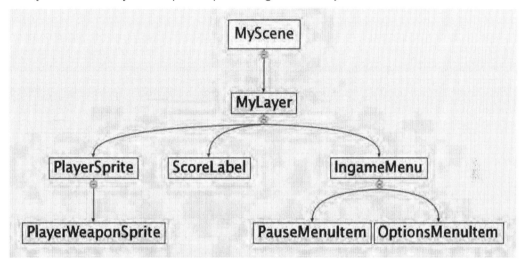

Figure 3–2. *The most important node classes in cocos2d. All node classes derive from CCNode, which defines the common properties and methods.*

CCNode

CCNode is the base class for all nodes. It's an abstract class that has no visual representation and defines all properties and methods common to all nodes.

Working with Nodes

The CCNode class implements all the methods to add, get, and remove child nodes. Here are some of the ways you can work with child nodes.

- To create a new node:

  ```
  CCNode* childNode = [CCNode node];
  ```

- To add the new node as child:

  ```
  [myNode addChild:childNode z:0 tag:123];
  ```

- To retrieve the child node:

  ```
  CCNode* retrievedNode = [myNode getChildByTag:123];
  ```

- To remove the child node by tag; `cleanup` will also stop any running actions:

  `[myNode removeChildByTag:123 cleanup:YES];`

- To remove the node if you have a pointer to it:

  `[myNode removeChild:retrievedNode];`

- To remove every child of the node:

  `[myNode removeAllChildrenWithCleanup:YES];`

- To remove myNode from its parent:

  `[myNode removeFromParentAndCleanup:YES];`

The z parameter in `addChild` determines the draw order of the node. The node with the lowest z value is drawn first; the one with the highest z value is drawn last. If multiple nodes have the same z value, they are simply drawn in the order they were added. Of course this only applies to nodes that have a visual representation, like sprites.

The `tag` parameter lets you can identify and obtain specific nodes at a later time using the `getChildByTag` method.

> **NOTE:** If several nodes end up with the same tag number, `getChildByTag` will return the first node with that tag number. The remaining nodes will be inaccessible. Make sure you use unique tag numbers for your nodes.
>
> Note that actions can have tags, too. Node and action tags do not conflict, however, so an action and a node can have the same tag number without any problem.

Working with Actions

Nodes can also run actions. I'll cover actions more in a bit. For now, just know that actions can move, rotate, and scale nodes and do other things with nodes over time.

- Here's an action declaration:

  ```
  CCAction* action = [CCBlink actionWithDuration:10 blinks:20];
  action.tag = 234;
  ```

- Running the action makes the node blink:

  `[myNode runAction:action];`

- If you need to access the action at a later time, you get it by its tag:

  `CCAction* retrievedAction = [myNode getActionByTag:234];`

- You can stop the action by tag:

  `[myNode stopActionByTag:234];`

- Or you can stop it by pointer:

```
[myNode stopAction:action];
```

- Or you can stop all actions running on this node:

```
[myNode stopAllActions];
```

Scheduled Messages

Nodes can schedule messages, which is Objective-C lingo for calling a method. In many cases, you'll want a particular update method to be running on a node in order to do some processing, like checking for collisions. The simplest way to schedule the particular update method to be called every frame is like this:

```
-(void) scheduleUpdates
{
        [self scheduleUpdate];
}

-(void) update:(ccTime)delta
{
        // this method is called every frame
}
```

Dead simple, isn't it? Notice that the update method has a fixed signature, meaning it's always defined exactly this way. The delta parameter is the elapsed time since the method was last called. This is the preferred way to schedule updates that should take place every frame, but there are reasons to use other update methods that give you more flexibility.

If you want a different method to be run, or if you don't want the method to be called every frame but every tenth of a second, you should use this method:

```
-(void) scheduleUpdates
{
        [self schedule:@selector(updateTenTimesPerSecond:) interval:0.1f];
}

-(void) updateTenTimesPerSecond:(ccTime)delta
{
        // this method is called according to its interval, ten times per second
}
```

Note that if interval is 0, you should use the scheduleUpdate method instead. However, the above code is the preferred choice if you ever need to unschedule a particular selector at a later time. The scheduleUpdate method won't let you do this.

The update method's signature is still the same; it receives a delta time as its only parameter. But this time it can be named any way you want, and it is called only every tenth of a second. This may be useful to check for win conditions if they are so complex you don't want to run them every frame. Or if you want something to happen after 10 minutes, you could schedule a selector with an interval of 600.

NOTE: The @selector(…) syntax may seem weird. It's the Objective-C way of referring to a specific method. The crucial thing here is not to overlook the colon at the end. It tells Objective-C to look for the method with the given name and exactly one parameter. If you forget to add the colon at the end, the program will still compile but it will crash later. In the Debugger Console, the error log will read "unrecognized selector sent to instance …".

The number of colons in @selector(…) must always match the number and names of the parameters of the method. For the following method:

```
-(void) example:(ccTime)delta sender:(id)sender flag:(bool)aBool
```

the corresponding @selector should be:

```
@selector(example:sender:flag:)
```

There's one major caveat with scheduling your own selectors, or with the @selector(…) keyword in general. By default, the compiler does not complain at all if the method's name doesn't exist. Instead, your app will simply crash when that selector is called. Since the call is done by cocos2d internally, you'll find it hard to figure out the cause of the problem. Luckily, there's a compiler warning you can enable. Figure 3–3 shows the "Undeclared Selector" warning enabled and the *Essentials* Xcode project for this chapter has it enabled as well.

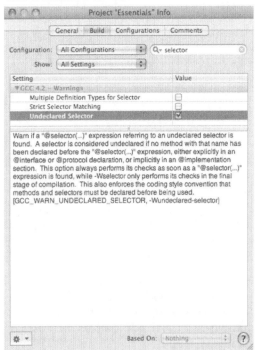

Figure 3–3. *Activating the Build Setting to warn about Undeclared Selectors.*

What's left is to show how to stop these scheduled methods from being called. You can do so by unscheduling them.

To stop all selectors of the node, even those scheduled with scheduleUpdate:

```
[self unscheduleAllSelectors];
```

To stop a particular selector, in this case the update method, do this instead:

```
[self unschedule:@selector(updateTenTimesPerSecond:)];
```

Note that this won't stop the update method scheduled by scheduleUpdate.

There's also a trick for scheduling and unscheduling selectors that's pretty useful. Quite often you'll find that in the scheduled method you want a particular method to no longer be called, without having to replicate the exact name and number of parameters, as they can change. Here's how you'd run a scheduled selector and stop it on the first call:

```
-(void) scheduleUpdates
{
        [self schedule:@selector(tenMinutesElapsed:) interval:600];
}

-(void) tenMinutesElapsed:(ccTime)delta
{
        // unschedule the current method by using the _cmd keyword
        [self unschedule:_cmd];
}
```

The keyword _cmd is shorthand for the current method. Effectively this stops the tenMinutesElapsed method from ever being called again. You can actually use _cmd for scheduling the selector as well. Let's assume you need a method called at varying intervals and this interval is changed each time the method is called. In this case, your code would look like this:

```
-(void) scheduleUpdates
{
        // schedule the first update as usual
        [self schedule:@selector(irregularUpdate:) interval:1];
}

-(void) irregularUpdate:(ccTime)delta
{
        // unschedule the method first
        [self unschedule:_cmd];

        // I assume you'd have some kind of logic other than random to determine
        // the next time the method should be called
        float nextUpdate = CCRANDOM_0_1() * 10;

        // then re-schedule it with the new interval using _cmd as the selector
        [self schedule:_cmd interval:nextUpdate];
}
```

Using the _cmd keyword will save you a lot of pain in the long run because it avoids the dreaded issue of scheduling or unscheduling the wrong selector.

There's one final scheduling issue to mention, and that's prioritizing updates. Have a look at the following code:

```
// in Node A
-(void) scheduleUpdates
{
        [self scheduleUpdate];
}

// in Node B
-(void) scheduleUpdates
{
        [self scheduleUpdateWithPriority:1];
}

// in Node C
-(void) scheduleUpdates
{
        [self scheduleUpdateWithPriority:-1];
}
```

This may take a moment to sink in. All nodes are still calling the same -(void) update:(ccTime)delta method for themselves. However, scheduling the update methods with a priority causes the one in Node C to be run first. Then the one in Node A is called because, by default, scheduleUpdate uses a priority of 0. Node B's update method is called last because it has the highest number. The update methods are called in the order from lowest priority number to highest.

You might wonder where that's useful. Well, to be honest it's rarely needed. I do know from experience there are some edge cases where it's handy, like applying forces to physics objects before or after the physics simulation itself is updated. The announcement of this feature supports this notion as it too mentions physics updates. And sometimes, usually late in the project, you may discover an odd bug that turns out to be a timing issue and it forces you to run the player's update method after all other objects have updated themselves.

Until you need to solve a particular problem by using prioritized updates, you can safely ignore them.

Scenes and Layers

Like CCNode, the CCScene and CCLayer classes have no visual representation and are used internally as abstract concepts for the starting point of the scene graph, which is always a CCScene-derived object. And CCLayer is typically used to group nodes together and to receive touch and accelerometer input if you enable it.

CCScene

A CCScene object is always the first node in the scene graph. Normally the only children of a CCScene are those derived from CCLayer, which in turn contain the individual game objects. Since the scene object itself in most cases doesn't contain any game-specific code and is rarely subclassed, it's most often created in a static method +(id) scene inside the CCLayer object. I already mentioned this method in Chapter 2, but here it is again to refresh your memory:

```
+(id) scene
{
        CCScene *scene = [CCScene node];
        CCLayer* layer = [HelloWorld node];
        [scene addChild:layer];

        return scene;
}
```

The very first place you'll create a scene is at the end of the AppDelegate's applicationDidFinishLaunching method. You use the Director to start the first scene using the runWithScene method:

```
// only use this to run the very first scene
[[CCDirector sharedDirector] runWithScene:[HelloWorld scene]];
```

In all other cases, you replace an existing scene with the aptly named replaceScene method:

```
// use replaceScene to change all subsequent scenes
[[CCDirector sharedDirector] replaceScene:[HelloWorld scene]];
```

> **NOTE:** If you run this code in the HelloWorld scene, it will work just fine. It will create a new instance of HelloWorld and replace the old one, effectively reloading the scene. However, don't try to reload the current scene by passing self as a parameter to replaceScene. This will freeze your game!

Scenes and Memory

Keep in mind that when you replace one scene with another, the new scene is loaded into memory before the old scene's memory is freed. This creates a short spike in memory usage. Replacing scenes is always a crucial point where you can run into memory warnings or straight into a crash related to not enough free memory. You should test scene switching early and often when your app uses a lot of memory.

> **NOTE:** cocos2d does a good job of cleaning up its own memory when you replace one scene with another. It removes all nodes, stops all actions, and unschedules all selectors. I mention this because sometimes I come across code that makes explicit calls to the respective removeAll cocos2d methods. Remember, if in doubt, trust cocos2d's memory management.

This issue becomes even more pronounced when you start using transitions. What happens then is that the new scene is created, the transition runs, and only after the transition has done its job is the old scene be removed from memory. It's good practice to add log statements to your scene, or respectively, to the layer that creates the scene:

```
-(id) init
{
        if ((self = [super init]))
        {
                CCLOG(@"%@: %@", NSStringFromSelector(_cmd), self);
        }
}

-(void) dealloc
{
        CCLOG(@"%@: %@", NSStringFromSelector(_cmd), self);

        // always call [super dealloc] in the dealloc method!
        [super dealloc];
}
```

Keep an eye on these log messages. If you ever notice that the dealloc log message is never sent when you switch from one scene to another, this is a huge warning sign. In that case, you're leaking the whole scene, not freeing its memory. Something like that is extremely unlikely to be caused by cocos2d itself. In almost all cases, it will boil down to retaining or not properly releasing nodes.

One thing you should never do is to add a node as child to the scene graph and then retain it yourself for some other purpose. Use cocos2d's methods to access node objects instead, or at the very least keep a weak reference to the pointer instead of retaining it. As long as you let cocos2d worry about managing the memory of nodes you should be fine.

Pushing and Popping Scenes

While I'm still talking about changing scenes, I should mention the pushScene and popScene methods of the Director, which can be useful tools. What they do is to run the new scene without removing the old scene from memory. The idea is to make changing scenes faster. But there's the conundrum: if your scenes are lightweight enough that they can share memory with each other, they'll load fast anyway. And if they are complex and thus slow to load, chances are they take away each other's precious memory—and memory usage quickly gets to a critical level.

The worst problem with pushScene and popScene is that you can stack them. You can push a scene and run a new scene. This new scene then pushes another scene that pushes yet another scene. If you're not extremely careful about managing your pushes and pops, you'll end up forgetting a pop or popping one scene too many. And this is besides the fact that all those scenes have to share the same memory.

There is one case where pushScene and popScene are very handy, and that's if you have one common scene that's used in many places, such as the Settings screen where you can change Music and Sound volume. You can push the Settings scene to display it, and the Settings scene's Back button then simply calls popScene and the game will return to the previous state. Whether you opened the Settings menu from the main menu, in-game, or someplace else, this technique works fine, and lets you avoid having to keep track of where the Settings menu was opened.

However, you need to test the Settings screen in all circumstances to make sure there's always enough memory available. Ideally, your Settings scene should be very lightweight.

To display the Settings scene from anywhere, use this code:

```
[[CCDirector sharedDirector] pushScene:[Settings scene]];
```

If you're inside the Settings scene when it should be closed, call popScene; this will return to the previous scene that's still in memory:

```
[[CCDirector sharedDirector] popScene];
```

CCTransitionScene

Transitions, meaning any class derived from CCTransitionScene, can give your game a really professional look.

> **NOTE:** Here's the warning in advance: not every transition is really useful in a game, even though they all look neat. What players care most about is the speed of a transition. Even just 3 seconds is quite a strain; I prefer to transition scenes within a second or completely avoid them altogether if it better fits the situation.
>
> What you should certainly try to avoid is picking random transitions when replacing scenes. Players don't care, and as game developers we know you just got a little over-excited by how cool the transitions are. If you don't know which transition is right for a particular change of scene, you shouldn't use any at all. In other words, just because you *can* doesn't mean you *should*.

Transitions only add one more line of code to replacing a scene, although admittedly that one line can be a long one given how long the names of transitions are and how they get even longer with the number of parameters they often require. Here's the very popular Fade Transition as an example; it fades to white in one second:

```
// initialize a transition scene with the scene we'd like to display next
CCFadeTransition* tran = [CCFadeTransition transitionWithDuration:1
                                              scene:[HelloWorld scene]
                                              withColor:ccWHITE];
// use the transition scene object instead of HelloWorld
[[CCDirector sharedDirector] replaceScene:tran];
```

You can use a CCTransitionScene with replaceScene and pushScene, but note, as I said earlier, that you can't use a transition with popScene.

There are a variety of transitions available, although most are variations of directions, as in where the transition moves to or from which side it starts. Here's a list of the currently available transitions, along with a short description for each.

- CCFadeTransition: Fade to a specific color and back.

- CCFadeTRTransition (three more variations): Tiles flip over to reveal new scene.

- CCJumpZoomTransition: Scene bounces and gets smaller, new scene does the reverse.

- CCMoveInLTransition (three more variations): Scene moves out, new scene moves in at the same time, either from left, right, top or bottom.

- CCOrientedTransitionScene (six more variations): A variety of transitions flipping the whole scene around

- CCPageTurnTransition: An effect like turning a page.

- CCRotoZoomTransition: Scene rotates and gets smaller, new scene does reverse.

- CCShrinkGrowTransition: Current scene shrinks, new scene grows over it.

- CCSlideInLTransition (three more variations): New scene slides over the current scene, either from left, right, top or bottom.

- CCSplitColsTransition (one variation): Columns of scene move up or down to reveal new scene.

- CCTurnOffTilesTransition: Tiles randomly replaced by tiles of new scene.

CCLayer

Sometimes you need more than one CCLayer in your scene. In that case, you need more layers as scenes are created like this:

```
+(id) scene
{
        CCScene* scene = [CCScene node];

        CCLayer* backgroundLayer = [HelloWorldBackground node];
        [scene addChild: backgroundLayer];
```

```
        CCLayer* layer = [HelloWorld node];
        [scene addChild:layer];

        CCLayer* userInterfaceLayer = [HelloWorldUserInterface node];
        [scene addChild: userInterfaceLayer];

        return scene;
}
```

An alternative would be to subclass CCScene and then create the layers and other objects in the scene's init method.

One case where you might want to use multiple layers per scene is if you have a scrolling background and a static frame surrounding the background, possibly including user interface elements. Using two separate layers makes it easy to move the background layer by simply adjusting the layer's position while the foreground layer remains in place. In addition, all objects of the same layer will be either in front or behind objects of another layer, depending on the z-order of the layers. Of course, you can achieve the same effect without layers, but it would require each individual object in the background to be moved separately. That's just ineffective so avoid it if you can.

Like scenes, layers have no dimension. Layers are primarily a grouping concept. For example, you can use any action with a layer and the action will affect all of the objects on the layer. That means you can move all layer objects around in unison, or rotate and scale them all at once. In general, use a layer if you need a group of objects to perform the same actions and behaviors. Moving all objects to scroll them is one such case; sometimes you might want to rotate them, or reorder them so they are drawn on top of other objects. If all these objects are children of a layer, you can simply change the layer's properties or run an action on the layer to affect all of its child nodes.

> **NOTE:** There is a recommendation not to use too many CCLayer objects per scene. This is often misunderstood. You can use as many layers as you want without affecting performance any more than using any other node. However, things change if the layer also accepts input, because receiving touch or accelerometer events are costly tasks. So you should not use too many layers receiving touch or accelerometer input. Preferably you should have just one layer receiving and handling input, and, where necessary, it should inform other nodes or classes about the input events received by forwarding the events.

Receiving Touch Events

The CCLayer class is designed to receive touch input but only if you explicitly enable it. To enable receiving touch events, set the property isTouchEnabled to YES:

```
self.isTouchEnabled = YES;
```

This is best done in the class's init method but it can be changed at any time.

Once the isTouchEnabled property is set, a variety of methods for receiving touch input will start to get called. These are the events received when a new touch begins, when a finger is moved on the touchscreen, and when the user lifts his finger off the screen. Cancelled touches are rare and you can safely ignore this method for the most part, or simply forward it to the ccTouchesEnded method.

- Called when a finger just begins touching the screen:

  ```
  -(void) ccTouchesBegan:(NSSet *)touches withEvent:(UIEvent *)event
  ```

- Called whenever the finger moves on the screen:

  ```
  -(void) ccTouchesMoved:(NSSet *)touches withEvent:(UIEvent *)event
  ```

- Called when a finger is lifted off the screen:

  ```
  -(void) ccTouchesEnded:(NSSet *)touches withEvent:(UIEvent *)event
  ```

- Called to cancel a touch:

  ```
  -(void) ccTouchesCancelled:(NSSet *)touches withEvent:(UIEvent *)event
  ```

Cancel events are rare and should behave just like touches ended in most cases.

In many cases, you'll want to know where a touch occurred. Since the touch events are received by the Cocoa Touch API, the location must be converted to OpenGL coordinates. The following is a method that does this for you:

```
-(CGPoint) locationFromTouches:(NSSet *)touches
{
        UITouch *touch = [touches anyObject];
        CGPoint touchLocation = [touch locationInView: [touch view]];
        return [[CCDirector sharedDirector] convertToGL:touchLocation];
}
```

This method works only with a single touch since it uses [touches anyObject]. To keep track of multi-touch locations, you have to keep track of each touch individually.

By default, the layer receives the same events as Apple's UIResponder class. Cocos2d also supports targeted touch handlers. The difference is that targeted touches receive only one touch at a time, in comparison to the UIResponder touch events that always receive a set of touches. The targeted touch handler simply splits those touches into separate events that, depending on your game's needs, may be easier to work with. More importantly, it allows you to remove certain touches from the event queue, specifying that you've handled this touch and don't want it to be forwarded to other layers. This makes it easy to sort out if touches are in a specific area of the screen; if they are, you mark the touch as claimed and all the remaining layers don't need to do this area check again.

To enable the targeted touch handler, add the following method to your layer's class:

```
-(void) registerWithTouchDispatcher
{
        [[CCTouchDispatcher sharedDispatcher] addTargetedDelegate:self
                                            priority:INT_MIN+1 swallowsTouches:YES];
}
```

> **NOTE:** If you leave the `registerWithTouchDispatcher` method empty, you won't receive any touches at all! If you want to keep the method but also want to use the default handler, you'll have to call `[super registerWithTouchDispatcher]` in this method.

Now, instead of using the default touch input methods, you'll be using a slightly different set of methods. They are almost equivalent with the exception of receiving a (`UITouch*`) touch instead of a (`NSSet*`) `touches` as the first parameter:

```
-(BOOL) ccTouchBegan:(UITouch *)touch withEvent:(UIEvent *)event {}
-(void) ccTouchMoved:(UITouch *)touch withEvent:(UIEvent *)event {}
-(void) ccTouchEnded:(UITouch *)touch withEvent:(UIEvent *)event {}
-(void) ccTouchCancelled:(UITouch *)touch withEvent:(UIEvent *)event {}
```

What's important to note here is that ccTouchBegan returns a BOOL value. If you return YES in that method, it means you don't want this particular touch to be propagated to other targeted touch handlers with a lower priority. You have effectively "swallowed" this touch.

Receiving Accelerometer Events

Like touch input, the accelerometer must be specifically enabled to receive accelerometer events:

```
self.isAccelerometerEnabled = YES;
```

Once more, there's a specific method to be added to the layer that receives the accelerometer events:

```
-(void) accelerometer:(UIAccelerometer *)accelerometer
```

```
didAccelerate:(UIAcceleration *)acceleration
{
        CCLOG(@"acceleration: x:%f / y:%f / z:%f",
                                acceleration.x, acceleration.y, acceleration.z);
}
```

You can use the `acceleration` parameter to determine the acceleration in any of the three directions.

CCSprite

CCSprite is certainly the most commonly used class. It uses an image to display the sprite onscreen. The simplest way to create a sprite is from a file that will be loaded into a CCTexture2D texture and assigned to the sprite. You have to add the image file to the Resources group in Xcode, otherwise the app will not be able to find the file:

```
CCSprite* sprite = [CCSprite spriteWithFile:@"Default.png"];
[self addChild:sprite];
```

Here's a question for you: where do you think this sprite will be positioned on the screen? Contrary to what you might be used to from other game engines, the texture is centered on the sprite's position. The sprite just initialized will be located at position 0,0, so it is positioned at the lower left corner of the screen. Because the sprite's texture is centered on the sprite's position, the texture will be only partially visible. Assuming the image is 80 x 30-pixels in size, you'd have to move the sprite to position 40,15 to make the s texture align perfectly with the lower left corner of the screen and be fully visible.

While unusual at first glance, centering the texture on the sprite does have great advantages. Once you start using the rotation or scale properties of the sprite, the sprite will stay centered on its position.

> **WARNING:** File names are case-sensitive on iOS devices! While you're on the simulator, the file name's case doesn't matter but when you switch over to testing on the device, it will most likely crash if the file name is actually something like @"default.PNG", as in the example.
>
> This has caused many developers serious headaches and it's another reason you should test on the device often. It's also a good idea to come up with a naming scheme for file names and stick to it. Personally, I keep them in lowercase, using dashes where needed to separate words.

Anchor Points Demystified

Every node has an anchor point but it only starts to make a difference if the node has a texture. By default, the anchorPoint property is at 0.5, 0.5 or half the size of the texture. It's a factor, a multiplier, and not a specific size in pixels.

The anchor point has nothing to do with the node's position, contrary to what you might think when you change the anchorPoint property and see the sprite change its position on screen. But that's a misperception. It's playing a trick on your mind because the node's position doesn't actually change; you're only moving the sprite's texture around!

The anchorPoint property merely defines the offset of the texture relative to the node's position. To calculate the texture offset, the texture width and height are simply multiplied by the anchor point. By the way, there's a read-only property anchorPointInPixels so you don't have to calculate the pixel offset yourself.

Setting the anchorPoint to 0,0 effectively places the texture's lower left corner at the node's position. In this code, the sprite image will neatly align with the lower left corner of the screen:

```
CCSprite* sprite = [CCSprite spriteWithFile:@"Default.png"];
sprite.anchorPoint = CGPointMake(0, 0);
[self addChild:sprite];
```

> **NOTE:** If you're tempted to change the anchor point to 0,0 for all your sprites because that's what you're used to from some other game engine, please don't. It's only going to hurt you later. It will make a lot of things more awkward, from rotation and scaling, to relative positions of child nodes, to distance checks and collision detection. You really, really want to have the anchorPoint at the center of the texture, even if you don't know it yet. Trust me.

Texture Dimensions

Texture dimensions deserve a special mention. iOS devices so far can work only with textures whose dimensions are a power of two, so the individual width and height of a texture can be 2, 4, 8, 16, 32, 64, 128, 256, 512, 1024, and on third-generation devices, even 2048 pixels. The textures don't need to be square, so a texture with a size of 8 x 1024 pixels is still perfectly fine.

This comes into play whenever you create a texture, for example by creating a sprite from an image file. Let's check the worst-case scenario right away by assuming you have an image that is 260 x 260-pixels in size with 32-bit colors. In memory, the texture should use around 270 KB, yet the texture is using a whopping 1 MB!

The almost fourfold increase stems from the fact that textures need to be powers of 2 in width and height, so the iOS device simply creates a texture with the smallest dimension that's still a power of 2 but large enough to contain the image. In the case of the 260 x 260 texture, the next best option is to create a 512 x 512-pixel texture in memory, which uses 1 MB of memory.

There's nothing you can do about this, other than creating images that are already powers of two from the start. The 260 x 260-pixel texture should really be a 256 x 256 texture instead so it doesn't waste that much memory. If you work with an artist, make sure she is aware of this issue.

In Chapter 6 I'll show you how you can alleviate this problem to a great extent by creating and using a Texture Atlas.

CCLabel

CCLabel is the simplest choice when it comes to displaying text on the screen. Here's how to create a CCLabel object to display some text:

```
CCLabel* label = [CCLabel labelWithString:@"text" fontName:@"AppleGothic"
```

```
fontSize:32];
[self addChild:label];
```

In case you're wondering which TrueType fonts are available on iOS devices, you'll find a list of fonts in the *Essentials* code project for this chapter.

Internally, the given TrueType font is used to render the text on a CCTexture2D texture. Since this is done every time the text changes, it's not something you should do every frame. Recreating a label's texture is really slow.

```
[label setString:@"new text"];
```

You'll also notice that if you change the text of a label, the label's text remains centered. This is because of the anchor point. In many cases you want to align labels left, right, up, or down, and you can use the anchorPoint property to easily achieve this. The following code shows how you can align a label by simply changing the anchorPoint property:

```
// align label to the right
label.anchorPoint = CGPointMake(1, 0.5f);
// align label to the left
label.anchorPoint = CGPointMake(0, 0.5f);
// align label to the top
label.anchorPoint = CGPointMake(0.5f, 1);
// align label to the bottom
label.anchorPoint = CGPointMake(0.5f, 0);

// use case: place label at top-right corner of the screen
// the label's text extends to the left and down and is always completely on screen
CGSize size = [[CCDirector sharedDirector] winSize];
label.position = CGPointMake(size.width, size.height);
label.anchorPoint = CGPointMake(1, 1);
```

Menus

You'll soon need some kind of button a user can press to perform an action, like going to another scene or toggling music on and off. This is where the CCMenu class comes into play. CCMenu accepts only CCMenuItem nodes as children.

Listing 3–2 shows the code for setting up a menu. You can find the menu code in the *Essentials* project in the MenuScene class.

Listing 3–2. *Creating Menus in cocos2d with Text and Image Menu Items*

```
CGSize size = [[CCDirector sharedDirector] winSize];

// set CCMenuItemFont default properties
[CCMenuItemFont setFontName:@"Helvetica-BoldOblique"];
[CCMenuItemFont setFontSize:26];

// create a few labels with text and selector
CCMenuItemFont* item1 = [CCMenuItemFont itemFromString:@"Go Back!" target:self

selector:@selector(menuItem1Touched:)];
```

```
// create a menu item using existing sprites
CCSprite* normal = [CCSprite spriteWithFile:@"Icon.png"];
normal.color = ccRED;
CCSprite* selected = [CCSprite spriteWithFile:@"Icon.png"];
selected.color = ccGREEN;
CCMenuItemSprite* item2 = [CCMenuItemSprite itemFromNormalSprite:normal
            selectedSprite:selected target:self selector:@selector(menuItem2Touched:)];

// create a toggle item using two other menu items (toggle works with images, too)
[CCMenuItemFont setFontName:@"STHeitiJ-Light"];
[CCMenuItemFont setFontSize:18];
CCMenuItemFont* toggleOn = [CCMenuItemFont itemFromString:@"I'm ON!"];
CCMenuItemFont* toggleOff = [CCMenuItemFont itemFromString:@"I'm OFF!"];
CCMenuItemToggle* item3 = [CCMenuItemToggle itemWithTarget:self
                selector:@selector(menuItem3Touched:) items:toggleOn, toggleOff, nil];

// create the menu using the items
CCMenu* menu = [CCMenu menuWithItems:item1, item2, item3, nil];
menu.position = CGPointMake(size.width / 2, size.height / 2);
[self addChild:menu];

// aligning is important, so the menu items don't occupy the same location
[menu alignItemsVerticallyWithPadding:40];
```

> **WARNING:** The lists of menu items always end with `nil` as the last parameter. This is a technical requirement. If you forget to add `nil` as the last parameter, your app will crash at that particular line.

It takes a fair bit of code to set up a menu. The first menu item is based on CCMenuItemFont and simply displays a string. When the menu item is touched, it calls the method menuItem1Touched. Internally, CCMenuItemFont simply creates a CCLabel. If you already have a CCLabel, you can use that with the CCMenuItemLabel class instead.

Likewise, there are two menu item classes for images; one is CCMenuItemImage, which creates an image from a file and uses a CCSprite internally, and the other is one I've used here, CCMenuItemSprite. This class takes existing sprites as input, which I think is more convenient because it you can use the same image and simply tint its color to achieve a highlighting effect when touched.

CCMenuItemToggle accepts exactly two CCMenuItem-derived objects and, when touched, will toggle between the two items. You can use either text labels or images with CCMenuItemToggle.

Finally, CCMenu itself is created and positioned. Since the menu items are all children of CCMenu, they will be positioned relative to the menu. To keep them from stacking up on each other, you have to call one of CCMenu's align methods, like alignItemsVerticallyWithPadding as I've done at the end of Listing 3–2.

Since CCMenu is a node containing all menu items, you can use actions on the menu to let it scroll in and out. This makes your menu screens appear less static, which is usually a good thing. See the *Essentials* project for an example. In the meantime take a look at Figure 3–4 to see what our current menu looks like.

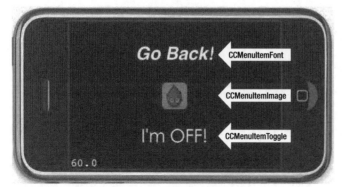

Figure 3–4. *This is the menu produced by the code in Listing 3–2. What you can't see is that the text labels change size and the sprite changes color when touched.*

Actions

Actions are lightweight classes that are used on nodes to perform certain, well, actions. They allow you to move, rotate, scale, tint, fade, and do a lot of other things with a node. Because they work with every node, you can use them on sprites, labels, even menus or whole scenes! That's what makes them so powerful.

Since most actions happen over time, like a rotation for three seconds, you'd normally have to write an update method and add variables to store the intermediate results. Actions wrap this kind of logic for you and turn it into simple, parameterized methods:

```
// I want myNode to move to 100, 200 and arrive there in 3 seconds
CCMoveTo* move = [CCMoveTo actionWithDuration:3 position:CGPointMake(100, 200)];
[myNode runAction:move];
```

Actions come in two flavors. Instant actions are basically the same as setting a node property like visible or flipX. Interval actions run over a period of time, like the move action above. By the way, you don't have to remove either type of action. Once an action has completed its task, it will remove itself from the node automatically and releases the memory it uses.

Repeating Actions

You can also have actions or even a whole sequence of actions repeat forever. You can create endlessly looping animations this way. This code lets a node rotate forever like an endlessly spinning wheel:

```
CCRotateBy* rotateBy = [CCRotateBy actionWithDuration:2 angle:360];
CCRepeatForever* repeat = [CCRepeatForever actionWithAction:rotateBy];
[myNode runAction:repeat];
```

Ease Actions

Actions become even more powerful by using CCEaseAction class actions. Ease actions allow you to modify the effect of an action over time. For example, if you use a CCMoveTo action on a node, the node will move the whole distance at the same speed until it has arrived. With CCEaseAction, you can have the node start slow and speed up towards the target, or vice versa. Or you can let it move past the target location a little and then bounce back. Ease actions create very dynamic animations that are normally very time-consuming to implement. The following code shows how an ease action is used to modify the behavior of a regular action. The rate parameter determines how pronounced the effect of the ease action is, and should be greater than 1 to see any effect.

```
// I want myNode to move to 100, 200 and arrive there in 3 seconds
CCMoveTo* move = [CCMoveTo actionWithDuration:3 position:CGPointMake(100, 200)];
// this time the node should slowly speed up and then slow down as it moves
CCEaseInOut* ease = [CCEaseInOut actionWithAction:move rate:4];
[myNode runAction:ease];
```

> **NOTE:** In the example, the ease action is run on the node, not the move action. It's all too easy to forget to change the runAction line when you're working with actions. It's a common mistake that happens even to the most experienced cocos2d developers. If you notice your actions aren't working as expected or not at all, double-check that you're actually running the correct action. And if the correct actions are used but you're still not seeing the desired result, verify that it's the correct node running the action. This is another common mistake.

Cocos2d implements the following CCEaseAction classes:

- CCEaseBackIn, CCEaseBackInOut, CCEaseBackOut
- CCEaseBounceIn, CCEaseBounceInOut, CCEaseBounceOut
- CCEaseElasticIn, CCEaseElasticInOut, CCEaseElasticOut
- CCEaseExponentialIn, CCEaseExponentialInOut, CCEaseExponentialOut
- CCEaseIn, CCEaseInOut, CCEaseOut
- CCEaseSineIn, CCEaseSineInOut, CCEaseSineOut

In Chapter 4 I'll use a number of these ease actions in the DoodleDrop project, so you can see what effect they have.

Action Sequences

Normally, when you add several actions to a node, they all perform their duties at the same time. For example, you could have an object rotate and fade out at the same time by adding the corresponding actions. But what if you want to run the actions one after the other?

Sometimes it's more useful to sequence actions, and that's where CCSequence comes in. You can use any number and type of actions in a sequence, which makes it easy to have a node move to a target location and, at arrival, have it rotate around and then fade out, each action followed by the next one until the sequence is complete.

Here's how to cycle a label's colors from red to blue to green:

```
CCTintTo* tint1 = [CCTintTo actionWithDuration:4 red:255 green:0 blue:0];
CCTintTo* tint2 = [CCTintTo actionWithDuration:4 red:0 green:0 blue:255];
CCTintTo* tint3 = [CCTintTo actionWithDuration:4 red:0 green:255 blue:0];
CCSequence* sequence = [CCSequence actions:tint1, tint2, tint3, nil];
[label runAction:sequence];
```

You can also use a CCRepeatForever action with the sequence:

```
CCSequence* sequence = [CCSequence actions:tint1, tint2, tint3, nil];
CCRepeatForever* repeat = [CCRepeatForever actionWithAction:sequence];
[label runAction:repeat];
```

> **NOTE:** As with menu items, a list of actions always ends with nil. If you forget to add nil as the last parameter, the line creating the CCSequence will crash!

Instant Actions

You might wonder why there are instantaneous actions based on the CCInstantAction class, when you could just as well change the node's property to achieve the same effect. For example, there are instant actions to flip the node, to place it at a specific location, or to toggle its visible property.

The reason these actions are useful is because of sequences. Sometimes in a sequence of actions you have to change a certain property of the node, like visibility or position, and then continue with the sequence. Instant actions make this possible. True, they are rarely used—with one exception: CCCallFunc actions.

When using an action sequence, you may want to be notified at certain times, for example when the sequence has ended, and then perhaps start another sequence immediately thereafter. To do this you can make use of three versions of CCCallFunc actions that will send a message whenever it's their turn in the sequence. Let's rewrite the color cycle sequence so that it calls a method each time one of the CCTintTo actions has done its job:

```
CCCallFunc* func = [CCCallFunc actionWithTarget:self selector:@selector(onCallFunc)];
CCCallFuncN* funcN = [CCCallFuncN actionWithTarget:self
                                        selector:@selector(onCallFuncN:)];
CCCallFuncND* funcND = [CCCallFuncND actionWithTarget:self
                          selector:@selector(onCallFuncND:data:) data:(void*)self];

CCSequence* seq = [CCSequence actions:tint1, func, tint2, funcN, tint3, funcND, nil];
[label runAction:seq];
```

This sequence will call the methods in the following code one after another. The sender parameter will always be derived from CCNode; it's the node that's running the actions. The data parameter can be used in any way you want, including passing values, structs, or other pointers. You only have to properly cast the data pointer.

```
-(void) onCallFunc
{
        CCLOG(@"end of tint1!");
}

-(void) onCallFuncN:(id)sender
{
        CCLOG(@"end of tint2! sender: %@", sender);
}

-(void) onCallFuncND:(id)sender data:(void*)data
{
        // be careful when casting pointers like this!
        // you have to be 100% sure the object is of this type!
        CCSprite* sprite = (CCSprite*)data;
        CCLOG(@"end of sequence! sender: %@ - data: %@", sender, sprite);
}
```

Of course CCCallFunc also works with CCRepeatForever sequences. Your methods will be called repeatedly at the appropriate time.

Cocos2d Test Cases

Did you know that cocos2d comes with a lot of sample code? In your cocos2d-iphone folder, you'll find a project aptly named cocos2d-iphone that contains a lot of test targets you can build and run. You can see how things work, then check the code to see how it's implemented.

Conclusion

Wow! That was a lot to take in! I don't expect you to remember all of this chapter's content at once. Feel free to come back at any time to look again at cocos2d's scene graph and how to use the various CCNode classes. I wrote this chapter to be a good reference whenever you need it.

Armed with this chapter's knowledge alone and a fair bit of motivation on your side, you could be starting to write your own games now.

You know what, let's do this together. Read on to the next chapter and I'll walk you through your first complete game project!

Chapter 4

Your First Game

In this chapter you'll build your first complete game. It won't win any awards, but you'll learn how to get the essential elements of cocos2d to work together. I'll guide you through the individual steps, so you'll also learn a bit about working with Xcode along the way.

The game is the inversion of the famous Doodle Jump game, aptly named Doodle Drop. The player's goal is to avoid falling obstacles for as long as possible by rotating the device to move the player sprite. Take a look at the final version in Figure 4–1 to get an idea of what you'll be creating in this chapter.

Figure 4–1. *The final version of the DoodleDrop game.*

Step-By-Step Project Setup

Fire up Xcode now and I'll walk you through the steps to create your first cocos2d game. In Xcode, select **File ➤ New Project…** and choose the cocos2d Application template as shown in Figure 4–2. When asked to enter a name for the new project, enter *DoodleDrop* and, if necessary, find a suitable location to save the project. Xcode will automatically create a subfolder named *DoodleDrop,* so you don't have to create that folder.

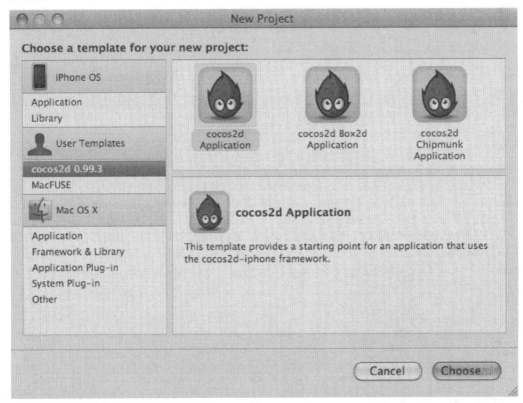

Figure 4–2. *Create the project from the cocos2d Application template.*

Xcode should present you with a project view like the one in Figure 4–3. I've already unfolded the *Classes* and *Resources* groups because that's where you'll be adding the source code and game resource files respectively. Anything that's not source code is considered to be a resource, be it an image, an audio file, a text file, or a plist. The grouping is not strictly necessary, but it does make it easier for you to navigate the project if you keep similar files grouped together.

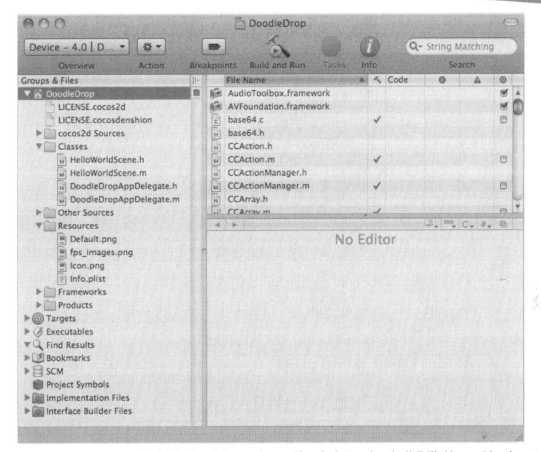

Figure 4–3. *Let the games begin! The DoodleDrop project at this point is based on the HelloWorld cocos2d project template. Make sure you add subsequent files to the Classes and Resources groups accordingly to keep your game project organized.*

The next step you're faced with is a decision: do you start working with the HelloWorldScene because it's there already, possibly renaming it later on? Or do you go through the extra steps to create your own scene to replace the HelloWorldScene? I chose the latter because eventually you'll have to add new scenes anyway, so it's a good idea to learn the ropes here and now and start with a clean slate.

Make sure the Classes group is selected and then select **File ➤ New File…** or right-click the classes folder and select **Add ➤ New File…** to open the New File dialog shown in Figure 4–4. Since cocos2d comes with class templates for the most important nodes, it would be a shame not to use them. From the cocos2d User Templates, select the CCNode class and make sure it's set to be a **Subclass of CCLayer**.

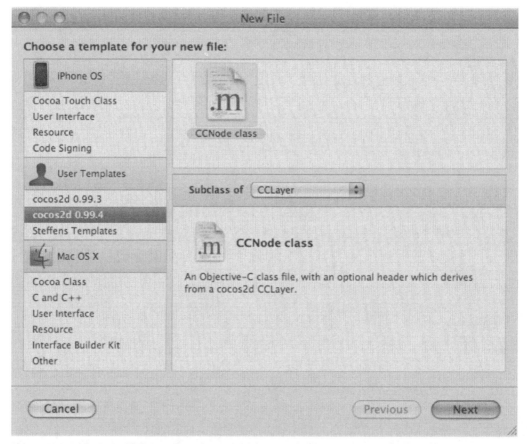

Figure 4–4. *Adding new CCNode derived classes is best done using the class templates provided by cocos2d. In this case, we want the CCNode class to be a subclass of CCLayer since we're setting up a new scene.*

The New File dialog opens, as shown in Figure 4–5. I prefer to name classes by function and in a generic way. I'm using *GameScene.m* in this case. It's going to be the scene where the DoodleDrop gameplay takes place, so that name seems appropriate. Be sure that the **Also create "GameScene.h"** checkbox is checked, as well as the DoodleDrop Target checkbox. Targets are Xcode's way of creating more or less different versions of the executable. For example, the iPad version of a game is usually created as a separate Target. In this case we have only one target, but once you create an iPad Target you want to make sure that, for example, the iPad's high resolution images aren't accidentally added to the iPhone/iPod Touch Target.

NOTE: Not reviewing the Target checkboxes can lead to all kinds of issues, from compile errors to "file not found" errors or crashes during gameplay when files haven't been added to the targets that need them. Or you might simply waste space by adding files to targets that don't need them at all, for example by adding iPad and iPhone 4 high-res images to regular iPhone/iPod Touch targets.

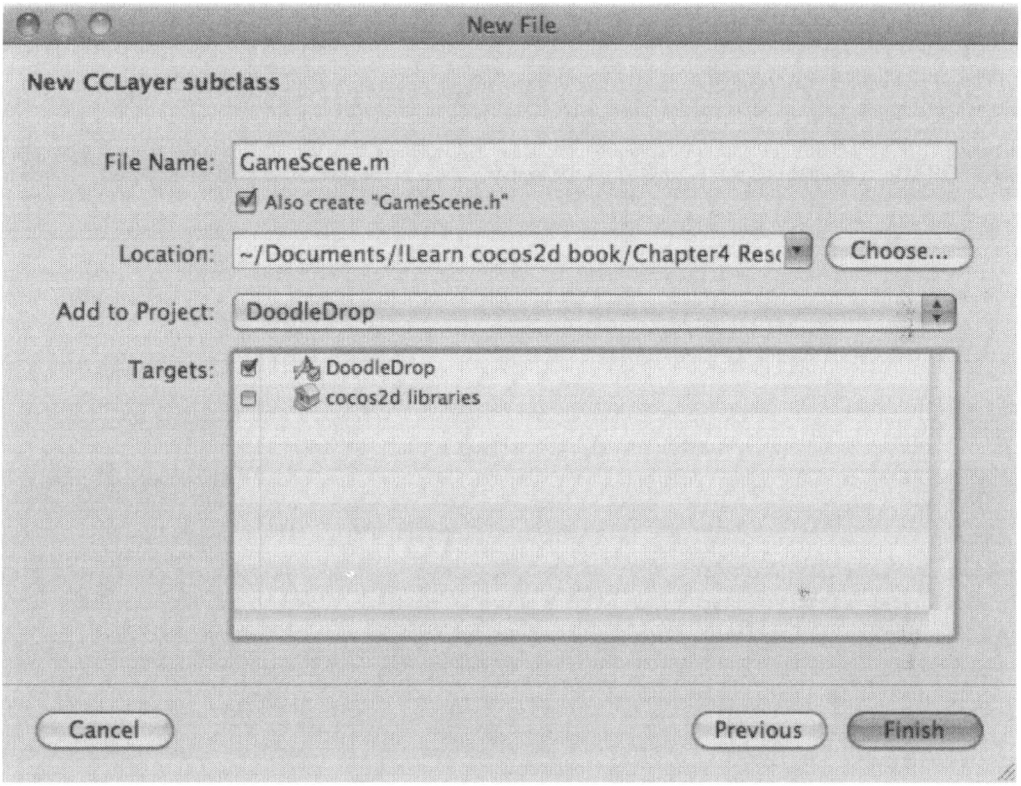

Figure 4–5. *Naming the new scene and making sure it's added to the appropriate target(s)*

At this point, our GameScene class is empty and the first thing we need to do to set it up as a scene is to add the +(id) scene method to it. The code we'll plug in is essentially the same as in Chapter 3, with only the layer's class name changed. What you'll almost always need in any class are the -(id) init and -(void) dealloc methods, so it makes sense to add them right away. I'm also a very cautious programmer and decided to add the logging statements introduced in Chapter 3. The resulting *GameScene.h* is shown in Listing 4–1 and *GameScene.m* is in Listing 4–2.

Listing 4–1. *GameScene.h with the Scene Method*

```
#import <Foundation/Foundation.h>
#import "cocos2d.h"

@interface GameScene : CCLayer
{
}

+(id) scene;

@end
```

Listing 4–2. *GameScene.m with the Scene Method and Standard Methods added, Including Logging*

```
#import "GameScene.h"

@implementation GameScene

+(id) scene
{
        CCScene *scene = [CCScene node];
        CCLayer* layer = [GameScene node];
        [scene addChild:layer];
        return scene;
}

-(id) init
{
        if ((self = [super init]))
        {
                CCLOG(@"%@: %@", NSStringFromSelector(_cmd), self);
        }

        return self;
}

-(void) dealloc
{
        CCLOG(@"%@: %@", NSStringFromSelector(_cmd), self);

        // never forget to call [super dealloc]
        [super dealloc];
}

@end
```

Now you can safely delete the HelloWorldScene class. When asked, select the **Also Move to Trash** option to remove the file from the hard drive as well, not just from the Xcode project. Select both files and choose **Edit ➤ Delete**, or right-click the files and choose **Delete** from the context menu. With the HelloWorldScene class gone, you have to modify the DoodleDropAppDelegate.m to change any references to HelloWorldScene to GameScene. Listing 4–3 highlights the necessary changes to the #import and runWithScene statements. I also changed the device orientation to Portrait mode since the game is desgined to work best in that mode.

Listing 4–3. *Changing DoodleDropAppDelegate.m File to Use the GameScene Class Instead of HelloWorldScene.*

```
// replace the line #import "HelloWorldScene.h" with this one:
#import "GameScene.h"

- (void) applicationDidFinishLaunching:(UIApplication*)application
{
        // Sets Portrait mode
        [director setDeviceOrientation:kCCDeviceOrientationPortrait];

        // replace HelloWorld with GameScene
        [[CCDirector sharedDirector] runWithScene: [GameScene scene]];
}
```

Compile and run, and you should end up with … a blank scene. Success! If you run into any problems, compare your project with the DoodleDrop01 project that accompanies this book.

Adding the Player Sprite

Next you'll add the player sprite and use the accelerometer to control its actions. To add the player image, select the Resources group in Xcode and select Project ➤ Add to Project… or, alternatively, right-click and from the context menu pick Add ➤ Existing Files… to open the file picker dialog. The player image *alien.png* is located in the Resources folder of the DoodleDrop projects supplied with the book. You can also choose your own image, as long as it's 64 x 64 pixels in size.

> **NOTE:** The preferred image format for iOS games is PNG, Portable Network Graphics. It's a compressed file format but, unlike JPG, the compression is lossless, retaining all pixels of the original image unchanged. While you can also save JPG files without compression, the same image in PNG format is typically smaller than an uncompressed JPG file. This affects only the app size, however, not memory (RAM) usage of the textures.

Xcode will then ask you details about how and where to add the file(s), as in Figure 4–6. Make sure the Add To Targets checkboxes are set for each target that will use the file(s), which in this case is only the DoodleDrop target. The defaults are good enough, but when you start working on your own and possibly bigger projects, you'll want to develop a good understanding of these settings. This is fundamental knowledge for working with Xcode. Apple's Xcode documentation describes how files are managed in Xcode projects: http://developer.apple.com/mac/library/documentation/ DeveloperTools/Conceptual/XcodeProjectManagement/130-Files_in_Projects/ project_files.html

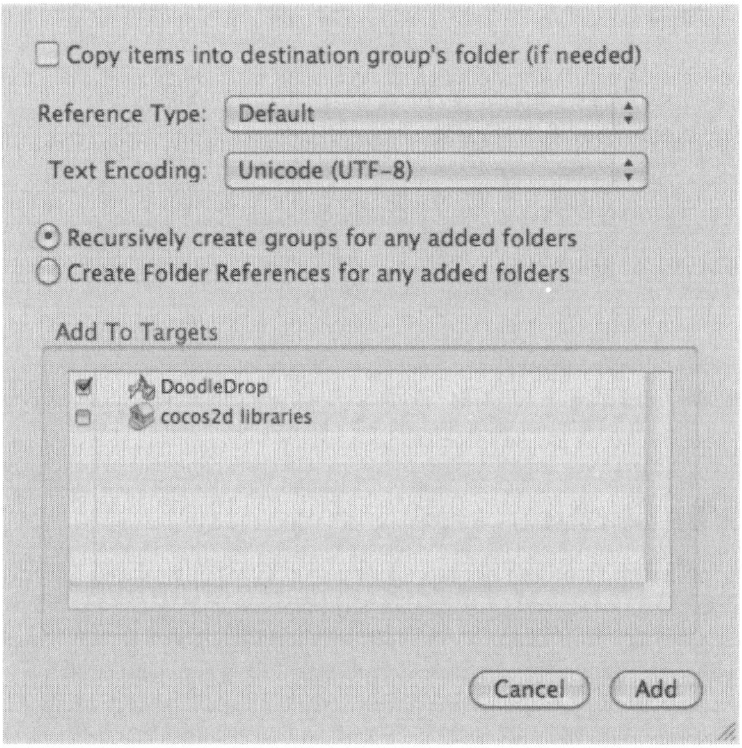

Figure 4–6. *You'll see this dialog whenever you add resource files. In most cases you should use these default settings.*

Now we'll add the player sprite to the game scene. I decided to add it as a CCSprite* member variable to the GameScene class. This is easier for now and the game is simple enough for everything to go into the same class. Generally, that's not the recommended approach and the projects following this one will create separate classes for individual game components as a matter of good code design.

Listing 4–4 shows the addition of the CCSprite* member to the GameScene header file.

Listing 4–4. *The CCSprite* Player Is Added as a Member Variable to the GameScene Class.*

```
#import <Foundation/Foundation.h>
#import "cocos2d.h"

@interface GameScene : CCLayer
{
        CCSprite* player;
}

+(id) scene;

@end
```

Listing 4–5 contains the code I've added to the init method to initialize the sprite, assign it to the member variable, and position it at the bottom center of the screen. I've also enabled accelerometer input.

Listing 4–5. *Enabling Accelerometer Input and Creating and Positioning the Player Sprite.*

```
-(id) init
{
        if ((self = [super init]))
        {
                CCLOG(@"%@: %@", NSStringFromSelector(_cmd), self);

                self.isAccelerometerEnabled = YES;

                player = [CCSprite spriteWithFile:@"alien.png"];
                [self addChild:player z:0 tag:1];

                CGSize screenSize = [[CCDirector sharedDirector] winSize];
                float imageHeight = [player texture].contentSize.height;
                player.position = CGPointMake(screenSize.width / 2, imageHeight / 2);
        }

        return self;
}
```

The player sprite is added as child with a tag of 1, which will later be used to identify and separate the player sprite from all other sprites. Notice that I don't retain the player sprite. Since we'll add it as child to the layer, cocos2d will retain it, and since the player sprite is never removed from the layer, that's sufficient to keep the player sprite without specifically retaining it. Not retaining an object whose memory is managed by another class or object is called keeping a weak reference.

> **NOTE:** Remember, file names on iOS devices are case-sensitive. If you try to load *Alien.png* or *ALIEN.PNG*, it will work in the simulator but not on any iOS device because the real name is *alien.png* in all lowercase. That's why it's a good idea to stick to a naming convention like rigorously keeping all file names in all lowercase.

You set the initial position of the player sprite by centering the x position at half the screen width, which puts the sprite in the center horizontally. Vertically we want the bottom of the player sprite's texture to align with the bottom of the screen. If you remember from the previous chapter, you know that the sprite texture is centered on the node's position. Positioning the sprite vertically at 0 would cause the bottom half of the sprite texture to be below the screen. That's not what we want; we want to move it up by half the texture height.

This is done by the call to [player texture].contentSize.height, which returns the sprite texture's content size. What exactly is the content size? In Chapter 3, I mentioned that the texture dimensions on the iPhone can only be powers of two. But the actual image size may be less than the texture size. For example, this is the case if the image is 100 x 100 pixels while the texture has to be 128 x128 pixels. The contentSize property of the texture returns the original image's size of 100 x 100 pixels. In most cases, you'll want to work with the content size, not the texture size.

By taking half of the image height and setting this as the position on the y axis, the sprite image will align neatly with the bottom of the screen.

> **NOTE:** It's good practice to avoid using fixed positions wherever you can. If you simply set the player position to 160,32, you are making two assumptions you should avoid. First, you're assuming the screen width will be 320 pixels, but that will not hold true for every iOS device. Second, you're assuming that the image height is 64 pixels, but that might change too. Once you start to make assumptions like these, you're forming a habit to do so throughout the project.
>
> The way I wrote the positioning code involves a bit more typing, but in the long run this pays off big time. You can deploy to different devices and it'll work, and you can use different image sizes and it'll work. No need to change this particular code anymore. One of the most time-consuming tasks a programmer faces is having to change code that was based on assumptions.
>
> Imagine yourself three months down the road with lots of images and objects added to your game, having to change all those fixed numbers to create an iPad version that obviously also requires images of different sizes. Then doing the same thing again to adjust the game to the iPhone 4's Retina Display. At that point, you have three different Xcode projects you need to maintain and add features to. Eventually it will lead to "copy & paste hell," which is even more undesirable—don't go there!

Accelerometer Input

Last step, then we should be done tilting the player sprite around. As I demonstrated in Chapter 3, you have to add the accelerometer method to the layer that receives accelerometer input. Here I use the `acceleration.x` parameter and add it to the player's position, multiplying by 10 is to speed up the player's movement.

```
-(void) accelerometer:(UIAccelerometer *)accelerometer
                        didAccelerate:(UIAcceleration *)acceleration
{
        CGPoint pos = player.position;
        pos.x += acceleration.x * 10;
        player.position = pos;
}
```

Notice something odd? I wrote three lines where one should suffice:

```
        // ERROR: lvalue required as left operand of assignment
        player.position.x += acceleration.x * 10;
```

However, unlike other programming languages such as Java, C++, and C#, writing something like `player.position.x += value` won't work with Objective-C properties.

The problem lies in how properties work in Objective-C and also how assignment works in the C language, on which Objective-C is based.

The statement `player.position.x` is actually a call to the position getter method [`player position`], which means you're actually retrieving a temporary position and then trying to change the x member of the temporary `CGPoint`. But the temporary `CGPoint` would then get thrown away. The position setter [`player setPosition`] simply will not be called automagically. You can only assign to the `player.position` property directly, in this case a new `CGPoint`. In Objective-C you'll have to live with this unfortunate issue— and possibly change programming habits if you come from a Java, C++ or C# background.

First Test Run

Your project should now be at the same level as the one in the DoodleDrop02 folder of the code provided with this chapter. Give it a try now. Make sure you choose to run the app on the device, as you won't get accelerometer input from the simulator. Test out how the accelerometer input behaves in this version.

If you haven't installed your development provisioning profiles in Xcode for this particular project yet, you'll get a CodeSign error. Code signing is required to run an app on an iOS device. Please refer to Apple's documentation to learn how to create and install the necessary development provisioning profiles (`https://developer.apple.com/iphone/manage/provisioningprofiles/howto.action`).

Player Velocity

Notice how the accelerometer input isn't quite right? It's reacting slowly and the motion isn't fluid. That's because the player sprite doesn't experience true acceleration and deceleration. Let's fix that now. The accompanying code changes are found in the DoodleDrop03 project.

The concept for implementing acceleration and deceleration is not to change the player's position directly but to use a separate `CGPoint` variable as a velocity vector. Every time an accelerometer event is received, the velocity variable accumulates input from the accelerometer. Of course, that means we also have to limit the velocity to an arbitrary maximum, otherwise it'll take too long to decelerate. The velocity is then added to the player position every frame, regardless of whether accelerometer input was received or not.

NOTE: Why not use actions to move the player sprite? Well, move actions are a bad choice whenever you want to change an object's speed or direction very often, say multiple times per second. Actions are designed to be relatively long-lived objects, so creating new ones frequently creates additional overhead in terms of allocating and releasing memory. This can quickly drain a game's performance.

Worse yet, actions don't work at all if you don't give them any time to do their work. That's why adding a new action to replace the previous one every frame won't show any effect whatsoever. Many cocos2d developers have stumbled across this seemingly odd behavior.

For example, stopping all actions and then adding a new MoveBy action to an object every frame will not make it move at all! The MoveBy action will only change the object's position in the next frame. But that's when you're already stopping all actions again, and adding another new MoveBy action. Repeat ad infinitum but the object will simply not move at all. It's like the clichéd donkey: push it too hard and it'll become a stubborn, immobile object.

Let's go through the code changes. The `playerVelocity` variable is added to the header:

```
@interface GameScene : CCLayer
{
        CCSprite* player;
        CGPoint playerVelocity;
}
```

If you wonder why I'm using a `CGPoint` instead of `float`: who's to say you'll never want to accelerate up or down a little? So it doesn't hurt to be prepared for future expansions.

Listing 4–6 shows the accelerometer code, which I changed to use the velocity instead of updating the player position directly. It introduces three new design parameters for the amount of deceleration, the accelerometer sensitivity, and the maximum velocity. Those are values that don't have an optimum; you need to tweak them and find the right settings that works best with your game's design, hence the name "design parameters".

Deceleration works by reducing the current velocity before adding the new accelerometer value multiplied by the sensitivity. The lower the deceleration, the quicker the player can change the alien's direction. The higher the sensitivity, the more responsive the player will react to accelerometer input. These values interact with each other since they modify the same value, so be sure to tweak only one value at a time.

Listing 4–6. *GameScene Header Gets* playerVelocity

```
-(void) accelerometer:(UIAccelerometer *)accelerometer
                                    didAccelerate:(UIAcceleration *)acceleration
{
        // controls how quickly velocity decelerates (lower = quicker to change
direction)
        float deceleration = 0.4f;
        // determines how sensitive the accelerometer reacts (higher = more sensitive)
        float sensitivity = 6.0f;
```

```
        // how fast the velocity can be at most
        float maxVelocity = 100;

        // adjust velocity based on current accelerometer acceleration
    playerVelocity.x = playerVelocity.x * deceleration + acceleration.x * sensitivity;

        // we must limit the maximum velocity of the player sprite, in both directions
        if (playerVelocity.x > maxVelocity)
        {
                playerVelocity.x = maxVelocity;
        }
        else if (playerVelocity.x < - maxVelocity)
        {
                playerVelocity.x = - maxVelocity;
        }
}
```

Now playerVelocity will be changed, but how do you add the velocity to the player's position? You do so by scheduling the update method in the GameScene init method, by adding this line:

```
// schedules the -(void) update:(ccTime)delta method to be called every frame
[self scheduleUpdate];
```

You also need to add the -(void) update:(ccTime)delta method as shown in Listing 4–7. The scheduled update method is called every frame and that's where we add the velocity to the player position. This way we get a smooth constant movement in either direction regardless of the frequency of accelerometer input.

Listing 4–7. *Updating the Player's Position with the Current Velocity*

```
-(void) update:(ccTime)delta
{
        // Keep adding up the playerVelocity to the player's position
        CGPoint pos = player.position;
        pos.x += playerVelocity.x;

        // The Player should also be stopped from going outside the screen
        CGSize screenSize = [[CCDirector sharedDirector] winSize];
        float imageWidthHalved = [player texture].contentSize.width * 0.5f;
        float leftBorderLimit = imageWidthHalved;
        float rightBorderLimit = screenSize.width - imageWidthHalved;

        // preventing the player sprite from moving outside the screen
        if (pos.x < leftBorderLimit)
        {
                pos.x = leftBorderLimit;
                playerVelocity = CGPointZero;
        }
        else if (pos.x > rightBorderLimit)
        {
                pos.x = rightBorderLimit;
                playerVelocity = CGPointZero;
        }

        // assigning the modified position back
        player.position = pos;
}
```

A boundary check prevents the player sprite from leaving the screen. Once again we have to take the player texture's `contentSize` into account, since the player position is at the center of the sprite image but we don't want either side of the image to be off the screen. For this, we calculate the `imageWidthHalved` and then use it to check if the newly updated player position is within the left and right border limits. The code may be a bit verbose at this point, but that makes it easier to understand. And that's it for with the player accelerometer input logic.

> **NOTE:** The `contentSize` width is not divided by two but rather multiplied by 0.5 in order to calculate imageWidthHalved. This is a conscious choice and leads to the same results because any division can be rewritten as a multiplication.
>
> The update method is called in every frame, and every piece of code that runs in every frame should be running at top speed. And since the ARM CPUs of the iOS devices don't support division operations in hardware, multiplications are generally a bit faster. It's not going to be noticeable in this case, but it's a good habit to get into since, unlike other (premature) optimizations, it doesn't make the code harder to read or maintain.

Adding Obstacles

This game isn't any good until we add something for the player to avoid. The *DoodleDrop04* project introduces an abomination of nature: a six-legged man-spider. Who wouldn't want to avoid that?

As with the player sprite, you should add the *spider.png* to the Resources group. Then the *GameScene.h* file gets three new member variables added to its interface. A `spiders` CCArray whose class reference is shown in Listing 4–9, and the `spiderMoveDuration` and `numSpidersMoved`, which are used in Listing 4–12:

```
@interface GameScene : CCLayer
{
        CCSprite* player;
        CGPoint playerVelocity;

        CCArray* spiders;
        float spiderMoveDuration;
        int numSpidersMoved;
}
```

And in the GameScene init method add the call to the initSpiders method discussed next, right after scheduleUpdate:

```
-(id) init
{
        if ((self = [super init]))
        {
            ...
```

```
            [self scheduleUpdate];
            [self initSpiders];
        }
        return self;
    }
}
```

After that a fair bit of code is added to the GameScene class, beginning with the initSpiders method in Listing 4–8, which is creating the spider sprites.

Listing 4–8. *For Easier Access, Spider Sprites Are Initialized and Added to a CCArray.*

```
-(void) initSpiders
{
        CGSize screenSize = [[CCDirector sharedDirector] winSize];

        // using a temporary spider sprite is the easiest way to get the image's size
        CCSprite* tempSpider = [CCSprite spriteWithFile:@"spider.png"];
        float imageWidth = [tempSpider texture].contentSize.width;

        // Use as many spiders as can fit next to each other over the whole screen
                                                              width.
        int numSpiders = screenSize.width / imageWidth;

        // Initialize the spiders array using alloc.
        spiders = [[CCArray alloc] initWithCapacity:numSpiders];

        for (int i = 0; i < numSpiders; i++)
        {
                CCSprite* spider = [CCSprite spriteWithFile:@"spider.png"];
                [self addChild:spider z:0 tag:2];

                // Also add the spider to the spiders array.
                [spiders addObject:spider];
        }
        // call the method to reposition all spiders
        [self resetSpiders];
}
```

There are a few things to note. I create a tempSpider CCSprite only to find out the sprite's image width, which is then used to decide how many spider sprites can fit next to each other. The easiest way to get an image's dimensions is by simply creating a temporary CCSprite. Note that I did not add the tempSpider as child to any other node. This means that its memory will be released automatically.

This is in contrast to the spiders array I'm using to hold references to the spider sprites. This array must be created using alloc; otherwise, its memory would be released and subsequent access to the sprites array would crash the app with an EXC_BAD_ACCESS error. And since I took control over managing the sprites' array memory, I must not forget to release the spiders array in the dealloc method, as shown here:

```
-(void) dealloc
{
        CCLOG(@"%@: %@", NSStringFromSelector(_cmd), self);

        // The spiders array must be released, it was created using [CCArray alloc]
        [spiders release];
        spiders = nil;
```

```
        // Never forget to call [super dealloc]!
        [super dealloc];
}
```

The CCArray class is, at this time of writing, an undocumented but fully supported class of cocos2d. You can find the CCArray class files in the cocos2d/Support group in the Xcode project. It's used internally by cocos2d and is similar to Apple's NSMutableArray class—except that it performs better. The CCArray class implements a subset of the NSArray and NSMutableArray classes and also adds new methods to initialize a CCArray from an NSArray. It also implements fastRemoveObject and fastRemoveObjectAtIndex methods by simply assigning the last object in the array to the deleted position, in order to avoid copying parts of the array's memory. This is faster but it also means objects in CCArray will change positions, so if you rely on a specific ordering of objects, you shouldn't use the fastRemoveObject methods. In Listing 4–9 you can see the full CCArray class reference because it doesn't implement all of the methods of NSArray and NSMutableArray while adding its own.

Listing 4–9. *CCArray Class Reference*

```
+ (id) array;
+ (id) arrayWithCapacity:(NSUInteger)capacity;
+ (id) arrayWithArray:(CCArray*)otherArray;
+ (id) arrayWithNSArray:(NSArray*)otherArray;

- (id) initWithCapacity:(NSUInteger)capacity;
- (id) initWithArray:(CCArray*)otherArray;
- (id) initWithNSArray:(NSArray*)otherArray;

- (NSUInteger) count;
- (NSUInteger) capacity;
- (NSUInteger) indexOfObject:(id)object;
- (id) objectAtIndex:(NSUInteger)index;
- (id) lastObject;
- (BOOL) containsObject:(id)object;

#pragma mark Adding Objects

- (void) addObject:(id)object;
- (void) addObjectsFromArray:(CCArray*)otherArray;
- (void) addObjectsFromNSArray:(NSArray*)otherArray;
- (void) insertObject:(id)object atIndex:(NSUInteger)index;

#pragma mark Removing Objects

- (void) removeLastObject;
- (void) removeObject:(id)object;
- (void) removeObjectAtIndex:(NSUInteger)index;
- (void) removeObjectsInArray:(CCArray*)otherArray;
- (void) removeAllObjects;
- (void) fastRemoveObject:(id)object;
- (void) fastRemoveObjectAtIndex:(NSUInteger)index;

- (void) makeObjectsPerformSelector:(SEL)aSelector;
- (void) makeObjectsPerformSelector:(SEL)aSelector withObject:(id)object;

- (NSArray*) getNSArray;
```

At the end of Listing 4–8, the method [self resetSpiders] is called; this method is shown in Listing 4–10. The reason for separating initialization of the sprites and positioning them is that eventually there will be a game over, after which the game will need to be reset. The most efficient way to do so is to simply move all game objects back to their initial positions. However, that may stop being feasible once your game scene gets to a certain complexity. Eventually, it'll be easier to simply reload the whole scene, at the cost of having the player wait for the scene to reload.

Listing 4–10. *Resetting Spider Sprite Positions*

```
-(void) resetSpiders
{
        CGSize screenSize = [[CCDirector sharedDirector] winSize];

        // Get any spider to get its image width
        CCSprite* tempSpider = [spiders lastObject];
        CGSize size = [tempSpider texture].contentSize;

        int numSpiders = [spiders count];
        for (int i = 0; i < numSpiders; i++)
        {
                // Put each spider at its designated position outside the screen
                CCSprite* spider = [spiders objectAtIndex:i];
                spider.position = CGPointMake(size.width * i + size.width * 0.5f,
                                                screenSize.height + size.height);

                [spider stopAllActions];
        }

        // Unschedule the selector just in case. If it isn't scheduled it won't do
                                                                        anything.
        [self unschedule:@selector(spidersUpdate:)];

        // Schedule the spider update logic to run at the given interval.
        [self schedule:@selector(spidersUpdate:) interval:0.7f];
}
```

Once again I get one of the existing spiders temporarily to get its image size. I don't create a new sprite here since there are already existing sprites of the same kind, and since all spiders use the same image with the same size, I don't even care which sprite I'm getting. So I simply choose the get the last spider from the array.

Each spider's position is then modified so that together they span the entire width of the screen. Half of the image size's width is added, and once again this is due to the sprite's texture being centered on the node's position. As for the height, each sprite is also set to be one image size above the upper screen border. This is an arbitrary distance, as long as the image isn't visible, which is all I want to achieve. Because the spider might still be moving when the reset occurs, I'll also stop all of its actions at this point.

> **TIP:** To save a few CPU cycles, it's good practice not to use method calls in the conditional block of `for` or other loops if it's not strictly necessary. In this case I created a variable numSpiders to hold the result of `[spiders count]` and I use that in the conditional check of the `for` loop. The count of the array remains the same during the for loop's iterations because the array itself isn't modified in the loop. That's why I can cache this value and save the repeated calls to `[spiders count]` during each iteration of the `for` loop.

I'm also scheduling the `spidersUpdate:` selector to run every 0.7 seconds, which is how often another spider will drop down from the top of the screen. But before doing so, I make sure the same selector is unscheduled, just to be safe. The `resetSpiders` method may be called while `spidersUpdate:` is still scheduled and I don't want the method to be called twice, effectively doubling the spider drop-down rate. The `spidersUpdate:` method, shown in Listing 4–11, randomly picks one of the existing spiders, checks if it is idle, and lets it fall down the screen by using a sequence of actions.

Listing 4–11. *The spidersUpdate: Method Frequently Lets a Spider Fall*

```
-(void) spidersUpdate:(ccTime)delta
{
        // Try to find a spider which isn't currently moving.
        for (int i = 0; i < 10; i++)
        {
                int randomSpiderIndex = CCRANDOM_0_1() * [spiders count];
                CCSprite* spider = [spiders objectAtIndex:randomSpiderIndex];

                // If the spider isn't moving it won't have any running actions.
                if ([spider numberOfRunningActions] == 0)
                {
                        // This is the sequence which controls the spiders' movement
                        [self runSpiderMoveSequence:spider];

                        // Only one spider should start moving at a time.
                        break;
                }
        }
}
```

I don't let any listing pass without some curiosity, do I? In this case, you might wonder why I'm iterating exactly 10 times to get a random spider. The reason is that I don't know if the randomly generated index will get me a spider that isn't moving already, so I want to be reasonably sure that eventually a spider is randomly picked that is currently idle. If after 10 tries—and this number is arbitrary—I did not have the luck to get an idle spider chosen randomly, I'll simply skip this update and wait for the next.

I could brute-force my way and just keep trying to find an idle spider using a do/while loop. However, it's possible that all spiders could be moving at the same time, since this depends on design parameters like the frequency with which new spiders are being dropped. In that case, the game would simply lock up, looping endlessly trying to find an idle spider. Moreover, I'm not so keen on trying too hard; it really doesn't matter much for this game if I'm unable to send another spider falling down for a couple of seconds. That said, if you check out the DoodleDrop04 project, you'll see I added a logging statement that will print out how many retries it took to find an idle spider.

Since the movement sequence is the only action the spiders perform, I simply check if the spider is running any actions at all, and if not, I assume it is idle. Which brings us to the runSpiderMoveSequence in Listing 4–12.

Listing 4–12. *Spider Movement Is Handled by an Action Sequence.*

```
-(void) runSpiderMoveSequence:(CCSprite*)spider
{
        // Slowly increase the spider speed over time.
        numSpidersMoved++;
        if (numSpidersMoved % 8 == 0 && spiderMoveDuration > 2.0f)
        {
                spiderMoveDuration -= 0.1f;
        }

        // This is the sequence which controls the spiders' movement.
        CGPoint belowScreenPosition = CGPointMake(spider.position.x,
                                      -[spider texture].contentSize.height);
        CCMoveTo* move = [CCMoveTo actionWithDuration:spiderMoveDuration
                                             position:belowScreenPosition];
        CCCallFuncN* call = [CCCallFuncN actionWithTarget:self
                                    selector:@selector(spiderBelowScreen:)];
        CCSequence* sequence = [CCSequence actions:move, call, nil];
        [spider runAction:sequence];
}
```

The runSpiderMoveSequence method keeps track of the number of dropped spiders. Every eighth spider, the spiderMoveDuration is decreased and thus any spider's speed is increased. In case you are wondering about the % operator, it's called the modulo operator. The result is the remainder of the division operation, meaning if numSpidersMoved is divisible by 8 the result of the modulo operation will be 0.

The action sequence consists only of a CCMoveTo action and a CCCallFuncN action. It could be improved to let spiders drop down a bit, wait, and then drop all the way, as evil six-legged man-spiders would normally do. I leave this improvement up to you. For now it's only important to know that I chose the CCCallFuncN variant because I want the spiderBelowScreen method to be called with the spider sprite as sender parameter. This way I get a reference to the spider that has reached its destination and I don't have to jump through hoops to find the right spider. Listing 4–13 reveals how it's done by resetting the spider position back to just above the top of the screen whenever a spider has reached its destination just below the screen.

Listing 4–13. *Resetting a Spider Position so It Can Fall Back Down Again*

```
-(void) spiderBelowScreen:(id)sender
{
        // Make sure sender is actually of the right class.
        NSAssert([sender isKindOfClass:[CCSprite class]], @"sender is not a CCSprite!");
        CCSprite* spider = (CCSprite*)sender;
```

```
    // move the spider back up outside the top of the screen
    CGPoint pos = spider.position;
    CGSize screenSize = [[CCDirector sharedDirector] winSize];
    pos.y = screenSize.height + [spider texture].contentSize.height;
    spider.position = pos;
}
```

> **NOTE:** Being a defensive programmer, I've added the NSAssert line to make sure that sender is of the right class, since I'm making the assumption that sender will be a CCSprite but it might not be one.
>
> Indeed, when I first ran this code I forgot to use CCCallFuncN and actually used a CCCallFunc, which led to sender being nil, since CCCallFunc doesn't pass the sender parameter. NSAssert caught this case, too. With sender being nil, the method isKindOfClass was never called and the return value became nil, causing the NSAssert to trigger. It wasn't the error I expected, but NSAssert caught it anyway. With that information, it was easy to figure out what I was doing wrong and fix it.

Once I'm sure that sender is of the class CCSprite, I can cast it to CCSprite* and use it to adjust the sprite's position. The process should be familiar by now.

So far, so good. You might want to try out the game and play it a little. I think you'll quickly notice what's still missing. Hint: read the next headline.

Collision Detection

You may be surprised to see that collision detection can be as simple as in Listing 4–14. Admittedly, this only checks the distance between the player and all spiders, which makes this type of collision detection a radial check. For this type of game, it's sufficient. The call to [self checkForCollision] is added to the end of the -(void) update:(ccTime)delta method.

Listing 4–14. *A Simple Range-Check or Radial Collision-Check Suffices.*

```
-(void) checkForCollision
{
    // Assumption: both player and spider images are squares.
    float playerImageSize = [player texture].contentSize.width;
    float spiderImageSize = [[spiders lastObject] texture].contentSize.width;
    float playerCollisionRadius = playerImageSize * 0.4f;
    float spiderCollisionRadius = spiderImageSize * 0.4f;

    // This collision distance will roughly equal the image shapes.
    float maxCollisionDistance = playerCollisionRadius + spiderCollisionRadius;

    int numSpiders = [spiders count];
    for (int i = 0; i < numSpiders; i++)
    {
        CCSprite* spider = [spiders objectAtIndex:i];
```

```
if ([spider numberOfRunningActions] == 0)
{
        // This spider isn't even moving so we can skip checking it.
        continue;
}

// Get the distance between player and spider.
float actualDistance = ccpDistance(player.position, spider.position);

// Are the two objects closer than allowed?
if (actualDistance < maxCollisionDistance)
{
        // No game over, just reset the spiders.
        [self resetSpiders];
}
        }
    }
}
```

The image sizes of the player and spider are used as hints for the collision radii. The approximation is good enough for this game. If you check the DoodleDrop05 project, you'll also notice that I've added a debug drawing method that renders the collision radii for each sprite.

> **NOTE:** The correct plural of radius is radii. You can also say radiuses without being expelled from the country, though I wouldn't dare say it in the vicinity of programmers.

I'm iterating over all the spiders but ignore those that aren't moving at the moment because they'll definitely be out of range. The distance between the current spider and the player is calculated by the ccpDistance method. This is another undocumented but fully supported cocos2d method. You can find these and other useful math functions in the CGPointExtension files in the cocos2d/Support group in the Xcode project.

The resulting distance is then compared to the sum of the player's and the spider's collision radius. If the actual distance is smaller than that, a collision has occurred. Since no game over has been implemented, I chose to simply reset the spiders.

Score Label

The game needs some kind of scoring mechanism. I decided to add a simple time-lapse counter as score. I start by adding the score's Label in the init method of the GameScene class:

```
scoreLabel = [CCLabel labelWithString:@"0" fontName:@"Arial" fontSize:48];
scoreLabel.position = CGPointMake(screenSize.width / 2, screenSize.height);

// Adjust the label's anchorPoint's y position to make it align with the top.
scoreLabel.anchorPoint = CGPointMake(0.5f, 1.0f);

// Add the score label with z value of -1 so it's drawn below everything else
 [self addChild:scoreLabel z:-1];
```

I consciously chose a CCLabel object, which would likely be the first choice for most beginning cocos2d programmers. I'll show you how quickly these label objects rear their ugly heads, though. Add the following code anywhere in the update: method so that the score label will be updated like a stopwatch counter every second.

```
// Update the Score (Timer) once per second.
totalTime += delta;
int currentTime = (int)totalTime;
if (score < currentTime)
{
        score = currentTime;
        [scoreLabel setString:[NSString stringWithFormat:@"%i", score]];
}
```

The delta parameter of the update: method is continuously added to the totalTime member variable, to keep track of the time that has passed. Because totalTime is a floating point variable, I simply assign it to an integer variable, effectively removing the fractional part. That makes it possible to compare the score with the currentTime; if the score is lower, currentTime becomes the new score and the CCLabel's string is updated.

And that's where things get ugly. In the previous chapter I mentioned that updating a CCLabel's text is slow. The whole texture is recreated using iOS font rendering methods and they take their time, besides allocating a new texture and releasing the old one. If you play this version of the game on the device, you may notice how the spiders seem to jump a little every time the score label changes. The game is no longer running smoothly.

If you want to see this effect more pronounced, uncomment just the line with the if statement so that [scoreLabel setString:…] is run every frame. On my iPhone 3GS, the framerate suddenly drops from a previous constant 60 frames per second to below 30—all this because of one measly CCLabel updated every frame!

But keep in mind that CCLabel is only slow when changing its string frequently. If you create the CCLabel once and never change it, it's just as fast as any other CCSprite of the same dimensions.

Introducing CCBitmapFontAtlas and Hiero

Labels that update fast at the expense of more memory usage, like any other CCSprite, are the specialty of the CCBitmapFontAtlas class. I've replaced the CCLabel with a CCBitmapFontAtlas in DoodleDrop07. It's relatively straightforward; besides changing the declaration of the scoreLabel variable from CCLabel to CCBitmapFontAtlas in the header file, you only have to change the line in the init method as shown here.

```
scoreLabel = [CCBitmapFontAtlas bitmapFontAtlasWithString:@"0"
                                              fntFile:@"bitmapfont.fnt"];
```

> **NOTE:** Bitmap fonts are a great choice for games because they are fast, but they do have a major disadvantage. The size of any bitmap font is fixed. If you need the same font but bigger or smaller in size, you can scale the `CCBitmapFontAtlas`—but you lose image quality. The other option is to create a separate font file with the new size, but this uses up more memory since each bitmap font comes with its own texture, even if only the font size changed.

But there's a catch, obviously. You need to add the *bitmapfont.fnt* file as well as the accompanying *bitmapfont.png,* which are both in the project's Resources folder. More importantly, you do want to create your own bitmap fonts sooner or later. The tool to use for that is called Hiero, written by Kevin James Glass. It's a free Java Web application and is available from `http://slick.cokeandcode.com/demos/hiero.jnlp`.

The downside is, it's a free Java Web application. It will ask you to trust the application because of a missing security certificate. On the other hand, many developers use the tool and so far there has been no evidence that the application is untrustworthy. If you prefer to use a different program, some developers use BMFont to great success. But as a Windows program, it requires a Windows computer or Windows installed in a virtual machine on your Mac. That's why it's not more widely used in the Mac developer community. You can download BMFont from `www.angelcode.com/products/bmfont/`.

Figure 4–7 shows the setup I used to create *bitmapfont.fnt.* You can load the *bitmapfont.hiero* file from the Resources folder of the DoodleDrop07 project to see the same setup. The basic process is relatively straightforward. You pick a font from the list, enter the characters you need in the Sample Text field, then save the file as BMFont file. Since Hiero is a Java Web application, you won't find its **File** menu in the regular menu bar but in the top left corner of the application window, just like in a Windows application. It's also a bit quirky in that it tends to forget to add file extensions when saving, leaving you to guess which file format the file really is. There are only two choices, though. The *.hiero* files are Hiero's internal format storing the current editor settings, while the *.fnt* files are the output files that cocos2d's `CCBitmapFontAtlas` class can read.

The remaining settings are completely optional. I decided to add Gradient and Shadow effects to the font to make it more colorful and to give it a 3D look. From the **Effects** menu in the top right corner you can select an effect, then click on the **Add** button. A new effect will be added to the list below, where you can tweak the parameters of all effects. The changes are displayed in the Rendering view. If you don't like an effect, click on the **X** button next to its name to remove it.

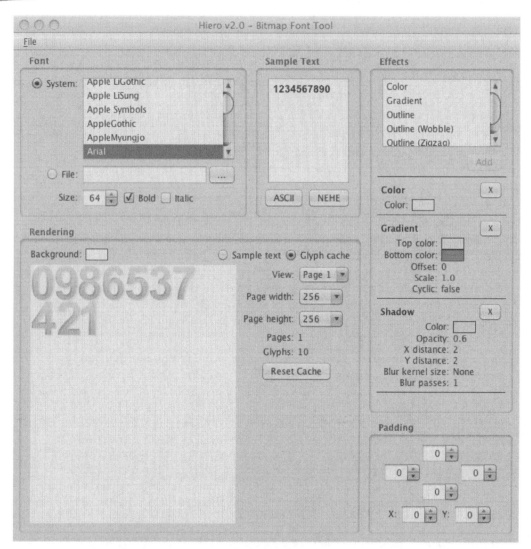

Figure 4–7. *The Hiero Bitmap Font Tool allows you to create bitmap fonts from any TrueType font. It creates a .fnt file that you can use directly with the CCBitmapFontAtlas class of cocos2d.*

The Rendering view in the lower left corner contains several settings that you can use to trim the image files Hiero creates. If you use only a few letters like I did, you want to set the page width and height to the smallest size, in this case 256 pixels, and then click **Reset Cache** to apply the new settings. This creates smaller image files and consumes less memory. For more complex fonts, Hiero will create several image files. This works just fine with `CCBitmapFontAtlas`, but don't forget to add all the *.png* files Hiero creates.

Notice that I've chosen to create my bitmap font using only the characters I need, in this case only digits. Since the image files created by Hiero are always at least 256 x 256 pixels in size for each font, there's only so much memory you can save. It actually wouldn't hurt to add a few more letters by typing them into the Sample Text field, there's still plenty of room.

If you'd like to learn more about Hiero, check out the tutorial on my web site, which covers how to use Hiero in full (www.learn-cocos2d.com/knowledge-base/tutorial-bitmap-fonts-hiero/).

> **NOTE:** If you try to display characters using a CCBitmapFontAtlas, which are not available in the *.fnt* file, they will simply be skipped and not displayed. For example, if you do [label setString:@"Hello, World!"] but your bitmap font contains only lowercase letters and no punctuation characters, you'll see the string "ello orld" displayed instead.

Adding Audio

I've added some audio to complete this game. In the *Resources* folder of the DoodleDrop07 project, you'll find a couple of audio files named *blues.mp3* and *alien-sfx.caf* that you can add to your project. The best choice and the easiest way to play audio files in cocos2d is by using the SimpleAudioEngine. Audio support is not an integral part of cocos2d; this is the domain of CocosDenshion, like the physics engines a third-party addition to cocos2d. For that reason, you have to add the corresponding header files whenever you use the CocosDenshion audio functionality, like so:

```
#import "GameScene.h"
#import "SimpleAudioEngine.h"
```

You'll find playing music and audio using the SimpleAudioEngine is straightforward, as shown here.

```
[[SimpleAudioEngine sharedEngine] playBackgroundMusic:@"blues.mp3" loop:YES];
[[SimpleAudioEngine sharedEngine] playEffect:@"alien-sfx.caf"];
```

For music, MP3 files are the preferred choice. Note that you can play only one MP3 file in the background at a time. Technically, it's possible to play two or more MP3 files, but only one can be decoded in hardware. The extra strain on the CPU is undesirable for games, so playing multiple MP3 files at the same time is out of the question for most.

For sound effects, I've had only good experiences with the CAF format.

If you want to quickly convert audio files from one format to another, possibly changing some basic settings like sampling rate, I can recommend just the tool. It's called SoundConverter and was developed by Steve Dekorte. The tool is free to use for files up to 500 KB in size and the license to use SoundConverter without restrictions is just $15. You can download SoundConverter from http://dekorte.com/projects/shareware/SoundConverter/

NOTE: If you ever find yourself in the situation where an audio file just won't play or results in a garbled mess of noise, don't worry. There are countless audio applications and numerous audio codecs that all create their own variations of the respective formats. Some are unable to play on iOS devices but play fine otherwise. Typically, the way you can fix this is to open the audio file and save it again, either by using a sound converter like the aptly named SoundConverter or the audio application of your choice. Usually, after this the file will be able to play just fine on the iOS device.

Porting to iPad

With all coordinates taking the screen's size into account, the game should simply scale up without any problems when running it on the iPad's bigger screen. And it does. Just like that. In contrast, if you had been using fixed coordinates you'd be facing a serious re-work of your game.

Porting an iPhone project is a simple process. Select the target in the Groups & Files pane that you want to convert and select **Project ➤ Upgrade Current Target for iPad…**, which will bring up the dialog in Figure 4–8.

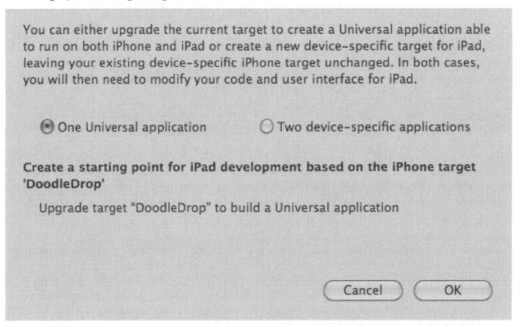

Figure 4–8. *Upgrading a target for iPad gives you two choices. In short, the universal application saves you time but requires you to add both iPhone and iPad assets to the same target, increasing the app's download size.*

For a simple game, the default One Universal application is fine. It does have the drawback that all assets are added to the same target, increasing the app's size. But the app can be run on both the iPhone and iPad.

The other option lets you keep game assets separate, but you end up with two apps, which you'll have to submit individually. More importantly, if an iTunes user wants both the iPhone and iPad versions, he'll have to buy both.

Choose One Universal application and run the code. On the device, the app will automatically detect which device is connected and run the appropriate version. If you want to try it out in the iPad Simulator, just select the iPad Simulator 3.2 as the Active Executable as in Figure 4–9.

Figure 4–9. *To run the new universal app in the iPad Simulator, make it the Active Executable.*

Conclusion

I hope you had fun building this first game. It was surely a lot to take in, but I'd rather err on the side of too much information than too little.

At this point, you've learned how to create your own game-layer class and how to work with sprites. You've used the accelerometer to control the player and added velocity to allow the player sprite to accelerate and decelerate, giving it a more dynamic feel.

I also introduced you to the undocumented CCArray class, cocos2d's replacement for NSMutableArray. This should be your preferred choice when you need to store a list of data. Simple radial collision detection using the distance check method from the likewise undocumented CGPointExtensions was also on the menu.

And for dessert you had a potpourri of labels, bitmap fonts, and the Hiero Bitmap Font Tool, garnished with some audio programming.

What's left? Maybe going through the source code for this chapter. I've added a finalized version of this game that includes some gameplay improvements, a startup menu, and a game-over message.

There's just one thing about the DoodleDrop project I haven't mentioned yet: it's all in one class. For a small project this may suffice, but it'll quickly get messy as you move on to implement more features. You need to add some structure to your code design. The next chapter will arm you with cocos2d programming best practices and show you how to lay out your code and the various ways information can be passed between objects if they are no longer in the same class.

Chapter 5

Game Building Blocks

The game DoodleDrop in the previous chapter was written to be easy to understand if you're new to cocos2d. If you're a more experienced developer, though, you probably noticed that there is no separation of code; everything is in just one file. Clearly, this doesn't scale and if you're going to make bigger, more exciting games than DoodleDrop, you'll have to find a suitable way to structure your code. Otherwise, you might end up with one class driving your game's logic. The code size can quickly grow to thousands of lines, making it hard to navigate and tempting to change anything from anywhere, very likely introducing subtle and hard to find bugs.

Each new project demands its own code design. In this chapter I'd like to introduce you to some of the building blocks for writing more complex cocos2d games. The code foundation laid out in this chapter will then be used to create the side-scrolling shooter game we'll be building in the next few chapters.

Working with Multiple Scenes

The DoodleDrop game had only one scene and one layer. More complex games will surely need several scenes and multiple layers. How and when to use them will become second nature for you. Let's see what's involved.

Adding More Scenes

The basics still apply. In Listings 4-1 and 4-2 in the previous chapter, I outlined the basic code needed to create a scene. Adding more scenes is a matter of adding more classes built on that same basic code. It's when you're transitioning between scenes that things get a little more interesting. There's a set of three methods in CCNode that get called for every node when you're replacing a scene via the CCDirector replaceScene method.

The onEnter and onExit methods get called at certain times during a scene change, depending on whether a CCTransitionScene is used. You must always call the super implementation of these methods, to avoid input problems and memory leaks. Take a look at Listing 5–1, and take note that all of these methods call the super implementation.

Listing 5–1. *The onEnter and onExit Methods*

```
-(void) onEnter
{
        // Called right after a node's init method is called.
        // If using a CCTransitionScene: called when the transition begins.

        [super onEnter];
}

-(void) onEnterTransitionDidFinish
{
        // Called right after onEnter.
        // If using a CCTransitionScene: called when the transition has ended.

        [super onEnterTransitionDidFinish];
}

-(void) onExit
{
        // Called right before node's dealloc method is called.
        // If using a CCTransitionScene: called when the transition has ended.

        [super onExit];
}
```

> **NOTE:** If you don't make the call to the super implementation in the onEnter methods, your new scene may not react to touch or accelerometer input. If you don't call super in onExit, the current scene may not be released from memory. Since it's easy to forget this, and the resulting behavior doesn't lead you to realize that it may be related to these methods, it's important to stress this point. You can see this behavior in the ScenesAndLayer01 project.

These methods are useful whenever you need to do something in any node right before a scene is changed, or right after. The difference from simply writing the same code in a node's init or dealloc method is that the scene is already fully set up during onEnter, and it still contains all nodes during onExit.

This can be important. For example, if you perform a transition to change scenes, you may want to pause certain animations or hide user interface elements until the transition finishes. Here's the sequence in which these methods get called, based on the logging information from the ScenesAndLayers02 project.

1. scene: OtherScene

2. init: <OtherScene = 066B2130 | Tag = -1>

3. onEnter: <OtherScene = 066B2130 | Tag = -1>

4. // Transition is running here …

5. onExit: <FirstScene = 0668DF40 | Tag = -1>

6. onEnterTransitionDidFinish: <OtherScene = 066B2130 | Tag = -1>

7. dealloc: <FirstScene = 0668DF40 | Tag = -1>

At first, OtherScene's +(id) scene method is called to initialize the CCScene and the CCLayer it contains. The OtherScene CCLayer's init method is then called, directly followed by the onEnter method in line 3. In line 4, the transition is sliding the new scene in, and when it's done the FirstScene onExit method gets called, followed by onEnterTransitionDidFinish in OtherScene.

Note that the FirstScene dealloc method is called last. This means that during onEnterTransitionDidFinish, the previous scene is still in memory. If you want to allocate memory-intensive nodes at this point, you'll have to schedule a selector to wait at least one frame before doing the memory allocations, to be certain that the previous scene's memory is released. Another strategy would be to release as much memory as possible in the previous scene's onExit method.

Loading Next Paragraph, Please Stand By

Sooner or later you'll face noticeable loading times during scene transitions. As you add more content, loading times will correspondingly increase. Creating a new scene actually happens before the scene transition starts. If you have very complex code or load a lot of assets in the new scene's init or onEnter methods, there will be an obvious delay before the transition begins. This is especially problematic if the new scene takes more than one second to load and the user initiated the scene change by pressing a button. The user may get the impression that the game has locked up, or frozen. The way to alleviate this problem is to add another scene in between: a loading scene. You'll find an example implementation in the *ScenesAndLayers03* project.

In effect, the LoadingScene acts as a intermediate scene. It is derived from the cocos2d CCScene class. You don't have to create a new LoadingScene for each transition; you can use one scene for which you simply specify the target scene you'd like to be loaded. An enum works best for this; it's defined in the *LoadingScene* header file shown in Listing 5–2.

Listing 5–2. *LoadingScene.h*

```
typedef enum
{
        TargetSceneINVALID = 0,
        TargetSceneFirstScene,
        TargetSceneOtherScene,
        TargetSceneMAX,
} TargetScenes;

// LoadingScene is derived directly from Scene. We don't need a CCLayer for this scene.
@interface LoadingScene : CCScene
{
        TargetScenes targetScene_;
}
```

```
+(id) sceneWithTargetScene:(TargetScenes)targetScene;
-(id) initWithTargetScene:(TargetScenes)targetScene;
```

> **TIP:** It is good practice to set the first enum value to be an INVALID value, unless you intend to make the first the default. Variables in Objective-C are initialized to 0 automatically unless you specify a different value.
>
> In addition, you can also add a MAX or NUM entry at the end of the enum if you intend to iterate over every enum value, as in:
>
> ```
> for (int i = TargetSceneINVALID + 1; i < TargetScenesMAX; i++) { .. }
> ```
>
> In the case of the LoadingScene it's not necessary, but I tend to add these entries merely out of habit, even if I don't need them.

This brings me to the LoadingScene class implementation of the *ScenesAndLayers03* project in Listing 5–3. You'll notice that the scene is initialized differently, and that it uses scheduleUpdate to delay replacing the LoadingScene with the actual target scene.

Listing 5–3. *The LoadingScene Class Uses a Switch to Decide Whether to Load the Target Scene*

```
+(id) sceneWithTargetScene:(TargetScenes)targetScene;
{
        // This creates an autorelease object of the current class (self ==
                                                                LoadingScene)
        return [[[self alloc] initWithTargetScene:targetScene] autorelease];
}

-(id) initWithTargetScene:(TargetScenes)targetScene
{
        if ((self = [super init]))
        {
                targetScene_ = targetScene;

                CCLabel* label = [CCLabel labelWithString:@"Loading ..."
                                                fontName:@"Marker Felt" fontSize:64];
                CGSize size = [[CCDirector sharedDirector] winSize];
                label.position = CGPointMake(size.width / 2, size.height / 2);
                [self addChild:label];

                // Must wait one frame before loading the target scene!
                [self scheduleUpdate];
        }

        return self;
}

-(void) update:(ccTime)delta
{
        [self unscheduleAllSelectors];

        // Decide which scene to load based on the TargetScenes enum.
        switch (targetScene_)
```

```
    {
        case TargetSceneFirstScene:
                [[CCDirector sharedDirector] replaceScene:[FirstScene scene]];
                break;
        case TargetSceneOtherScene:
                [[CCDirector sharedDirector] replaceScene:[OtherScene scene]];
                break;

        default:
                // Always warn if an unspecified enum value was used
                NSAssert2(nil, @"%@: unsupported TargetScene %i",
                                NSStringFromSelector(_cmd), targetScene_);
                break;
    }
}
```

Because the LoadingScene is derived from CCScene and requires a new parameter passed to it, it's no longer sufficient to call [CCScene node]. The sceneWithTargetScene method first allocates self, calls the initWithTargetScene method, and returns the new object as autorelease. This is the same way cocos2d initializes its own classes, and it's the reason you can rely on cocos2d objects being autoreleased. If you're deriving your own classes, you should always add the appropriate static autorelease initializers, like in this case sceneWithTargetScene.

The init method simply stores the target scene in a member variable, creates the "Loading..." label, and runs scheduleUpdate.

> **CAUTION:** Why not just call replaceScene right inside the init method? There are two rules about that. Rule number one is: never call CCDirector's replaceScene in a node's init method. Rule number two is: follow rule number one. The reason: it crashes. The Director can't cope with replacing a scene from a node that is currently being initialized.

The update method then uses a simple switch statement based on the provided TargetScenes enum to determine which scene is to be replaced. The default switch contains an NSAssert, which always triggers when the default case is hit. This is good practice because you'll be editing and expanding this list several times, and if you forgot to update the switch statement with a new case, you'll be notified of that.

This is a very simple LoadingScene implementation that you can use in your own games. Simply extend the enum and switch statement with more target scenes, or use the same target scene multiple times but with different transitions. But as I mentioned before, don't overdo the transitions just because they're cool-looking.

Using the LoadingScene has an important effect regarding memory. Since you're replacing the existing scene with the lightweight LoadingScene, and then replacing the LoadingScene with the actual target scene, you're giving cocos2d enough time to free up the previous scene's memory. Effectively there's no longer any overlap with two complex scenes in memory at the same time, reducing spikes in memory usage during scene changes.

Working with Multiple Layers

The project *ScenesAndLayers04* illustrates how multiple layers can be used to scroll the contents of a game's objects layer while the content of the user interface layer, where it says "Here be your Game Scores" (see Figure 5–1), remains static. You'll learn how multiple layers can cooperate and react only to their own touch input, as well as how to access the various layers from any node.

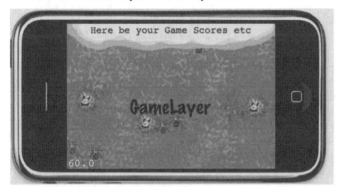

Figure 5–1. *The ScenesAndLayers04 project. So far, so normal.*

I'll start by putting the `MultiLayerScene` together in the `init` method. If you skim over the code in Listing 5–4, you'll barely notice anything different from what we've done so far.

Listing 5–4. *Initializing the MultiLayerScene*

```
-(id) init
{
        if ((self = [super init]))
        {
                multiLayerSceneInstance = self;

                // The GameLayer will be moved, rotated and scaled independently
                GameLayer* gameLayer = [GameLayer node];
                [self addChild:gameLayer z:1 tag:LayerTagGameLayer];
                gameLayerPosition = gameLayer.position;

                    // The UserInterfaceLayer remains static and relative to the screen
                                                                                    area.
                UserInterfaceLayer* uiLayer = [UserInterfaceLayer node];
                [self addChild:uiLayer z:2 tag:LayerTagUserInterfaceLayer];
        }

        return self;
}
```

> **TIP:** It's worth mentioning that I've started using enum values for tags, like LayerTagGameLayer. This has the advantage over using numbers in that you can actually read whose tag it is, instead of having to remember which layer had tag number 7 assigned to it. It also shows that the actual tag values are not important; what's important is that you use the same value consistently for the same node. Using a human-readable tag makes that task easier and less error prone. The same goes for action tags, of course.

You may have noticed the variable multiLayerSceneInstance and that it gets self assigned. A bit strange, isn't it? What would that be good for? If you recall from Chapter 3, I explained how to create a singleton class. In this case, I'll turn the MultiLayerScene class into a singleton. See Listing 5–5 and if you want, compare it with Listing 3-1 to spot the differences.

Listing 5–5. *Turning the MultiLayerScene into a Semi-Singleton Object.*

```
static MultiLayerScene* multiLayerSceneInstance;

+(MultiLayerScene*) sharedLayer
{
        NSAssert(multiLayerSceneInstance != nil, @"MultiLayerScene not available!");
        return multiLayerSceneInstance;
}

-(void) dealloc
{
        // MultiLayerScene will be deallocated now, you must set it to nil
        multiLayerSceneInstance = nil;

        // don't forget to call "super dealloc"
        [super dealloc];
}
```

Simply put, the multiLayerSceneInstance is a static global variable that will hold the current MultiLayerScene object during its lifetime. When the layer is deallocated, the variable is set back to nil to avoid crashes, as the multiLayerSceneInstance variable would be pointing to an already released object after the dealloc method. The reason for this semi-singleton is that you'll be using several layers, each with its own child nodes, but you still need to somehow access the main layer. It's a very comfortable way to give access to the main layer to other layers and nodes of the current scene.

> **CAUTION:** This semi-singleton only works if there is only ever one instance of MultiLayerScene allocated at any one time. It also can't be used to initialize MultiLayerScene, unlike a regular singleton class.

Access to the GameLayer and UserInterfaceLayer is granted through property getter methods, for ease of use. The properties are defined in Listing 5–6, which shows the relevant part from *MultiLayerScene.h*.

Listing 5–6. *Property Definitions for Accessing the GameLayer and UserInterfaceLayer*

```
@property (readonly) GameLayer* gameLayer;
@property (readonly) UserInterfaceLayer* uiLayer;
```

The properties are defined as `readonly`, since we only ever want to retrieve the layers, never set them through the property. Their implementation in Listing 5–7 is a straightforward wrapper to the `getChildByTag` method, but they also perform a safety check just in case, verifying that the retrieved object is of the correct class.

Listing 5–7. *Implementation of the Property Setters*

```
-(GameLayer*) gameLayer
{
        CCNode* layer = [self getChildByTag:LayerTagGameLayer];
        NSAssert([layer isKindOfClass:[GameLayer class]], @"%@: not a GameLayer!",
                                                NSStringFromSelector(_cmd));
        return (GameLayer*)layer;
}

-(UserInterfaceLayer*) uiLayer
{
        CCNode* layer = [[MultiLayerScene sharedLayer] getChildByTag:LayerTagUILayer];
        NSAssert([layer isKindOfClass:[UserInterfaceLayer class]],
                                @"%@: not a UILayer!", NSStringFromSelector(_cmd));
        return (UserInterfaceLayer*)layer;
}
```

This makes it easy to access the various layers from any node of the `MultiLayerScene`.

■ To access the "scene" layer of `MultiSceneLayer`:

```
MultiSceneLayer* sceneLayer = [MultiSceneLayer sharedLayer];
```

■ To access the other layers through the scene layer:

```
GameLayer* gameLayer = [sceneLayer gameLayer];
UserInterfaceLayer* uiLayer = [sceneLayer uiLayer];
```

■ As an alternative, because of the @property definition, you can also use the dot accessor:

```
GameLayer* gameLayer = sceneLayer.gameLayer;
UserInterfaceLayer* uiLayer = sceneLayer.uiLayer;
```

The `UserInterfaceLayer` and `GameLayer` classes both handle touch input, but independently. To achieve the correct results, we need to use `TargetedTouchHandlers`, and by using the `priority` parameter we can make sure that the `UserInterfaceLayer` gets to look at a touch event before the GameLayer. The `UserInterfaceLayer` uses the `isTouchForMe` method to determine if it should handle the touch, and it will return `YES` from the `ccTouchBegan` method if it did handle the touch. This will keep other targeted touch handlers from receiving this touch. Listing 5–8 illustrates the important bits of the touch event code for the `UserInterfaceLayer`.

Listing 5–8. *Touch input Processing Using TargetedTouchDelegate*

```
// Register TargetedTouch handler with higher priority than GameLayer
-(void) registerWithTouchDispatcher
{
        [[CCTouchDispatcher sharedDispatcher] addTargetedDelegate:self priority:-1
                                                   swallowsTouches:YES];
}

// Checks if the touch location was in an area that this layer wants to handle as input.
-(bool) isTouchForMe:(CGPoint)touchLocation
{
        CCNode* node = [self getChildByTag:UILayerTagFrameSprite];
        return CGRectContainsPoint([node boundingBox], touchLocation);
}

-(BOOL) ccTouchBegan:(UITouch*)touch withEvent:(UIEvent *)event
{
        CGPoint location = [MultiLayerScene locationFromTouch:touch];
        bool isTouchHandled = [self isTouchForMe:location];
        if (isTouchHandled)
        {
                CCNode* node = [self getChildByTag:UILayerTagFrameSprite];
                NSAssert([node isKindOfClass:[CCSprite class]], @"node is not a
                                                                 CCSprite");

                // Highlight the UI layer's sprite for the duration of the touch
                ((CCSprite*)node).color = ccRED;

                // Access the GameLayer via MultiLayerScene.
                GameLayer* gameLayer = [MultiLayerScene sharedLayer].gameLayer;

                // Run Actions on GameLayer … (code removed for clarity)
        }

        return isTouchHandled;
}

-(void) ccTouchEnded:(UITouch*)touch withEvent:(UIEvent *)event
{
        CCNode* node = [self getChildByTag:UILayerTagFrameSprite];
        NSAssert([node isKindOfClass:[CCSprite class]], @"node is not a CCSprite");
        ((CCSprite*)node).color = ccWHITE;
}
```

In registerWithTouchDispatcher, the UserInterfaceLayer registers itself as targeted touch handler with a priority of -1. Because GameLayer uses the same code but with a priority of 0, the UserInterfaceLayer will be the first layer to receive touch input.

In ccTouchBegan, the first thing to do is to check if this touch is of relevance to the UserInterfaceLayer. The isTouchForMe method implements a simple "point in boundingBox" check via CGRectContainsPoint to see if the touch began on the uiframe sprite. There are more useful methods available in CGGeometry to test intersection, containing points or equality. Please refer to Apple's documentation to learn more about the CGGeometry methods

(http://developer.apple.com/mac/library/documentation/GraphicsImaging/Reference
/CGGeometry/Reference/reference.html).

If the touch location check determines that the touch is on the sprite, ccTouchBegan will
return YES, signaling that this touch event was used and should not be processed by
other layers with a targeted touch delegate of lower priority.

Only if the isTouchForMe check fails will the GameLayer receive the touch input and use it
to scroll itself when the user moves a finger over the screen. You can compare
GameLayer's input handling code in Listing 5–9.

Listing 5–9. *GameLayer Receives the Remaining Touch Events and Uses Them to Scroll Itself*

```
-(void) registerWithTouchDispatcher
{
        [[CCTouchDispatcher sharedDispatcher] addTargetedDelegate:self priority:0
                                                      swallowsTouches:YES];
}

-(BOOL) ccTouchBegan:(UITouch*)touch withEvent:(UIEvent *)event
{
        lastTouchLocation = [MultiLayerScene locationFromTouch:touch];

        // Stop the move action so it doesn't interfere with the user's scrolling.
        [self stopActionByTag:ActionTagGameLayerMovesBack];

        // Always swallow touches, GameLayer is the last layer to receive touches.
        return YES;
}

-(void) ccTouchMoved:(UITouch*)touch withEvent:(UIEvent *)event
{
        CGPoint currentTouchLocation = [MultiLayerScene locationFromTouch:touch];

        // Take the difference of the current to the last touch location.
        CGPoint moveTo = ccpSub(lastTouchLocation, currentTouchLocation);

        // Then reverse to give the impression of moving the background
        moveTo = ccpMult(moveTo, -1);

        lastTouchLocation = currentTouchLocation;

        // Adjust the layer's position accordingly, and with it all child nodes.
        self.position = ccpAdd(self.position, moveTo);
}

-(void) ccTouchEnded:(UITouch*)touch withEvent:(UIEvent *)event
{
        // Move the game layer back to its designated position.
        CCMoveTo* move = [CCMoveTo actionWithDuration:1 position:gameLayerPosition];
        CCEaseIn* ease = [CCEaseIn actionWithAction:move rate:0.5f];
        ease.tag = ActionTagGameLayerMovesBack;
        [self runAction:ease];
}
```

Since GameLayer is the last layer to receive input, it doesn't need to do any `isTouchForMe` checks and simply swallows all touches.

Using the `ccTouchMoved` event, the difference between the previous and current touch location is calculated. It is then reversed by multiplying it by -1 to change the effect from moving the camera over the background, to moving the background under the camera. If you have a hard time imagining what I mean by this, try out the *ScenesAndLayers04* project, and then try it out a second time, commenting out the `moveTo = ccpMult(moveTo, -1);` line. You'll notice the second time that every finger movement moves the layer in the opposite direction.

In `ccTouchEnded`, the layer is then simply moved back to its center position automatically when the user lifts the finger off the screen. Figure 5–2 shows this project in action with the whole GameLayer rotated and zoomed out. Every game object on the `GameLayer` abides by every movement, rotation, and scaling of the `GameLayer` automatically, whereas the `UserInterfaceLayer` always stays put.

Figure 5–2. *The utility of multiple layers becomes clear once the GameLayer is zoomed out and rotated, with all its nodes adhering to the layer's behavior, while the UserInterfaceLayer on top remains in place unaffected.*

How to Best Implement Levels

So far we've examined multiple scenes and multiple layers. Now you want to cover what, levels?

Well, the concept of levels is very common in many games, so I don't think I need to explain that. What's much harder is deciding which approach best serves a level-based game. In cocos2d you can go either way, choosing a new scene for each level, or using separate layers to manage multiple levels. Both have their uses and which one to choose depends mostly on what purpose levels serve in your game.

Scenes as Levels

The most straightforward approach is to run each level as a separate scene. You can either create a new Scene class for each level, or choose to initialize one common

LevelScene class and pass as a parameter the level number or other information necessary to load the correct level data.

This approach works best if you have clearly separated levels and most everything that happens within a level is no longer relevant or needed after the player has progressed through that level. Maybe you'll keep the player's score and the number of lives left, but that's about it. The user interface is probably minimal and non-interactive, and likely is purely informative without any interactive elements other than a pause button.

I imagine this approach works best for twitch-based action game levels.

Layers as Levels

Using separate layers in the same scene to load and display levels is an approach that's recommended if you have a complex user interface that should not be reset when a level changes. You might even want to keep the player and other game objects in the exact same positions and states when changing levels.

You'll probably have a number of variables that keep the current game state and user interface settings, such as an inventory. It would be more work to save and restore these game settings and reset all visual elements than to switch out one layer with another within the same scene.

This may be the ideal solution for a hidden object or adventure game, where you move from room to room, especially if you want to replace the level contents using an animation that moves in or out beneath the user interface.

The CCMultiplexLayer class may be the ideal solution for such an approach. It can contain multiple nodes but only one will be active at any given time. Listing 5–10 shows an example of using the CCMultiplexLayer class. The only drawback is that you can't transition between the layers. There's only one layer visible at a time which makes any transition effects impossible.

Listing 5–10. *Using the CCMultiplexLayer Class to Switch Between Multiple Layers*

```
CCLayer* layer1 = [CCLayer node];
CCLayer* layer2 = [CCLayer node];
CCMultiplexLayer* mpLayer = [CCMultiplexLayer layerWithLayers:layer1, layer2, nil];

// Switches to layer2 but keeps layer1 as child of mpLayer.
[mpLayer switchTo:1];

// Switches to layer1, removes layer2 from mpLayer and releases its memory.
// After this call you must not switch back to layer2 (index: 1) anymore!
[mpLayer switchToAndReleaseMe:0];
```

CCColorLayer

In the ScenesAndLayers project, so far the background is simply a black screen. You can see it when you scroll to the edge of the grassy background image, or tap on the "user interface" to have the GameLayer zoom out. To change the background color, cocos2d provides a `CCColorLayer`, which is added to the ScenesAndLayers05 project and works like this:

```
// Set background color to magenta. The most unobtrusive color imaginable.
CCColorLayer* colorLayer = [CCColorLayer layerWithColor:ccc4(255, 0, 255, 255)];
[self addChild:colorLayer z:0];
```

If you're somewhat familiar with OpenGL it may seem like overkill to add a separate layer just to change the background color. You can achieve the same effect using OpenGL, like this:

```
glClearColor(1, 0, 1, 1);
```

But please test this with your game's scene transitions first, since changing the `glClearColor` can have an adverse effect on scene transitions. For example, when using `CCFadeTransition`, the clear color will shine through regardless of the color you use to initialize `CCFadeTransition`.

Subclassing Game Objects from CCSprite

Very often your game objects will implement logic of their own. It makes sense to create a separate class for each type of game object. This could be your player character, various enemy types, bullets, missiles, platforms, and about everything else that can be individually placed in a game's scene and needs to run logic of its own.

The question then is, where to subclass from?

A lot of developers choose the seemingly obvious route of subclassing `CCSprite`. I don't think that's a good idea. The relationship of subclassing is a "is a" relationship. Think closely, is your player character a `CCSprite`? Are all of your enemy characters `CCSprites`?

At first the answer seems logical: of course they are sprites! That's what they use to display themselves. But wait a second. Could they be something else other than `CCSprite`? For all I know, game characters can also be characters in the literal sense. In Rogue-like games, your player character is an @. So would that character be a `CCLabel` then?

I think the confusion comes from `CCSprite` being the most widely used class to display anything onscreen. But the true relationship of your game characters to `CCNode` classes is a "has a" relationship. Your player class "has a" `CCSprite` it uses to display itself. In a Rogue-like game, the player character class "has a" `CCLabel` to display itself. And if you want to get fancy, as in OpenGL and lots of particle effects, your player class "has a" system of particle effects to represent it visually on screen.

The distinction becomes even clearer when you think of why you'd normally subclass the `CCSprite` class: in general, to add new features to the `CCSprite` class—for example, to have a `CCSprite` class that uses a `CCRenderTexture` to modify how it is displayed based on what is beneath it on the screen.

What would you add to the CCSprite class if you subclassed it for your player object? Input handling, animating the player, collision detection; in general: game logic. None of these things belong to a CCSprite class.

You may still be wondering why this has any relevance, or why you should care? Consider the case where you want your player to have several visual representations that it should be able to switch to seamlessly. If the player needs to morph from one sprite to another using FadeIn/FadeOut actions, you're going to have to use two sprites. Or if you want your game objects to appear on different parts of the screen at the same time, for example in a game like Asteroids where the Asteroid leaving the top of the screen should also show up partially at the bottom of the screen. You need two sprites to do this, and that's just one reason why composition (or aggregation) is preferable to subclassing (or inheritance). Inheritance causes tight coupling between classes, with changes to parent classes potentially introducing bugs and anomalies in subclasses. The deeper the class hierarchy, the more code will reside in base classes, which amplifies the problem.

Another good reason is that a game object encapsulates its visual representation, If the logic is self-contained, only the game object itself should ever change any of the CCNode properties, such as position, scale, rotation, or even running and stopping actions. One of the core problems many game developers face sooner or later is that their game objects are directly manipulated by outside influences. For example, you may inadvertently create situations where the scene's layer, the user interface, and the player object itself all change the player sprite's position. This is undesirable. You want all of the other systems to notify the player object to change its position, giving the player object itself the final say about how to interpret these commands, whether to apply them, modify them, or ignore them.

Composing Game Objects using CCSprite

Let's try this out. Instead of creating a new class derived from a CCNode class, create it from Objective-C's base class NSObject. Figure 5–3 shows you which Cocoa Touch class template to choose.

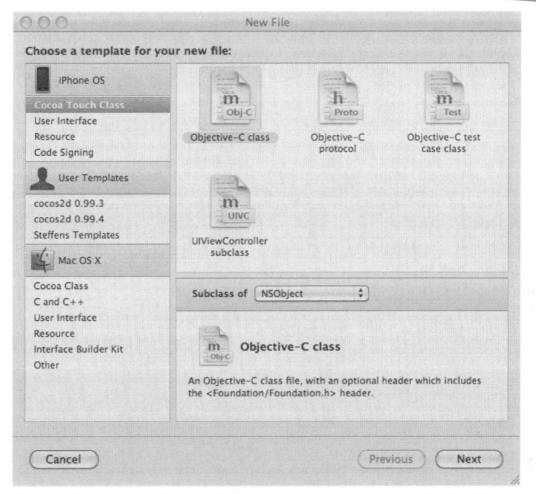

Figure 5–3. *Start a new game object by subclassing* NSObject *instead of a* CCNode-*based class like* CCSprite.

I decided to turn the spiders in the ScenesAndLayers05 project into a class of their own. The class is simply called Spider. Listing 5–11 reveals the Spider class's header file.

Listing 5–11. *The Spider Class Interface.*

```
// Don't forget to #import the cocos2d header when subclassing from NSObject!
#import "cocos2d.h"

@interface Spider : NSObject
{
        CCSprite* spiderSprite;
}

+(id) spiderWithParentNode:(CCNode*)parentNode;
-(id) initWithParentNode:(CCNode*)parentNode;

@end
```

When you subclass from NSObject, you need to manually add the #import "cocos2d.h" line to avoid compile errors. It's not automatically added since you're not starting from one of the cocos2d class templates. You can see that the CCSprite used to display is added as a member variable to the class and is named spiderSprite. This is called *composition* since you compose the Spider class of a CCSprite used to display it, and later possibly other objects and variables.

The Spider class in Listing 5–12 has a static autorelease initializer like any CCNode class. This mimics cocos2d's memory management scheme and it is good practice to follow that. You will also notice that I did not use [self scheduleUpdate]. That method is defined by CCNode but the Spider class is not deriving from a CCNode class. Instead, I have to make use of cocos2d's undocumented CCScheduler class, which is also used internally by CCNode. This also requires that I manually unschedule the update selector in the dealloc method.

Listing 5–12. *The Spider Class Implementation*

```
#import "Spider.h"

@implementation Spider

// Static autorelease initializer, mimics cocos2d's memory allocation scheme.
+(id) spiderWithParentNode:(CCNode*)parentNode
{
        return [[[self alloc] initWithParentNode:parentNode] autorelease];
}

-(id) initWithParentNode:(CCNode*)parentNode
{
        if ((self = [super init]))
        {
                CGSize screenSize = [[CCDirector sharedDirector] winSize];

                spiderSprite = [CCSprite spriteWithFile:@"spider.png"];
                spiderSprite.position = CGPointMake(CCRANDOM_0_1() *
                                screenSize.width, CCRANDOM_0_1() * screenSize.height);
                [parentNode addChild:spiderSprite];

                // Manually schedule update via the undocumented CCScheduler class.
                [[CCScheduler sharedScheduler] scheduleUpdateForTarget:self priority:0
                                                                        paused:NO];
        }

        return self;
}

-(void) dealloc
{
        // Must manually unschedule, it is not done automatically.
        [[CCScheduler sharedScheduler] unscheduleUpdateForTarget:self];

        [super dealloc];
}
```

```
-(void) update:(ccTime)delta
{
        numUpdates++;
        if (numUpdates > 50)
        {
                numUpdates = 0;
                [spiderSprite stopAllActions];

                // Let the Spider move randomly.
                CGPoint moveTo = CGPointMake(CCRANDOM_0_1() * 200 - 100,
                                             CCRANDOM_0_1() * 100 - 50);
                CCMoveBy* move = [CCMoveBy actionWithDuration:1 position:moveTo];
                [spiderSprite runAction:move];
        }
}

@end
```

The Spider class now uses its own game logic to move the spiders around on the screen. Granted, it won't win any prices at this year's Artificial Intelligence Symposium; it's just meant as an example.

Up to this point I've led you to believe you can receive Touch input only on CCLayer nodes, but this is not entirely true. In fact, any class can receive touch input using the CCTouchDispatcher directly. It only needs to implement either the CCStandardTouchDelegate or CCTargetedTouchDelegate protocols. You'll find these changes in the *ScenesAndLayers06* project, and the protocol definition added to the header file is shown in Listing 5–13.

Listing 5–13. *The CCTargetedTouchDelegate Protocol*

```
@interface Spider : NSObject <CCTargetedTouchDelegate>
{
        ...
}
```

The implementation in Listing 5–14 highlights the changes made to the Spider class. The Spider class now reacts to targeted touch input. Whenever you tap a spider, it will quickly move away from your finger. Contrary to common perceptions, Spiders are usually more afraid of humans than the other way around, exceptions notwithstanding.

Just like with the CCScheduler, the Spider class is registered with CCTouchDispatcher to receive input but must also be removed on dealloc. Otherwise, the scheduler or touch dispatcher would still keep a reference to the Spider class even though it was released from memory. This would cause a crash shortly thereafter.

Listing 5–14. *The Changed Spider Class*

```
-(id) initWithParentNode:(CCNode*)parentNode
{
        if ((self = [super init]))
        {
                ...
```

```
            // Manually schedule update via the undocumented CCScheduler class.
            [[CCScheduler sharedScheduler] scheduleUpdateForTarget:self priority:0
                                                              paused:NO];

            // Manually add this class as receiver of targeted touch events.
            [[CCTouchDispatcher sharedDispatcher] addTargetedDelegate:self
                                             priority:-1 swallowsTouches:YES];
        }

        return self;
}

-(void) dealloc
{
        // Must manually unschedule, it is not done automatically!
        [[CCScheduler sharedScheduler] unscheduleUpdateForTarget:self];

        // Must manually remove this class as touch input receiver!
        [[CCTouchDispatcher sharedDispatcher] removeDelegate:self];

        [super dealloc];
}

// Extract common logic into a separate method accepting parameters.
-(void) moveAway:(float)duration position:(CGPoint)moveTo
{
        [spiderSprite stopAllActions];
        CCMoveBy* move = [CCMoveBy actionWithDuration:duration position:moveTo];
        [spiderSprite runAction:move];
}

-(void) update:(ccTime)delta
{
        numUpdates++;
        if (numUpdates > 50)
        {
                numUpdates = 0;

                // Move at regular speed.
                CGPoint moveTo = CGPointMake(CCRANDOM_0_1() * 200 - 100,
                                             CCRANDOM_0_1() * 100 - 50);
                [self moveAway:2 position:moveTo];
        }
}

-(BOOL) ccTouchBegan:(UITouch *)touch withEvent:(UIEvent *)event
{
        // Check if this touch is on the Spider's sprite.
        CGPoint touchLocation = [MultiLayerScene locationFromTouch:touch];
        BOOL isTouchHandled = CGRectContainsPoint([spiderSprite boundingBox],
                                                  touchLocation);
        if (isTouchHandled)
        {
```

```
                    // Reset move counter.
                    numUpdates = 0;

                    // Move away from touch loation rapidly.
                    CGPoint moveTo;
                    float moveDistance = 60;
                    float rand = CCRANDOM_0_1();

                    // Randomly pick one of four corners to move away to.
                    if (rand < 0.25f)
                            moveTo = CGPointMake(moveDistance, moveDistance);
                    else if (rand < 0.5f)
                            moveTo = CGPointMake(-moveDistance, moveDistance);
                    else if (rand < 0.75f)
                            moveTo = CGPointMake(moveDistance, -moveDistance);
                    else
                            moveTo = CGPointMake(-moveDistance, -moveDistance);

                    // Move quickly:
                    [self moveAway:0.1f position:moveTo];
            }

        return isTouchHandled;
}
```

I decided to improve the move logic by extracting the functionality into a separate method. The straightforward way would have been to just copy the existing code from the update method to the ccTouchBegan method. However, copy-and-paste is evil. If you join the Cult of Programmology, be aware that it is considered a deadly sin to duplicate existing code. Using copy-and-paste is very easy, which makes it so tempting. But whenever you duplicate code, you duplicate the effort needed to change that code later on. Consider the case where you duplicate the same sequence of actions four times and you need to change the duration of one of the actions. You can't change it once, you have to change it four times, and more importantly you have to test the change four times.

Using methods to extract common functionality and exposing what needs to be flexible as parameters is indeed a very simple task. I hope that the moveAway method in Listing 5–14 illustrates my point well. It does not contain much code, but even the smallest amount of duplicated code increases your time spent on maintaining your code.

The ccTouchBegan method takes the touch location and checks via the CGRectContainsPoint if the touch location is inside the spider sprite's boundingBox. If so, it handles the touch and runs the code that lets the spider move away quickly in one of four directions.

In summary, using an NSObject as base class makes a few things odd or maybe inconvenient at first glance. The benefits may not become visible until you start creating larger projects. It is OK if you prefer to subclass CCNode classes like CCSprite for now. But when you get more proficient—and more ambitious—please come back to this chapter again and try this approach. It leads to a better code structure and more clearly separated boundaries and responsibilities of the individual game elements.

Curiously Cool CCNode Classes

Please remain seated as I walk you through a few more CCNode derived classes that fulfill very specific purposes. They are CCProgressTimer, CCParallaxNode, CCRibbon, and CCMotionStreak.

CCProgressTimer

In the *ScenesAndLayers07* project, I've added a CCProgressTimer node to the UserInterfaceLayer class. The progress timer class is useful for any kind of progress display, like a loading bar or the time it takes an icon to become available again. Think of the action buttons in World of Warcraft and their recast timer. The progress timer takes a sprite and, based on a percentage, displays only a part of it to visualize some kind of progress in your game. See Listing 5–15 for how to initialize the CCProgressTimer node.

Listing 5–15. *Initializing a CCProgressTimer Node*

```
// Progress timer is a sprite only partially displayed to visualize some kind of progress.
CCProgressTimer* timer = [CCProgressTimer progressWithFile:@"firething.png"];
timer.type = kCCProgressTimerTypeRadialCCW;
timer.percentage = 0;
[self addChild:timer z:1 tag:UILayerTagProgressTimer];

// The update is needed for the progress timer.
[self scheduleUpdate];
```

The timer type is from the CCProgressTimerType enum defined in *CCProgressTimer.h*. You can choose between radial, vertical, and horizontal progress timers. But there's one caveat: the timer doesn't update itself. You have to change the timer's percentage value frequently to update the progress. That's why I included the scheduleUpdate in Listing 5–15. The implementation of the update method that does the actual progressing is shown in Listing 5–16. The CCProgressTimer node's percentage property must be frequently updated as needed—it won't progress by itself automatically. The progress here is simply the passing of time. Isn't that what games are all about?

Listing 5–16. *The Implementation of the update Method*

```
-(void) update:(ccTime)delta
{
        CCNode* node = [self getChildByTag:UILayerTagProgressTimer];
        NSAssert([node isKindOfClass:[CCProgressTimer class]], @"node is not a
                                                        CCProgressTimer");

        // Updates the progress timer
        CCProgressTimer* timer = (CCProgressTimer*)node;
        timer.percentage += delta * 10;
        if (timer.percentage >= 100)
        {
                timer.percentage = 0;
        }
}
```

CCParallaxNode

Parallaxing is an effect used in 2D games to give the impression of depth, created by using layered images that move at different rates. The images in the foreground move faster relative to the images in the background. Cocos2d has a specialized node you can use to create this effect. The code to create a CCParallaxNode in Listing 5–17 is also in the *ScenesAndLayers08* project.

Listing 5–17. *The CCParallaxNode Requires a Lot of Setup Work, but the Results Are Worth It*

```
// Load the sprites for each parallax layer, from background to foreground.
CCSprite* para1 = [CCSprite spriteWithFile:@"parallax1.png"];
CCSprite* para2 = [CCSprite spriteWithFile:@"parallax2.png"];
CCSprite* para3 = [CCSprite spriteWithFile:@"parallax3.png"];
CCSprite* para4 = [CCSprite spriteWithFile:@"parallax4.png"];

// Set the correct offsets depending on the screen and image sizes.
para1.anchorPoint = CGPointMake(0, 1);
para2.anchorPoint = CGPointMake(0, 1);
para3.anchorPoint = CGPointMake(0, 0.6f);
para4.anchorPoint = CGPointMake(0, 0);
CGPoint topOffset = CGPointMake(0, screenSize.height);
CGPoint midOffset = CGPointMake(0, screenSize.height / 2);
CGPoint downOffset = CGPointZero;

// Create a parallax node and add the sprites to it.
CCParallaxNode* paraNode = [CCParallaxNode node];
[paraNode addChild:para1 z:1 parallaxRatio:CGPointMake(0.5f, 0)

positionOffset:topOffset];
[paraNode addChild:para2 z:2 parallaxRatio:CGPointMake(1, 0) positionOffset:topOffset];
[paraNode addChild:para3 z:4 parallaxRatio:CGPointMake(2, 0) positionOffset:midOffset];
[paraNode addChild:para4 z:3 parallaxRatio:CGPointMake(3, 0) positionOffset:downOffset];
[self addChild:paraNode z:0 tag:ParallaxSceneTagParallaxNode];

// Move the parallax node to show the parallaxing effect.
CCMoveBy* move1 = [CCMoveBy actionWithDuration:5 position:CGPointMake(-160, 0)];
CCMoveBy* move2 = [CCMoveBy actionWithDuration:15 position:CGPointMake(160, 0)];
CCSequence* sequence = [CCSequence actions:move1, move2, nil];
CCRepeatForever* repeat = [CCRepeatForever actionWithAction:sequence];
[paraNode runAction:repeat];
```

To create a CCParallaxNode, you first create the desired CCSprite nodes that make up the individual parallaxing images, then you have to properly position them on the screen. In this case, I chose to modify their anchor points instead as it was easier to align the sprites with the screen borders. The CCParallaxNode is created like any other node, but its children are added using a special initializer. With it you specify the parallaxRatio, which is a CGPoint used as multiplier for any movement of the CCParallaxNode. In this case, the CCSprite para1 would move at half the speed, para2 at normal speed, para3 at double the speed of the CCParallaxNode, and so on.

Using a sequence of CCMoveBy actions, the CCParallaxNode is moved from left to right and back. You will notice how the clouds in the background move slowest while the trees and gravel in the foreground scroll by the fastest. This gives the illusion of depth.

> **NOTE:** You can't modify the positions of individual child nodes once they are added to the CCParallaxNode. You can only scroll as far as the largest and fastest-moving image before the background shows through. You can see this effect if you modify the CCMoveBy actions to scroll a lot further. You can increase the scrolling distance by adding more of the same sprites with the appropriate offsets. But if you require endless scrolling in one or both directions, you will have to implement your own parallax system. In fact, this is what we're going to do in Chapter 7.

CCRibbon

The CCRibbon node creates a band of images, like a chain, or as in Figure 5–4, like a millipede crawling over the parallaxing scene in the *ScenesAndLayers09* project.

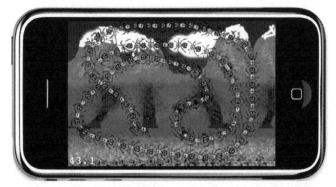

Figure 5–4. *Nasty. A CCRibbon of spiders. Looks like a millipede crawling over the screen of the ScenesAndLayers09 project. Do you dare to touch it to draw your own sequence of images using the CCRibbon node?*

The CCRibbon class, together with touch input, can be used to create the line-drawing effects of popular games. Listing 5–18 shows how the CCRibbon is implemented with the touch events. What's notable is that you can't remove individual points from a CCRibbon. You can only remove the whole CCRibbon by removing it as child from its parent. The width and length parameters of the CCRibbon initializer determine how big individual ribbon elements are drawn. In this case I chose to make is as big as the *spider.png* image, which is 32 pixels wide and high. If you choose other values, the image will be scaled up or down accordingly.

Listing 5–18. *The CCRibbon Class*

```
-(void) resetRibbon
{
        // Removes the ribbon and creates a new one.
        [self removeChildByTag:ParallaxSceneTagRibbon cleanup:YES];
        CCRibbon* ribbon = [CCRibbon ribbonWithWidth:32 image:@"spider.png"
                                 length:32 color:ccc4(255, 255, 255, 255) fade:0.5f];
        [self addChild:ribbon z:5 tag:ParallaxSceneTagRibbon];
```

```
}

-(CCRibbon*) getRibbon
{
        CCNode* node = [self getChildByTag:ParallaxSceneTagRibbon];
        NSAssert([node isKindOfClass:[CCRibbon class]], @"node is not a CCRibbon");

        return (CCRibbon*)node;
}

-(void) addRibbonPoint:(CGPoint)point
{
        CCRibbon* ribbon = [self getRibbon];
        [ribbon addPointAt:point width:32];
}

-(BOOL) ccTouchBegan:(UITouch*)touch withEvent:(UIEvent *)event
{
        [self addRibbonPoint:[MultiLayerScene locationFromTouch:touch]];
        return YES;
}
-(void) ccTouchMoved:(UITouch*)touch withEvent:(UIEvent *)event
{
        [self addRibbonPoint:[MultiLayerScene locationFromTouch:touch]];
}
-(void) ccTouchEnded:(UITouch*)touch withEvent:(UIEvent *)event
{
        [self resetRibbon];
}
```

CCMotionStreak

CCMotionStreak is essentially a wrapper around CCRibbon. It causes the CCRibbon elements to more or less slowly fade out and disappear after you've drawn them. Try it out in the *ScenesAndLayers10* project.

As you can see in Listing 5–19, you use it almost identically to CCRibbon, except that the CCRibbon is now a property of CCMotionStreak. The fade parameter determines how fast ribbon elements fade out; the smaller the number, the quicker they disappear. The minSeg parameter seems to have no discernable effect, although an interesting graphical glitch occurs if you set it to negative values.

Listing 5–19. *The CCMotionStreak Lets the Ribbon's Elements Fade Out, Creating a Streak Effect*

```
-(void) resetMotionStreak
{
        // Removes the CCMotionStreak and creates a new one.
        [self removeChildByTag:ParallaxSceneTagRibbon cleanup:YES];
        CCMotionStreak* streak = [CCMotionStreak streakWithFade:0.7f minSeg:10
                        image:@"spider.png" width:32 length:32 color:ccc4(255, 0, 255, 255)];
        [self addChild:streak z:5 tag:ParallaxSceneTagRibbon];
}

-(void) addMotionStreakPoint:(CGPoint)point
{
```

```
        CCMotionStreak* streak = [self getMotionStreak];
        [streak.ribbon addPointAt:point width:32];
}
```

Conclusion

In this chapter you learned more about scenes and layers—how and when to use them and for what. I explained why it's usually not a good idea to subclass game objects directly from CCSprite, and I showed you how to create a game object class that doesn't derive from any CCNode class at all, but from NSObject.

Finally, you learned how to use specialized CCNode classes like CCProgressTimer, CCParallaxNode, CCRibbon, and CCMotionStreak.

You now have enough knowledge about cocos2d to start creating more complex games, like the side-scrolling shooter I'm preparing you for. And with complex games come complex graphics, including animations. How to handle all of these sprites efficiently both in terms of memory and performance is the topic of the next chapter.

Chapter **6**

Sprites In-Depth

In this chapter I'll focus on working with sprites. There are numerous ways to create sprites from single files and Texture Atlases. I will also explain how to create and play sprite animations.

A *Texture Atlas* is a regular texture that contains more than one image. Often it is used to store all animation frames of a single character in one texture, but it is not limited to that. In fact, you can place any image into a Texture Atlas. The goal is to get as many images as possible into each Texture Atlas. To help create a Texture Atlas, most cocos2d developers rely on the Zwoptex tool, which I'll also introduce in this chapter.

Sprite batching is a technique for speeding up the drawing of sprites. It speeds up drawing identical sprites, but is most effective when using a Texture Atlas. If you use a Texture Atlas along with sprite batching, you can draw all of the images in that Texture Atlas in one draw call.

A *draw call* is the process of transmitting the necessary information to the graphics hardware in order to render a texture or parts of it. When you are using CCSprites, each CCSprite will cause one draw call. The overhead for each draw call can add up so much that it can decrease the frame rate by roughly 15 percent or more (unless you are using a CCSpriteBatchNode instead, which functions like an extra layer to which you can add sprite nodes that use the same texture).

The lessons you'll learn in this chapter will become the foundation for the parallax-scrolling shoot-'em-up game that I'll be discussing in Chapters 7 and 8.

CCSpriteBatchNode

Every time a texture is drawn on the screen, the graphics hardware has to prepare the rendering, render the graphics, and clean up after rendering. There is an inherent overhead caused by starting and ending the rendering of a single texture. This can be alleviated by letting the graphics hardware know that you have a group of sprites that should be rendered using the same texture. In that case, the graphics hardware will perform the preparation and cleanup steps only once for a group of sprites.

Figure 6–1 shows an example of this kind of batch rendering. As you can see, there are hundreds of identical bullets on the screen. If you rendered them each one at a time, your frame rate would drop by at least 15 percent in this case. With a CCSpriteBatchNode, you can avoid the repeated effort.

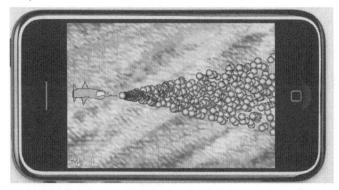

Figure 6–1. *Drawing many CCSprite nodes using the same texture is more efficient when they are added to a CCSpriteBatchNode.*

As a refresher, here's how you'd create a CCSprite the normal way:

```
CCSprite* sprite = [CCSprite spriteWithFile:@"bullet.png"];
[self addChild:sprite];
```

Listing 6–1 changes the creation of the same CCSprite to use a CCSpriteBatchNode instead. Of course, just adding one CCSprite to it won't give you any benefit, so I'll be adding a number of sprites using the same texture to the CCSpriteBatchNode.

Listing 6–1. *Creating Multiple CCSprites and Adding Them to a CCSpriteBatchNode to Render Them Faster*

```
CCSpriteBatchNode* batch = [CCSpriteBatchNode batchNodeWithFile:@"bullet.png"];
[self addChild:batch];

for (int i = 0; i < 100; i++)
{
        CCSprite* sprite = [CCSprite spriteWithFile:@"bullet.png"];
        [batch addChild:bullet];
}
```

You will notice that in Listing 6–1 the CCSpriteBatchNode takes a file as an argument, even though the CCSpriteBatchNode itself isn't displayed. It's more like a CCLayer in that regard, except that you can only add CCSprite nodes to it. The reason it takes an image file as argument is that all CCSprite nodes added to the CCSpriteBatchNode must use the same texture. If you make that mistake, you'll see the following error message in the debugger console:

```
SpriteBatches[13879:207] *** Terminating app due to uncaught exception
'NSInternalInconsistencyException', reason: 'CCSprite is not using the same texture id'
```

When to Use the CCSpriteBatchNode

The CCSpriteBatchNode can be used whenever you display two or more CCSprites of the same kind. The more CCSprites you can group together, the greater the benefit of using CCSpriteBatchNode will be.

There are limitations, however. Since all the CCSprite nodes are added to the CCSpriteBatchNode, all CCSprite nodes added to it will be drawn at the same z-order (depth). If your game is supposed to have bullets flying behind and in front of enemies, you would have to use two CCSpriteBatchNodes to group the bullet sprites of the lower and the higher z-order independently.

Another drawback is that all CCSprites added to the CCSpriteBatchNode need to use the same texture. But that also means that the CCSpriteBatchNode becomes most important when you are using a Texture Atlas. With a Texture Atlas you are not limited to drawing only one image; instead you can add a number of different images to the same Texture Atlas and draw all of these images using the same CCSpriteBatchNode, speeding up the rendering of all the images of the same Texture Atlas.

The issue of z-ordering in this case also is less prevalent since you can specify the z-order of CCSprite nodes within the CCSpriteBatchNode. If all your game's images can fit into the same Texture Atlas, you could compose almost your entire game using just a single CCSpriteBatchNode (although this will be the rare exception).

Think of the CCSpriteBatchNode as similar to a CCLayer, except that it only accepts CCSprite nodes using the same texture. With that mindset I'm sure you'll find the right places to use the CCSpriteBatchNode.

Demo Projects

There are four projects—named *Sprites01* through *Sprites04*—that are intended as a demonstration of using a CCSpriteBatchNode. They are the first steps toward the scrolling shoot-'em-up game that I'll discuss in Chapter 7. Since developers often start by using just the CCSprite node, and then improve the code to support CCSpriteBatchNode, I found it interesting to show exactly this process and how the code changes along the way.

The projects use two classes, named Ship and Bullet, both derived from CCSprite, to illustrate how a project may be changed from using regular CCSprite objects to a CCSpriteBatchNode.

A Common and Fatal Mistake

The *Sprites01* project shows a common trap developers new to Objective-C can quickly find themselves in. It's easy to make this mistake but hard to figure out the cause and how to fix it. I'll spare you the headache. Take a look at Listing 6–2; do you see what's wrong with this code?

Listing 6–2. *A Commonly Made Fatal Mistake When Subclassing CCSprite (or Other Classes for That Matter)*

```
-(id) init
{
        if ((self = [super initWithFile:@"ship.png"]))
        {
                [self scheduleUpdate];
        }
        return self;
}
```

No, it's not about `scheduleUpdate`, that's just to throw you off guard. The problem lies in the fact that the `-(id) init` method is the default initializer, which is eventually called by any other specialized initializer like `initWithFile`. Can you imagine now what's wrong with the code?

Well, `initWithFile` will eventually call the default initializer, `-(id) init`. Then, since this class's implementation overrides it, it will call `[super initWithFile: ..]` again. Repeat ad infinitum.

The solution is very simple. As shown in Listing 6–3, it is sufficient to give the initializer method a different name—something other than `-(id) init`.

Listing 6–3. *Fixing the Infinite Loop Caused by the Code in Listing 6–2*

```
-(id) initWithShipImage
{
        if ((self = [super initWithFile:@"ship.png"]))
        {
                [self scheduleUpdate];
        }
        return self;
}
```

> **CAUTION:** In general you should never call anything but `[super init]` in the default initializer `-(id) init` to avoid this problem. If you have to call `[super initWith...]` in your class's initializer method, then you should name the initializer method accordingly, as `-(id) initWith...` (e.g., like `-(id) initWithShipImage` as in Listing 6–3).

Bullets Without a SpriteBatch

The *Sprites02* project creates a new `CCSprite` for each `Bullet`. Since the ship sprite is adding the bullets, the most peculiar thing is in Listing 6–4, in which the ship is shooting the bullets one per frame—it does not add them to itself; otherwise, all the flying bullets would mimic the ship's movement.

Listing 6–4. *The Ship Shooting the Bullets*

```
-(void) update:(ccTime)delta
{
        // Keep creating new bullets
        Bullet* bullet = [Bullet bulletWithShip:self];
```

```
        // Add the bullets to the ship's parent
        [[self parent] addChild:bullet z:1 tag:GameSceneNodeTagBullet];
}
```

The Bullet sprites are added to the ship's parent for the simple reason that adding them to the ship would make all flying bullets positioned at an offset to the ship. This means that if the ship were to move—which I suppose you will want eventually; otherwise, this would be a really boring game—all the flying bullets would change their positions relative to the ship, as if they were somehow attached to it.

The bullets also use an update method to update their position and to remove themselves at some point. Although sprites aren't drawn if they are outside the screen, they still consume memory and CPU power, so it's a necessity to remove any stray objects that leave the screen area at some point in time. In this case, you simply check the bullet's position against the right side of the screen, as shown in Listing 6–5.

Listing 6–5. *Moving and Removing the Bullets*

```
-(void) update:(ccTime)delta
{
        self.position = ccpAdd(self.position, velocity);

        if (self.position.x > outsideScreen)
        {
                [self removeFromParentAndCleanup:YES];
        }
}
```

The bullet position is updated by simply adding a velocity vector to its position. The velocity simply determines how many pixels to move in each direction every frame. This is much more effective than using CCMoveTo or CCMoveBy actions in this case. It avoids some overhead and the problem that actions are time-based. If the ship were to move closer to the right side of the screen, the move actions would cause the bullets to move more slowly since they need to travel a shorter distance in the same time.

Introducing the CCSpriteBatchNode

In the *Sprites03* project, the CCSpriteBatchNode for bullets has been added. I decided to add it to the GameScene itself, since bullets are not supposed to be added to the Ship class. Since the Ship class has no access to the GameScene, I also needed to add the pseudo-singleton accessor sharedGameScene to allow the ship to get to the CCSpriteBatchNode, as shown in Listing 6–6.

Listing 6–6. *The GameScene Gets a CCSpriteBatchNode for Bullets and Accessors for the Ship Class*

```
static GameScene* instanceOfGameScene;
+(GameScene*) sharedGameScene
{
        NSAssert(instanceOfGameScene != nil, @" instance not yet initialized!");
        return instanceOfGameScene;
}

-(id) init
{
```

```
        if ((self = [super init]))
        {
                instanceOfGameScene = self;

                ...

                CCSpriteBatchNode* batch = [CCSpriteBatchNode
                                        batchNodeWithFile:@"bullet.png"];
                [self addChild:batch z:1 tag:GameSceneNodeTagBulletSpriteBatch];
        }
        return self;
}

-(void) dealloc
{
        instanceOfGameScene = nil;
        [super dealloc];
}

-(CCSpriteBatchNode*) bulletSpriteBatch
{
        CCNode* node = [self getChildByTag:GameSceneNodeTagBulletSpriteBatch];
        NSAssert([node isKindOfClass:[CCSpriteBatchNode class]], @"not a SpriteBatch");
        return (CCSpriteBatchNode*)node;
}
```

> **CAUTION:** I know this singleton and the additional accessor method bulletSpriteBatch may not be to everyone's liking. Why didn't I simply pass the CCSpriteBatchNode as a pointer to the Ship class, either in the initializer or via a property?
>
> One reason is that the Ship does not own the bullet sprite batch, and therefore it should not keep a reference to it. Moreover, if the Ship class even retains the sprite batch, it could cause your whole scene to not be deallocated if you're not careful. Nodes should never retain other nodes that do not belong to them.

Now the Ship class can add the bullets to the sprite batch directly by using the sharedGameScene and bulletSpriteBatch accessors. This is shown in Listing 6–7.

Listing 6–7. *GameScene Gets a CCSpriteBatchNode for Bullets and Accessors for the Ship Class*

```
-(void) update:(ccTime)delta
{
        Bullet* bullet = [Bullet bulletWithShip:self];
        [[[GameScene sharedGameScene] bulletSpriteBatch] addChild:bullet z:1
                                        tag:GameSceneNodeTagBullet];
}
```

Optimizations

While I'm optimizing this code, why not get rid of the unnecessary memory allocations and releases caused by the Bullet class? Because you can define a limit for the number of bullets that can be on the screen at the same time, and then create this number of bullets up front, you can avoid allocating and releasing bullets during game play. Since the bullets share the same texture, the additional memory used by having a greater number of bullets reside in memory at all times is negligible. Listing 6–8 shows the changes to GameScene's init method implemented in the *Sprites04* project.

Listing 6–8. *Creating a Reasonable Number of Bullet Sprites Up Front Avoids Unnecessary Memory Allocations During Game Play*

```
CCSpriteBatchNode* batch = [CCSpriteBatchNode batchNodeWithFile:@"bullet.png"];
[self addChild:batch z:1 tag:GameSceneNodeTagBulletSpriteBatch];

// Create a number of bullets up front and reuse them whenever necessary.
for (int i = 0; i < 400; i++)
{
        Bullet* bullet = [Bullet bullet];
        bullet.visible = NO;
        [batch addChild:bullet];
}
```

All the bullets are made invisible since we don't use them just yet. The GameScene class gets a new method in Listing 6–9 that allows it to shoot bullets from the ship by reactivating inactive bullets in sequence. This process is often referred to as *object pooling*. Shooting is now rerouted through the GameScene since it contains the CCSpriteBatchNode used for the bullets. Once an inactive bullet has been selected, it is instructed to shoot itself.

Listing 6–9. *Shooting Is Now Rerouted*

```
-(void) shootBulletFromShip:(Ship*)ship
{
        CCArray* bullets = [self.bulletSpriteBatch children];

        CCNode* node = [bullets objectAtIndex:nextInactiveBullet];
        NSAssert([node isKindOfClass:[Bullet class]], @"not a bullet!");

        Bullet* bullet = (Bullet*)node;
        [bullet shootBulletFromShip:ship];

        nextInactiveBullet++;
        if (nextInactiveBullet >= [bullets count])
        {
                nextInactiveBullet = 0;
        }
}
```

By keeping the reference counter nextInactiveBullet, each shot uses the sprite-batched bullet from that index. Once all bullets have been shot once, the index is reset. This works fine as long as the number of bullets in the pool is always greater than the maximum number of bullets on the screen.

The Bullet class's shoot method in Listing 6–10 only performs the necessary steps to reinitialize a bullet, including rescheduling its update selector. Most importantly, the Bullet is set to be visible again. Its position and velocity are also reset. The Bullet class's shoot method simply resets the relevant variables such as position and velocity, and then sets the bullet to be visible. Once the bullet has reached the end of its lifetime, it's simply set to not be visible again.

Listing 6–10. *The Bullet Class's Shoot Method Reinitializing a Bullet*

```
-(void) shootBulletFromShip:(Ship*)ship
{
        float spread = (CCRANDOM_0_1() - 0.5f) * 0.5f;
        velocity = CGPointMake(1, spread);

        outsideScreen = [[CCDirector sharedDirector] winSize].width;

        self.position = CGPointMake(ship.position.x + ship.contentSize.width * 0.5f,
                                                                ship.position.y);

        self.visible = YES;

        [self scheduleUpdate];
}

-(void) update:(ccTime)delta
{
        self.position = ccpAdd(self.position, velocity);

        if (self.position.x > outsideScreen)
        {
                self.visible = NO;
                [self unscheduleAllSelectors];
        }
}
```

Sprite Animations the Hard Way

Now brace yourself. I'd like to show you how sprite animations work. They are another good reason to use CCSpriteBatchNode, because you can put all animation frames into the same texture to conserve memory. It's quite a bit of code actually, as you'll see in Listing 6–11 and in the *Sprites05* project. After that, I'll show you how to create the same animation using a Texture Atlas, and how that is cutting down the amount of code you'll have to write.

Listing 6–11. *Adding an Animation to the Ship Without Using a Texture Atlas Requires Quite a Bit of Code*

```
// Load the ship's animation frames as textures and create a sprite frame
NSMutableArray* frames = [NSMutableArray arrayWithCapacity:5];
for (int i = 0; i < 5; i++)
{
        // Create a texture for the animation frame
        NSString* file = [NSString stringWithFormat:@"ship-anim%i.png", i];
        CCTexture2D* texture = [[CCTextureCache sharedTextureCache] addImage:file];

        // The whole image should be used as the animation frame
        CGSize texSize = [texture contentSize];
        CGRect texRect = CGRectMake(0, 0, texSize.width, texSize.height);

        // Create a sprite frame from the texture
```

```
                    CCSpriteFrame* frame = [CCSpriteFrame frameWithTexture:texture rect:texRect
                                                                 offset:CGPointZero];
            [frames addObject:frame];
    }
```

```
// Create an animation object from all the sprite animation frames
CCAnimation* anim = [CCAnimation animationWithName:@"move" delay:0.08f frames:frames];
```

```
// Run the animation by using the CCAnimate action and loop it with CCRepeatForever
CCAnimate* animate = [CCAnimate actionWithAnimation:anim];
CCRepeatForever* repeat = [CCRepeatForever actionWithAction:animate];
[self runAction:repeat];
```

All that just to create a sprite animation with five frames? I'm afraid so. I'll walk you through the code backward this time, which may explain the setup better. At the very end we're using a CCAnimate action to play an animation. In this case we're also using a CCRepeatForever action to loop the animation.

The CCAnimate action uses a CCAnimation object (which is a container for animation frames), defines the delay between each individual frame, and gives the animation a name. The name is useful because you can also store animations inside a CCSprite node, as shown in Listing 6–12. You can then access a particular animation by name.

Listing 6–12. *The CCSprite Class Can Store Animations for You, Which Can Be Retrieved by Name*

```
CCAnimation* anim = [CCAnimation animationWithName:@"move" delay:1 frames:frames];
```

```
// Store the animation in the CCSprite node
[mySprite addAnimation:anim];
```

```
// Sometime later: retrieve the move animation from the CCSprite node
CCAnimation* moveAnim = [mySprite animationByName:@"move"];
```

Going back to Listing 6–11, notice the for loop. This is where it gets complicated. The CCAnimation class must be initialized with an NSArray containing CCSpriteFrame objects. A *sprite frame* consists only of a reference to a texture, a rectangle that defines the area of the texture that should be drawn, and a position offset where that rectangle is positioned within the texture. I want the whole image to be displayed in this case, so the offset is zero and the texture rectangle equals the texture's contentSize property—in other words, the size of the actual image contained in the texture.

Now, the CCSpriteFrame unfortunately doesn't take an image file name as input, it only accepts existing CCTexture2D objects. The texture is created using the CCTextureCache singleton's addImage method, normally used to preload images as textures into memory without having to create a CCSprite or other object. The file name is constructed using NSString's stringWithFormat method, which allowed me to use the loop variable i to be appended to the file name, instead of having to write out all five file names.

To recap, from top to bottom, here's how you can create and run a sprite animation:

1. Create NSMutableArray.

2. For each animation frame:

    a. Create a CCTexture2D for each image.

    b. Create a CCSpriteFrame using the CCTexture2D.

    c. Add each CCSpriteFrame to the NSMutableArray.

3. Create a CCAnimation using the frames in the NSMutableArray.

4. Optionally, add the CCAnimation to a CCSprite.

5. Use a CCAnimate action to play the animation.

Shh, calm down—no need to take that Valium. If you pack your animation frames into a Texture Atlas, things will get a bit easier and more efficient at the same time. More helpful is to encapsulate all this code into a helper method and stick to a naming convention for your animation files.

Animation Helper Category

Since the code to create the animation frames and the animation is common to all animations, you should consider encapsulating this into a helper method. I have done so in the project Sprite05_WithAnimHelper. Instead of using static methods, I decided to extend the CCAnimation class using an Objective-C feature called a *category*. It offers a way to add methods to an existing class without having to modify the original class. The only downside is that with a category you cannot add member variables to the class, you can only add methods. The following code is the @interface for the CCAnimation category, which I simply named Helper:

```
@interface CCAnimation (Helper)
+(CCAnimation*) animationWithFile:(NSString*)name frameCount:(int)frameCount
                                                        delay:(float)delay;
@end
```

The @interface for a Objective-C category uses the same name as the class it extends, and adds a category name within parentheses. The category name is like a variable name and thus cannot contain spaces or other characters you can't use in variables, like punctuation characters for example. The @interface also must not contain curly brackets, since adding member variables to a category is not possible and not allowed.

The actual @implementation for the CCAnimation category uses the same schema as the @interface by appending the category name in parentheses after the class name. Everything else is just like writing regular class methods; in this case, my extension method is named animationWithFile, and takes the file name, the number of frames, and the animation delay as input:

```
@implementation CCAnimation (Helper)
```

```
// Creates an animation from single files
+(CCAnimation*) animationWithFile:(NSString*)name frameCount:(int)frameCount
delay:(float)delay
{
        // Load the animation frames as textures and create the sprite frames
        NSMutableArray* frames = [NSMutableArray arrayWithCapacity:frameCount];
        for (int i = 0; i < frameCount; i++)
        {
                // Assuming all animation files are named "nameX.png"
                NSString* file = [NSString stringWithFormat:@"%@%i.png", name, i];
                CCTexture2D* texture = [[CCTextureCache sharedTextureCache]
                                                              addImage:file];

                // Assuming that image file animations always use the whole image
                CGSize texSize = texture.contentSize;
                CGRect texRect = CGRectMake(0, 0, texSize.width, texSize.height);
                CCSpriteFrame* frame = [CCSpriteFrame frameWithTexture:texture
                                               rect:texRect offset:CGPointZero];

                [frames addObject:frame];
        }

        // Return an animation object from all the sprite animation frames
        return [CCAnimation animationWithName:name delay:delay frames:frames];
}

@end
```

Here's how the naming convention comes into play. The Ship's animations have the base name ship-anim followed by a consecutive number starting with 0 and ending in the *.png* file extension. For example, the file names for the Ship's animation are named *ship-anim0.png* through *ship-anim4.png*. If you create all your animations using that naming scheme, you can use the preceding CCAnimation extension method for all of your animations.

> **TIP:** I can't help but notice that a lot of developers and artists have a habit of consecutively naming files with a fixed number of digits, by adding leading zeros where necessary. For example, you might be tempted to name your files *my-anim001* through *my-anim024*. I think this habit goes back to the good-old computer operating systems that were incapable of natural sorting, and thus incorrectly sorted file names with consecutive numbers. Those days are long gone, and you'll actually make it harder for the programmer to load files named like that in a for loop, since you'll have to take into account how many leading zeros should be prepended. There is a nice formatting shortcut, %03i, to prepend zeros so that the number is always at least three digits long. However, I think it's better in our modern world to just name file names consecutively without prepending any leading zeros. You gain a little bit of simplicity and peace of mind.

This simplifies the code used to create an animation from individual files a lot:

```
// The whole shebang is now encapsulated into a Category extension method
CCAnimation* anim = [CCAnimation animationWithFile:@"ship-anim" frameCount:5
                                                     delay:0.08f];
```

Essentially this cuts down the number of lines from nine to just this one. As the file name, you only need to pass the base name of your animation—in this case `ship-anim`. The helper method adds the consecutive numbers based on the `frameCount` parameter and also appends the *.png* file extension. It also uses the base name as the name for the animation, so that both are in sync all the time, and you don't have to remember alternate names for what is the same animation. Previously I named the ship's animation "move." Now it's called "ship-anim," inline with the file names. You can now access the animation stored within a `CCSprite` by using its base name like so:

```
[shipSprite addAnimation:anim];
CCAnimation* shipAnim = [shipSprite animationByName:@"ship-anim"];
```

The `animationWithFile` helper method makes two assumptions: animation image file names are consecutively numbered beginning with 0, and the files must be *.png* files. It's up to you whether you want to stick to this exact naming convention or change it to accommodate your own needs. For example, you might find it more convenient to start numbering your animations starting with 1 instead of 0. In that case you'll have to change the `for` loop so that the name string is formatted with `i + 1`. The important part is to stick to whatever naming convention you choose, to make your life (and your code) easier.

You should take away three things from this:

- Encapsulate commonly used code by defining your own methods.
- Use Objective-C categories to add methods to existing classes.
- Define resource file naming conventions to support your code.

Working with Texture Atlases

Texture Atlases help conserve precious memory, and they also help speed up the rendering of sprites. Since a Texture Atlas is nothing but a big texture, you can render all the images it contains using a `CCSpriteBatchNode`, thus reducing the draw call overhead. Using Texture Atlases is a win-win for both memory usage and performance.

What Is a Texture Atlas?

So far, for all the sprites used, I simply loaded the image file they need to display. Internally, this image becomes the sprite's texture, which contains the image, but the texture width and height always have to be a power of 2—for example, 1024×128 or 256×512. The texture size is increased automatically to conform to this rule, possibly taking up more memory than the image size would suggest. For example, an image with dimensions of 140×600 becomes a texture with the dimensions 256×1024 in memory. This texture is wasting a lot of precious memory, and the amount of wasted memory becomes significant if you have several such images and you load them each into individual textures.

That's where the Texture Atlas comes in. It is simply an image that is already aligned to a power-of-2 dimension and contains multiple images. Each image contained in the Texture Atlas has a sprite frame that defines the rectangle area the image is at within the Texture Atlas. In other words, a sprite frame is a `CGRect` structure that defines which part of the Texture Atlas should be used as the sprite's image. These sprite frames are saved in a separate *.plist* file so that cocos2d can render very specific images from a large Texture Atlas texture.

Introducing Zwoptex

Packing images into a Texture Atlas and noting the rectangular sprite frames they occupy would be a monumental task if it weren't for Zwoptex, a 2D sprite-packing tool (shown in Figure 6–2). The Zwoptex desktop app is available as a paid version for $24.95 at the time of this writing. The seven-day trial version can be downloaded here from `http://zwoptexapp.com`.

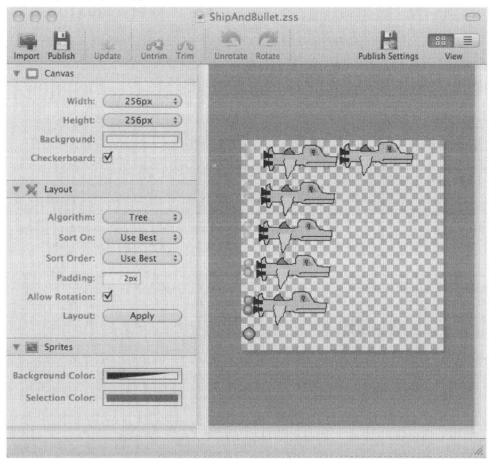

Figure 6–2. *The Zwoptex desktop app with the ship's animation frames already packed into a Texture Atlas*

If you don't need the latest features, such as 2048×2048-pixel textures, sprite updates that don't require you to remove and readd them, and the ability to allow sprites to be rotated so that they fit better into the texture, then you can use the Flash version of Zwoptex (Figure 6–3), which preceded the Zwoptex desktop app. You can use the Flash version online by visiting http://zwoptexapp.com/flashversion.

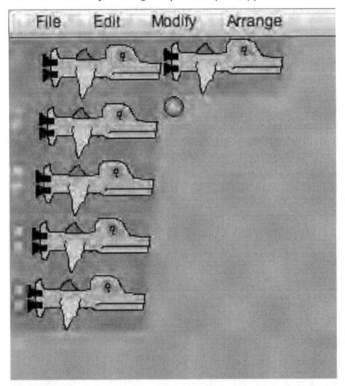

Figure 6–3. *The Zwoptex Flash version is still available online. It's not as fancy or powerful as the desktop app, but it's free.*

In this chapter I will focus on the Zwoptex desktop app, but the same Texture Atlas can be created with the Flash version.

Creating a Texture Atlas with Zwoptex Desktop

Working with Zwoptex is very straightforward and involves only a few steps, as illustrated in Figure 6–4. It's tweaking the settings to get the most optimized Texture Atlas possible that takes time.

Click import and add
multiple image files.

Choose the smallest possible Canvas size still
allows all images to be placed without overlap.

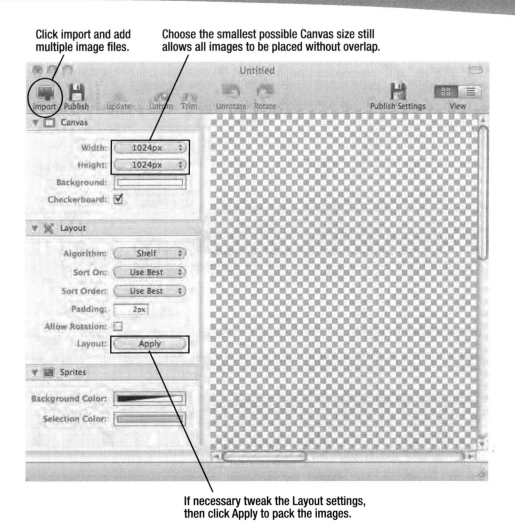

If necessary tweak the Layout settings,
then click Apply to pack the images.

Figure 6–4. *The process of working with Zwoptex is straightforward.*

First you'll have to add the images you want to add to the Texture Atlas. You can always add more at a later time, or remove existing ones. Click the **Import** button, or from the **File** menu choose **Import Sprites**, and then select one or more images. Zwoptex can load images from the most common graphics formats. In this case we will add all ship images and animation frames, as well as the bullet image. They can be found in the *Sprites06 Resource* folder.

After adding the images, you'll see them stuck together in the upper-left corner. The first thing you should do is to click the **Apply** button in the **Layout** pane to lay out the sprites according to the current layout settings. In some cases you can optimize the layout of the Texture Atlas to allow for more images by finding the best settings through experimentation. This can be a time-consuming process and usually leads to very similar end results, so I recommend not to spend too much time with it. In particular, the **Sort On** and **Sort Order** settings can be left at **Use Best**.

You should experiment with the canvas width or height, and then click **Apply** to apply the layout settings again to see if all images still fit into the Texture Atlas. The goal is to create a Texture Atlas with the smallest possible canvas size that can still contain all desired images without overlap.

> **CAUTION:** Unless you develop your game exclusively for iPhone 3GS, iPad, or iPhone 4 and future devices, you should not use a canvas width or height of 2048. Older devices only support texture dimensions up to a maximum of 1024×1024 pixels.

There's one crucial detail you should watch out for when changing the canvas size. If the canvas size is too small and some images overlap because there is not enough space left, as shown in Figure 6–5, you will only notice this because Zwoptex adds a selection rectangle on the overlapping images in the upper-left corner. Sometimes this automatic selection can be hard to spot—it's a very indirect indicator. But it's also a good feature because you can then simply delete these images, or move them. You can click and drag any image in the Texture Atlas to manually lay out the images. This is not recommended, however, since you can easily cause images to overlap accidentally, and you'll lose manual layout the next time you click the **Apply** button.

Zwoptex's rotation attempts in Figure 6–5 don't quite work. You can see by the selection rectangle appearing after applying the layout, and by the overlapping images at the top-left corner, that the settings for canvas width and height are too small to fit all images into this Texture Atlas.

The **Allow Rotation** check box in the **Layout** pane allows Zwoptex to rotate images by 90 degrees. Sometimes this helps fit in more images, especially if there are images that are significantly wider than tall, or vice versa.

Rotation does not affect how the sprites are displayed. Cocos2d takes the rotation of images in a Texture Atlas into account and rotates the image back to its regular orientation before displaying it.

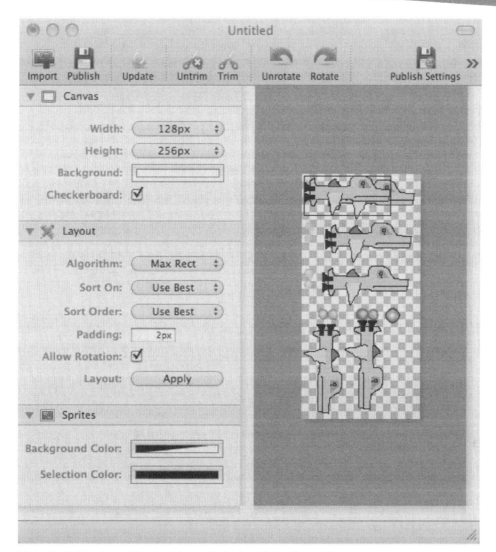

Figure 6–5. *Zwoptex rotates some images to try to optimize the used space.*

CAUTION: If you manually rotate some images and then click the Apply button in the **Layout** pane with **Allow Rotation** checked, you may lose those sprites' rotations.

The same goes for the trimming of images. After you added and laid out the ship animation images from the *Sprites06* project's *Resources* folder, you may have noticed that the images do not align. Zwoptex removes any excess transparent borders from images to make them as small as possible to save space in the Texture Atlas. Don't worry, cocos2d will take this offset into account and display these trimmed images at the correct positions.

In case you are wondering about the **Padding** setting, it determines how many pixels of space is left between all images. The default of 2 pixels ensures that all the images in the Texture Atlas can be drawn without any artifacts. With less padding, images can show stray pixels around their borders when they are displayed in your game. The amount and color of these stray pixels depends on surrounding pixels from other images in the Texture Atlas. This is a technical issue that has to do with how the graphics hardware filters textures, and the only solution is to leave a certain amount of padding between all images in a Texture Atlas.

After you've done a quick initial layout of the images, you'll be able to see approximately how much space in the Texture Atlas is still unused. You can then add more images, since your goal should be to create as few Texture Atlases as possible with the most images and the least amount of wasted space. But if you have only a few images, the next best option should be to reduce the texture size (or *canvas*, in Zwoptex terms).

When you are done creating your Texture Atlas and all images fit without overlap, you should save it by selecting **File ➤ Save**. This will save the Zwoptex settings in a ZSS file. Then click the **Publish** button, and Zwoptex will create the *.png* and *.plist* files, which are needed for cocos2d in the same folder as the ZSS file.

Using the Texture Atlas with Cocos2d

The first thing you should do is add the new Texture Atlas to the Xcode project's Resource group. Don't add the Zwoptex settings file with the extension *.zss* or *.zssxml* to your Xcode project. Cocos2d only needs the *.png* and *.plist* files for the Texture Atlas. The code in Listing 6–13 now replaces the code in Listing 6–11.

Listing 6–13. *The Ship Class Now Uses the Texture Atlas for Its Initial Frame and the Animation*

```
// Load the Texture Atlas sprite frames; this also loads the Texture with the same name
CCSpriteFrameCache* frameCache = [CCSpriteFrameCache sharedSpriteFrameCache];
[frameCache addSpriteFramesWithFile:@"ship-and-bullet.plist"];

// Loading the ship's sprite using a sprite frame name (e.g., the file name)
if ((self = [super initWithSpriteFrameName:@"ship.png"]))
{
        // Load the ship's animation frames
        NSMutableArray* frames = [NSMutableArray arrayWithCapacity:5];
        for (int i = 0; i < 5; i++)
        {
                NSString* file = [NSString stringWithFormat:@"ship-anim%i.png", i];
                CCSpriteFrame* frame = [frameCache spriteFrameByName:file];
                [frames addObject:frame];
        }

        // Create an animation object from all the sprite animation frames
        CCAnimation* anim = [CCAnimation animationWithName:@"move" delay:0.08f
                                                                  frames:frames];

        // Run the animation by using the CCAnimate action
        CCAnimate* animate = [CCAnimate actionWithAnimation:anim];
        CCRepeatForever* repeat = [CCRepeatForever actionWithAction:animate];
        [self runAction:repeat];
}
```

At the very beginning of the code, I assigned the `sharedSpriteFrameCache` to a local variable. The only reason to do so is that the `[CCSpriteFrameCache sharedSpriteFrameCache]` singleton accessor is pretty lengthy to write.

To load a Texture Atlas, you use the `CCSpriteFrameCache`'s method `addSpriteFramesWithFile`, and pass it the name of the *.plist* file for this Texture Atlas. The `CCSpriteFrameCache` will load the sprite frames, and will also try to load the texture with the same name, but ending in *.png*.

> **NOTE:** If you're using a large Texture Atlas texture—with dimensions of 512×512 or higher— you should load this texture before game play begins. It will take a moment to load such a large texture (in the worst case it will freeze the game for a few seconds).

Because the `Ship` class derives from `CCSprite` and because I wanted it to use the *ship.png* image from the Texture Atlas, I changed its initialization to use the `initWithSpriteFrameName` method. This is identical to the code that initializes a regular `CCSprite` from a Texture Atlas using a sprite frame name.

```
CCSprite* sprite = [CCSprite spriteWithSpriteFrameName:@"ship.png"];
```

If you load several Texture Atlases and only one contains the sprite frame with the name *ship.png*, cocos2d will still find that frame and use the correct texture for the sprite. In essence, you work with the sprite frames by name as if they were the image's file names, but you do not need to know which texture contains the actual image (unless you use a `CCSpriteBatchNode`, of course, which requires that all of its children use the same texture).

In Listing 6–13 I could get rid of most of the extra code required to initialize a `CCSpriteFrame` object. There's no need anymore to load a `Texture2D` and define the texture's dimensions. Instead I simply call `[CCSpriteFrame spriteFrameByName:file]` to create the file with the corresponding name.

The remaining code hasn't changed. But the result on screen has, unfortunately. The ship has now magically moved toward the center of the screen even though the image itself hasn't changed. The cause is not so obvious, but easy to fix. Here's the code for the initialization of the `Ship` class before the fix:

```
Ship* ship = [Ship ship];
ship.position = CGPointMake(ship.texture.contentSize.width / 2, screenSize.height / 2);
[self addChild:ship];
```

The cause for this odd behavior is that the ship's position depends on the ship texture's `contentSize`. Since the texture the ship uses is now the much larger Texture Atlas, the `contentSize` of the texture has also changed. You can fix that by using the sprite's `contentSize` instead of the texture's. This is a subtle difference that only comes to light when you're using a Texture Atlas:

```
Ship* ship = [Ship ship];
ship.position = CGPointMake(ship.contentSize.width / 2, screenSize.height / 2);
[self addChild:ship];
```

Updating the CCAnimation Helper Category

While the code to create a CCAnimation could be reduced significantly by using a Texture Atlas, it's still worthwhile to encapsulate this code into the CCAnimationHelper class. After all, one line of code is still less than five lines, especially if you would otherwise use the same five lines of code everywhere. Without further ado, Listing 6–14 shows the extended CCAnimation Helper interface declaration, which adds the animationWithFrame method.

Listing 6–14. *The @interface for the CCAnimation Helper Category*

```
@interface CCAnimation (Helper)
+(CCAnimation*) animationWithFile:(NSString*)name frameCount:(int)frameCount
                                                    delay:(float)delay;
+(CCAnimation*) animationWithFrame:(NSString*)frame frameCount:(int)frameCount
                                                    delay:(float)delay;

@end
```

This code is essentially the same method using the same parameters, except that this method uses sprite frames instead of file names. The implementation is nothing spectacular, and is very similar to the animationWithFile method shown in Listing 6–15.

Listing 6–15. *The animationWithFrame Helper Method Makes It Easier to Create an Animation*

```
// Creates an animation from sprite frames
+(CCAnimation*) animationWithFrame:(NSString*)frame frameCount:(int)frameCount
delay:(float)delay
{
        // load the ship's animation frames as textures and create a sprite frame
        NSMutableArray* frames = [NSMutableArray arrayWithCapacity:frameCount];
        for (int i = 0; i < frameCount; i++)
        {
                NSString* file = [NSString stringWithFormat:@"%@%i.png", frame, i];
                CCSpriteFrameCache* frameCache = [CCSpriteFrameCache
                                                sharedSpriteFrameCache];
                CCSpriteFrame* frame = [frameCache spriteFrameByName:file];
                [frames addObject:frame];
        }

        // Return an animation object from all the sprite animation frames
        return [CCAnimation animationWithName:frame delay:delay frames:frames];
}
```

The big plus is now, once again, that you can create an animation from a Texture Atlas using sprite frame names with just one line of code:

```
// Create an animation object from all the sprite animation frames
CCAnimation* anim = [CCAnimation animationWithFrame:@"ship-anim" frameCount:5
                                                    delay:0.08f];
```

The much, much bigger plus is, however, that you can now work with your animations as single files and only later create a Texture Atlas. All you have to do is to change one line of code from using animationWithFile to the animationWithFrame method. This allows you to quickly prototype animations using individual files, and only when you're satisfied will you pack the animation frames into a Texture Atlas and load the animation images from it.

You'll find this code in the project *Sprites06_WithAnimHelper*.

All into One and One for All

If you can (and I'm sure you can), you should add all your game's images into one Texture Atlas, or as few as possible. It is more effective to use three Texture Atlases with dimensions of 1024×1024 than 20 smaller ones.

Unlike code, which you should separate into logical components, with a Texture Atlas, your goal should be to put as many images as possible into the same Texture Atlas while trying to reduce the wasted space of each Texture Atlas as much as possible.

It may seem logical to use one Texture Atlas for your player's images; another for monster A, B, and C and their animations; and so on. However, that is only helpful if you have a huge number of images and you want to be selective about which images to load into memory at any one time. One such scenario might be a shoot-'em-up game with different worlds where you know that each world has separate types of enemies. In that case, it makes sense not to mix-and-match enemies of different worlds into the same Texture Atlas.

As long as your game's images can fit into three or four Texture Atlases of 1024×1024 size, you should just put all the images into those Texture Atlases and load them up front. This will use 12 to 16MB of memory for your textures. Your actual program code and other assets such as audio files don't take up that much space, so you should be able to keep these Texture Atlases in memory even on older iOS devices with just 128MB of RAM.

Once you pass that point, however, you need a better strategy to handle your texture memory. One such strategy, as mentioned above, could be to divide your game's images into worlds, and only load the Texture Atlases needed for the current world. This will introduce a short delay when a new world is loaded, and would be a good use for the LoadingScene I described in Chapter 5.

Since cocos2d automatically caches all images, you'll need a way to specifically unload textures that you know you don't need. In most cases you can rely on cocos2d to do that for you:

```
[[CCSpriteFrameCache sharedSpriteFrameCache] removeUnusedSpriteFrames];
[[CCTextureCache sharedTextureCache] removeUnusedTextures];
```

Obviously you should call these methods only when there are unused textures that you want to be removed. This is typically done after changing scenes, and should not be done during game play. Keep in mind that changing scenes causes the previous scene to be deallocated only after the new scene has been initialized. This means you can't use the removeUnused methods in the init method of a scene—that is, unless you use the LoadingScene from Chapter 5 in between two scenes, in which case you should extend it so that it removes unused textures before replacing itself with the new scene.

If you absolutely want to remove all textures from memory before loading new ones, you should use the purge methods instead:

```
[CCSpriteFrameCache purgeSharedSpriteFrameCache];
[CCTextureCache purgeSharedTextureCache];
```

Do It Yourself

I must confess, I'm a little proud of the doodles I created for this book. It's nowhere near what an artist can do for you, but there's an inherent satisfaction that stems from a do-it-yourself attitude.

You may think that with my experience it would be easy to make these artworks. No, it's not. But I do know my limitations (actually, one limitation: I am no good at art, period). The point is that in this book, I did not strive for the artwork to look good (or even any better than what a five-year-old could do—yes, I'm that immature when it comes to art). However, you should by all means try creating your own art, and audio for that matter. Just don't spend too much time on it—only enough that it conveys what your game is about.

I focused on creating artwork that I could make in a very short time, and I aimed to find the simplest way I could create images and animations that get my point across. If your game's design calls for lifelike pixel art animations, you might not want to do those yourself if you don't know how. On the other hand, if your game can be understood and played even with crooked animations and doodles, then by all means create your own art. Not only will this give your game a unique look, it will also be much easier to have an artist later on replace your game's artwork by providing the artist with all the images to draw over.

Since you have all the artwork, you can still give the images to an artist to draw over and replace your programmer's art. If only the image contents are replaced, you don't even have to change your game's code.

I already mentioned that I use the free Seashore program for image-editing purposes. You can download it here: `http://seashore.sourceforge.net`.

But when it comes to animations and pixel art, there's no way you should pass up on the free and open source program Pixen. Figure 6–6 gives you an impression of Pixen's animation editor. You can download Pixen here: `http://opensword.org/Pixen`.

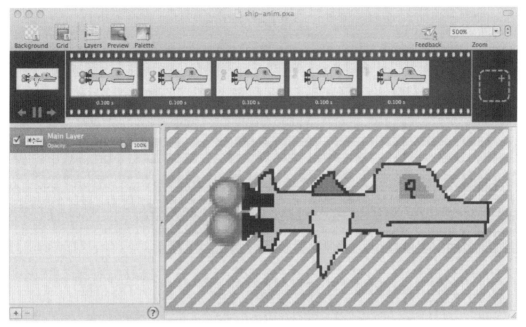

Figure 6–6. *The ship animation in Pixen's easy-to-use but powerful animation editor*

And as for audio production, if you want to pull off your own tunes and sound effects, a good place to start is GarageBand, which you'll find already installed on your Mac. You only need a microphone to record some noises, and then spend some time tweaking them and use them wherever you find them appropriate (or inappropriate, as the case may be, seeing how popular fart and burp sounds are for the iPhone). If you don't want to make your own audio, you can also search online for free and low-cost audio files— for example, on www.soundsnap.com and similar web sites.

> **CAUTION:** Be wary of sprite and audio collections downloaded from the Internet. There are places where you can download ready-made game assets for "free." But simply "free" doesn't mean that you are allowed to redistribute the files, or use them in a commercial product like a game sold on the App Store. Unless the assets come with an explicit license file allowing redistribution and use in commercial products, or you get the express permission of the original author, you should only use them as placeholders for the final artwork and audio.

Conclusion

In this chapter you learned how to use a CCSpriteBatchNode to render multiple sprites using the same texture faster, whether that texture is a single image or a sprite frame of a Texture Atlas.

Subclassing your game objects from CCSprite also introduces a few subtle differences and stumbling blocks, which I demonstrated earlier in this chapter, before I moved on to show you how to create sprite animations. Since the code to create animations is very complex, I gave you the solution in the form of a CCAnimationHelper category.

I also showed you how to work with Texture Atlases and why and how you should use them. Of course, one can't say "Texture Atlas" without mentioning Zwoptex in the same sentence. It's hands-down the best tool to create and modify Texture Atlases, and if you don't want to spend money on it, you can always use the somewhat outdated and less elegant Flash version.

Finally, I hoped encourage you to created your own art and audio. After all, doing everything by yourself can be a great delight.

In the next chapter, you'll be working on your next game, as we work on making the shooter game playable.

Chapter 7

Scrolling with Joy

Continuing with the beginnings of the game from the previous chapter, I now want to turn it into something resembling an actual shoot-'em-up game. The very first thing will be to make the player's ship controllable. Acceleromater controls don't make sense in this case; a virtual joypad would be much more appropriate. But instead of reinventing the wheel, we'll be using a cool source code package called SneakyInput to add a virtual joypad to this cocos2d game.

Moving the player's ship around is just one thing. We also want the background to scroll, to give the impression of moving into a certain direction. For this to happen we'll implement our own solution for parallax scrolling, since CCParallaxNode is too limited in that it does not allow an infinitely scrolling parallax background.

In addition, I'll illustrate what you've learned about Texture Atlases and sprite batching in the previous chapter. There will be one Texture Atlas containing all of the game's graphics since there's no need to group the images separately when using a Texture Atlas.

Advanced Parallax Scrolling

I mentioned before that CCParallaxNode is limited in that it doesn't allow infinite scrolling. For this shooting game, we'll add a ParallaxBackground node, which will do just that. Moreover, it will use a CCSpriteBatchNode to speed up the rendering of the background images.

Creating the Background As Stripes

First, I would like to illustrate how I created the background stripes that will create the parallaxing effect. This is crucial to understanding how the Texture Atlas created by Zwoptex can help you save memory and performance, but also save time positioning the individual stripes. Take a look at Figure 7–1; it shows the background layer as I drew it in Seashore as a 480×320 image. This image is also in the *Resources* folder of the *ScrollingWithJoy01* project, as *background-parallax.xcf*.

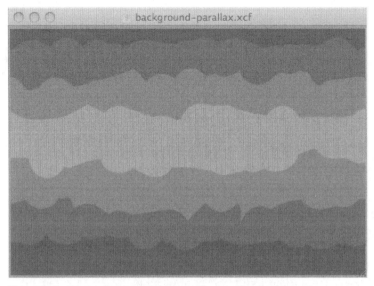

Figure 7–1. *The source image for the parallax scrolling background*

Each of these stripes is on its own layer in the image-editing program Seashore. In Figure 7–2 you can see the various layers, and if you look in the *Resources* folder you'll notice that there are images named *bg0.png* through *bg6.png*, which correspond to the seven individual stripes that make up the background.

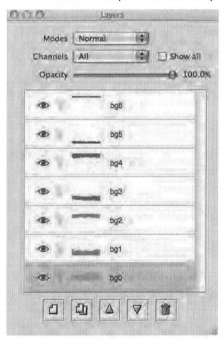

Figure 7–2. *Each stripe of the background is on its own layer. This helps in creating the individual images and positioning them in the game.*

There are several reasons for creating the parallax background image in this way. You can create the image as a whole, but you're able to save each layer to an individual file. All of these files will be 480×320 pixels in size, which may seem wasteful at first. But you're not adding the individual images to the game; instead you'll be adding them to a Texture Atlas. Since Zwoptex removes the surrounding transparent space of each image, it will shrink the individual stripes down to a bare minimum. You can see this in Figure 7–3.

NOTE: The background images are designed with a regular iPhone's screen size of 480×320 pixels in mind. To support iPad and Retina Display resolutions, you would have to create additional background images at the respective resolutions.

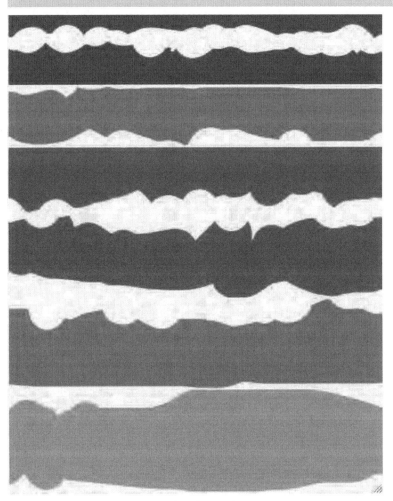

Figure 7–3. *The background stripes in a Texture Atlas*

Splitting the stripes into individual images is not only going to be helpful for drawing the images at the correct z-order. Strictly speaking, the images *bg5.png* and *bg6.png* can be at the same z-order since they do not overlap, yet I chose to save them into separate files. In Figure 7–3 you can see these two files as the two topmost stripes. You'll notice how little space they actually use up in the Texture Atlas, and that's because Zwoptex was able to remove most of the surrounding transparent parts of these images. Now suppose I left both these stripes in the same 480×320 image—one would be at the top and the other at the bottom of the image, with a big gaping hole of transparency in between them. Zwoptex is not able to remove the transparent part between these two sprites, so they would have remained as a 480×320 image in the Texture Atlas, which is a lot more space than they take up as individual images.

Splitting the stripes into individual images also helps to maintain a high frame rate. The iOS devices are very limited in *fill rate* (i.e., the number of pixels they can draw every frame). Since images can overlap each other, and they frequently do, the iOS device will often have to draw the same pixel several times in every frame. The extreme scenario would be a full-screen image that is on top of another full-screen image. You can only see one of the two images, but the device actually has to draw both. The technical term for that is *overdraw*. Separating the background into individual stripes with as little overlap as possible reduces the number of pixels drawn.

Re-creating the Background in Code

You may be wondering by now how you can put these images back together in the source code without spending a lot of time properly positioning these stripped-down images. The answer is you don't have to. Since all these images were saved as full-screen images, Zwoptex will remember the image offsets. All you really have to do is to center each of these images on the screen, and they will be at the correct place.

Let's take a look at the code for the ParallaxBackground node newly added to the *ScrollingWithJoy01* project. The header file is pretty straightforward:

```
@interface ParallaxBackground : CCNode
{
        CCSpriteBatchNode* spriteBatch;
        Int numSprites;s
}
@end
```

I only chose to keep a reference to the CCSpriteBatchNode around because I will be accessing it in the code frequently. Storing a node as a member variable is faster than asking cocos2d for the node via the getNodeByTag method. If you do that every frame it saves you a few CPU cycles. Nothing too dramatic, and certainly not worth keeping several hundreds of member variables around. It's a minor optimization that is just very convenient in this case.

In the init method of the ParallaxBackground class, the CCSpriteBatchNode is created, and all seven background images are added from the Texture Atlas, as shown in Listing 7–1.

Listing 7–1. *Loading the Background Images*

```
CGSize screenSize = [[CCDirector sharedDirector] winSize];

// Get the game's texture atlas texture by adding it
CCTexture2D* gameArtTexture = [[CCTextureCache sharedTextureCache]
                                            addImage:@"game-art.png"];

spriteBatch = [CCSpriteBatchNode batchNodeWithTexture:gameArtTexture];
[self addChild:spriteBatch];

numSprites = 7;

// Add the six different layer objects and position them on the screen
for (int i = 0; i < numSprites; i++)
{
        NSString* frameName = [NSString stringWithFormat:@"bg%i.png", i];
        CCSprite* sprite = [CCSprite spriteWithSpriteFrameName:frameName];
        sprite.position = CGPointMake(screenSize.width / 2, screenSize.height / 2);
        [spriteBatch addChild:sprite z:i];
}
```

You'll see that first of all, I'm adding the *game-art.png* Texture Atlas image to CCTextureCache. Actually, the Texture Atlas has already been added in the GameScene class, so why would I add it a second time here? The reason is simply that I need the CCTexture2D object to create the CCSpriteBatchNode, and adding the same image another time is the only way to retrieve an already cached image from the CCTextureCache. This doesn't load the texture a second time; the CCTextureCache singleton knows that the texture is already loaded and returns the cached version, which is a fast operation. It's just a bit unusual that there is no specific getTextureByName method, but that's the way it is.

With the CCSpriteBatchNode created and set up, the next step is to load the seven individual background images. I deliberately chose to number them from 0 to 6 so that I can use stringWithFormat to create the file names as strings in a very effective way:

```
NSString* frameName = [NSString stringWithFormat:@"bg%i.png", i];
```

With that sprite frameName, I create a CCSprite as usual and then position it at the center of the screen:

```
sprite.position = CGPointMake(screenSize.width / 2, screenSize.height / 2);
```

Of course, once you create an iPad version of this project, the images won't fit anymore since they were designed for a screen of 480×320 resolution. If you want to create an iPad version, you can follow the exact same steps, except make your original image 1024×768 in size.

> **TIP:** It takes surprisingly little effort to re-create the source image in cocos2d, and it's all thanks
> to Zwoptex saving the image offsets for you. It's also a great way to create your game screen
> layouts. You can have an artist design each screen as separate layers, as many as are needed.
> Then each layer is exported as an individual full-screen file with transparency. Next you create a
> Texture Atlas from these files and end up having the artist-envisioned screen design in cocos2d
> with no hassle of positioning individual files and no wasted memory either.

Because the `ParallaxBackground` class is derived from `CCNode`, I only need to add it to
the `GameScene` layer to add the `ParallaxBackground` to the game, like this:

```
ParallaxBackground* background = [ParallaxBackground node];
[self addChild:background z:-1];
```

This replaces the `CCColorLayer` and the background `CCSprite`, which were placeholders
from the previous chapter.

Moving the ParallaxBackground

In the *ScrollingWithJoy01* project, I also added a quick-and-dirty scrolling of the
background stripes. It does show a parallax effect, although the images quickly leave
the screen, revealing the blank background behind them. Figure 7–4 isn't exactly what I
had in mind, but I'm getting there.

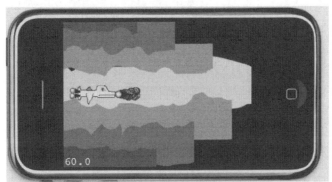

Figure 7–4. *The background stripes are moving, but it doesn't look too good. Somehow they need to be
repeating.*

Still, Listing 7–2 shows that the code to make the background scroll as a first test is
surprisingly simple.

Listing 7–2. *Moving the Background Stripes*

```
-(void) update:(ccTime)delta
{
        CCSprite* sprite;
        CCARRAY_FOREACH([spriteBatch children], sprite)
        {
                CGPoint pos = sprite.position;
```

```
                pos.x -= (scrollSpeed + sprite.zOrder) * (delta * 20);
                sprite.position = pos;
        }
}
```

Every background image's x position gets subtracted a bit every frame to scroll it from right to left. By how much an image moves depends on the predefined scrollSpeed plus the sprite's zOrder. The delta multiplier is used to make the scrolling speed independent of the frame rate, which is then multiplied by 20 to make the scrolling reasonably fast. Images that are closer to the screen scroll faster. However, using the zOrder property causes the stripes that should be at the same visual depth to scroll at different speeds.

The position is also multiplied by the *delta time* to make the scrolling speed independent of the frame rate. The delta time itself is just a tiny fraction—it's the time between two calls to the update method. At exactly 60 frames per second (fps), it's 1/60 of a second, which is a delta time of 0.167 seconds. For that reason I multiply delta by 20 just to get a reasonably fast scroll; otherwise, the images would be moving too slowly.

Parallax Speed Factors

Somehow the stripes of the same color need to scroll at the same speed, and the stripes should repeat so that the background doesn't show up. My solutions to these issues are in the *ScrollingWithJoy02* project.

The first change is regarding the scrolling speed. I decided to use a CCArray to store the speed factor with which individual stripes move. There are other solutions, but this allows me to illustrate a key issue of CCArray and in fact all iPhone SDK collection classes: they can only store objects, never values such as integers and floating-point numbers.

The way around this is to box numbers into an NSNumber object. The following code is the newly added CCArray* speedFactors, which stores floating-point values. The array is defined in the ParallaxBackground class header:

```
@interface ParallaxBackground : CCNode
{
        CCSpriteBatchNode* spriteBatch;

        int numStripes;
        CCArray* speedFactors;
        float scrollSpeed;
}
@end
```

Then it is filled with factors in the init method of the ParallaxBackground class. Notice how NSNumber numberWithFloat is used to store a float value inside the array:

```
// Initialize the array that contains the scroll factors for individual stripes
speedFactors = [[CCArray alloc] initWithCapacity:numStripes];
[speedFactors addObject:[NSNumber numberWithFloat:0.3f]];
[speedFactors addObject:[NSNumber numberWithFloat:0.5f]];
[speedFactors addObject:[NSNumber numberWithFloat:0.5f]];
[speedFactors addObject:[NSNumber numberWithFloat:0.8f]];
```

```
[speedFactors addObject:[NSNumber numberWithFloat:0.8f]];
[speedFactors addObject:[NSNumber numberWithFloat:1.2f]];
[speedFactors addObject:[NSNumber numberWithFloat:1.2f]];
NSAssert([speedFactors count] == numStripes, @"speedFactors count mismatch!");
```

The final assert is simply a safety check for human error. Consider that you may be adding or removing stripes from the background for whatever reason but might forget to adjust the number of values you're adding to the speedFactors array. If you forget to modify the speedFactors initialization, the assert will remind you of it, instead of potentially crashing the game seemingly at random.

In Figure 7–5 you can see which speed factor is applied to which stripe. Stripes with higher speed factors move faster than those with a slower speed factors, which creates the parallax effect.

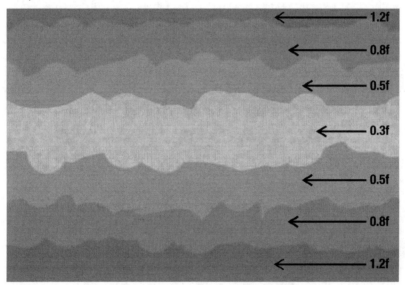

Figure 7–5. *The speed factors applied to each background stripe*

The speedFactors array is created with alloc, so its memory must also be released, which is done in the newly added dealloc method:

```
-(void) dealloc
{
    [speedFactors release];
    [super dealloc];
}
```

To use the newly introduced speed factors, the update method has been changed to this:

```
-(void) update:(ccTime)delta
{
    CCSprite* sprite;
    CCARRAY_FOREACH([spriteBatch children], sprite)
    {
        NSNumber* factor = [speedFactors objectAtIndex:sprite.zOrder];
```

```
                CGPoint pos = sprite.position;
                pos.x -= scrollSpeed * [factor floatValue] * (delta * 50);
                sprite.position = pos;
        }
}
```

Based on the sprite's zOrder property, a speed factor NSNumber is obtained from the speedFactors array. This will be multiplied by the scrollSpeed to speed up or slow down the movement of individual stripes. You can't multiply the NSNumber object directly because it is a class instance storing a primitive data type such as float, int, char, or others. NSNumber has a floatValue method that returns the floating-point value, but it supports a number of different methods. You could also use intValue, even though this NSNumber stores a floating-point value. It is essentially the same as casting a float to an int. Once again, the delta time is also factored in to make the scrolling speed independent of the frame rate.

By using the speedFactors array and giving the same-colored stripes the same factor, the background stripes will now move as expected. But there's still the issue of making endless scrolling.

Scrolling to Infinity and Beyond

Also in *ScrollingWithJoy02* is the first step toward endless scrolling. As you can see in Listing 7–3, I simply added seven more background stripes to the CCSpriteBatchNode, although with a slightly different setup.

Listing 7–3. *Adding Offscreen Background Images*

```
// Add seven more stripes, flip them, and position them next to their neighbor stripe
for (int i = 0; i < numStripes; i++)
{
        NSString* frameName = [NSString stringWithFormat:@"bg%i.png", i];
        CCSprite* sprite = [CCSprite spriteWithSpriteFrameName:frameName];

        // Position the new sprite one screen width to the right
        sprite.position = CGPointMake(screenSize.width + screenSize.width / 2,
                                                  screenSize.height / 2);

        // Flip the sprite so that it aligns perfectly with its neighbor
        sprite.flipX = YES;

        // Add the sprite using the same tag offset by numStripes
        [spriteBatch addChild:sprite z:i tag:i + numStripes];
}
```

The idea is to add one more stripe of the same type each. They are positioned so that they align with the right end of the first stripe's position. In effect, this doubles the total width of the background stripes, and that will be enough for endless scrolling. But I'll get to that shortly.

First I need to point out that the new neighboring images are flipped along their X axes. This is done so that the images match visually where they are aligned, to avoid any sharp edges. The new images also get a different tag number, one that is offset by the number of stripes in use. This way it will be easy to get to the neighboring stripe by either adding or deducting numStripes from the tag number.

Right now, the background image scrolls just a bit longer before showing the blank canvas behind the images. The project *ScrollingWithJoy03* completes the effort and adds totally infinite scrolling. But first the anchorPoint property of the stripes needs to change to make things a little easier. The x position is now simply at 0:

```
sprite.anchorPoint = CGPointMake(0, 0.5f);
sprite.position = CGPointMake(0, screenSize.height / 2);
```

The same goes for the secondary, flipped stripes, which now only need to be offset by the screen width:

```
sprite.anchorPoint = CGPointMake(0, 0.5f);
sprite.position = CGPointMake(screenSize.width, screenSize.height / 2);
```

The stripes' anchorPoint is changed from its default (0.5f, 0.5f) to (0, 0.5f). This makes it easier to work with the sprites, since in this particular case you don't want to have to take into account that that texture's origin and the sprite's x position aren't at the same location. Figure 7–6 shows how this makes it easier to calculate the x position.

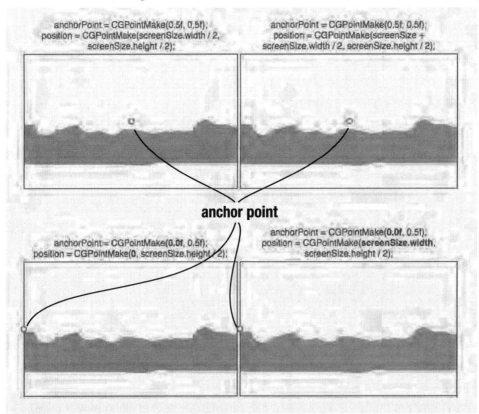

Figure 7–6. *Anchor point moved to the left for simplicity*

You can see in Listing 7–4 how this is helpful in the changed `update` method, which now gives us endless scrolling.

Listing 7–4. *Moving the Image Pairs Seamlessly*

```
-(void) update:(ccTime)delta
{
        CCSprite* sprite;
        CCARRAY_FOREACH([spriteBatch children], sprite)
        {
                NSNumber* factor = [speedFactors objectAtIndex:sprite.zOrder];

                CGPoint pos = sprite.position;
                pos.x -= scrollSpeed * [factor floatValue];

                // Reposition stripes when they're out of bounds
                if (pos.x < -screenSize.width)
                {
                        pos.x += screenSize.width * 2;
                }

                sprite.position = pos;
        }
}
```

The stripes' x position now only needs to be checked if it is less than negative screen width, and if it is it is, multiplied by twice the screen width. Essentially, this moves the sprite that has just left the screen on the left side to the right side, just outside the screen. This repeats forever with the same two sprites, giving the effect of endless scrolling.

> **TIP:** Notice that the background of the screen scrolls, but the ship stays in place. Inexperienced game developers often have the misconception that everything on the screen needs to be scrolling to achieve the effect of game objects passing by the player character as he progresses through the game world. Instead, you can much more easily create the illusion of objects moving on the screen by moving the background layers but keeping the player character fixed in place. Popular examples of games that make use of this visual illusion are Super Turbo Action Pig, Canabalt, Super Blast, Doodle Jump, and Zombieville USA. Typically, the game objects scrolling into view are randomly generated shortly before they appear, and when they leave the screen they are removed from the game.

Fixing the Flicker

So far, so good. There's only one issue remaining. If you look closely, you may notice that from time to time a vertical, black line appears on the stripes. That's where they align with each other. This line appears due to rounding errors in their positions. From time to time, a 1-pixel-wide gap can appear for just a fraction of a second. It's still noticeable, and something you should get rid of for a commercial-quality game.

The simplest solution is to overlap the stripes by 1 pixel. In the *ScrollingWithJoy04* project I changed the initial positions for the flipped background stripes by subtracting 1 pixel from the x position:

```
sprite.position = CGPointMake(screenSize.width - 1, screenSize.height / 2);
```

This also requires updating the stripe-repositioning code in the `update` method so that the stripe is positioned 2 pixels further to the left than before:

```
// Reposition stripes when they're out of bounds
if (pos.x < -screenSize.width)
{
        pos.x += (screenSize.width * 2) - 2;
}
```

Why 2 pixels? Well, since the initial position of the flipped stripes is already moved to the left by 1 pixel, we have to move all of them 2 pixels to the left each time they flip around to maintain the same distance and to keep the overlap of 1 pixel.

An alternative solution would be to update only the position of the currently leftmost sprite, and then find the sprite that is aligned to the right of it and offset it by exactly the screen width. This way you also avoid the rounding errors. Figure 7–7 shows the finished result.

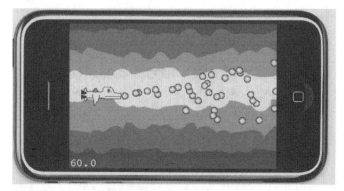

Figure 7–7. *The result: An infinitely scrolling parallax background*

Repeat, repeat, repeat

There's another neat trick that deserves mention in this chapter. You can set any texture to repeat over a certain rectangular area. If you make this area big enough, you can have this texture repeat nearly endlessly. At least several thousand pixels or dozens of screen areas can be covered with a repeating texture, with no penalty to performance or memory usage.

The trick is to use the `GL_REPEAT` texture parameter supported by OpenGL. But it only works with square images that are exactly a power of 2, like 32×32 or 128×128 pixels. Listing 7–5 shows the code.

Listing 7–5. *Repeating Background with GL_REPEAT*

```
CGRect repeatRect = CGRectMake(-5000, -5000, 5000, 5000);
CCSprite* sprite = [CCSprite spriteWithFile:@"square.png" rect:repeatRect];
ccTexParams params =
{
        GL_LINEAR,
        GL_LINEAR,
        GL_REPEAT,
        GL_REPEAT
};
[sprite.texture setTexParameters:&params];
```

In this case, the sprite must be initialized with a `rect` that determines the area the sprite will occupy. The `ccTexParams` struct is initialized with the wrap parameters set to `GL_REPEAT`. Don't worry if that doesn't mean anything to you. These OpenGL parameters are then set on the sprite's texture using the `CCTexture2D` method `setTexParameters`.

The result is a tiled area repeating the same *square.png* image over and over again. If you move the sprite, the whole area covered by the `repeatRect` is moved. You could use this trick to remove the bottommost background stripe and replace it with a smaller image that simply repeats. I'll leave that up to you as an exercise.

A Virtual Joypad

Since the iOS devices all use a touchscreen for input and have no buttons, D-pads, or analog joypads like conventional mobile gaming devices, we need something called a virtual joypad. This emulates the behavior of digital or analog thumbsticks by allowing you to touch the screen where the digipad or thumbstick is displayed and move your finger over it to control the action on the screen. Buttons are also designated areas of the touchscreen that you can tap or hold to cause actions on screen. Figure 7–8 shows a virtual joypad in action.

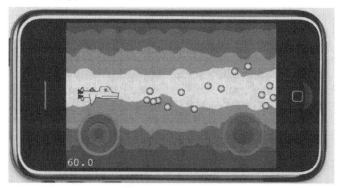

Figure 7–8. *A skinned analog thumbstick and fire button created with SneakyInput*

Introducing SneakyInput

Over time, many a developer has faced the problem of implementing a virtual joypad. There are many ways to go about this, and even more ways to fail at it. But why spend time on that if there's a ready-to-use solution?

This is generally sound advice. Before you program anything that seems reasonably common that others might have worked on before, always check first if there isn't a general purpose solution available that you can just use instead of having to spend a lot of time creating it yourself. In this case, SneakyInput is just too good to be ignored.

SneakyInput was created by Nick Pannuto, with skinning examples by CJ Hanson. SneakyInput is open source software and free to download, but if you like this product please consider making a donation to Nick Pannuto at this link: `http://pledgie.com/campaigns/9124`.

The SneakyInput source code is hosted on github, a social coding web site, at this link: `http://github.com/sneakyness/SneakyInput`.

It may not be immediately obvious what you have to do to download the source code from github. When you browse to the web site and click any of the files, you'll see the actual source code displayed in your browser. But you want the full source code project, not individual files. What you do is locate the **Download Source** button in the upper-right corner of the web site. You then choose one of the archive types—it doesn't really matter which—and save the file to your computer and extract it.

At this point you might want to open the SneakyInput Xcode project and compile it. Since SneakyInput comes together with cocos2d integrated into the project, it's possible that the cocos2d version used by SneakyInput may not be the most current version. You may then experience the "base SDK missing" issue I mentioned in Chapter 2. To fix this issue you'll have to open the Info panel of the SneakyInput project and choose an appropriate base SDK from the **General** tab. If the project is up and running, you'll see an analog pad and a button as simple circles. The analog virtual thumbstick moves the Hello World label on the screen, while the button changes the label's colors on touch.

Figure 7–9 shows the SneakyInput sample project running in the iPhone Simulator. The sample project includes a virtual analog thumbstick that controls the Hello World label's position, and a button in the lower-right corner that changes the label's color when touched. The buttons aren't skinned; they use the `ColoredCircleSprite` class.

Figure 7–9. *The SneakyInput sample project*

But of course the sticks and buttons can also be skinned. Skinning, sometimes referred to as *texturing*, means using images from textures instead of flat colors to display the sticks and buttons.

Integrating SneakyInput

I already have a project fully set up and functioning—in this case *ScrollingWithJoy05*. I don't want to use the project provided by SneakyInput. How do I get it to work with my project?

This is an issue that isn't limited to SneakyInput, but possibly any source code project you can download that comes already bundled with its own version of cocos2d. In most cases, and as long as the programming language of that source code is Objective-C, you only have to figure out which of the project's files are necessary and add them to your own project. There's no clear guideline, however, since every project is different.

I can tell you which files you need to add to your project regarding SneakyInput, however. It consists at its core of five classes:

- SneakyButton and SneakyButtonSkinnedBase
- SneakyJoystick and SneakyJoystickSkinnedBase
- ColoredCircleSprite (optional)

The remaining files are not needed but serve as references. Figure 7–10 shows the selection I've made in the **Add Existing Files** dialog. My rationale for not including certain classes was by first making an educated guess and then seeing if I was right by compiling the project after having added the files I believed to be necessary.

The HelloWorldScene class is created by a cocos2d project template and most likely doesn't contain anything but example code. Of course, I already have an AppDelegate in my project, so I don't need to be adding SneakyInput's AppDelegate class—it might be in conflict with the existing AppDelegate. Then there are two classes explicitly suffixed with Example, which indicates that these files are not core classes for SneakyInput, but further example code.

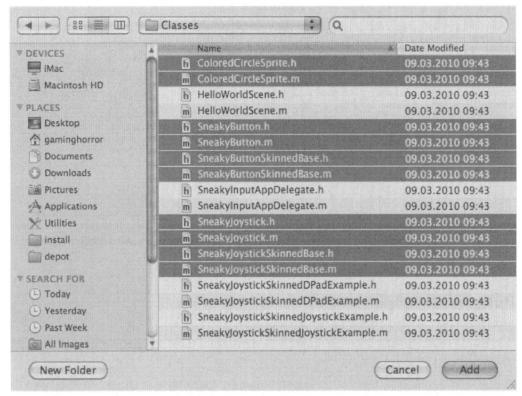

Figure 7–10. *These files are needed to get SneakyInput to work in your own project; the other files are only used for example code.*

Touch Button to Shoot

Let's try this. With the SneakyInput source code added to the project *ScrollingWithJoy05*, the first goal is to add a button that allows the player to shoot bullets from the player's ship. I'm going to add a separate `InputLayer` class to the project, which is derived from `CCLayer` and added to the `GameScene` class. In Listing 7–6, I updated the `scene` method to add the new `InputLayer` to it, and I'm giving both layers a tag just in case I need to identify them later on.

Listing 7–6. *Adding the InputLayer to the GameScene*

```
+(id) scene
{
        CCScene* scene = [CCScene node];
        GameScene* layer = [GameScene node];
        [scene addChild:layer z:0 tag:GameSceneLayerTagGame];
        InputLayer* inputLayer = [InputLayer node];
        [scene addChild:inputLayer z:1 tag:GameSceneLayerTagInput];
        return scene;
}
```

The new tags are defined in the `GameScene` header file as follows:

```
typedef enum
{
        GameSceneLayerTagGame = 1,
        GameSceneLayerTagInput,
} GameSceneLayerTags;
```

With the `InputLayer` in place, the next step is to add the header files for the SneakyInput files we want to use to the *InputLayer.h* header file. I'm not picky, and we're probably going to use most of the classes, so I simply added all of the SneakyInput header files:

```
#import <Foundation/Foundation.h>
#import "cocos2d.h"

// SneakyInput headers
#import "ColoredCircleSprite.h"
#import "SneakyButton.h"
#import "SneakyButtonSkinnedBase.h"
#import "SneakyJoystick.h"
#import "SneakyJoystickSkinnedBase.h"

@interface InputLayer : CCLayer
{
        SneakyButton* fireButton;
}
@end
```

In addition, I added a `SneakyButton` member variable for easier access to the button I'm going to create now. This is done in the `addFireButton` method in Listing 7–7.

Listing 7–7. *Creating a SneakyButton*

```
-(void) addFireButton
{
        float buttonRadius = 80;
        CGSize screenSize = [[CCDirector sharedDirector] winSize];

        fireButton = [[[SneakyButton alloc] initWithRect:CGRectZero] autorelease];
        fireButton.radius = buttonRadius;
        fireButton.position = CGPointMake(screenSize.width - buttonRadius,
                                                         buttonRadius);
        [self addChild:fireButton];
}
```

The `CGRect` parameter of the button's `initWithRect` method isn't used by `SneakyButton`, which is why I'm simply passing `CGRectZero`. The actual touch code uses the `radius` property to determine if the button should react to the touch. The button in this case should be neatly tucked into the lower-right corner. Subtracting the `buttonRadius` from the screen width and setting its height to `buttonRadius` places it exactly at the desired location.

> **TIP:** The use of the `buttonRadius` variable allows you to change the radius of the button in one place, instead of having to update several values in several places. This is not only extra work for a value you might want to tweak several times before you get it exactly the way you want to. It can also introduce subtle bugs, because you're a human and you tend to forget things, like changing that one value over there. Suddenly the button is offset—or worse, the input doesn't match the button's location.

The `InputLayer` class schedules the `update` method:

```
[self scheduleUpdate];
```

The `update` method is used to check if the button is touched or not:

```
-(void) update:(ccTime)delta
{
        if (fireButton.active)
        {
                CCLOG(@"FIRE!!!");
        }
}
```

Instead of shooting a bullet, I wanted to keep things simple for now and simply log a successful button press. If you try the *ScrollingWithJoy05* project now, you'll notice that there isn't any button drawn. Yet when you touch the screen at the lower-right corner you'll see the FIRE!!! message appear in the debugger console. So all is well and right, except that the button can't be seen—which we'll need to fix.

Skinning the Button

Eeeww! No, it's not what you think. *Skinning* in computer graphics refers to giving an otherwise featureless object a texture or simply a different look. In this case we want to actually see our button, so we need an image for that.

I also prefer to add cocos2d-style static initializers to external classes using a category, as done in the last chapter. This helps avoid potentially forgetting to send `alloc` or autorelease messages to a `SneakyButton` object. I'll start with that by adding a SneakyExtensions class to the *ScrollingWithJoy06* project and then stripping the header file down to this:

```
#import <Foundation/Foundation.h>

// SneakyInput headers
#import "ColoredCircleSprite.h"
#import "SneakyButton.h"
#import "SneakyButtonSkinnedBase.h"
#import "SneakyJoystick.h"
#import "SneakyJoystickSkinnedBase.h"

@interface SneakyButton (Extension)
+(id) button;
+(id) buttonWithRect:(CGRect)rect;
@end
```

Once more, all the SneakyInput headers are added because I plan to make more categories for every SneakyInput class that doesn't conform to regular cocos2d initializers. In this case, a SneakyButton category named Extension is added, which adds two methods, named button and buttonWithRect. They are implemented as shown in Listing 7–8.

Listing 7–8. *A Category with SneakyButton Autorelease Initializers*

```
#import "SneakyExtensions.h"

@implementation SneakyButton (Extension)
+(id) button
{
        return [[[SneakyButton alloc] initWithRect:CGRectZero] autorelease];
}

+(id) buttonWithRect:(CGRect)rect
{
        return [[[SneakyButton alloc] initWithRect:rect] autorelease];
}
@end
```

They simply wrap the alloc and autorelease calls. Also, I decided to add a simple, parameterless button initializer because the CGRect parameter isn't really used anyway. This allows me to initialize the fireButton in a straightforward manner:

```
fireButton = [SneakyButton button];
```

It's just a little extra effort for more convenience and cleaner code. I'll be adding more convenience methods to SneakyExtensions without discussing them in the book, as the principle is the same.

Now my mind is at peace and I can start skinning the button. I created four button images that are 100×100 pixels in size—twice the final button radius of 50 that I'm going with. The button images come in four variations: Default, Pressed, Activated, and Disabled. The default state is what the button looks like when it isn't pressed, which should make it obvious what the Pressed state is. The Activated state only comes into play for toggle buttons, meaning the toggle button is *active*, or *on*. The Disabled image is used if the button currently has no function. For example, when the ship's weapons are overheated and you can't shoot for a few seconds, you could disable the button and it would show the Disabled image. For the shoot button, I only needed to use the Default and Pressed images. Listing 7–9 shows the updated addFireButton method.

Listing 7–9. *Replacing Listing 7–7 with a Skinned Button*

```
float buttonRadius = 50;
CGSize screenSize = [[CCDirector sharedDirector] winSize];

fireButton = [SneakyButton button];
fireButton.isHoldable = YES;

SneakyButtonSkinnedBase* skinFireButton = [SneakyButtonSkinnedBase skinnedButton];
skinFireButton.position = CGPointMake(screenSize.width - buttonRadius, buttonRadius);
skinFireButton.defaultSprite = [CCSprite spriteWithSpriteFrameName:
                                          @"button-default.png"];
```

```
skinFireButton.pressSprite = [CCSprite spriteWithSpriteFrameName:
                                               @"button-pressed.png"];
skinFireButton.button = fireButton;
[self addChild:skinFireButton];
```

I initialized the `fireButton` as usual except that I made it holdable, which means you can keep it pressed down for a continuous stream of bullets. It also doesn't set the `radius` property anymore, since the images of the `SneakyButtonSkinnedBase` class determine the radius now. Keep in mind that I added a category to `SneakyButtonSkinnedBase` in the `SneakyExtension` source files created earlier. The `skinnedButton` initializer is in there, and wraps the `alloc` and `autorelease` messages.

Instead of positioning the `fireButton`, the skinned button is now used to position the button on the screen; the actual button is updated accordingly by `SneakyButtonSkinnedBase`.

At this point it makes sense to also write the firing code; Listing 7–10 shows the `update` method now sending the fire message to the `GameScene` class.

Listing 7–10. *Shooting Bullets Whenever the Fire Button Is Active*

```
-(void) update:(ccTime)delta
{
        totalTime += delta;

        if (fireButton.active && totalTime > nextShotTime)
        {
                nextShotTime = totalTime + 0.5f;

                GameScene* game = [GameScene sharedGameScene];
                [game shootBulletFromShip:[game defaultShip]];
        }

        // Allow faster shooting by quickly tapping the fire button
        if (fireButton.active == NO)
        {
                nextShotTime = 0;
        }
}
```

The two `ccTime` variables, `totalTime` and `nextShotTime`, are used to limit the amount of bullets the ship will emit to two per second. If the fire button is not active (meaning that it isn't pressed), the `nextShotTime` is set to 0 so that the next time you press the button a shot is guaranteed to be fired. Tap the button quickly and you should be able to shoot more bullets than with continuous fire.

Controlling the Action

You can't fly a ship without some form of input. This is where `SneakyJoystick` will give us a helping hand (I mean a helping virtual thumbstick). Behold, *ScrollingWithJoy07* is here!

As usual, the first thing I did was add another Extension category to the new classes so I could initialize them like any other CCNode. For the joystick, I'll go right ahead and create a skinned one in the addJoystick method in Listing 7–11.

Listing 7–11. *Adding a Skinned Joystick*

```
-(void) addJoystick
{
        float stickRadius = 50;

        joystick = [SneakyJoystick joystickWithRect:CGRectMake(0, 0, stickRadius,
                                                        stickRadius)];
        joystick.autoCenter = YES;
        joystick.hasDeadzone = YES;
        joystick.deadRadius = 10;

        SneakyJoystickSkinnedBase* skinStick = [SneakyJoystickSkinnedBase
                                                        skinnedJoystick];
        skinStick.position = CGPointMake(stickRadius * 1.5f, stickRadius * 1.5f);
        skinStick.backgroundSprite = [CCSprite spriteWithSpriteFrameName:
                                                        @"button-disabled.png"];
        skinStick.backgroundSprite.color = ccGREEN;
        skinStick.thumbSprite = [CCSprite spriteWithSpriteFrameName:
                                                        @"button-disabled.png"];
        skinStick.thumbSprite.scale = 0.5f;
        skinStick.joystick = joystick;
        [self addChild:skinStick];
}
```

The SneakyJoystick is initialized with a CGRect, and contrary to the SneakyButton, the CGRect is actually used to determine the joystick's radius. I set the joystick to autoCenter so that the thumb controller jumps back to the neutral position, like most real-world game controllers. The dead zone is also enabled; this is a small area defined by the deadRadius, in which you can move the thumb controller without any effect. This gives users a certain radius where they can keep the thumb controller centered. Without the dead zone, it would be almost impossible to center the thumb controller manually.

The SneakyJoystickSkinnedBase is positioned a small distance away from the edge of the screen. The button's position and size may not be ideal for the game, but it allows me to better demonstrate the controls. If you align the thumb controller with the screen edges, it's too easy to inadvertently move your finger off the touchscreen and thus lose control of the ship. For the images, I decided to use *button-disabled.png* and simply give the background sprite a green color, while the thumbSprite is scaled down to half the size.

TIP: Gray areas are useful! I mean gray images like *button-disabled.png*. By using just grayscale colors, you can colorize the image using the `color` property of the sprite. You can create red, green, yellow, blue, magenta, and other colored versions of the same image, saving both download size and in-game memory. The only drawback is that it will be a flat color, so instead of shades of gray your image will be using shades of red. This trick works best with images that are supposed to be shades of a single color.

You want the thumbstick on the screen to be used to control the ship, of course. As usual, the `update` method processes the input, as shown in Listing 7–12.

Listing 7–12. *Moving the Ship Based on Joystick Input*

```
-(void) update:(ccTime)delta
{
        …

        // Moving the ship with the thumbstick
        GameScene* game = [GameScene sharedGameScene];
        Ship* ship = [game defaultShip];

        // Velocity must be scaled up by a factor that feels right
        CGPoint velocity = ccpMult(joystick.velocity, 200);
        if (velocity.x != 0 && velocity.y != 0)
        {
                ship.position = CGPointMake(ship.position.x + velocity.x * delta,
                                           ship.position.y + velocity.y * delta);
        }
}
```

I have added a `defaultShip` accessor method to the `GameScene` class in the meantime, so that the `InputLayer` has access to the ship. The `velocity` property of the joystick is used to change the ship's position, but not without scaling it up. The `velocity` values are a tiny fraction of a pixel, so multiplying the velocity using cocos2d's `ccpMult` method, which takes a `CGPoint` and a float factor, is necessary for the joypad velocity to have a noticeable effect. The scale factor is arbitrary; it's just a value that feels good for this game.

To ensure smooth movement even if the `update` method is called at uneven intervals, the `update` method's `delta` parameter is factored in as well. The `delta` parameter is passed by cocos2d and contains the time elapsed since the `update` method was last called. This isn't strictly necessary, but it's good practice. If you don't do it, you run the risk that the ship will move more slowly whenever the frame rate drops below 60 fps. Tiny things like these can be pretty annoying to players, and as game developers our goal is the exact opposite of annoying players.

At this point, it is still possible to move the ship outside the screen area. I bet you'd like for the ship to stay on the screen as much as I do. And you may be tempted to add this code directly to the `InputLayer` where the ship's position is updated. That brings up a question: do you want to prevent the joystick input from moving the ship outside the screen, or do you want to prevent the ship from ever being able to move outside the screen? The latter is the more general solution and preferable in this case. To do so, you only need to override the `setPosition` method in the Ship class, as shown in Listing 7–13.

Listing 7–13. *Overriding the Ship's setPosition Method*

```
// Override setPosition to keep the ship within bounds
-(void) setPosition:(CGPoint)pos
{
        CGSize screenSize = [[CCDirector sharedDirector] winSize];
        float halfWidth = contentSize_.width * 0.5f;
        float halfHeight = contentSize_.height * 0.5f;

        // Cap the position so the ship's sprite stays on the screen
        if (pos.x < halfWidth)
        {
                pos.x = halfWidth;
        }
        else if (pos.x > (screenSize.width - halfWidth))
        {
                pos.x = screenSize.width - halfWidth;
        }

        if (pos.y < halfHeight)
        {
                pos.y = halfHeight;
        }
        else if (pos.y > (screenSize.height - halfHeight))
        {
                pos.y = screenSize.height - halfHeight;
        }

        // Must call super with the new position
        [super setPosition:pos];
}
```

Every time the ship's position is updated, the preceding code performs the check to see if the ship's sprite is still inside the screen boundaries. If not, then the x or y coordinate is set to a distance of half the `contentSize` away from the respective screen border.

Because `position` is a property, the `setPosition` method gets called by this code:

```
ship.position = CGPointMake(200, 100);
```

The dot notation is shorthand for getter and setter messages to Objective-C properties, and it can be rewritten:

```
[ship setPosition:CGPointMake(200, 100)];
```

You can override other base class methods in this way to change the behavior of your game objects. For example, if an object is only allowed to be rotated between 0 and 180 degrees, you would override the `setRotation:(float)rotation` method and add the code to limit the rotation to it.

Digital Controls

What if an analog controller doesn't fit your game? You can turn the `SneakyJoystick` class into a digital controller as well, often referred to as a D-pad. The necessary code changes are minimal. You can find them in the *ScrollingWithJoy08* project or right here:

```
joystick = [SneakyJoystick joystickWithRect:CGRectMake(0, 0, stickRadius, stickRadius)];
joystick.autoCenter = YES;

// Now with fewer directions
joystick.isDPad = YES;
joystick.numberOfDirections = 8;
```

The dead zone properties have been removed—they are not needed for a digital controller. The joystick is set to digital controls by setting the `isDPad` property to `YES`. You can also define the number of directions. While D-pads regularly have four directions, in many games you can keep two directions pressed at the same time to have the character move in a diagonal direction. To achieve the same effect, the `numberOfDirections` property is set to 8. `SneakyJoystick` automatically ensures that these directions are evenly divided onto the thumb pad controller. Of course, you will get strange results if you set the number of directions to 6, but then again, maybe that's exactly what you need to travel across a hexagonal tile map.

An Alternative: GPJoystick

SneakyInput isn't the only popular solution to adding virtual thumbstick controls and buttons to a cocos2d game. There's also GPJoystick, which you might be interested in. It's a commercial product, but offered at a very low price. You can find it here: `http://wrensation.com/?p=36`.

If you want to get an idea of how GPJoystick works and how it differs from SneakyInput, then you should watch the YouTube screencast video about GPJoystick by YouTube user SDKTutor, who also happens to feature several video tutorials about cocos2d (see `www.youtube.com/user/SDKTutor`).

Conclusion

In this chapter you learned several tricks to make an effective parallax scrolling background. Not only did you learn to scroll the background infinitely and without flickering edges, but you also learned how to properly separate the parallax layers so that Zwoptex can cut down on any unnecessary transparent areas while keeping the image's offset so you don't have to fumble with positioning the parallax layers.

The downside to this approach is that it is specific to a certain screen resolution. If you wanted to create an iPad version, for example, you could use the same process, except you'd have to create the image at a 1024×768 resolution. I'll leave that up to you as an exercise.

The second half of this chapter introduced you to SneakyInput, an open source project to add virtual thumbsticks and buttons to any cocos2d game. It may not be perfect, but it's good enough for most games, and it definitely beats writing your own virtual thumbstick code.

The ship is now controllable and stays within the screen's boundaries, and it's able to shoot with the press of a button—but the game is still lacking something. A shoot-'em-up isn't a shoot-'em-up without something to shoot down, is it? The next chapter addresses that lack.

Chapter 8

Shoot 'em Up

What does a game of this kind need above all else? Something to shoot up and bullets to evade. In this chapter you'll be adding enemies to the game and even a boss monster.

Both enemies and player will use the new `BulletCache` class to shoot a variety of bullets from the same pool. The cache class reuses inactive bullets to avoid constantly allocating and releasing bullets from memory. Likewise, enemies will use their own `EnemyCache` class because they, too, will appear in greater numbers on the screen.

Obviously the player will be able to shoot these enemies. I will also introduce the concept of component-based programming, which allows you to extend the game's actors in a modular way. Besides shooting and moving components, we also create a healthbar component for the boss monster. After all, a boss monster should not be an instant kill but require several hits before it is destroyed.

Adding the BulletCache Class

The `BulletCache` class is the one-stop shop for creating new bullets in the *ShootEmUp01* project. Previously all of this code was in the `GameScene` class but it shouldn't be the responsibility of the `GameScene` to manage and create new bullets. Listing 8–1 shows the new `BulletCache` header file, and it now contains the `CCSpriteBatchNode` and the inactive bullets counter:

Listing 8–1. *The @interface of the* BulletCache *Class*

```
#import <Foundation/Foundation.h>
#import "cocos2d.h"

@interface BulletCache : CCNode
{
    CCSpriteBatchNode* batch;
    int nextInactiveBullet;
}

-(void) shootBulletAt:(CGPoint)startPosition velocity:(CGPoint)velocity
                                      frameName:(NSString*)frameName;
@end
```

To refactor the bullet-shooting code out of the GameScene class, I needed to move both the initialization and the method to shoot bullets to the new BulletCache class (Listing 8–2). Along the way I decided to keep the CCSpriteBatchNode in a member variable instead of using the CCNode getChildByTag method every time I need the sprite batch object. It's a minor performance optimization. Since I'll be adding the BulletCache class as child to the GameScene, I can simply add the sprite batch node to the BulletCache class.

> **NOTE:** There's little harm in increasing the depth of the scene hierarchy by adding an in-between CCNode like BulletCache. If you're concerned about scene hierarchy depth, the alternative would be to add the sprite batch node to the GameScene class as usual and use an accessor method to get to the sprite batch node in the BulletCache class. But the additional function call overhead could possibly void any performance gain. If in doubt, always prefer to make your code more readable, then refactor later to improve performance where necessary, and only where necessary.

Listing 8–2. *The BulletCache Maintains a Pool of Bullets for Reuse*

```
#import "BulletCache.h"
#import "Bullet.h"

@implementation BulletCache

-(id) init
{
        if ((self = [super init]))
        {
                // get any bullet image from the Texture Atlas we're using
                CCSpriteFrame* bulletFrame = [[CCSpriteFrameCache
                        sharedSpriteFrameCache] spriteFrameByName:@"bullet.png"];

                // use the bullet's texture
                batch = [CCSpriteBatchNode batchNodeWithTexture:bulletFrame.texture];
                [self addChild:batch];

                // Create a number of bullets up front and re-use them
                for (int i = 0; i < 200; i++)
                {
                        Bullet* bullet = [Bullet bullet];
                        bullet.visible = NO;
                        [batch addChild:bullet];
                }
        }

        return self;
}

-(void) shootBulletAt:(CGPoint)startPosition velocity:(CGPoint)velocity
                                        frameName:(NSString*)frameName
{
        CCArray* bullets = [batch children];
        CCNode* node = [bullets objectAtIndex:nextInactiveBullet];
        NSAssert([node isKindOfClass:[Bullet class]], @"not a Bullet!");
```

```
            Bullet* bullet = (Bullet*)node;
            [bullet shootBulletAt:startPosition velocity:velocity frameName:frameName];

            nextInactiveBullet++;
            if (nextInactiveBullet >= [bullets count])
            {
                    nextInactiveBullet = 0;
            }
}
@end
```

The shootBulletAt method has changed the most as you can see. It now takes three parameters: startPosition, velocity, and frameName instead of a pointer to the Ship class. It then passes on these parameters to the Bullet class's shootBulletAt method, which I had to refactor as well:

```
-(void) shootBulletAt:(CGPoint)startPosition velocity:(CGPoint)vel
                                                frameName:(NSString*)frameName
{
        self.velocity = vel;
        self.position = startPosition;
        self.visible = YES;

        // change the bullet's texture by setting a different SpriteFrame to be
                                                                        displayed
        CCSpriteFrame *frame = [[CCSpriteFrameCache sharedSpriteFrameCache]
                                                spriteFrameByName:frameName];
        [self setDisplayFrame:frame];

        [self scheduleUpdate];
}
```

Both velocity and position are now directly assigned to the bullet. This means that the code calling the shootBulletAt method has to determine the position, direction, and speed of the bullet. This is exactly what I wanted: full flexibility for shooting bullets, including changing the bullet's sprite frame by using the setDisplayFrame method. Since the bullets are all in the same Texture Atlas and thus use the same texture, all it needs to change which bullet is displayed is to set the desired sprite frame. In effect, this is simply going to render a different part of the texture and comes at no extra cost.

While I was in the Bullet class, I also fixed the boundary issues the bullets would have had—that only bullets moving outside the right side of the screen would have been set invisible and put back on the waiting list. By using the CGRectIntersectsRect check with the bullet's boundingBox and the screenRect in the update method, any bullet having moved completely outside the screen area will be marked for reuse:

```
// When the bullet leaves the screen, make it invisible
if (CGRectIntersectsRect([self boundingBox], screenRect) == NO)
{
        …
}
```

The screenRect variable itself is now stored for convenience and performance reasons as a static variable, so it can be accessed by other classes and doesn't need to be recreated for each use. Static variables like screenRect are available in the class implementation file where they are declared. They are like global variables to the class; any class instance can read and modify the variable, as opposed to class member variables, which are local to every class instance. Since the screen size never changes during gameplay and all Bullet instances need to use this variable, it makes sense to store it in a static variable for all class instances. The first bullet to be initialized sets the screenRect variable. The CGRectIsEmpty method checks if the screenRect variable is still uninitialized; since the variable is static, I only want to initialize it once.

```
static CGRect screenRect;

…

// make sure to initialize the screen rect only once
if (CGRectIsEmpty(screenRect))
{
        CGSize screenSize = [[CCDirector sharedDirector] winSize];
        screenRect = CGRectMake(0, 0, screenSize.width, screenSize.height);
}
```

With these changes implemented, what's left is to clean up the GameScene by removing any of the methods and member variables previously used for shooting bullets. Specifically, I need to replace the CCSpriteBatchNode initialization with the initialization of the BulletCache class:

```
BulletCache* bulletCache = [BulletCache node];
[self addChild:bulletCache z:1 tag:GameSceneNodeTagBulletCache];
```

I also need to add a bulletCache accessor so other classes can access the BulletCache instance through the GameScene:

```
-(BulletCache*) bulletCache
{
        CCNode* node = [self getChildByTag:GameSceneNodeTagBulletCache];
        NSAssert([node isKindOfClass:[BulletCache class]], @"not a BulletCache");
        return (BulletCache*)node;
}
```

The InputLayer can now use the new BulletCache class, and uses it to shoot the player's bullets. The bullet properties, such as starting position, velocity, and the sprite frame to use, are now passed by the shooting code in the update method of the InputLayer:

```
if (fireButton.active && totalTime > nextShotTime)
{
        nextShotTime = totalTime + 0.5f;

        GameScene* game = [GameScene sharedGameScene];
        Ship* ship = [game defaultShip];
        BulletCache* bulletCache = [game bulletCache];

        // Set the position, velocity and spriteframe before shooting
        CGPoint shotPos = CGPointMake(ship.position.x + [ship contentSize].width * 0.5f,
                                                            ship.position.y;
        float spread = (CCRANDOM_0_1() - 0.5f) * 0.5f;
```

```
        CGPoint velocity = CGPointMake(1, spread);
        [bulletCache shootBulletAt:shotPos velocity:velocity frameName:@"bullet.png"];
}
```

This short refactoring session adds much-needed flexibility to shooting bullets. I'm sure you can imagine how enemies can now use the very same code to shoot their own bullets.

What about Enemies?

At this point, there's only a fuzzy idea about what the enemies are, what they do, and what their behavior will be. That's the thing with enemies—you never quite know what they're up to.

In the case of games, that means going back to the drawing board, planning out what you want the enemies to do, and then deducing from that plan what you need to program. Contrary to real life, you have full control over the enemies. Doesn't that make you feel powerful? But before you or anyone can have fun, you need to come up with a plan for world domination.

I already created the graphics for three different types of enemies. At this point, I know only that at least one of them is supposed to be a boss monster. Take a look at Figure 8–1 and try to imagine what these enemies could be up to.

Figure 8–1. *The graphics used as the game's enemy characters. The Gingerbread Man, the volatile Snake, and the Blob Monster, aka da Boss.*

Before you start programming, you should have a good understanding of which behaviors the enemies will have in common, so that you program those parts only once. Eliminating code duplication is the single most important goal of clean code design.

Let's see what we know for sure is common to all enemies:

- Shoots bullets
- Has logic that determines when and where to shoot what bullet

- Can be hit by player's bullets

- Can not be hit by other enemy's bullets

- Can take one or more hits (has health)

- Has a specific behavior and movement pattern

- Has a specific behavior or animation when destroyed

- Will appear outside the screen area and move inside

- Will not leave the screen area once inside

When you look at that list, you may notice that some of these attributes also apply to the player's ship. It certainly can shoot bullets; we may want it to sustain multiple hits; and it should have a specific behavior or animation when destroyed. It makes sense to consider the player's ship as just a special type of enemy and take it into consideration as well.

Looking at this feature set, I see three possible approaches. I could create one class that contains all the code for the Ship, the enemies, and the Boss monster. Certain parts of the code would run conditionally, depending on the type of enemy. For example, the shooting code may have different code paths for each type of game object. With a limited number of different objects, this approach works reasonably well—but it doesn't scale. As you add more and more types of game objects, you end up with a bigger and fatter class containing all of the game logic code. Any change to any part of that class has the potential to cause undesirable side effects in enemies' or even the player Ship's behavior. Determining which code path to execute depending on a type variable is quite reminiscent of pure C programming and doesn't make use of the object-oriented nature of the Objective-C programming language. But if used judiciously, it's a very powerful concept even today.

The second approach is to create a class hierarchy with the `Entity` class as the base class, then derive a Ship, two monsters, and a boss monster class from it. This is what a lot of programmers actually do and it also works reasonably well for a small number of game objects. But in essence, it's little different from the first approach, in that common code often ends up piling up in the base `Entity` class when it is needed by some of the subclasses, but not all of them. It takes a turn for the worse as soon as that code in the `Entity` class starts to add switches based on the type of the enemy, to skip parts of the code or execute code paths specific to that type of enemy. That's the same problem of the first C-style programming approach. With a little care, you can make sure the code specific to an enemy is part of that enemy's class, but it's all too easy to end up making most changes in the `Entity` class itself.

The third option is to use a component system. This means that individual code paths are separated from the `Entity` class hierarchy and only added to the subclasses that need the components, such as a healthbar component. Since component-based development would justify a book on its own, and is likely to be overkill for a small project like this shoot 'em up game, I'll use a mixture of the class hierarchy approach and component design to at least give you an idea how compositing game objects out of individual parts works in principle and what the benefits are.

I do want to point out that there is no one best approach to code design. Certain choices are entirely subjective and depend on personal preferences and experience. Working code is often preferable to clean code if you're willing to refactor your codebase often as you learn more about the game you're making. Experience allows you to make more of these decisions up front in the planning stage, enabling you to create more complex games faster. So if that's your goal, start by making and completing smaller games and slowly push yourself to new limits and new challenges. It's a learning process, and unfortunately the easiest way to kill your motivation is to be over-ambitious. There's a reason why every seasoned game programmer will tell a beginner to start simple and to recreate classic arcade games like Tetris, Pac-Man, or Asteroids first.

The Entity Class Hierarchy

For the base class I created the Entity class in the *ShootEmUp02* project. Entity is a generic class derived from CCSprite, which only contains the setPosition code of the Ship class to keep all instances of Entity inside the screen. I made just a small improvement to this code so that objects outside the screen area are allowed to move inside, but once inside, they can no longer leave the screen area. In this Shoot'em Up example game, the enemies won't pass by you; they'll stop mid-screen in order to illustrate the EnemyCache, introduced shortly. The screen area check simply checks if the screen rectangle fully contains the sprite's boundingBox, and only if that's the case will the code to keep the sprite inside the screen rectangle run:

```
-(void) setPosition:(CGPoint)pos
{
        // If the current position is outside the screen no adjustments should be made!
        // This allows entities to move into the screen from outside.
        if (CGRectContainsRect([GameScene screenRect], [self boundingBox]))
        {
            …
        }

        [super setPosition:pos];
}
```

The Ship class has been replaced with ShipEntity. Since the Entity base class now contains the setPosition code, the only thing left in ShipEntity is the initWithShipImage method. It's the same as before so I won't recreate it here.

The EnemyEntity Class

I do need to go more in depth with the EnemyEntity class and what it does, starting with the header file in Listing 8–3.

Listing 8–3. *The @interface of the EnemyEntity Class*

```
#import <Foundation/Foundation.h>
#import "Entity.h"

typedef enum
{
        EnemyTypeBreadman = 0,
        EnemyTypeSnake,
        EnemyTypeBoss,

        EnemyType_MAX,
} EnemyTypes;

@interface EnemyEntity : Entity
{
        EnemyTypes type;
}

+(id) enemyWithType:(EnemyTypes)enemyType;
+(int) getSpawnFrequencyForEnemyType:(EnemyTypes)enemyType;
-(void) spawn;
@end
```

Nothing too exciting here. The EnemyTypes enum is used to differentiate between the three different types of enemies currently supported, with EnemyType_MAX used as the upper limit for loops, as you'll see soon. The EnemyEntity class has a member variable that stores the type, so that I can use switch statements to branch the code depending on the type of enemy as needed.

The implementation of EnemyEntity contains a lot of code I'd like to discuss, so I'll split the discussion into several topics and present only the relevant code, beginning with the initWithType method in Listing 8–4.

Listing 8–4. *Initializing an Enemy with a Type*

```
-(id) initWithType:(EnemyTypes)enemyType
{
        type = enemyType;

        NSString* frameName;
        NSString* bulletFrameName;
        int shootFrequency = 300;
        switch (type)
        {
                case EnemyTypeBreadman:
                        frameName = @"monster-a.png";
                        bulletFrameName = @"candystick.png";
                        break;
                case EnemyTypeSnake:
                        frameName = @"monster-b.png";
```

```
                    bulletFrameName = @"redcross.png";
                    shootFrequency = 200;
                    break;
            case EnemyTypeBoss:
                    frameName = @"monster-c.png";
                    bulletFrameName = @"blackhole.png";
                    shootFrequency = 100;
                    break;

            default:
                    [NSException exceptionWithName:@"EnemyEntity Exception"
                                     reason:@"unhandled enemy type" userInfo:nil];
    }

    if ((self = [super initWithSpriteFrameName:frameName]))
    {
            // Create the game logic components
            [self addChild:[StandardMoveComponent node]];

            StandardShootComponent* shootComponent =
                                    [StandardShootComponent node];
            shootComponent.shootFrequency = shootFrequency;
            shootComponent.bulletFrameName = bulletFrameName;
            [self addChild:shootComponent];

            // enemies start invisible
            self.visible = NO;

            [self initSpawnFrequency];
    }

    return self;
}
```

The code begins by setting variables, depending on the enemy type, using a switch statement to provide default values for each type of enemy—the sprite frame name to use, the name of the bullet sprite frame, and the shooting frequency. The default case of the switch statement throws an exception because that option usually results from adding a new enemy type to the EnemyTypes enum without extending this switch statement accordingly. Safeguarding your switch statements in this way so that no default case will be accepted is a good strategy to avoid spending too much debugging time on simple human errors. And you are a human being, right? So you're prone to forget these things. I know I am. Instead of wondering why your new enemy doesn't move, or shoots the wrong bullets, you'll get a crash that waves a big red flag saying: "Hey, you forgot to update me!"

It's also perfectly fine to run code before the assignment to self, as long as you don't forget to call a [super init…] method eventually. Otherwise the super class won't be properly initialized and that can lead to strange bugs and crashes.

The component classes created and added to EnemyEntity contain exchangeable code. I'll get to components soon; for the moment just know that the StandardMoveComponent allows the enemy to move while the StandardShootComponent allows it to, you guessed it, shoot.

Let's focus our attention now on the `initSpawnFrequency` method. The relevant code is shown in Listing 8–5.

Listing 8–5. *Controlling the Spawning of Enemies*

```
static CCArray* spawnFrequency;

-(void) initSpawnFrequency
{
        // initialize how frequent the enemies will spawn
        if (spawnFrequency == nil)
        {
                spawnFrequency = [[CCArray alloc] initWithCapacity:EnemyType_MAX];
                [spawnFrequency insertObject:[NSNumber numberWithInt:80]
                                                    atIndex:EnemyTypeBreadman];
                [spawnFrequency insertObject:[NSNumber numberWithInt:260]
                                                    atIndex:EnemyTypeSnake];
                [spawnFrequency insertObject:[NSNumber numberWithInt:1500]
                                                    atIndex:EnemyTypeBoss];

                // spawn one enemy immediately
                [self spawn];
        }
}

+(int) getSpawnFrequencyForEnemyType:(EnemyTypes)enemyType
{
        NSAssert(enemyType < EnemyType_MAX, @"invalid enemy type");
        NSNumber* number = [spawnFrequency objectAtIndex:enemyType];
        return [number intValue];
}

-(void) dealloc
{
        [spawnFrequency release];
        spawnFrequency = nil;

        [super dealloc];
}
```

We store the spawn frequency values for each type of enemy in a static `spawnFrequency` `CCArray`. It's a static variable because the spawn frequency isn't needed for each enemy but only for each enemy type. The first `EnemyEntity` instance that executes the `initSpawnFrequency` method will find that the `spawnFrequency` `CCArray` is `nil`, and so initializes it.

Since a `CCArray` can only store objects and not primitive data types like integers, the values have to be wrapped into an `NSNumber` class using the `numberWithInt` initializer. I chose to use `insertObject` here instead of `addObject` because it not only ensures that the values will have the same index as the enemy type defined in the enum, it also tells any other programmer looking at this code that the index used has a meaning. In this case, the index is synonymous with the enemy type. Although it's technically unnecessary to specify the index here, it helps to show which value is used for which enemy type.

Of course, the dealloc method releases the spawnFrequency CCArray, and it also sets it to nil, which is very important. Being a static variable, the first EnemyEntity object to run its dealloc method will release the spawnFrequency's memory. If it wasn't set to nil immediately thereafter, the next EnemyEntity running its dealloc method would try the same, and thus over-release the spawnFrequency CCArray, leading to a crash. On the other hand, if the spawnFrequency variable is nil, any message sent to it, like the release message, will simply be ignored. I said it before but it can't be repeated often enough: sending messages to nil objects is perfectly fine in Objective-C; the message will simply be ignored.

Spawning an entity is done by the spawn method:

```
-(void) spawn
{
        // Select a spawn location just outside the right side of the screen
        CGRect screenRect = [GameScene screenRect];
        CGSize spriteSize = [self contentSize];
        float xPos = screenRect.size.width + spriteSize.width * 0.5f;
        float yPos = CCRANDOM_0_1() * (screenRect.size.height - spriteSize.height) +
                                                        spriteSize.height * 0.5f;
        self.position = CGPointMake(xPos, yPos);

        // Finally set yourself to be visible, this also flag the enemy as "in use"
        self.visible = YES;
}
```

Because an EnemyCache is used to create all instances of enemies up front, the whole spawning process is limited to choosing a random y position just outside the right side of the screen, and then setting the EnemyEntity sprite to be visible. The visible status is used elsewhere in the project, specifically by component classes, to determine if the EnemyEntity is currently in use. If it's not visible, it can be spawned to make it visible but it should only run its game logic code while it's visible.

The EnemyCache Class

I just mentioned the EnemyCache class. By its name, it should remind you of the BulletCache class, which also holds a number of pre-initialized objects for fast and easy reuse. This avoids creating and releasing objects during gameplay that can be a source of minor performance hiccups. Especially for action games, those small glitches can have a devastating effect on the player's experience. With that said, let's look at the unspectacular header file of the EnemyCache in Listing 8–6.

Listing 8–6. *The @interface of the EnemyCache Class*

```
#import <Foundation/Foundation.h>
#import "cocos2d.h"

@interface EnemyCache : CCNode
{
        CCSpriteBatchNode* batch;
        CCArray* enemies;
```

```
            int updateCount;
}
@end
```

After the `spriteBatch,` which contains all the enemy sprites, there's an `enemies` `CCArray` that stores a list of enemies of each type. The `updateCount` variable is increased every frame and used to spawn enemies at regular intervals. The `init` method of the `EnemyCache` is quite similar to the `BulletCache` init with its initialization of the `CCSpriteBatchNode`:

```
-(id) init
{
        if ((self = [super init]))
        {
                // get any image from the Texture Atlas we're using
                CCSpriteFrame* frame = [[CCSpriteFrameCache sharedSpriteFrameCache]
                                            spriteFrameByName:@"monster-a.png"];
                batch = [CCSpriteBatchNode batchNodeWithTexture:frame.texture];
                [self addChild:batch];

                [self initEnemies];
                [self scheduleUpdate];
        }

        return self;
}
```

But since the code for initializing the enemies is a bit more complex, I extracted it into its own method, as shown in Listing 8–7.

Listing 8–7. *Initializing the Pool of Enemies for Later Reuse*

```
-(void) initEnemies
{
        // create the enemies array containing further arrays for each type
        enemies = [[CCArray alloc] initWithCapacity:EnemyType_MAX];

        // create the arrays for each type
        for (int i = 0; i < EnemyType_MAX; i++)
        {
                // depending on enemy type the array capacity is set
                // to hold the desired number of enemies
                int capacity;
                switch (i)
                {
                        case EnemyTypeBreadman:
                                capacity = 6;
                                break;
                        case EnemyTypeSnake:
                                capacity = 3;
                                break;
                        case EnemyTypeBoss:
                                capacity = 1;
                                break;

                        default:
```

```
                                    [NSException exceptionWithName:
                                                @"EnemyCache Exception"
                                                reason:@"unhandled enemy type"
                                                userInfo:nil];
                            break;
                }

                // no alloc needed since the enemies array will retain anything added to
it
                CCArray* enemiesOfType = [CCArray arrayWithCapacity:capacity];
                [enemies addObject:enemiesOfType];
        }

        for (int i = 0; i < EnemyType_MAX; i++)
        {
                CCArray* enemiesOfType = [enemies objectAtIndex:i];
                int numEnemiesOfType = [enemiesOfType capacity];

                for (int j = 0; j < numEnemiesOfType; j++)
                {
                        EnemyEntity* enemy = [EnemyEntity enemyWithType:i];
                        [batch addChild:enemy z:0 tag:i];
                        [enemiesOfType addObject:enemy];
                }
        }
}

-(void) dealloc
{
        [enemies release];
        [super dealloc];
}
```

The interesting part here is that the CCArray* enemies itself contains more CCArray* objects, one per enemy type. It's what's called a two-dimensional array. The member variable enemies requires the use of alloc, because otherwise its memory would be freed after leaving the initEnemies method. In contrast, the CCArray* objects added to the enemies CCArray do not need to be created using alloc, because the enemies CCArray, retains the objects added to it.

The initial capacity of each enemiesOfType CCArray also determines how many enemies of that type can be on screen at once. In this way you can keep the maximum number of enemies on screen under control. Each enemiesOfType CCArray is then added to enemies CCArray using addObject, just like any other object. If you want, you can create deep hierarchies in this way. As a matter of fact, the cocos2d node hierarchy is built on CCNode classes containing CCArray* children member variables that can contain more CCNode classes and so on.

I split the array initialization and the creation of enemies into separate loops even though both could be done in the same loop. They are simply different tasks and should be kept separate. The additional overhead of going through all enemy types once again is negligible.

Based on the initial capacity set in the CCArray initialization loop, the desired number of enemies are created, added to the CCSpriteBatchNode, and then added to the corresponding enemiesOfType CCArray. While the enemies could also be accessed through the CCSpriteBatchNode, keeping references to the enemy entities in separate arrays makes it easier to process them during later activities such as spawning, as shown in Listing 8–8.

Listing 8–8. *Spawning Enemies*

```
-(void) spawnEnemyOfType:(EnemyTypes)enemyType
{
        CCArray* enemiesOfType = [enemies objectAtIndex:enemyType];

        EnemyEntity* enemy;
        CCARRAY_FOREACH(enemiesOfType, enemy)
        {
                // find the first free enemy and respawn it
                if (enemy.visible == NO)
                {
                        //CCLOG(@"spawn enemy type %i", enemyType);
                        [enemy spawn];
                        break;
                }
        }
}

-(void) update:(ccTime)delta
{
        updateCount++;

        for (int i = EnemyType_MAX - 1; i >= 0; i--)
        {
                int spawnFrequency = [EnemyEntity getSpawnFrequencyForEnemyType:i];

                if (updateCount % spawnFrequency == 0)
                {
                        [self spawnEnemyOfType:i];
                        break;
                }
        }
}
```

The update method increases a simple update counter. It does not take into effect the actual time passed, but since the variances are typically minimal, it's a fair tradeoff to make life a bit easier. This for loop oddly starts at EnemyType_MAX - 1 and runs until i is negative. The only purpose for this is that higher-numbered EnemyTypes have spawn precedence over lower-numbered EnemyTypes. If a boss monster is scheduled to appear at the same time as a Snake, the Boss will be spawned. Otherwise it could happen that the Snake takes the Boss' spawn slot by trying to spawn at the same time, blocking the Boss from ever spawning. It's a side-effect of the spawning logic and I leave it up to you to extend and improve this code, as you'll probably have to do anyway if you decide to write your own version of a classic shoot 'em up game.

The spawnFrequency is obtained from EnemyEntity's getSpawnFrequencyForEnemyType method:

```
+(int) getSpawnFrequencyForEnemyType:(EnemyTypes)enemyType
{
        NSAssert(enemyType < EnemyType_MAX, @"invalid enemy type");
        NSNumber* number = [spawnFrequency objectAtIndex:enemyType];
        return [number intValue];
}
```

First the method asserts that the enemyType number is actually within the defined range. Then the NSNumber object for that enemy type is obtained and returned as intValue.

The modulo operator % returns the remainder left after the division of the two operands updateCount and spawnFrequency. This means an enemy is spawned only when updateCount can be evenly divided by spawnFrequency, resulting in a remainder of 0.

The spawnEnemyOfType method then gets the CCArray from the enemies CCArray, which contains the list of enemiesOfType, another CCArray. You can now iterate over only the desired enemy types, rather than having to go through all sprites added to the CCSpriteBatchNode. As soon as one enemy is found that is not visible, its spawn method is called. If all enemies of that type are visible, the maximum number of enemies is currently onscreen and no further enemies are spawned, effectively limiting the number of enemies of a type on screen at any time.

The Component Classes

Component classes are intended as plug-ins for game logic. If you add a component to an entity, the entity will execute the behavior of the component: moving, shooting, animating, showing a healthbar, and so on. The big benefit is that you program these components to work generically almost automatically, because they interact with the parent CCNode class and should make as few assumptions about the parent class as possible. Of course, in some cases a component requires the parent to be an EnemyEntity class, but then you can still use it with any EnemyEntity.

Component classes can also be configured depending on the class that's using the component. As an example for component classes, let's take a look at the StandardShootComponent initialization in the EnemyEntity class:

```
StandardShootComponent* shootComponent = [StandardShootComponent node];
shootComponent.shootFrequency = shootFrequency;
shootComponent.bulletFrameName = bulletFrameName;
[self addChild:shootComponent];
```

The variables shootFrequency and bulletFrameName have been set previously based on the EnemyType. By adding the StandardShootComponent to the EnemyEntity class, the enemy will shoot specific bullets at certain intervals. Since this component makes no assumptions about the parent class, you could even add an instance of it to the ShipEntity class and have your player's ship shoot automatically at specific intervals! Or by simply activating and deactivating specialized shooting components, you can create the effect of changing weapons for the player with very little code. You just program the shooting code in isolation, then plug it into a game entity and add some parameters to it. The only logic left for programming the switching of weapons is simply when to deactivate which components. What's more, you can reuse these components in other games if they make sense. Components are great for writing reusable code and are a standard mechanism in many, many game engines. If you'd like to learn more about game components, please refer to this blog post on my web site (www.learn-cocos2d.com/2010/06/prefer-composition-inheritance/).

Let's look at the StandardShootComponent's source code, starting with the header file:

```
#import <Foundation/Foundation.h>
#import "cocos2d.h"

@interface StandardShootComponent : CCSprite
{
        int updateCount;
        int shootFrequency;
        NSString* bulletFrameName;
}

@property (nonatomic) int shootFrequency;
@property (nonatomic, copy) NSString* bulletFrameName;

@end
```

There are two things of note. The first is that StandardShootComponent is derived from CCSprite, even though it doesn't use any texture. That is a workaround because all EnemyEntity objects are added to a CCSpriteBatchNode, which can contain only CCSprite-based objects. This also extends to any child node of the EnemyEntity class; thus the StandardShootComponent needs to inherit from CCSprite to satisfy the requirement of the CCSpriteBatchNode.

Next there's an NSString* pointer, bulletFrameName, with a corresponding @property. If you look closely, you'll notice the keyword copy in the @property definition. That means assigning an NSString to this property will create a copy of it. This is important for strings since they are generally autoreleased objects and we want to make sure this string is ours. We could also retain it, but the problem is, if the source NSString were to be changed, this would also change the bulletFrameName, which would be undesirable in this case. Of course, with the copy keyword comes the responsibility to release the bulletFrameName memory on dealloc, as seen in the implementation in Listing 8–9.

Listing 8–9. *The StandardShootComponent Implementation in Its Entirety*

```
#import "StandardShootComponent.h"
#import "BulletCache.h"
#import "GameScene.h"

@implementation StandardShootComponent

@synthesize shootFrequency;
@synthesize bulletFrameName;

-(id) init
{
        if ((self = [super init]))
        {
                [self scheduleUpdate];
        }
```

```
        return self;
}

-(void) dealloc
{
        [bulletFrameName release];
        [super dealloc];
}

-(void) update:(ccTime)delta
{
        if (self.parent.visible)
        {
                updateCount++;

                if (updateCount >= shootFrequency)
                {
                        updateCount = 0;

                        GameScene* game = [GameScene sharedGameScene];
                        CGPoint startPos = ccpSub(self.parent.position,
                                CGPointMake(self.parent.contentSize.width * 0.5f, 0));
                        [game.bulletCache shootBulletFrom:startPos
                                                    velocity:CGPointMake(-2, 0)
                                                    frameName:bulletFrameName];
                }
        }
}
@end
```

The actual shooting code first checks if the parent is visible, because if the parent isn't visible, the code obviously shouldn't shoot. The BulletCache is what shoots the bullet, using the bulletFrameName provided to the component and a fixed velocity. For the start position, the component's position itself is irrelevant. Instead, the parent position and contentSize properties are used to calculate the correct starting position: in this case, at the left side of the enemy's sprite.

This bullet startPos works reasonably well for regular enemies, but for the boss it would be cooler if the bullets were shot from its mouth or nose. I'll leave it up to you to add another property to this component with which to set the bullet startPosition. Alternatively, you could also create a separate BossShootComponent and add this only to boss enemies to create more complex shooting patterns. The same goes for StandardMoveComponents, which for the boss might require hovering at a certain position at the right side of the screen.

Shooting Things

I almost forgot—you actually want to shoot the enemies, right? Well, in the *ShootEmUp03* project, you can!

The ideal starting point to check if a bullet has hit something is in the BulletCache class. I've added just the method to do that. Actually, I've added three methods, two of them public; the third is private to the class and combines the common code (see Listing 8–10). The idea behind using the two wrapper methods, isPlayerBulletCollidingWithRect and isEnemyBulletCollidingWithRect, is to hide the internal detail of determining which kinds of bullets are used for collision checks. You could also expose the usePlayerBullets parameter to other classes, but doing so would only make it harder to eventually change the parameter from a bool to an enum, in case you want to introduce a third type of bullet.

Listing 8–10. *Checking for Collisions with Bullets*

```
-(bool) isPlayerBulletCollidingWithRect:(CGRect)rect
{
        return [self isBulletCollidingWithRect:rect usePlayerBullets:YES];
}

-(bool) isEnemyBulletCollidingWithRect:(CGRect)rect
{
        return [self isBulletCollidingWithRect:rect usePlayerBullets:YES];
}

-(bool) isBulletCollidingWithRect:(CGRect)rect usePlayerBullets:(bool)usePlayerBullets
{
        bool isColliding = NO;

        Bullet* bullet;
        CCARRAY_FOREACH([batch children], bullet)
        {
                if (bullet.visible && usePlayerBullets == bullet.isPlayerBullet)
                {
                        if (CGRectIntersectsRect([bullet boundingBox], rect))
                        {
                                isColliding = YES;

                                // remove the bullet
                                bullet.visible = NO;
                                break;
                        }
                }
        }

        return isColliding;
}
```

Only visible bullets can collide, of course, and by checking the bullet's isPlayerBullet property, we ensure that enemies can't shoot themselves. The actual collision test is a simple CGRectIntersectsRect test and if the bullet has actually hit something, the bullet itself is also set to be invisible to make it disappear.

The EnemyCache class holding all EnemyEntity objects is the perfect place to call this method to check if any enemy was hit by a player bullet. The class has a new checkForBulletCollisions class, which is called from its update method:

```
-(void) checkForBulletCollisions
{
        EnemyEntity* enemy;
```

```
CCARRAY_FOREACH([batch children], enemy)
{
        if (enemy.visible)
        {
                BulletCache* bulletCache = [[GameScene sharedGameScene]
                                                        bulletCache];
                CGRect bbox = [enemy boundingBox];
                if ([bulletCache isPlayerBulletCollidingWithRect:bbox])
                {
                        // This enemy got hit ...
                        [enemy gotHit];
                }
        }
}
}
```

Here again it's convenient to be able to iterate over all the enemy entities in the game, skipping those that are currently not visible. Using each enemy's boundingBox to check with the BulletCache isPlayerBulletCollidingWithRect method, we can quickly find if an enemy got hit by a player bullet. If so, the EnemyEntity method gotHit is called, which simply sets the enemy to be invisible.

I'll leave it as an exercise for you to implement the player's ship being hit by enemy bullets. You'll have to schedule an update method in ShipEntity, then implement the checkForBulletCollisions method and call it from the update method. You'll have to change the call to isPlayerBulletCollidingWithRect to isEnemyBulletCollidingWithRect and decide how you want to react to being hit by a bullet, for example by playing a sound effect.

A Healthbar for the Boss

The boss monster shouldn't be an easy, one-hit kill. It also should give the player feedback about its health by displaying a healthbar that decreases with each hit. The first step towards a healthbar is adding the hitPoints member variable to the EnemyEntity class, which tells us how many hits the enemy can take before being destroyed. The initialHitPoints variable stores the maximum hit points, since after an enemy gets killed we need to be able to restore the original hit points. This is the changed header file in the EnemyEntity class:

```
@interface EnemyEntity : Entity
{
        EnemyTypes type;
        int initialHitPoints;
        int hitPoints;
}

@property (readonly, nonatomic) int hitPoints;
```

To display the healthbar, a component class is ideal as it provides a plug-and-play solution. The header file for the HealthbarComponent proves to be highly unspectacular:

```
#import <Foundation/Foundation.h>
#import "cocos2d.h"
```

```
@interface HealthbarComponent : CCSprite
{
}

-(void) reset;

@end
```

The implementation of the `HealthbarComponent` class is more interesting, as Listing 8–11 shows.

Listing 8–11. *The HealthBarComponent Updates Its* `scaleX` *Property Based on the Enemy's Remaining Hit Points*

```
#import "HealthbarComponent.h"
#import "EnemyEntity.h"

@implementation HealthbarComponent

-(id) init
{
        if ((self = [super init]))
        {
                self.visible = NO;
                [self scheduleUpdate];
        }

        return self;
}

-(void) reset
{
        float parentHeight = self.parent.contentSize.height;
        float selfHeight = self.contentSize.height;
        self.position = CGPointMake(self.parent.anchorPointInPixels.x,
                                                     parentHeight + selfHeight);
        self.scaleX = 1;
        self.visible = YES;
}

-(void) update:(ccTime)delta
{
        if (self.parent.visible)
        {
                NSAssert([self.parent isKindOfClass:[EnemyEntity class]],
                                                     @"not a EnemyEntity");
                EnemyEntity* parentEntity = (EnemyEntity*)self.parent;
                self.scaleX = parentEntity.hitPoints /
                                                     (float)parentEntity.initialHitPoints;
        }
        else if (self.visible)
        {
                self.visible = NO;
        }
}
@end
```

The healthbar turns its visible state on and off to be in line with its parent EnemyEntity object. The reset method places the healthbar sprite at the proper location just above the head of the EnemyEntity's sprite. Since a decrease in health is displayed by modifying the scaleX property, it, too, needs to be reset to its default state.

In the update method and when its parent is visible, the HealthbarComponent first asserts that the parent is of class EnemyEntity. Since this component relies on certain properties only available in the EnemyEntity class and its subclasses, we need to make sure that it's the right parent class. We modify the scaleX property as a percentage of the current hit points divided by the initial hit points. Since there's currently no way of telling when the hit points change, the calculation is done every frame, regardless of whether it's needed. The overhead here is minimal, but for more complex calculations, a call to the HealthbarComponent from the onHit method of the EnemyEntity class would be preferable.

> **NOTE:** The parentEntity.initialHitPoints is cast to float. If I hadn't done this, the division would be an integer division that would always result in 0 since integers can't represent fractional numbers and are always rounded down. Casting the divisor to a float data type ensures that floating point division is done and the desired result is returned.

In the init method of the EnemyEntity, the HealthbarComponent is added if the enemy type is EnemyTypeBoss:

```
if (type == EnemyTypeBoss)
{
        HealthbarComponent* healthbar = [HealthbarComponent
                                        spriteWithSpriteFrameName:@"healthbar.png"];
        [self addChild:healthbar];
}
```

The spawn method has been extended to include resetting the hit points to their initial value and calling the reset method of any possible HealthbarComponent added to the entity. I omitted the explicit check if the enemy is a boss type here simply because the HealthbarComponent is universal and could be used by any type of enemy.

```
-(void) spawn
{
        // Select a spawn location just outside the right side of the screen
        CGRect screenRect = [GameScene screenRect];
        CGSize spriteSize = [self contentSize];
        float xPos = screenRect.size.width + spriteSize.width * 0.5f;
        float yPos = CCRANDOM_0_1() * (screenRect.size.height - spriteSize.height) +
                                                spriteSize.height * 0.5f;
        self.position = CGPointMake(xPos, yPos);

        // Finally set yourself to be visible, this also flag the enemy as "in use"
        self.visible = YES;

        // reset health
        hitPoints = initialHitPoints;
```

```
        // reset certain components
        CCNode* node;
        CCARRAY_FOREACH([self children], node)
        {
                if ([node isKindOfClass:[HealthbarComponent class]])
                {
                        HealthbarComponent* healthbar = (HealthbarComponent*)node;
                        [healthbar reset];
                }
        }
}
```

Conclusion

Creating a complete and polished game is quite an effort, one that involves a lot of refactoring, changing working code to improve its design and to allow for more features existing in harmony with each other.

In this chapter, you learned the value of classes like BulletCache and EnemyCache, which manage all instances of certain classes so that you have easy access to them from one central point. And pooling objects together also helps to improve performance.

The Entity class hierarchy serves as just one example of how you can divide your classes without requiring each game object to be its own class. By using component classes and cocos2d's node hierarchy to your advantage, you can create plug-and-play classes with very specific functionality. This helps you to construct your game objects using composition rather than inheritance. It's a much more flexible way to write game logic code and leads to better code reuse.

Finally, you learned how to shoot enemies and how the BulletCache and EnemyCache classes help perform such tasks in a straightforward manner. And the HealthbarComponent provided the perfect example of the component system at work.

The game to this point leaves a couple things open for you to build on. First and foremost, the player doesn't get hit yet. And you might want to add a healthbar to the Snake monster, and write specialized move and shoot components for the boss monster's behavior. Overall, it's an excellent starting point for your own side-scrolling game, just waiting for you to improve on it.

In the next chapter I'll show you how to add visual eye-candy to the Shoot'em Up game by using Particle Effects.

Chapter 9

Particle Effects

To create special visual effects, game programmers often make use of *particle systems*. Particle systems work by emitting vast numbers of tiny particles and rendering them efficiently, much more efficiently than if they were sprites. This allows you to simulate effects like rain, fire, snow, explosions, vapor trails, and many more.

Particle systems are driven by a great number of properties. By great I mean about 30 properties, which all influence not only the appearance and behavior of individual particles, but the whole particle effect. The particle effect is the totality of all particles working together to create a particular visual outcome. One particle alone does not make a fire effect; ten still don't get close enough. You would want several dozens, if not hundreds, of particles to work together in just the right way to create the fire effect.

Creating convincing particle effects is a trial-and-error process. Trying out all the various properties in source code and tweaking a particle system by compiling the game, seeing what it looks like, then making changes and repeating this process is cumbersome to say the least. That's where a particle design tool comes in handy, and I know just the right one: it's called Particle Designer and I'll explain how it works in this chapter.

Example Particle Effects

Cocos2d comes with a number of built-in particle effects that give you a good idea of the kinds of effects they'll produce. You can use them as placeholders in your game or subclass and modify the examples defined in the *CCParticleExamples.m* file if you just want to apply some minor tweaks. The good thing about them is that you don't need any outside help; you create the example particle effects as if they were simple CCNode objects. As a matter of fact, they are actually derived from CCNode.

I created a project called *ParticleEffects01* that shows all the cocos2d example particle effects. You can cycle through the examples by quickly tapping the screen and you can also drag and move them with your finger. Many particle effects look totally different as soon as they start moving, so what seems like just a huge blob of particles may well work as an engine exhaust effect if it is moving.

There's only one type of effect that can't be moved, and these are one-time effects like the CCParticleExplosion shown in Figure 9–1. What's special about this effect is that it emits all its particles at once and then just stops emitting. All other particle effects run continuously, always creating new particles while those that have exceeded their lifetime are removed. The challenge in that situation is to balance the total number of particles that are on screen.

Figure 9–1. *The CCParticleExplosion is an example effect provided by cocos2d.*

Listing 9–1 shows the relevant methods used in the *ParticleEffects01* example project. By using the current particleType variable in the switch statement, the corresponding built-in particle effect is created. Note that a CCParticleSystem pointer is used to store the particles, so I only need to use the addChild code once at the end of the runEffect method. Every example particle effect is derived from CCParticleSystem.

Listing 9–1. *Using the Built-in Effects*

```
-(void) runEffect
{
        // remove any previous particle FX
        [self removeChildByTag:1 cleanup:YES];

        CCParticleSystem* system;

        switch (particleType)
        {
                case ParticleTypeExplosion:
                        system = [CCParticleExplosion node];
                        break;
                case ParticleTypeFire:
                        system = [CCParticleFire node];
                        break;
                case ParticleTypeFireworks:
                        system = [CCParticleFireworks node];
                        break;
                case ParticleTypeFlower:
                        system = [CCParticleFlower node];
                        break;
                case ParticleTypeGalaxy:
                        system = [CCParticleGalaxy node];
                        break;
```

```
            case ParticleTypeMeteor:
                    system = [CCParticleMeteor node];
                    break;
            case ParticleTypeRain:
                    system = [CCParticleRain node];
                    break;
            case ParticleTypeSmoke:
                    system = [CCParticleSmoke node];
                    break;
            case ParticleTypeSnow:
                    system = [CCParticleSnow node];
                    break;
            case ParticleTypeSpiral:
                    system = [CCParticleSpiral node];
                    break;
            case ParticleTypeSun:
                    system = [CCParticleSun node];
                    break;

            default:
                    // do nothing
                    break;
    }

    [self addChild: system z:1 tag:1];

    [label setString:NSStringFromClass([system class])];
}

-(void) setNextParticleType
{
    particleType++;
    if (particleType == ParticleTypes_MAX)
    {
            particleType = 0;
    }
}
```

> **NOTE:** The NSStringFromClass method is very helpful in this example for printing out the name of the class without having to enter dozens of matching strings. It's one of the cool runtime features of the Objective-C language that you're able to get a class's name as a string. Try to do that in C++ and you'll be biting your toenails.
>
> For gameplay code, the NSStringFromClass and related methods hardly play any role, but they're very helpful debugging and logging tools. You can find a complete list and description of these methods in Apple's Foundation Function Reference: http://developer.apple.com/mac/library/documentation/Cocoa/Reference/Foundation/Miscellaneous/Foundation_Functions/Reference/reference.html.

If you use one of these example effects in your own project, you might be shocked to see ugly, square pixels. Figure 9–2 shows this effect very clearly. This occurs because the built-in particle effects try to load a specific texture named *fire.png,* which is distributed with cocos2d-iphone in the *Resources/Images* folder. You can still create very good particle effects even without a texture, provided that the particle sizes remain fairly small. But to see the built-in particle effects as they were intended, you need to add the *fire.png* image to your Xcode project.

Figure 9–2. *If your example particle effects, like this CCParticleFireworks, display huge, square particles, you forgot to add the fire.png image to your Xcode project.*

Creating a Particle Effect the Hard Way

You can easily create your own subclass of the CCParticleSystem class. What's not so easy is creating a convincing particle effect with it, let alone one that comes close to what you originally envisioned. Following is the list of properties grouped by function that determine the particle system's look and behavior:

- emitterMode = gravity
    - gravity, centerOfGravity
    - radialAccel, radialAccelVar
    - speed, speedVar
    - tangentialAccel, tangentialAccelVar
- emitterMode = radius
    - startRadius, startRadiusVar, endRadius, endRadiusVar
    - rotatePerSecond, rotatePerSecondVar
- duration
- posVar
- positionType
- startSize, startSizeVar, endSize, endSizeVar
- angle, angleVar
- life, lifeVar

- emissionRate

- startColor, startColorVar, endColor, endColorVar

- blendFunc, blendAdditive

- texture

As you can imagine, there's a lot to tweak here. And, of course, there's a lot to understand in the first place about what each of these properties do. Let's start at the beginning, which requires creating a new class derived from CCParticleSystem.

Actually, you should subclass either from CCPointParticleSystem or from CCQuadParticleSystem. Point particles are a bit faster on first- and second-generation iOS devices but don't perform well on third- and fourth-generation devices like the iPhone 3GS, iPad, and iPhone 4. This is due to the change in CPU architecture. The ARMv7 CPU architecture used in third- and fourth-generation devices introduced optimizations and new features, such as a vector floating-point processor and a SIMD instruction set (NEON), and the CCQuadParticleSystem takes advantage of these.

If in doubt, use the CCQuadParticleSystem since it performs well on all devices and creates exactly the same visual effects. Or let cocos2d make that decision for you based on the build target. You'll see how in the *ParticleEffectSelfMade* file I've added to the *ParticleEffects02* project, shown in Listing 9–2.

Listing 9–2. *Subclassing from the Optimal Particle System Class*

```
#import <Foundation/Foundation.h>
#import "cocos2d.h"

// Depending on the targeted device the ParticleEffectSelfMade class will either derive
// from CCPointParticleSystem or CCQuadParticleSystem
@interface ParticleEffectSelfMade : ARCH_OPTIMAL_PARTICLE_SYSTEM
{
}
@end
```

The preprocessor definition ARCH_OPTIMAL_PARTICLE_SYSTEM, instead of an actual class name, is used to determine during compilation which of the two particle systems this class should subclass from. The definition in cocos2d is based on the processor architecture and results either in a CCQuadParticleSystem or CCPointParticleSystem:

```
// build each architecture with the optimal particle system
#ifdef __ARM_NEON__
        // armv7
        #define ARCH_OPTIMAL_PARTICLE_SYSTEM CCQuadParticleSystem
#elif __arm__ || TARGET_IPHONE_SIMULATOR
        // armv6 or simulator
        #define ARCH_OPTIMAL_PARTICLE_SYSTEM CCPointParticleSystem
#else
        #error(unknown architecture)
#endif
```

Now let's look at the implementation of the self-made particle effect, which uses all available properties. I'll attempt to explain each of them, but it's much better to see it for yourself and experiment with the parameters, so I encourage you to tweak the properties in this project. In the *ParticleEffects02* project (Listing 9–3), you'll also find comments describing each parameter in brief.

Listing 9–3. *Manually Setting a Particle System's Properties*

```
#import "ParticleEffectSelfMade.h"

@implementation ParticleEffectSelfMade
-(id) init
{
        return [self initWithTotalParticles:250];
}

-(id) initWithTotalParticles:(int)numParticles
{
        if ((self = [super initWithTotalParticles:numParticles]))
        {
                self.duration = kCCParticleDurationInfinity;
                self.emitterMode = kCCParticleModeGravity;

                // some properties must only be used with a specific emitterMode!
                if (self.emitterMode == kCCParticleModeGravity)
                {
                        self.gravity = CGPointMake(-50, -90);
                        self.centerOfGravity = CGPointMake(-15, 0);
                        self.radialAccel = -90;
                        self.radialAccelVar = 20;
                        self.tangentialAccel = 120;
                        self.tangentialAccelVar = 10;
                        self.speed = 15;
                        self.speedVar = 4;
                }
                else if (self.emitterMode == kCCParticleModeRadius)
                {
                        self.startRadius = 100;
                        self.startRadiusVar = 0;
                        self.endRadius = 10;
                        self.endRadiusVar = 0;
                        self.rotatePerSecond = -180;
                        self.rotatePerSecondVar = 0;
                }

                self.position = CGPointZero;
                self.posVar = CGPointZero;
                self.positionType = kCCPositionTypeFree;

                self.startSize = 40.0f;
                self.startSizeVar = 0.0f;
                self.endSize = kCCParticleStartSizeEqualToEndSize;
                self.endSizeVar = 0;

                self.angle = 0;
                self.angleVar = 0;

                self.life = 5.0f;
                self.lifeVar = 1.0f;

                self.emissionRate = 30;
```

```
            self.totalParticles = 250;

            startColor.r = 1.0f;
            startColor.g = 0.25f;
            startColor.b = 0.12f;
            startColor.a = 1.0f;
            startColorVar.r = 0.0f;
            startColorVar.g = 0.0f;
            startColorVar.b = 0.0f;
            startColorVar.a = 0.0f;
            endColor.r = 0.0f;
            endColor.g = 0.0f;
            endColor.b = 0.0f;
            endColor.a = 1.0f;
            endColorVar.r = 0.0f;
            endColorVar.g = 0.0f;
            endColorVar.b = 1.0f;
            endColorVar.a = 0.0f;

            self.blendFunc = (ccBlendFunc){GL_SRC_ALPHA, GL_DST_ALPHA};
            // or use this shortcut to set the blend func to: GL_SRC_ALPHA, GL_ONE
            //self.blendAdditive = YES;

            self.texture = [[CCTextureCache sharedTextureCache]
                                                addImage:@"fire.png"];
        }
        return self;
}
@end
```

Variance Properties

You'll notice that many properties have companion properties suffixed with Var. These are variance properties, and they determine the range of fuzzyness that is allowed for the corresponding property. Take, for example, the properties life = 5 and lifeVar = 1. These values mean that on average each particle will live for 5 seconds. The variance allows a range of 5-1 to 5+1. So each particle will get a random lifetime between 4 to 6 seconds.

If you don't want any variation, set the Var variable to 0. Variation is what gives particle effects their organic, fuzzy behavior and appearance. But variation can also be confusing when you design a new effect, so unless you have some experience I recommend starting out with a particle effect that has little or no variance.

Number of Particles

Let's get acquainted with particles by starting with the total number of particles in the particle effect, controlled by the totalParticles property. The totalParticles variable is usually set by the initWithTotalParticles method, but can be changed later. The number of particles has a direct impact both on the look of the effect and on performance.

```
-(id) init
{
        return [self initWithTotalParticles:250];
}
```

Use too few particles and you won't get a nice glow, but it may be sufficient to sprinkle a few stars around the player's head when he runs into a wall. Use too many particles and it might not be what you want either, as many particles are rendered on top of one another and possibly blended so you basically end up with a white blob. Furthermore, using too many particles easily kills your framerate. There's a reason why the Particle Designer tool won't let you create effects with more than 2,000 particles.

> **TIP:** In general, you should aim to achieve the desired effect with the smallest number of particles. Particle size also plays an important role—the smaller the size of individual particles, the better the performance will be.

Emitter Duration

The duration property determines how long particles will be emitted. If set to 2, it will create new particles for 2 seconds and then stop. It's that simple:

```
self.duration = 2.0f;
```

If you'd like the particle effect node to be automatically removed from its parent node once the particle system has stopped emitting particles and the last particles have vanished, set the autoRemoveOnFinish property to YES:

```
self.autoRemoveOnFinish = YES;
```

The autoRemoveOnFinish property is a convenience feature that is only meaningful if used in conjunction with particle systems that don't run infinitely. Cocos2d defines a constant kCCParticleDurationInfinity (equals: -1) for infinitely running particle effects. The majority of particle effects fall into that category.

```
self.duration = kCCParticleDurationInfinity;
```

Emitter Modes

There are two emitter modes: gravity and radius, controlled by the emitterMode property. These two modes create fundamentally different effects even if most of the parameters are the same, as you can see when you compare Figure 9–3 with Figure 9–4. Both modes use several exclusive properties that must not be set if they are not supported by the current mode, otherwise you'll receive a runtime exception from cocos2d like this:

```
ParticleEffects[6332:207] *** Terminating app due to uncaught exception
            'NSInternalInconsistencyException', reason: 'Particle Mode should be Radius'
```

Emitter Mode: Gravity

Gravity mode lets particles fly toward or away from a center point. Its strength is that it allows very dynamic, organic effects. You can set gravity mode with this line:

```
self.emitterMode = kCCParticleModeGravity;
```

Gravity mode uses the following exclusive properties, which can be used only when emitterMode is set to kCCParticleModeGravity:

```
self.centerOfGravity = CGPointMake(-15, 0);
self.gravity = CGPointMake(-50, -90);
self.radialAccel = -90;
self.radialAccelVar = 20;
self.tangentialAccel = 120;
self.tangentialAccelVar = 10;
self.speed = 15;
self.speedVar = 4;
```

The centerOfGravity determines the offset as a CGPoint from the node's position where new particles appear. The name is a bit misleading in that the actual center of gravity is the node's position, and centerOfGravity is an offset to that center of gravity. The gravity property then determines the speed with which particles accelerate in the x and y directions. For the center of gravity have any impact, the gravity of the particles shouldn't be too high and the centerOfGravity should not be offset too far. The above values give you a good working example that you can tweak.

The radialAccel property defines how fast particles accelerate the further they move away from the emitter. This parameter can also be negative, which makes particles slow down as they move away. The tangentialAccel property is similar in that it lets particles rotate around the emitter and speed up as they move away. Negative values let the particles spin clockwise, positive values spin them counterclockwise.

The speed property should be fairly obvious—it's simply the speed of the particles. It has no particular unit of measurement.

Figure 9–3 shows an example particle effect using gravity mode.

Figure 9–3. *The ParticleEffectSelfMade from the ParticleEffects02 project in gravity mode*

Emitter Mode: Radius

Radius mode causes particles to rotate in a circle. It also allows you to create spiral effects with particles either rushing inward or rotating outward. You set radius mode with this line:

```
self.emitterMode = kCCParticleModeRadius;
```

Like gravity mode, radius mode has exclusive properties, which can be used only when emitterMode is set to kCCParticleModeRadius:

```
self.startRadius = 100;
self.startRadiusVar = 0;
self.endRadius = 10;
self.endRadiusVar = 0;
self.rotatePerSecond = -180;
self.rotatePerSecondVar = 0;
```

The startRadius property determines how far away from the particle effect node's position the particles will be emitted. Likewise, the endRadius determines the distance from the node's position the particles will rotate toward. If you want to achieve a perfect circle effect, you can set endRadius to the same as the startRadius using this constant:

```
self.endRadius = kCCParticleStartRadiusEqualToEndRadius;
```

Using the rotatePerSecond property you can influence the direction the particles move and the speed with which they move, and thus the number of times they rotate around if startRadius and endRadius are different.

The same particle effect that was shown in Figure 9–3 using gravity mode is shown in Figure 9–4 using radius mode, and you'll notice how different it looks, despite all other properties—except for the exclusive ones—being the same. To test this, uncomment the following line in the ParticleEffects02 project:

```
//self.emitterMode = kCCParticleModeRadius;
```

Figure 9–4. *The very same effect using radius mode looks completely different.*

Particle Position

By moving the node, you also move the effect. But the effect also has a posVar property that determines the variance in the position where new particles will be created. By default, both are at the center of the node:

```
self.position = CGPointZero;
self.posVar = CGPointZero;
```

A very important aspect of particle positions is whether existing particles should move relative to the node's movement, or if they should not be influenced at all by the node's position. For example, if you have a particle effect that creates stars around your player-character's head, you would want the stars to follow the player as he moves around. You can achieve this effect by setting this property:

```
self.positionType = kCCPositionTypeGrouped;
```

On the other hand, if you want to set your player on fire and you want the particles to create a trail-like effect as the player moves around, you should set the positionType property like this:

```
self.positionType = kCCPositionTypeFree;
```

The free movement is best used with effects like steam, fire, engine exhaust smoke, and similar effects that move around with the object they are attached to, and should give the impression of not being connected to the object that emits these particles.

Particle Size

The size of particles is given in pixels using the startSize and endSize properties, which determine the size of the particles when they are emitted and how big they are when they are removed. The size of the particle gradually scales from startSize to endSize.

```
self.startSize = 40.0f;
self.startSizeVar = 0.0f;
self.endSize = kCCParticleStartSizeEqualToEndSize;
self.endSizeVar = 0;
```

The constant kCCParticleStartSizeEqualToEndSize can be used to ensure that the particle size does not change during a particle's lifetime.

Particle Direction

The direction in which particles are initially emitted is set with the angle property. A value of 0 means that particles will be emitted upward, but this is only true for gravity emitterMode. In radius emitterMode the angle property determines where on the startRadius the particles will be emitted; higher values will move the emission point counterclockwise along the radius.

```
self.angle = 0;
self.angleVar = 0;
```

Particle Lifetime

A particle's lifetime determines how many seconds it will take to transition from start to end, where the particle will simply fade out and disappear. The life property sets the lifetime of individual particles. Keep in mind that the longer particles live, the more particles will be onscreen at any given time. If the total number of particles is reached, no new particles will be spawned until some existing particles have died.

```
self.life = 5.0f;
self.lifeVar = 1.0f;
```

The emissionRate property directly influences how many particles are created per second. Together with the totalParticles property, it has a big impact on what the particle effect looks like.

```
self.emissionRate = 30;
self.totalParticles = 250;
```

In general, you will want to balance the emissionRate so that it matches the particle lifetime with the totalParticles allowed in the particle effect. You can do so by dividing totalParticles by life and set the result as the emissionRate:

```
self.emissionRate = self.totalParticles / self.life;
```

> **TIP:** By tweaking particle lifetime, the total number of particles allowed in the system, and the emissionRate, you can create burst effects by allowing the stream of particles to be frequently interrupted just because the number of particles on screen is limited and new particles are emitted relatively quickly. On the other hand, if you notice undesirable gaps in your particle stream, you need to either increase the number of allowed particles or preferably reduce the lifetime and/or emission rate. In that case you should use emissionRate = totalParticles / life.

Particle Color

Each particle can transition from a starting color to an end color, creating the vibrant colors particle effects are known for. You should at least set the startColor in a particle effect; otherwise the particles may not be visible at all since the default color is black. The colors are of type ccColor4F, a struct with four floating-point members: r, g, b, and a, corresponding to the colors red, green, and blue, as well as the alpha channel, which determines the color's opacity. The value range for each of these members goes from 0 to 1 with 1 being the full color. If you want a completely white particle color, you'd set all four r, g, b, and a members to 1.

```
startColor.r = 1.0f;
startColor.g = 0.25f;
startColor.b = 0.12f;
startColor.a = 1.0f;
startColorVar.r = 0.0f;
```

```
startColorVar.g = 0.0f;
startColorVar.b = 0.0f;
startColorVar.a = 0.0f;
endColor.r = 0.0f;
endColor.g = 0.0f;
endColor.b = 0.0f;
endColor.a = 1.0f;
endColorVar.r = 0.0f;
endColorVar.g = 0.0f;
endColorVar.b = 1.0f;
endColorVar.a = 0.0f;
```

Particle Blend Mode

Blending refers to the computation a particle's pixels go through before being displayed on screen. The property blendFunc takes a ccBlendFunc struct as input which provides the source and destination blend modes:

```
self.blendFunc = (ccBlendFunc){GL_SRC_ALPHA, GL_DST_ALPHA};
```

Blending works by taking the red, green, blue, and alpha of the source image (the particle) and mixing it with the colors of any images that are already on screen when the particle is rendered. In effect, the particle blends in a certain way with its background, and blendFunc determines how much and what colors of the source image are blended how much and with which colors of the background.

The blendFunc property has a very profound effect on how particles are displayed. By using a combination of the following blend modes for both source and target you can create rather bizarre effects, or simply cause the effect to render as black squares. There's lots of room for experimentation.

- GL_ZERO
- GL_ONE
- GL_SRC_COLOR
- GL_ONE_MINUS_SRC_COLOR
- GL_SRC_ALPHA
- GL_ONE_MINUS_SRC_ALPHA
- GL_DST_ALPHA
- GL_ONE_MINUS_DST_ALPHA

You'll find more information on the OpenGL blend modes and details about the blend calculations in the OpenGL ES documentation at www.khronos.org/opengles/documentation/opengles1_0/html/glBlendFunc.html.

The source and target blend modes GL_SRC_ALPHA and GL_ONE are frequently combined to create additive blending, resulting in very bright or even white colors where many particles are drawn on top of each other:

```
self.blendFunc = (ccBlendFunc){GL_SRC_ALPHA, GL_ONE};
```

Alternatively, you can simply set the blendAdditive property to YES, which is the same as setting blendFunc to GL_SRC_ALPHA and GL_ONE:

```
self.blendAdditive = YES;
```

The normal blend mode is set using GL_SRC_ALPHA and GL_ONE_MINUS_SRC_ALPHA which creates transparent particles:

```
self.blendFunc = (ccBlendFunc){GL_SRC_ALPHA, GL_ONE_MINUS_SRC_ALPHA};
```

Particle Texture

Without a texture, all particles would be flat, colored squares, as in Figure 9–2. To use a texture for a particle effect, provide one using the CCTextureCache method addImage, which returns the CCTexture2D for the given image file:

```
self.texture = [[CCTextureCache sharedTextureCache] addImage:@"fire.png"];
```

Particle textures look best if they are cloudlike and roughly spherical. It's often detrimental to the particle effect if the texture has high-contrast areas, resembling a particular shape or form, like the *redcross.png* from the Shoot 'em Up game. This makes it easier to see individual particles because they don't blend too well with each other. Some effects can use this to their advantage, like the aforementioned stars circling the player's head.

The most important aspect of particle textures is that the image must be at most 64x64 pixels in size. The smaller the texture size, the better it is for the performance of the particle effect.

Introducing the Particle Designer

The Particle Designer is an interactive tool for creating particle effects for cocos2d and iOS OpenGL applications. You can download the trial version at http://particledesigner.71squared.com.

This is an invaluable tool that will save you a lot of time creating particle effects. Its power is that you can immediately see what happens onscreen when you change a particle effect's properties. By default, the Particle Designer's user interface shows a visual list of particle effects. To edit a particular effect, select it and switch to the **Emitter Config** view (Figure 9–5) by either double-clicking it or clicking on the **Emitter Config** button in the upper right corner.

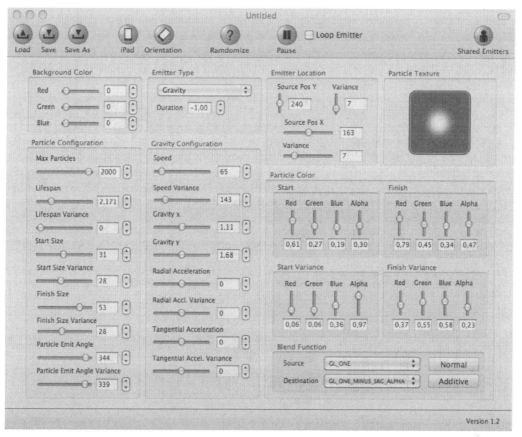

Figure 9–5. *Particle Designer is full of properties you can tweak interactively. A separate window (not pictured) shows the effect as you edit it.*

You should recognize these parameters from the description of the self-made particle effect properties. There are only few properties that are not available and can't be edited in Particle Designer. One is the positionType and another is the endRadiusVar property for the radius emitter mode. The latter means that you can't create particle effects that rotate outward in radius mode. But you can always load a Particle Designer effect and then tweak it in code by overriding certain properties. This is a minor nuisance compared to actually seeing onscreen how your effect changes as you move the sliders.

The only unusual control is the Particle Texture. There is no button to load an image and double-clicking the field doesn't do anything either. The trick here is that the Particle Texture box only accepts images that are dragged and dropped onto it. Just drag any image from Finder over to this box and the box will turn green, signaling that it will accept that image. Once you drop the image, it will be used by the particle effect. Note that Particle Designer will warn you if you use an image that is larger than 64x64 pixels. It will use the image anyway, but will scale the image down to 64x64 pixels, regardless of its original aspect ratio.

The Particle Designer preview window in Figure 9–6 looks just like the iPhone Simulator. It can also be set to the iPad screen size, and the orientation can be changed by clicking the **iPad/iPhone** and **Orientation** buttons in Particle Designer's menu bar, to the right of the **Load**, **Save**, and **Save As** buttons. By clicking and dragging inside the preview window, you can move the particle effect around, which helps to see how the effect might look on moving objects.

Notice that the Background Color settings are not part of the actual effect. They will change the background color of the preview window. This is useful if your game has bright colors and you want to design a dark or dim effect and still be able to see what you're doing.

Figure 9–6. *The Particle Designer has a preview window that looks like the iPhone Simulator. You can also set it to the iPad screen size and change its orientation. If you click and drag inside the screen you can even move the particle effect around to see what it might look like on moving objects.*

If you lack inspiration, you can always make use of the **Ramdomize** button. You can also ponder about the meaning of the word "ramdomize," which is how it's spelled in the Particle Designer. The Urban Dictionary tells me that ramdom is a cooler form of random. So I'm guessing the developers just thought their randomizer to be extra cool. Well, it's definitely inspiring even though it doesn't randomize all of the available properties. For example, **Ramdomize** will never change the Emitter Type, the Emitter Location, and many Emitter Type-specific parameters.

Once you found your inspiration, you'll want to slide the sliders and watch what happens in the preview window. Take your time and tweak an effect until you like it. Careful, though, it's a very captivating, even mesmerizing, activity and you'll easily find yourself making new particle effects just for the fun of it.

> **CAUTION:** Be careful when designing particle effects! First of all, keep in mind that your game has to calculate and render a lot of other things, too. If the effect you're currently designing runs at 60 FPS in Particle Designer's preview window, that doesn't mean it won't kill your framerate when you use it in your game. Always test new particle effects in your game and keep an eye on the framerate. Also make sure to run these tests on a device! Your game's performance in the iPhone/iPad Simulator is often misleading and thus must be regarded as completely irrelevant. The same goes for the Particle Designer preview window.

Using Particle Designer Effects

I'm assuming that, hours later, you've made the perfect particle effect and now you'd like to use that in cocos2d. I made mine and the first step is to save the particle effect. When you click on the **Save** or **Save As** button in Particle Designer, you'll be presented with a dialog as shown in Figure 9–7.

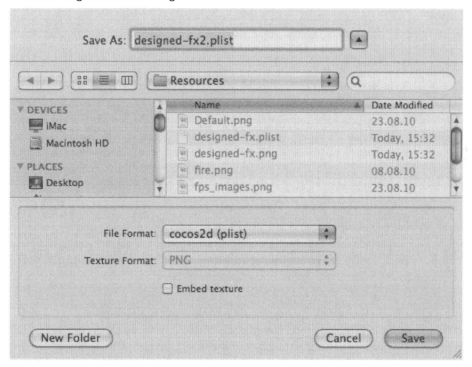

Figure 9–7. *Saving a particle effect from Particle Designer requires you set the File Format to cocos2d. Embedding the texture into the plist file is optional.*

For the saved particle effect to be usable by cocos2d, you must set the **File Format** to **cocos2d (plist)**. You can also check the **Embed texture** box, which will save the texture into the plist file. The benefit is that you only have to add the plist file to your Xcode project;

the downside is that you then can't change the effect's texture without loading the particle effect into Particle Designer.

After saving the effect, you have to add the effect plist and, if you didn't embed the texture, the effect's PNG file to your Xcode project's Resources group. In the *ParticleEffects03* project, I've added both variants, one effect with a separate PNG texture and another effect that has the texture embedded in the plist file.

Listing 9–4 shows how I modified the runEffect method to load the Particle Designer effects.

Listing 9–4. *Using a Particle Effect Created with Particle Designer*

```
-(void) runEffect
{
        // remove any previous particle FX
        [self removeChildByTag:1 cleanup:YES];

        CCParticleSystem* system;

        switch (particleType)
        {
                case ParticleTypeDesignedFX:
                        system = [CCQuadParticleSystem particleWithFile:@"fx1.plist"];
                        break;
                case ParticleTypeDesignedFX2:
                        system = [CCQuadParticleSystem particleWithFile:@"fx2.plist"];
                        system.positionType = kCCPositionTypeFree;
                        break;
                case ParticleTypeSelfMade:
                        system = [ParticleEffectSelfMade node];
                        break;

                default:
                        // do nothing
                        break;
        }

        CGSize winSize = [[CCDirector sharedDirector] winSize];
        system.position = CGPointMake(winSize.width / 2, winSize.height / 2);
        [self addChild:system z:1 tag:1];

        [label setString:NSStringFromClass([system class])];
}
```

You initialize a CCParticleSystem with a Particle Designer effect by using the particleWithFile method and providing the particle effect's plist file as parameter. In this case, I chose a CCQuadParticleSystem since it performs well on all iOS devices. You can also leave this decision to cocos2d by using the ARCH_OPTIMAL_PARTICLE_SYSTEM keyword in place of an actual class name:

```
system = [ARCH_OPTIMAL_PARTICLE_SYSTEM particleWithFile:@"fx1.plist"];
```

> **CAUTION:** Particle Designer effects must be initialized with either `CCQuadParticleSystem` or `CCPointParticleSystem`. Even though `CCParticleSystem`, the parent class for the aforementioned subclasses, implements the `particleWithFile` method, it won't display anything unless you use one of the subclasses, either Quad or Point particle systems, when loading Particle Designer effects.

As a side note, I moved the two lines that position the particle system node at the center of the screen outside of the `switch` case to avoid duplicating that code. As I mentioned before, it's always good practice to minimize the amount of code duplication, and this is one area where I've seen developers simply copying and pasting what's already there.

Sharing Particle Effects

What's very cool about Particle Designer is that you can share your creations with other Particle Designer users. From the Particle Designer menu, simply choose **Share** and then **Share Emitter** to open a dialog that lets you enter a title and description for your particle effect, as seen in Figure 9–8.

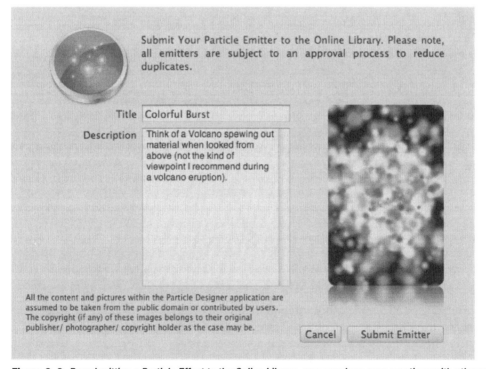

Figure 9–8. *By submitting a Particle Effect to the Online Library, you can share your creations with other users.*

In Figure 9–9, you can see the effect I just submitted in the lower right corner.

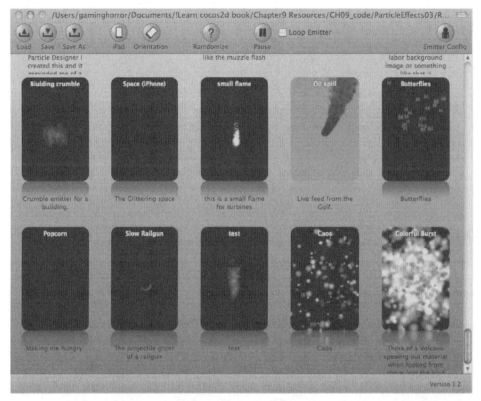

Figure 9–9. *The submitted effect quickly appears in the Online Library. The effect I just submitted is the one in the bottom right corner. Apparently my description was too long to fit in the display area.*

Shared particle effects may not always be perfect for your requirements, but they often provide good starting points for your own effects. They help you achieve the desired effect much faster and, at the very least, they can be an inspiration. I encourage you to scroll through the list of effects and try out as many as you can to gain a good sense of what's possible, what looks good, and what just doesn't work.

Shoot 'em Up with Particle Effects

I'd love to see some of these effects in the game! Let's take the Shoot 'em Up game to a new level. You'll find the results in this chapter's *ShootEmUp04* project, and in Figure 9–10.

In the EnemyEntity class, the gotHit method is the perfect place to add destructive particle explosions, as Listing 9–5 shows. I decided the boss monster should have its own particle effect, mostly because it's so big. And purple.

Listing 9–5. *Adding an Explosion Effect to the Shoot 'em Up Game*

```
-(void) gotHit
{
        hitPoints--;
        if (hitPoints <= 0)
```

```
    {
            self.visible = NO;

            // Play a particle effect when the enemy was destroyed
            CCParticleSystem* system;

            if (type == EnemyTypeBoss)
            {
                    system = [ARCH_OPTIMAL_PARTICLE_SYSTEM
                                            particleWithFile:@"fx-explosion2.plist"];
            }
            else
            {
                    system = [ARCH_OPTIMAL_PARTICLE_SYSTEM
                                            particleWithFile:@"fx-explosion.plist"];
            }

            // Set some parameters that can't be set in Particle Designer
            system.positionType = kCCPositionTypeFree;
            system.autoRemoveOnFinish = YES;
            system.position = self.position;

            [[GameScene sharedGameScene] addChild:system];
    }
}
```

The particle effects *fx-explosion.plist* and *fx-explosion2.plist* must be added as resources to the Xcode project. The particle system is initialized as before. Since the particle effect should and must be independent from the enemy that creates it, a few preparations are necessary. First, the autoRemoveOnFinish flag is set to YES so that the effect automatically removes itself. This works because both explosions run only for a short time. The effect also needs the current position of the enemy so that it's displayed at the correct position.

I add the particle effect to the GameScene because the enemy itself can't display the particle effect. To start, it's invisible, then it might be respawned very soon, which would interfere with the particle effect. But most importantly, all EnemyEntity objects are added to a CCSpriteBatchNode, which does not allow you to add anything but CCSprite objects. If the particle effect were added to the EnemyEntity object, a runtime exception would be inevitable.

As you play the game with the new particle effects, you may notice that the first time one of these effects displays, the gameplay stops for a short moment. That's because cocos2d is loading the particle effect's texture—a rather slow process, whether the texture is embedded into the plist, as in this case, or provided as a separate texture. To avoid that I've added a preloading mechanism to the GameScene: the init method now calls the preloadParticleEffect method for each particle effect used during gameplay:

```
// To preload the textures, play each effect once off-screen
[self preloadParticleEffects:@"fx-explosion.plist"];
[self preloadParticleEffects:@"fx-explosion2.plist"];
```

The preloadParticleEffects method simply creates the particle effect. Because the returned object is an autorelease object, its memory will be freed automatically. But the texture it loads will still be in the CCTextureCache.

```
-(void) preloadParticleEffects:(NSString*)particleFile
{
        [ARCH_OPTIMAL_PARTICLE_SYSTEM particleWithFile:particleFile];
}
```

If you chose not to embed the texture inside the particle effect plist file, you can preload the particle effect textures simply by calling the CCTextureCache addImage method:

```
[[CCTextureCache sharedTextureCache] addImage:particleFile];
```

Figure 9–10. *I killed the boss and I can't see a darn thing. But those particles are so beautiful!*

Conclusion

This chapter was truly a visual joyride! The stock effects provided by cocos2d give a good indication of what the particle effect is able to deliver. They're quick and easy to use.

But it was also excruciating to create a particle effect in source code. There are so many properties to tweak; some are exclusive to specific emitter modes; some have misleading names and they aren't exactly straightforward to figure out. With the explanation for each property, however, you should now have a good understanding how a particle effect is put together and what the most important parameters are.

We then saw how particle effects can shine with Particle Designer. This tool is extremely helpful—and lots of fun—to work with it. Suddenly, when you can move sliders and see the results immediately onscreen, it changes your whole view on particle effects, and even more so since you can share your creations with others, and experiment with other designer's effects.

Finally the Shoot 'em Up game got a makeover and now plays particle explosions when enemies are destroyed. This makes for a much more lively game.

In the next chapter I'll set the Shoot 'em Up game aside for a bit to tell you all you need to know about tilemaps.

Chapter 10

Working with Tilemaps

In the next two chapters I'll introduce you to the world of tile-based games. Whether you've been playing games since the age of classic role-playing games like Ultima or you've just recently joined your Facebook friends in Farmville, I'm sure you've already played a game that uses the tilemap concept for displaying its graphics.

In tilemap games, the graphics consist of a small number of images, called *tiles*, that align with each other; placing them on a grid allows us to build rather convincing game worlds. The concept is very attractive because it conserves memory as compared to drawing the whole world as individual textures, while still allowing a lot of variety.

This chapter will introduce general tilemap concepts by using the simplest tilemaps of all: *orthogonal tilemaps*. They are built from square or nonsquare rectangular tiles, and typically display the world in a top-down fashion. For example, the Ultima series has used tilemaps for a long time. The Ultima 1 through 5 series used square tiles and a top-down view; Ultima 6 and 7 then switched to a semiisometric perspective, but still used orthogonal tilemaps. Ultima 8: Pagan, is the only part in the series that uses an isometric tilemap to create a much more immersive game world. Isometric tilemaps are discussed in the next chapter.

I will also explain how to scroll a tilemap, how to keep it centered on a specific tile, and how to keep the screen within the tilemap area. The scrolling will be done by touching the tile you'd like to center the camera on, which means that you'll also learn how to determine which tile was touched.

What Is a Tilemap?

Tilemaps are 2D game worlds made of individual tiles. You can create large world maps with just a handful of images that all have the same dimensions. This means tilemaps are very efficient at conserving memory for large maps. It's no wonder that they first appeared in the early days of computer games. Many classic role-playing games used square tiles to create fantastic fantasy worlds. These games looked a bit like the tilemap in Figure 10–1.

Editing tilemaps is usually done with an editor, and the one directly supported by cocos2d is called Tiled (Qt) Map Editor. Tiled is free, open source, and allows you to edit both orthogonal and isometric tilemaps with multiple layers. Tiled also enables you to add trigger areas and objects, as well as define tile properties that you can use in code to determine what type of tile it is.

> **NOTE:** Qt refers to Nokia's Qt framework, on which Tiled is built. Since there is also a defunct Java version of Tiled, it's important to make this differentiation by writing Tiled (Qt). The Java version is no longer updated but contains a few extra features that may be worth checking out. But in this and the following chapter I will be using and discussing Tiled (Qt).

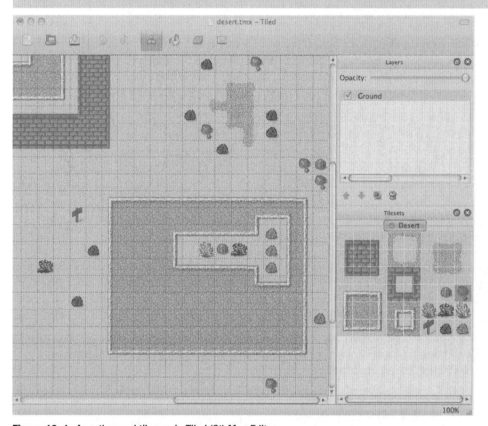

Figure 10–1. *An orthogonal tilemap in Tiled (Qt) Map Editor*

Over time, the square image tilemaps improved with the addition of tilemaps with transition tiles. For example, instead of placing a water tile next to a grass tile you can create a much smoother transition by adding mixed tiles (in this case, a tile that contains water on one side and grass on the other, with a shoreline in the middle). Without this feature, you would have to create a lot more tiles and carefully consider which tiles could transition to other tiles, to keep the number of tile variations in check. The result is worth the extra effort.

The tilemap in Figure 10–1 uses a good number of transitioning tiles. The Desert tileset has only four floor tile variations: desert, gravel stone (in the lower half of the tilemap), brick stone (in the upper-left area), and dirt (in the upper-right area). For three of these tiles (all except desert), there are 12 additional tiles for each to be able to transition them to the desert ground tile.

Tiles actually don't need to be square; you can create orthogonal tilemaps from rectangular images as well. These are most often used by Asian role-playing games, such as Dragon Quest 4 through 6. While still using an orthogonal perspective, it allowed the designers to create objects that are seemingly taller than wide. This creates and illusion of depth. Isometric tilemaps take this one step further by rotating the perspective by 45 degrees. By creating tiles in a seemingly 3D fashion, the game world gains visual depth. Isometric tilemaps are very effective in tricking our minds into believing that there really is a third dimension in this world, even though all of the images are still essentially flat. Isometric tilemaps achieve this impression of depth by using tile images that are drawn as diamond shapes (rhombuses) and allowing tiles closer to the viewer to draw over the tiles further away from the viewer. See Figure 10–2 for an example of an isometric tilemap.

Figure 10–2. *An isometric tilemap in Tiled (Qt) Map Editor*

Isometric maps prove that tilemaps don't need to be flat-looking. You can even achieve similar effects with square tilemaps, if the individual tiles are designed to be placed seamlessly on top of each other. For that reason, Tiled supports multiple layers of tiles to create a very convincing 3D look, as shown in Figure 10–3. The layering or stacking of tiles can also be used with isometric maps, as many of the Farmville fan videos show to great effect. Several Farmville users have used nothing but crop fields to build houses and even tall skyscrapers. The trick is to make use of an optical illusion that's very easy to achieve with isometric tilemaps.

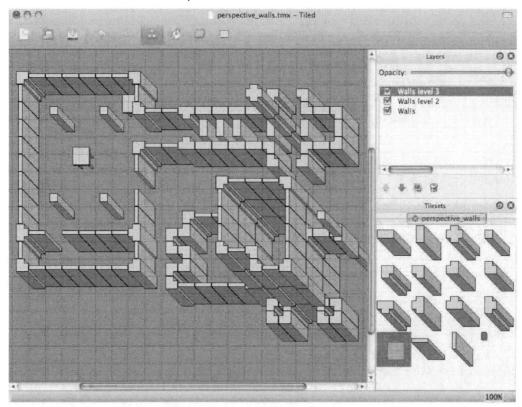

Figure 10–3. *A square tilemap designed to be used in multiple layers to give the impression of depth. This tilemap style has come to fame by Ultima 7.*

Preparing Images with Zwoptex

In the *Tilemap01* project for this chapter you'll find a number of square tile images in the *Resources/individual tile images* folder. Add all of these tile images to Zwoptex and set the Canvas size to 256×256 pixels—that's more than enough. Click the **Apply** button to arrange the tiles as Zwoptex sees fit. The result should look similar to Figure 10–4.

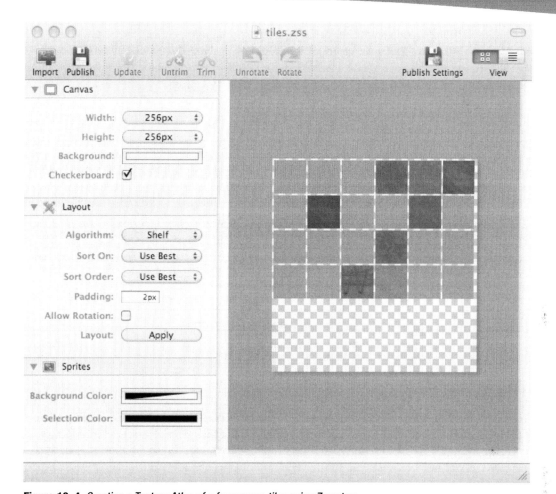

Figure 10–4. *Creating a Texture Atlas of a few square tiles using Zwoptex*

Notice that Zwoptex arranged the tiles in random order. Unfortunately, at the time of this writing, in Zwoptex v1.0.4 there is no way to arrange the tiles by name. If that were possible, the layout would match the file names on disk. This feature has been requested by a number of Zwoptex users, so sorting by name may be implemented in a future version. Check whether the version of Zwoptex you're using supports that feature, and if it does, take advantage of it by editing your tiles as individual images, and then use Zwoptex to create a sorted tileset from your tile images.

In the meantime, you might get by with these randomly sorted images. However, there is no guarantee that they will all stay in the same place when you add or remove tiles and click **Apply** again. Zwoptex may decide seemingly at random to reorder the position of the tiles. In use with the CCSpriteBatchNode, that poses no problems at all, however, since you refer to individual images by name.

For Tiled Map Editor, on the other hand, it is crucial that the tiles stay at the same position, since Tiled refers to individual tiles in the tileset by position and offset only.

That means that if tiles in the texture shift places, the tilemap in Tiled using this tileset texture will look completely different. The tilemap still refers to the same tile positions in the tileset, but instead of a grass tile there could now be a water tile at that position, for example.

The fix to this is to add empty tiles to fill a reasonably sized tileset texture (or at least as many as you need). The purpose of the empty tiles in Figure 10–3 is simply to give you a canvas to draw on. The idea is to add all the empty tiles to Zwoptex to create a tileset texture containing evenly spaced but empty tiles. Then you can close Zwoptex, and you won't need it again, since you can simply open the tilemap Texture Atlas in any image-editing program and draw over the nontransparent parts of the image. Zwoptex simply helps with the initial positioning of tiles in the tileset texture.

If you're a better artist than I am, you might also consider creating such a tilemap in an image program directly. What you need to make sure of is that the background of the image is transparent. This will avoid visual glitches at the borders of tiles when they are displayed in the game. Also, all the tiles need to be of the same width and height, and the space between individual tiles must be constant.

Doing that manually in an image program would have taken me more time than just creating a number of empty tiles and letting Zwoptex align them for me. It needs to be done only once, and it's quite convenient that way.

Tiled Map Editor

The most popular tool to create tilemaps for use with cocos2d is Tiled Map Editor. The TMX files it creates are natively supported by the cocos2d game engine. Tiled Map Editor is available for free, and at the time of this writing, version 0.5 is the most current. You can download Tiled from its home page, at www.mapeditor.org.

If you would like to support the development of Tiled, consider making a donation to the project's developer, Thorbjørn Lindeijer. You can donate to the project here: http://sourceforge.net/donate/index.php?group_id=161281.

Creating a New Tilemap

The first thing after you've downloaded, extracted, installed, and started Tiled is to go to the **View** menu and check both the **Tilesets** and **Layers** items. This will show the list of layers and the current tileset on the right side of the Tiled window. Then choose **File ➤ New** to create a new tilemap. This will bring up the New Map dialog pictured in Figure 10–5.

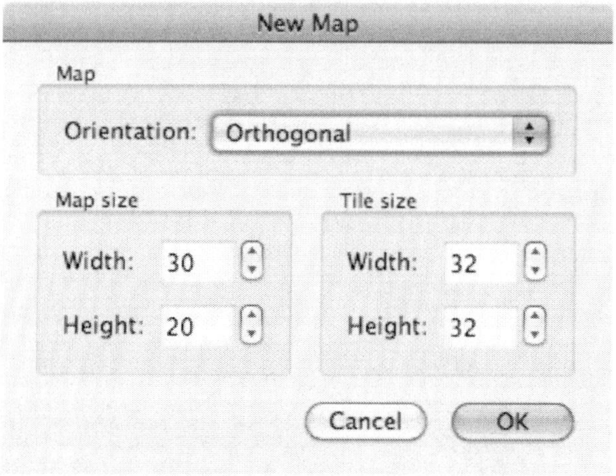

Figure 10–5. *Creating a new tilemap in Tiled*

Currently, Tiled supports orthogonal (rectangular) tilemaps as well as isometric tilemaps. The map size is given in tiles, not pixels. In this case, the new map will be 30×20 tiles, with the tile images having 32×32-pixel dimensions. It's crucial that the tile size matches the size of your tile images, or they will not align.

The new map will be completely empty, and there's no tileset loaded that you can draw from. You can add a tileset by selecting **Map ➤ New Tileset** from Tiled's menu. This will open the **New Tileset** dialog (shown in Figure 10–6), where you can browse for the proper tileset image. A tileset is just a name for an image containing multiple tiles with equal spacing, so you could also call it a Texture Atlas containing only images of the same size.

I will use the *dg_grounds32.png* tileset. These tiles were drawn by David E. Gervais and published under the Creative Commons License, meaning you are free to share and remix his work as long as you give credit to him. You can download more of his tilesets from this web site: `http://pousse.rapiere.free.fr/tome/index.htm`.

In Figure 10–6, I have already added the *dg_grounds32.png* tileset image by locating it through the **Browse** button in the *Resources* folder of the *Tilemap01* project. If you check the "**Use transparent color**" check box, transparent areas will simply be drawn in pink (the default color). You can leave this box unchecked for now since the tiles in use have no transparent areas.

The tile width and height are the dimensions of individual tiles in the tileset. They should match the tile size of 32×32 pixels, which you set when creating the new map. The **Margin** and **Spacing** settings determine how many pixels away from the image border the tiles are, and how many pixels of space are between them. In case of the *dg_grounds32.png*, there is no spacing at all, so I set both values to 0.

If you had your tiles aligned by Zwoptex to create a tileset texture, you must enter the pixel-padding value used by Zwoptex in the **Margin** and **Spacing** fields. By default Zwoptex uses a padding of 2 pixels.

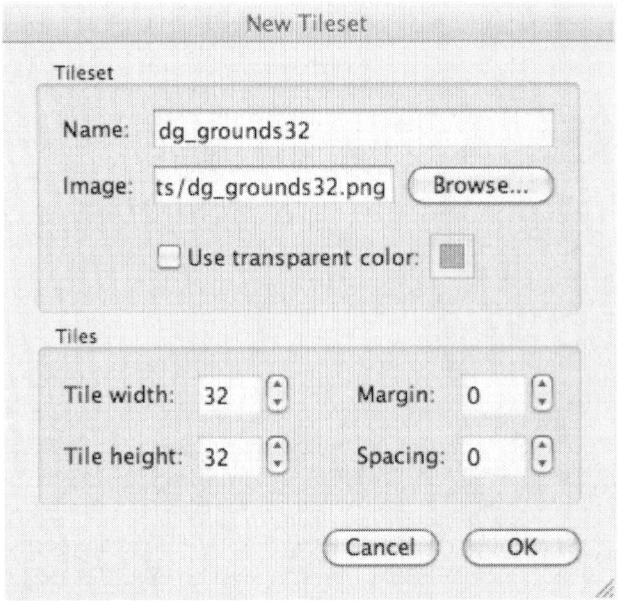

Figure 10–6. *Creating a new tileset from an image file*

When loading a new tileset image, make sure the tileset image is already located in your project's resource folder. You should then also make sure to save the tilemap TMX file to the same folder where the tileset image used by the tilemap is located. Otherwise, cocos2d might fail to load the tileset image; trying to load the TMX file will then cause a runtime exception. The culprit is that TMX files reference the tileset image relative to the location the TMX file is saved to. If they are not both in the same folder, cocos2d may be unable to find the image because the folder structure is not preserved when the app is installed in the simulator or on the device.

> **TIP:** TMX files are plain XML files, so you might want to peek inside if you're curious. If you see the image file referenced with parts of a path, then cocos2d is unlikely to load the referenced image file. The image reference should list just the image file name without any path components, like so: `<image source="tiles.png"/>`.

Designing a Tilemap

With the tileset loaded, you'll be faced with a blank map, an invitation for your creativity to come up with great ideas for a tilemap. What's even better is to get rid of the blank tilemap as the very first step. It's very helpful to start the tilemap with a default floor tile. I selected the **Bucket Fill tool** and picked a bright grass tile so that my tilemap is now a lush meadow—sort of. You can see it in Figure 10–7.

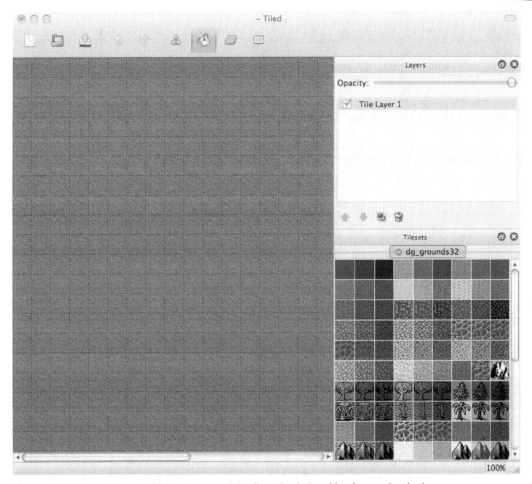

Figure 10–7. *An empty map with the dg_grounds32 tileset loaded, waiting for your inspiration*

Tiled uses four modes for editing the tilemap, indicated by the four rightmost icons on the toolbar. They are **Stamp Brush** (hotkey B), which allows you to draw the current selection in the tileset; **Bucket Fill** (hotkey F), which fills areas of connected, identical tiles; **Eraser** (hotkey E), which erases tiles; and **Rectangular Select** (hotkey R), with which you can select a range of tiles and then copy and paste the selection.

You'll spend most of your time picking a tile from the tileset and drawing it onto the tilemap with the **Stamp Brush** selected. Placing tile by tile you'll create your tile-based game world.

You can also edit tiles in multiple layers by adding more layers in the Layers view. From the menu, choose **Layer → Add Tile Layer** to create a new layer for tiles. Using multiple tile layers allows you to switch out areas of the tilemap in cocos2d. In the *TileMap01* example project, I'm using it to switch parts of the map between winter and summer.

You can also choose **Layer** → **Add Object Layer** to add a layer for adding objects. Objects in Tiled are simply rectangles that you can draw and later retrieve in code. You can use them to trigger certain events—for example, to spawn monsters when the player enters an area. I've added a few at random to show you how to work with them in cocos2d code.

Some functionality in Tiled is hidden in context menus. For example, the rectangle objects I just mentioned can be deleted by right-clicking them in the Tilemap view and selecting **Remove Object**. Note that you also need to have the object layer highlighted in the Layers list view for the context menu to appear.

You can also edit properties of objects, layers, and tiles by right-clicking them and clicking the corresponding **Properties** menu item. One use for that is to create an additional tile layer by using **Layer** ➤ **Add Tile Layer**. This will be a layer used to tell the game about certain properties of tiles. I called it GameEventLayer. With GameEventLayer selected, choose Map ➤ New Tileset and load *game-events.png* from the same folder as *dg_grounds32.png*. It only contains three tiles. Right-click one, select **Tile Properties**, and add the isWater property, as shown in Figure 10–8.

> **CAUTION:** Keep in mind that each tile layer creates some overhead, especially if you set tiles in multiple layers at the same location. This will cause both layers to be drawn and can adversely affect the game's performance. It is recommended to keep the number of tile layers to a minimum. Two to four tile layers should be sufficient for most games. Be sure to have a look at your game's frame rate on the device after you have added a new tile layer and drawn on it.

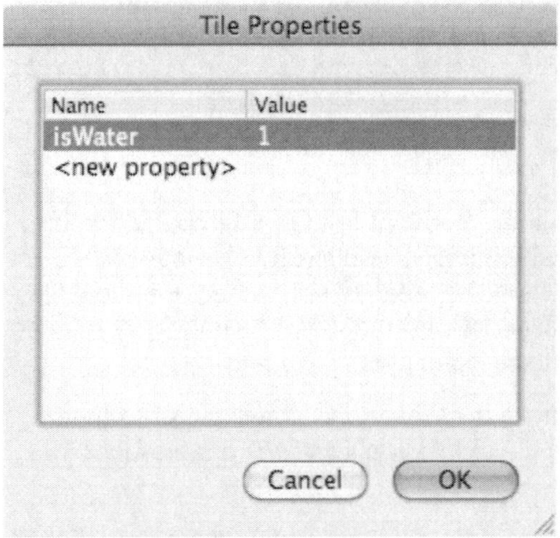

Figure 10–8. *Adding a tile property*

You can then draw over the tilemap using the tile to whose properties you just added the isWater property. Ideally, draw it over the river. If you want to see the tiles underneath what you're drawing, you can use the **Opacity** slider for the GameEventLayer in the Layers view. Or, click the layer's check box to hide or unhide everything drawn on this particular layer.

Just be sure to enable all layer check boxes before saving the TMX tilemap. Cocos2d does not load layers that are unchecked in Tiled.

When you're done with this, you should have a tilemap similar to the one in Figure 10–9. Save it in the same *TileMap01 Resources* folder where the tileset images are.

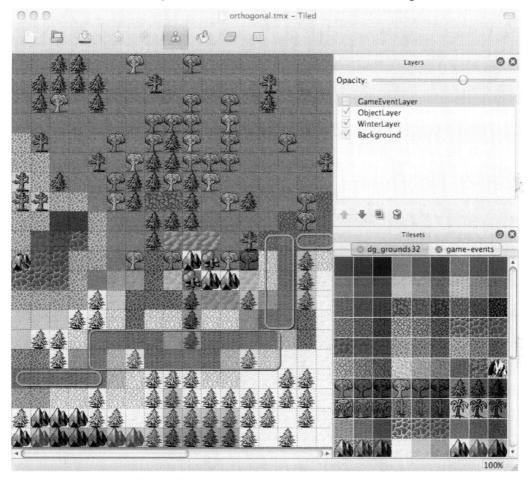

Figure 10–9. *A completed tilemap with three tile layers and a object layer*

Using Orthogonal Tilemaps with Cocos2d

To use TMX tilemaps with cocos2d, you first have to add the TMX file and the accompanying tileset image files as resources to your Xcode project. In the *TileMap01* project I added *orthogonal.tmx* along with the tilesets *dg_grounds32.png* and *game-events.png*. Loading and displaying the tilemap is very straightforward; the following code is from the `init` method of the `TileMapLayer` class:

```
CCTMXTiledMap* tileMap = [CCTMXTiledMap tiledMapWithTMXFile:@"orthogonal.tmx"];
[self addChild:tileMap z:-1 tag:TileMapNode];

CCTMXLayer* eventLayer = [tileMap layerNamed:@"GameEventLayer"];
eventLayer.visible = NO;
```

The CCTMXTiledMap class is initialized with the name of the TMX file and then added as a child with a tag so that it can be retrieved later. A member variable would of course work just as well. The next step is to retrieve the CCTMXLayer used for game events by using the layerNamed method and providing the name of the layer as it was named in Tiled. Because the game events layer will be used only as hints for code to determine properties of certain tiles, this layer should not be rendered at all. Note that if you uncheck the layer in Tiled, it won't be displayed, but you will also not have access to its tiles and tile properties either.

If you run the project now, you'll see a tilemap just like in Figure 10–10.

Figure 10–10. *The orthogonal tilemap in the iPhone Simulator*

Right now you can't do anything with the tilemap, but I'd like to change that. Moving on to the *TileMap02* project, I'd like to be able to find the isWater tiles. I've added the ccTouchesBegan method, as shown in Listing 10–1, in order to determine the tile that the player is touching.

Listing 10–1. *Determining a Tile's Properties*

```
-(void) ccTouchesBegan:(NSSet *)touches withEvent:(UIEvent *)event
{
        CCNode* node = [self getChildByTag:TileMapNode];
        NSAssert([node isKindOfClass:[CCTMXTiledMap class]], @"not a CCTMXTiledMap");
        CCTMXTiledMap* tileMap = (CCTMXTiledMap*)node;

        // Get the position in tile coordinates from the touch location
        CGPoint touchLocation = [self locationFromTouches:touches];
        CGPoint tilePos = [self tilePosFromLocation:touchLocation tileMap:tileMap];

        // Check if the touch was on water (e.g., tiles with isWater property)
        bool isTouchOnWater = NO;

        CCTMXLayer* eventLayer = [tileMap layerNamed:@"GameEventLayer"];
        int tileGID = [eventLayer tileGIDAt:tilePos];
```

```
    if (tileGID != 0)
    {
            NSDictionary* properties = [tileMap propertiesForGID:tileGID];
            if (properties)
            {
                    NSString* isWaterProperty = [properties valueForKey:@"isWater"];
                    isTouchOnWater = ([isWaterProperty boolValue] == YES);
            }
    }

    // Decide what to do depending on where the touch was
    if (isTouchOnWater)
    {
            [[SimpleAudioEngine sharedEngine] playEffect:@"alien-sfx.caf"];
    }
    else
    {
            // Get the winter layer and toggle its visibility
            CCTMXLayer* winterLayer = [tileMap layerNamed:@"WinterLayer"];
            winterLayer.visible = !winterLayer.visible;
    }
}
```

The CCTMXTiledMap is retrieved as usual. The location of the touch is first converted into screen coordinates and then used to retrieve the tilePos containing the indices into the tilemap at that specific screen location. I'll get to the tilePosFromLocation method in a minute. For now just know that it returns the index of the touched tile.

At this point I'd like to introduce the concept of global identifiers (GIDs) for tiles, which are unique integer numbers assigned to each tile used in a tilemap. The tiles in a map are consecutively numbered, starting with 1. A GID of 0 represents an empty tile. With the tileGIDAt method of the CCTMXLayer, you can determine the GID number of the tile at the given tile coordinates.

Next, the CCTMXLayer named GameEventLayer is obtained from the tilemap. This is the layer where I defined the isWater tile and drew it over the river tiles. The tileGIDAt method returns the unique identifier for this tile. If the identifier happens to be 0, it means there is no tile at this position on this layer—in that case, it's already clear that the touched tile can't be an isWater tile.

The CCTMXTiledMap has a propertiesForGID method, which returns an NSDictionary if there are properties available for the tile with the given identifier, or GID. This NSDictionary contains the properties edited in Tiled (see Figure 10–8). The dictionary stores any key/value pairs as NSString objects. If you want to see what's in a particular NSDictionary for debugging purposes, you can use a CCLOG statement like this:

```
CCLOG(@"NSDictionary 'properties' contains:\n%@", properties);
```

This will print out a line similar to the following in the debugger console window:

```
2010-08-30 19:50:52.344 Tilemap[978:207] NSDictionary 'properties' contains:
{
    isWater = 1;
}
```

You'll be dealing with a variety of NSDictionary objects while working with tilemaps. Logging its contents allows you to peek inside any NSDictionary, or any iPhone SDK collection class for that matter. This will come in handy at times.

Each property in an NSDictionary can be retrieved by its name through the NSDictionary method valueForKey, which returns an NSString. To get a bool value from the NSString, you can simply use the NSString's boolValue method. In much the same way, you can retrieve integer and floating-point values using NSString's intValue and floatValue methods, respectively.

At the end of ccTouchesBegan, I check if the touch was on water, and if so a sound is played. Otherwise, I retrieve the WinterLayer and toggle its visible property by negating it. Changing seasons has never been this simple! The effect should illustrate how you can use multiple layers in Tiled to achieve changes on a global scale without having to load a completely separate tilemap.

For more local changes to individual tiles, you can make use of the removeTileAt and setTileGID methods to remove or replace tiles of a specific layer during game play:

```
[winterLayer removeTileAt:tilePos];
[winterLayer setTileGID:tileGID at:tilePos];
```

Locating Touched Tiles

I mentioned the tilePosFromLocation method earlier, and I'll repeat the two relevant lines here:

```
// Get the position in tile coordinates from the touch location
CGPoint touchLocation = [self locationFromTouches:touches];
CGPoint tilePos = [self tilePosFromLocation:touchLocation tileMap:tileMap];
```

First, the position of the touch is mapped to screen coordinates. I've done this before, but since you'll be needing this code a lot, I've provided it in Listing 10–2 for your reference.

Listing 10–2. *Determining the Position of a Touch*

```
-(CGPoint) locationFromTouch:(UITouch*)touch
{
        CGPoint touchLocation = [touch locationInView: [touch view]];
        return [[CCDirector sharedDirector] convertToGL:touchLocation];
}

-(CGPoint) locationFromTouches:(NSSet*)touches
{
        return [self locationFromTouch:[touches anyObject]];
}
```

With the touch location converted to screen coordinates, the tilePosFromLocation method is called. It gets both the touch location and a pointer to the tileMap as parameters. The method in Listing 10–3 contains a bit of math, which I'll explain in a second—hold your breath:

Listing 10–3. *Converting Location to Tile Coordinates*

```
-(CGPoint) tilePosFromLocation:(CGPoint)location tileMap:(CCTMXTiledMap*)tileMap
{
        // Tilemap position must be subtracted, in case the tilemap is scrolling
        CGPoint pos = ccpSub(location, tileMap.position);

        // Cast to int makes sure that result is in whole numbers
        pos.x = (int)(pos.x / tileMap.tileSize.width);
        pos.y = (int)((tileMap.mapSize.height * tileMap.tileSize.height - pos.y) /
                                                        tileMap.tileSize.height);

        CCLOG(@"touch at (%.0f, %.0f) is at tileCoord (%i, %i)", location.x, location.y,
                                                    (int)pos.x, (int)pos.y);
        NSAssert(pos.x >= 0 && pos.y >= 0 && pos.x < tileMap.mapSize.width &&
                        pos.y < tileMap.mapSize.height,
                        @"%@: coordinates (%i, %i) out of bounds!",
                        NSStringFromSelector(_cmd), (int)pos.x, (int)pos.y);

        return pos;
}
```

Still with me? If you've worked with tilemaps before, this bit of code should be familiar, but if not, you may be at a loss. I'll explain. The first thing this method does is subtract the current `tileMap.position` from the touch location. The upcoming *Tilemap03* example project adds tilemap scrolling, so the tilemap's position will most likely not be at 0,0.

To make the viewpoint scroll further up (north) and to the right (east), you actually have to change its position by negative amounts. That is because the tilemap starts out at position 0,0, which positions the map's bottom-left corner at the very bottom left of the screen. The tilemap's 0,0 point coincides with the screen's 0,0 point initially. If you were to move the tilemap to position 100,100, it would seem as if the viewpoint were moving toward the left and down. The common mistake is to assume that you're moving the viewpoint, which you are not. The tilemap layer is what's moving, and to scroll further toward the center of the tilemap, you have to offset the tilemap by negative values.

The rest is simple math: to get the proper offset from the tilemap (whose position we know is always negative), we have to subtract the touch location and `tileMap.position`. The concrete number reveal that subtracting a negative number is actually an addition:

```
location(240, 160) - tileMap.position(-100, -100) = pos(340, 260)
```

With the tilemap layer moved –100,–100 pixels away from the screen's 0,0 point and the touch being at 240,160 pixels on the screen, the total offset of the touch location from the tilemap's position is 340,260 pixels away from the current `tileMap.position`.

With the scrolling offset taken into account, we can get the tile coordinates for the tile at this location into the tilemap. At this point, you have to consider that the tile coordinates' 0,0 tile is at the top-left corner of the tilemap. Contrary to screen coordinates, where the 0,0 point (point of origin) is at the lower-left corner, the tilemap coordinates start at the upper-left corner. Figure 10–11 shows the x,y coordinates of a series of tiles. The screenshot was made with the Tiled Java version by enabling View ➤ Show Coordinates, which is a feature that isn't available yet in the Tiled Qt version.

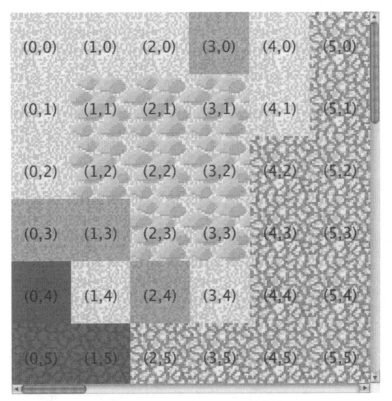

Figure 10–11. *The coordinate system of an orthogonal tilemap*

So as not to get confused, this is the line of code that calculates the tile coordinate's x position:

```
pos.x = (int)(pos.x / tileMap.tileSize.width);
```

The `tileMap.tileSize` property is the size of the tiles in the tileset, which in this case is 32×32 (see also Figure 10–6). If the touch were at the 340 x position, the calculation would reveal the following:

```
340 / 32 = 10.625
```

That can't be right, though. We're looking for a tile's x coordinate, which is never a fractional number! The reason is, of course, that the touch was somewhere inside the tile we're looking for (i.e., inside a 32×32 square area). The simple trick of casting the result to an int value will get rid of the fractional part and assign this to `pos.x`:

```
pos.x = (int)10.625        // pos.x == 10
```

Casting to an int will remove the fractional part. You can safely get rid of the fractional part because it's simply not relevant—actually it's harmful. If you didn't cast away the fractional part but used the noninteger coordinate, in this example 10.625, to try to retrieve the tile at a tile coordinate 10.625, you'd receive a runtime error because there is only a tile at x coordinates 10 and 11, not at 10.625.

A slightly more complicated calculation is used to get the tile's y coordinate:

```
pos.y = (int)((tileMap.mapSize.height * tileMap.tileSize.height - pos.y) /
tileMap.tileSize.height);
```

Note that the parentheses are important to make sure that the division is done last. In actual numbers, this calculation may be easier to understand. As shown in Figure 10–5, the `tileMap.mapSize` is 30×20 tiles, and as I mentioned earlier, `tileMap.tileSize` is 32×32 pixels. The calculation then looks like this:

```
pos.y = (int)((20 * 32 - 260) / 32)
```

Multiplying `tileMap.mapSize.height` with `tileMap.tileSize.height` returns the full height of the tilemap in pixels. This is necessary because the tilemap starts counting y coordinates from top to bottom, whereas screen y coordinates count from bottom to top. By calculating the bottommost y coordinate of the tilemap, and subtracting the current y position 260 from that, you get the correct y position of the touch into the tilemap, in pixels. And because it is a pixel coordinate, you need to divide by the `tileSize.height` and then cast down to an `int` value to get the tile's y coordinate.

The `CCLOG` and `NSAssert` lines are helpful for seeing the results of the calculation in the debugger console, as well as ensuring that tile coordinates never take on illegal values. It's both a learning tool and an insurance policy.

An Exercise in Optimization and Readability

Since the tilemap's size never changes, you can optimize the calculation a little to get the y tile coordinate by adding a member variable to the class's `@interface`, which will be used to store the tilemap's height in pixels:

```
float tileMapHeightInPixels;
```

You can then make the calculation to get the `tileMapHeightInPixels` just once in the init method, right after the tilemap is loaded:

```
CCTMXTiledMap* tileMap = [CCTMXTiledMap tiledMapWithTMXFile:@"orthogonal.tmx"];
tileMapHeightInPixels = tileMap.mapSize.height * tileMap.tileSize.height;
```

Then you can rewrite the calculation, saving a multiplication every time you call the `tilePosFromLocation` method:

```
pos.y = (int)((tileMapHeightInPixels - pos.y) / tileMap.tileSize.height);
```

It may not win any awards for best optimization ever—it's only a very tiny improvement in performance. But every bit counts, and it does make the calculation easier to read by taking away complexity and putting a readable variable name in its place.

Working with the Object Layer

The *orthogonal.tmx* tilemap I've created as an example tilemap for this chapter also contains an object layer, fittingly named `ObjectLayer`. You can create object layers in Tiled by choosing **Layer → Add Object Layer**. Then you can click inside the tilemap and draw rectangles. I think the name *object layer* is a bit unfortunate and misleading, because most games will use these rectangles as points of interest and trigger areas, and not as actual objects.

In the *Tilemap03* project, I've added a bit more code to the ccTouchesBegan method to interact with the object layer. Listing 10–4 shows the relevant part of the code, which follows directly after the isWater check:

Listing 10–4. *Detecting If a Touch Was Inside an ObjectLayer Rectangle*

```
// Check if the touch was within one of the rectangle objects
CCTMXObjectGroup* objectLayer = [tileMap objectGroupNamed:@"ObjectLayer"];

bool isTouchInRectangle = NO;
int numObjects = [objectLayer.objects count];
for (int i = 0; i < numObjects; i++)
{
        NSDictionary* properties = [objectLayer.objects objectAtIndex:i];
        CGRect rect = [self getRectFromObjectProperties:properties tileMap:tileMap];

        if (CGRectContainsPoint(rect, touchLocation))
        {
                isTouchInRectangle = YES;
                break;
        }
}
```

Because object layers are a different kind of layer, you can't get them via the layerNamed method of the tilemap. The object layer in cocos2d is the class CCTMXObjectGroup, another unfortunate naming mishap, since Tiled refers to it as an *object layer*, not an *object group*. In any case, you can get the CCTMXObjectGroup for the object layer named simply ObjectLayer by using the tilemap's objectGroupNamed method and specifying the object layer's name as defined in Tiled.

Next, I iterate over the objectLayer.objects NSMutableArray, which contains a list of NSDictionary items. Sound familiar? Yes, these are the same NSDictionary properties returned by the tilemap's propertiesForGID method, as shown earlier—except that the contents of these NSDictionary items are given by Tiled and not user editable. They simply contain the coordinates for each rectangle. The method getRectFromObjectProperties returns the rectangle:

```
-(CGRect) getRectFromObjectProperties:(NSDictionary*)dict
tileMap:(CCTMXTiledMap*)tileMap
{
        float x, y, width, height;

        x = [[dict valueForKey:@"x"] floatValue] + tileMap.position.x;
        y = [[dict valueForKey:@"y"] floatValue] + tileMap.position.y;
        width = [[dict valueForKey:@"width"] floatValue];
        height = [[dict valueForKey:@"height"] floatValue];

        return CGRectMake(x, y, width, height);
}
```

The keys x, y, width, and height are set by Tiled. I simply retrieve them from the NSDictionary via valueForKey and use the floatValue method to convert the values from NSString to actual floating-point numbers. The x and y values need to be offset with the tileMap's position, as the rectangles need to be moving along with the tilemap. At the end, a CGRect is returned by calling the CGRectMake convenience method.

The remaining code in ccTouchesBegan then simply checks if the touch location is contained in the rect via CGRectContainsPoint. If it is, the isTouchInRectangle flag is set to true and the for loop is aborted by using the break statement. There's no need to check another rectangle for containing the touch location. At the end of ccTouchesBegan, the isTouchInRectangle flag is then used to decide whether to play a particle effect at the touch location. So, this code is creating an explosion particle effect whenever you touch inside a rectangle:

```
if (isTouchOnWater)
{
        [[SimpleAudioEngine sharedEngine] playEffect:@"alien-sfx.caf"];
}
else if (isTouchInRectangle)
{
        CCParticleSystem* system = [CCQuadParticleSystem particleWithFile:
                                                  @"fx-explosion.plist"];
        system.autoRemoveOnFinish = YES;
        system.position = touchLocation;
        [self addChild:system z:1];
}
```

Drawing the Object Layer Rectangles

When you run the *Tilemap03* project, you'll notice that the object layer rectangles are drawn over the tilemap, as shown in Figure 10–12. This is not a standard feature of tilemaps or object layers. Instead, the rectangles are drawn using OpenGL ES code. Every CCNode has a -(void) draw method that you can override to add custom OpenGL ES code. I tend to use this a lot to debug my code visually by drawing lines, circles, and rectangles that may be used for collision and distance tests, among other things. In this case it's very useful to actually see where the object layer areas are. Visualizing such information beats looking up and comparing coordinates in the debugger. Our minds are much better at assessing visual information than at comparing and calculating numbers. Use this to your advantage!

Figure 10–12. *The tilemap with object layer rectangles displayed using OpenGL ES code*

The -(void) draw method just needs to be in the class, and it will be called automatically every frame. However, you should refrain from using the draw method to modify properties of nodes, as this can interfere with drawing the nodes. Listing 10–5 shows the draw method of the TileMapLayer class.

Listing 10–5. *Drawing ObjectLayer Rectangles*

```
-(void) draw
{
        CCNode* node = [self getChildByTag:TileMapNode];
        NSAssert([node isKindOfClass:[CCTMXTiledMap class]], @"not a CCTMXTiledMap");
        CCTMXTiledMap* tileMap = (CCTMXTiledMap*)node;

        // Get the object layer
        CCTMXObjectGroup* objectLayer = [tileMap objectGroupNamed:@"ObjectLayer"];

        // Make the line 3 pixels thick
        glLineWidth(3.0f);
        glColor4f(1, 0, 1, 1);

        int numObjects = [[objectLayer objects] count];
        for (int i = 0; i < numObjects; i++)
        {
                NSDictionary* properties = [[objectLayer objects] objectAtIndex:i];
                CGRect rect = [self getRectFromObjectProperties:properties
                                                        tileMap:tileMap];
                [self drawRect:rect];
        }

        glLineWidth(1.0f);
        glColor4f(1, 1, 1, 1);
}
```

First, I get the tilemap by its tag and then the CCTMXObjectGroup by using the objectGroupNamed method. I then set the line width to 3 pixels by using the OpenGL ES method glLineWidth, and set the color to purple by using glColor4f. This affects line thickness and color of all subsequent lines drawn with OpenGL ES—not just in the current method, but possibly other nodes that use OpenGL ES code for drawing (e.g., any of the convenience methods for drawing lines, circles, and polygons defined in cocos2d's *CCDrawingPrimitives.h* header file). That is why I reset `glLineWidth` and `glColor4f` after I'm done drawing. It is good style in OpenGL code to leave its state like you found it; otherwise, it might alter the way other draw code produces its output. OpenGL is a state machine, so every setting you change is remembered and may affect subsequent drawing methods. To avoid this, any OpenGL settings you change should be set back to a safe default after you're done drawing.

> **NOTE:** Code inside the `-(void) draw` method is always drawn at a z-order of 0. It is also drawn before all other nodes at z-order 0, which means that any OpenGL ES code will be overdrawn by other nodes if they are also at z-order 0. In the case of the object layer `draw` code, I had to add the `tileMap` at a z-order of −1 for the rectangles to be drawn over the tilemap.

Just like before, I iterate over all object layer objects, and get their properties from `NSDictionary` to get the `CGRect` of that object, which is then passed to the `drawRect` method. Unfortunately, cocos2d omitted this particular convenience method, but it's easy enough to add using `ccDrawLine`, as Listing 10–6 shows.

Listing 10–6. *Drawing a Rectangle*

```
-(void) drawRect:(CGRect)rect
{
        // The rect is drawn using four lines
        CGPoint pos1, pos2, pos3, pos4;
        pos1 = CGPointMake(rect.origin.x, rect.origin.y);
        pos2 = CGPointMake(rect.origin.x, rect.origin.y + rect.size.height);
        pos3 = CGPointMake(rect.origin.x + rect.size.width, rect.origin.y +
                                                            rect.size.height);
        pos4 = CGPointMake(rect.origin.x + rect.size.width, rect.origin.y);

        ccDrawLine(pos1, pos2);
        ccDrawLine(pos2, pos3);
        ccDrawLine(pos3, pos4);
        ccDrawLine(pos4, pos1);
}
```

For each corner of the rectangle, a `CGPoint` is created, which is then used in four `ccDrawLine` methods to draw the lines between the corners of the rectangle. You may want to remember this method and put it in a safe place, because you'll probably need it again.

Note that the `draw` and `drawRect` methods are enclosed in `#ifdef DEBUG` and `#endif` statements. This means that the object layer rectangles will not be drawn in release builds, because I only need them for debugging and illustration purposes—the end user should never see them.

```
#ifdef DEBUG
-(void) drawRect:(CGRect)rect
{
        ...
}

-(void) draw
```

```
{
    ...
}
#endif
```

Scrolling the Tilemap

The best part comes last: scrolling. It's actually straightforward because only the CCTMXTiledMap needs to be moved. In the *Tilemap04* project, I've added the call to the centerTileMapOnTileCoord method in ccTouchesBegan right after obtaining the tile coordinates of the touch:

```
-(void) ccTouchesBegan:(NSSet *)touches withEvent:(UIEvent *)event
{
    ...
    // Get the position in tile coordinates from the touch location
    CGPoint touchLocation = [self locationFromTouches:touches];
    CGPoint tilePos = [self tilePosFromLocation:touchLocation tileMap:tileMap];

    // Move tilemap so that the touched tile is at the center of the screen
    [self centerTileMapOnTileCoord:tilePos tileMap:tileMap];
    ...
}
```

Listing 10–7 shows the centerTileMapOnTileCoord method, which moves the tilemap so that the touched tile is at the center of the screen. It also stops the tilemap from scrolling further if any tilemap border already aligns with the screen edge.

Listing 10–7. *Centering the Tilemap on a Tile Coordinate*

```
-(void) centerTileMapOnTileCoord:(CGPoint)tilePos tileMap:(CCTMXTiledMap*)tileMap
{
    // Center tilemap on the given tile pos
    CGSize screenSize = [[CCDirector sharedDirector] winSize];
    CGPoint screenCenter = CGPointMake(screenSize.width * 0.5f, screenSize.height *
                                                                            0.5f);

    // Tile coordinates are counted from upper-left corner
    tilePos.y = (tileMap.mapSize.height - 1) - tilePos.y;

    // Point is now at lower-left corner of the screen
    CGPoint scrollPosition = CGPointMake(-(tilePos.x * tileMap.tileSize.width),
                                         -(tilePos.y * tileMap.tileSize.height));

    // Offset point to center of screen and center of tile
    scrollPosition.x += screenCenter.x - tileMap.tileSize.width * 0.5f;
    scrollPosition.y += screenCenter.y - tileMap.tileSize.height * 0.5f;

    // Make sure tilemap scrolling stops at the tilemap borders
    scrollPosition.x = MIN(scrollPosition.x, 0);
    scrollPosition.x = MAX(scrollPosition.x, -screenSize.width);
    scrollPosition.y = MIN(scrollPosition.y, 0);
    scrollPosition.y = MAX(scrollPosition.y, -screenSize.height);
```

```
        CCAction* move = [CCMoveTo actionWithDuration:0.2f position: scrollPosition];
        [tileMap stopAllActions];
        [tileMap runAction:move];
}
```

After obtaining the center position of the screen, I modify the `tilePos` y coordinate because tilemap coordinates are counted from top to bottom (see Figure 10–11), while screen coordinates increase from bottom up. In effect, I convert the `tilePos` y coordinate as if it were counted from bottom up. In addition, I subtract 1 from the map's height to account for the fact that tile coordinates are counted from 0. In other words, if the map's height were 10, only the tile coordinates 0 to 9 would be valid.

Next, the `scrollPosition` `CGPoint` is created, which will become the position the tilemap will be moved to. The first step is to multiply the tile coordinates with the tilemap's `tileSize`. You may be wondering why I negate the `tilePosInPixels` coordinates. It's simply because if I want the tiles to move from top right to bottom left, I have to move the tilemap down and to the left by decreasing the coordinates.

The next big block modifies the coordinates of the `scrollPosition` to center the tile on the screen's center point. You also need to take into account the center of the tile itself, which is why half the `tileSize` is deducted from the `screenCenter` offset.

By using the Objective-C language's `MIN` and `MAX` macros, it is ensured that the `scrollPosition` is kept within the bounds of the tilemap, so as to not reveal anything past the borders of the tilemap. `MIN` and `MAX` return the minimum and maximum values of their two parameters, respectively, and are a more compact and readable solution than conditional assignments using `if` and `else` statements.

Finally, a `CCMoveTo` action is used to scroll the tilemap node so that the touched tile is centered on the screen. The result is a tilemap that scrolls to the tile that you tap. You can use the same method to scroll to a tile of interest—for example, the player's position.

Conclusion

You should now have a fair understanding of what tilemaps are and how to work with Tiled Map Editor to create a tilemap with multiple layers and properties that can be used by your game.

Loading and displaying a tilemap with cocos2d is a simple task that quickly grows in complexity when it comes to obtaining tile and object layers, modifying them, and reading their properties. You also learned how to determine the tile coordinate of a touch location and how to use tile coordinates to scroll the tilemap, so that it centers the touched tile on the screen.

I even got you acquainted with custom drawing and a bit of OpenGL ES code to render the object layer rectangles on the tilemap for debugging purposes.

Isometric Tilemaps

With isometric tilemaps you can get the best of both worlds—using 2-dimensional graphics to achieve a 3-dimensional look. This is the reason isometric tilemap games are so widely popular. They allow you to create believable game worlds that seem to have spatial depth with relatively simple graphics and tools. Not to mention that 2D graphics require far less powerful devices than real 3D computer graphics.

Figure 11–1 shows an example screenshot of the isometric tilemap game we'll build in this chapter. You'll control a ninja character who sneaks around in this world, avoiding collisions with walls and mountains. The ninja will also be able to hide behind certain objects, like trees and cacti.

Figure 11–1. *An isometric tilemap game*

NOTE: All tilesets used in this chapter were created by David E. Gervais and published under the Creative Commons license. You can download more of his work at

http://pousse.rapiere.free.fr/tome/index.htm.

Designing Isometric Tile Graphics

Isometric tilemap games use an axonometric projection to give the impression of looking at the scenery from an angle, thus creating visual depth. Axonometric projection is the technical term for projecting a rotated three-dimensional object onto a two-dimensional plane. The image then becomes skewed but our minds still recognize it as a three-dimensional object.

In terms of tilemaps, if you take a look at Figure 11–2 you can see the concrete steps for creating an isometric projection of an orthogonal image. The square is first rotated by 45 degrees and then scaled down along its Y axis to give it its typical isometric diamond shape.

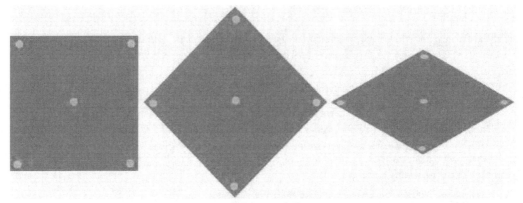

Figure 11–2. *An orthogonal turned isometric by rotating it by 45 degrees, then compressing it vertically*

However, Figure 11–2 is just the theoretical approach to illustrate the projection of the isometric shape. You can't turn an orthogonal image into an isometric image by simply rotating and compressing it because the rotation would affect the image content. It would just look flat and very wrong, just like Figure 11–3.

Figure 11–3. *Turning an orthogonal tileset into an isometric tileset—it's not that simple!*

Instead, consider the diamond shape created in Figure 11–2 as your drawing canvas of the floor. The simplest isometric tiles you can design are flat ground tiles. Just fill the diamond shape with a certain pattern and you get yourself usable isometric tiles. Figure 11–4 shows a number of flat-colored isometric tiles laid out next to each other, creating a ground floor pattern. Ground floor tiles are not impressive, and look very flat. Yet they are essential as the game world's background layer.

Figure 11–4. *Ground floor isometric tiles have no depth. They are used as solid surface areas.*

To add actual visual depth to an isometric tilemap, you need to have object tiles that extend beyond the diamond shape. The most commonly used approach is to draw three-dimensional objects as if they were viewed at a 45-degree angle, and draw them up and over the diamond shape, typically extending no more than one tile above. In the example in Figure 11–5 you can see this quite nicely by looking at the doorway. The door arch is drawn mostly over the isometric tile above the one the door's frame is standing on. This gives the door its visual depth.

Figure 11–5. *Add depth by drawing objects up to twice as high as the diamond shape.*

Isometric tilemaps allow object tiles to overlap one another because the tiles are drawn from back to front, which means that object tiles closer to the viewer will always be drawn over tiles behind them, adding to the feeling of depth. But this approach requires careful design of individual tiles and the tilemap itself, because too much overlap or overlapping the wrong tiles can quickly destroy the illusion of depth.

As a good practice, try not to overlap object tiles that have wildly different shapes, but do use the same or similar color palette. In the case of Figure 11–5, for example, you would not want to place the crystal tile directly behind the doorway. The loss in contrast and merging outlines of these tiles could easily destroy the perception of depth.

Likewise, while you can create isometric object tiles that span much higher than twice the tile height, it's very hard to create a convincing 3D look if objects appear very high because the player will only see a part of the tilemap. If you were building a huge castle whose walls span a dozen tiles high, and the player approached them from below, the walls could easily be mistaken for a large section of ground floor. You can even end up creating optical illusions like the drawings of M. C. Escher because the isometric tiles do not get smaller the further away from the screen they are. So there's always a fine line between what works and what doesn't when designing isometric tiles and tilemaps.

Figure 11–6 shows a finely crafted isometric tileset named *dg_iso32.png,* which contains a good variation of ground floor tiles, object tiles like walls, trees, and houses, as well as adornment objects or items that can be placed on any ground tile. The tiles in this set are each 54x49 pixels in size. The height can be chosen arbitrarily; it can be more or less than 49 pixels and depends on how much overlap between tiles you like in your tilemap. The actual height of the diamond shape is 27 pixels. This will become important when you create the tilemap in Tiled.

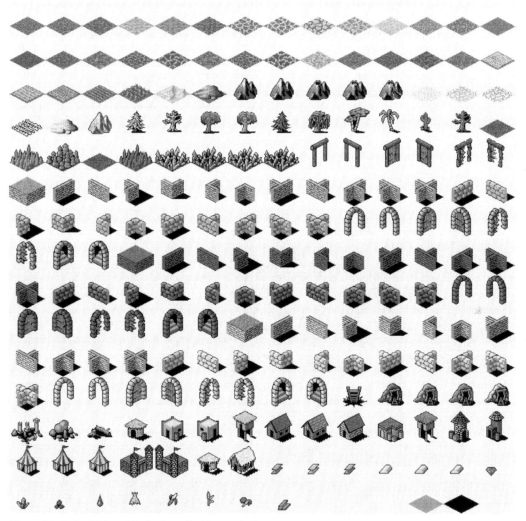

Figure 11–6. *David Gervais's finely crafted isometric tileset*

Isometric Tilemap Editing with Tiled

I'll use the Tiled Map Editor once again to create the isometric tilemap. The basic tilemap editing is the same as with orthogonal maps, but there are certain crucial steps to correctly set up a new isometric tilemap and load an isometric tileset.

Creating a New Isometric Tilemap

Open up Tiled and choose File ➤ New to bring up the New Map dialog in Figure 11–7. The orientation should obviously be set to Isometric and the Map size is set to 30 tiles wide and high, just right for our example project. The odd thing here is the Tile size width and height, which seem to be off a bit. I already mentioned that the individual tiles in the *dg_iso32.png* are 54x49 pixels. The size of the diamond shape, which you have to consider when laying down tiles, is 54x27 pixels. Yet the tile size in the New Map dialog is 52x26.

This offset is on purpose, because isometric tiles are designed to overlap each other a little. In this case—and actually in most other isometric tilesets as well—the size of the tiles in the Tiled isometric map must be 2 pixels less wide and 1 pixel less high than the actual size of the diamond shapes in the tileset.

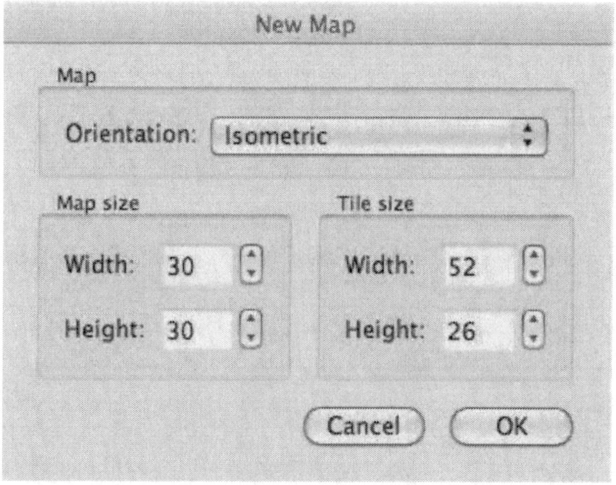

Figure 11–7. *Create a new isometric tilemap in Tiled.*

The goal of this (-2, -1) offset is to have straight lines at the edges of the tilemap and avoid the background showing through. It's necessary because it is impossible to design diamond shapes that are placed at the same distance from each other and do not overlap.

If you see any artifacts like the ones in Figure 11–8, you have set the wrong tile size when creating a new isometric map. You can find this erroneous tilemap as *isometric-no-offset.tmx* in the Tilemap05 project's resources folder, for illustration purposes.

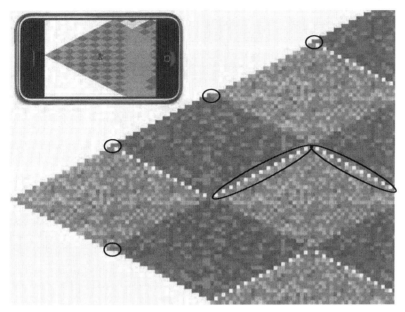

Figure 11–8. *Artifacts like these indicate a tile-size offset problem.*

If you did make a mistake and picked incorrect offsets, and you don't want to lose the tilemap you've just spent hours designing, or if you have other reasons to want to tweak the tilemap size or tileset size, there's a simple way to do this. The following trick makes it easy to experiment with various offsets until you get it just right. Select the TMX file in your Xcode project and you'll see that it's a plain-text XML file. At the beginning of the file you'll find the map section:

```
<map version="1.0" orientation="isometric" width="30" height="30" tilewidth="54"

tileheight="27">
```

You can edit the tilewidth and tileheight parameters until you've found the correct offsets for the tilemap. Likewise, if you're having problems determining the tile size of the isometric tileset you're using, you can modify the tilewidth and tileheight parameters of the tileset(s):

```
<tileset firstgid="1" name="dg_iso32" tilewidth="54" tileheight="49">
  <image source="dg_iso32.png"/>
</tileset>
```

Just make sure to reload the TMX file in Tiled after you made any manual changes to it, because Tiled will not automatically update the file.

Creating a New Isometric Tileset

Next you need to load a tileset containing isometric tiles. For this chapter I will be using the *dg_iso32.png* tileset image found in the *Tilemap05* project's resources folder. In Tiled, choose **Map ➤ New Tileset…** and browse to the *dg_iso32.png* file.

Notice that Tiled will set default Tile width and height according to the settings in the New Map dialog, shown in Figure 11–7. For isometric tilemaps, the defaults will always need to be corrected due to the overlap of isometric tiles. As I mentioned earlier, the *dg_iso32.png* tileset uses a tile width of 54 pixels and a tile height of 49 pixels. Note that you have to use the full canvas height of the isometric tiles, not the diamond shape height of 27 pixels. Figure 11–9 shows the correct setup for this tileset.

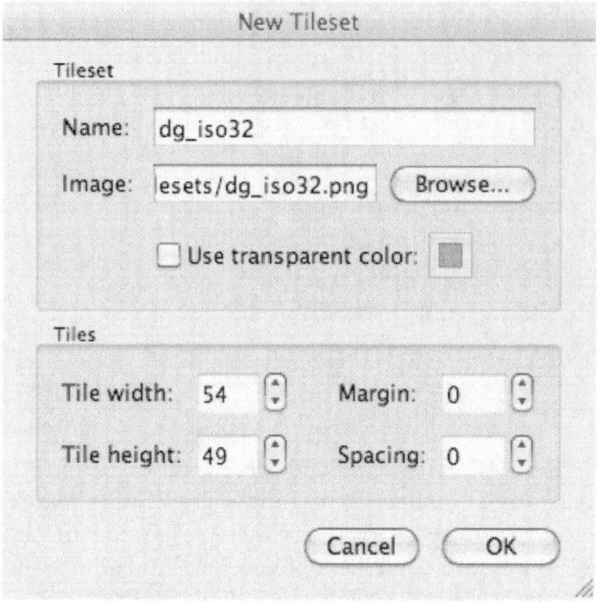

Figure 11–9. *Adding the Tileset with width 54 pixels and height 49 pixels*

Laying Down Some Ground Rules

The most important rule for designing isometric maps is that you're going to need at least two layers so that game characters can walk behind certain tiles. One layer is for flat ground objects and floor tiles, and the other is for all other objects that either overlap other tiles or that are not fully opaque, such as items. In the tileset of Figure 11–6, the first two rows are ground tiles and need to be placed on the Ground floor, whereas in row three the mountains as well as almost all tiles in row 4 and after need to be placed on the Objects layer.

In Tiled, add two new layers via **Layer ➤ Add Tile Layer…** and name them "Ground" and "Objects." Make sure that the Objects layer is drawn on top of the Ground layer. When designing your tilemap, you should take great care to lay down only fully opaque, flat floor tiles on the Ground layer. All other tiles have to be placed on the Objects layer.

In the past, cocos2d had issues with properly displaying game characters and other sprites behind partially occluding tiles in tilemaps. One part of the solution has been to add a special property named cc_vertexz to Tiled layers. I'll explain the solution in more detail shortly; for now, select the Ground layer and click **Layer ➤ Layer Properties….** Add a new property named `cc_vertexz` and set its value to -1000. Do the same with the Objects layer but instead of entering -1000, enter the string "automatic" (without the quotes), as in Figure 11–10.

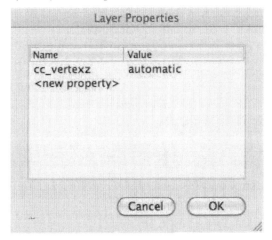

Figure 11–10. *The Objects layer needs the cc_vertexz property set to automatic.*

Now you can spend some time designing a nice-looking tilemap, or simply load the one I designed in the *Tilemap05* project. Be sure to put only floor tiles on the Ground layer, and only overlapping and transparent tiles on the Objects layer. When you're done, you should have a nice-looking tilemap like the one in Figure 11–11.

Figure 11–11. *A completed isometric tilemap in Tiled using David Gervais's tileset*

Isometric Game Programming

Let's use this isometric tilemap in a cocos2d game. As you might expect, some things will have to change compared to working with orthogonal tilemaps. In particular, you need to set up cocos2d properly to allow isometric tiles to partially occlude game characters. Determining a touched tile also requires different code than from orthogonal tilemaps, and when scrolling, you can no longer stop scrolling at the borders of the tilemap because the tilemap itself has a diamond shape.

Loading the Isometric Tilemap in Cocos2d

This is easy. Compared to orthogonal tilemaps, you don't need to change anything except to load the *isometric.tmx* file instead of *orthogonal.tmx*.

```
CCTMXTiledMap* tileMap = [CCTMXTiledMap tiledMapWithTMXFile:@"isometric.tmx"];
[self addChild:tileMap z:-1 tag:TileMapNode];
tileMap.position = CGPointMake(-500, -300);
```

I do set the isometric tilemap's position to -500, -300 right away, assuming the tilemap size is 30x30 tiles. This approximately centers the screen on the lower corner of the small village on the north of the tilemap in Figure 11–11. I did this to illustrate the following point about properly setting up Cocos2D for isometric tilemaps, and in Figure 11–12 you can see there's something obviously wrong with the tilemap.

Setup Cocos2d for Isometric Tilemaps

If you followed the creation of the tilemap thus far, and you have set the `cc_vertexz` properties on the Ground and Objects layers in Tiled as described earlier, the resulting tilemap may look like the one in Figure 11–12. Somehow, the Ground layer is zoomed far out and tiles from the Objects layer seem to be floating in mid-air. It looks like a scary place to be.

Figure 11–12. *Without 2D Projection the ground layer will render incorrectly.*

The way to fix this and to enable proper rendering of overlapping sprites requires cocos2d to be initialized in a different way from how the cocos2d Application template in Xcode sets things up. By default, to setup cocos2d the template adds the following macro to the application delegate's applicationDidFinishLaunching method:

```
CC_DIRECTOR_INIT();
```

The macro CC_DIRECTOR_INIT is defined in *ccMacros.h*. It initializes cocos2d in a standard way, which is fine for most games but fails to work properly with isometric tilemap games. In the *Tilemap05* project, the macro is replaced by more verbose initialization code for cocos2d, shown in Listing 11–1.

Listing 11–1. *Manually Initializing cocos2d's* EAGLView

```
window = [[UIWindow alloc] initWithFrame:[[UIScreen mainScreen] bounds]];
if ([CCDirector setDirectorType:kCCDirectorTypeDisplayLink] == NO)
      [CCDirector setDirectorType:kCCDirectorTypeNSTimer];

CCDirector *director = [CCDirector sharedDirector];
[director setAnimationInterval:1.0/60];
EAGLView *glView = [EAGLView viewWithFrame:[window bounds]
                pixelFormat:kEAGLColorFormatRGB565
                depthFormat:GL_DEPTH_COMPONENT24_OES
                preserveBackbuffer:NO];
[director setOpenGLView:glView];
[window addSubview:glView];
[window makeKeyAndVisible];

// this fixes the zoomed out ground layer:
[director setProjection:kCCDirectorProjection2D];
```

The procedure is always the same for every game, which is why the most common use case was provided with the CC_DIRECTOR_INIT macro. However, in this case you need to change certain parameters of the EAGLView during cocos2d initialization, so you can't rely on that macro. You have to change two things: first you need to enable the OpenGL depth buffer to allow a more fine-grained control over the z ordering of objects. Second, the CCDirector has to use a 2D projection to work with the depth buffer.

You first create a UIWindow, then decide on a CCDirector type to use and set the animation interval to 60 frames per second. This is the default behavior.

The EAGLView line is important because for overlapping tiles to render properly, a depth buffer must be specified with the depthFormat parameter. In this case it's GL_DEPTH_COMPONENT24_OES, which creates a depth buffer of 24 bits. To conserve memory, you can also use a 16-bit depth buffer, which may also be sufficient.

Depth buffering allows OpenGL to determine whether a certain pixel is in front or behind another pixel, so it can decide whether to actually draw the new pixel or discard it. This comes at a cost of additional memory usage—around 500 KB for a 24-bit depth buffer—but it allows sprites and tiles to correctly overlap one another.

After the glView has been created, it's assigned to the CCDirector, added as subview to the window, and then the window is made visible.

The other really important line in the initialization is setProjection, which puts cocos2d in 2D projection mode. This changes a couple of OpenGL parameters that affect the way cocos2d renders nodes. In this case, it fixes the issue in Figure 11–12 where the ground floor is not rendered as expected, with the result in Figure 11–13. But it also enables you to finely tune the z-order of sprites by using the `vertexZ` property rather than the `zOrder` property of sprites. I'll talk about that more later in this chapter.

Figure 11–13. *With 2D projection, the ground layer is displayed as expected.*

Locating an Isometric Tile

The next thing to do is to determine from a touch location the coordinates of the touched tile. This is done in the *Tilemap06* project.

If you refer back to Figure 10-11 in the previous chapter, you'll recall that the tilemap indices of orthogonal tilemaps have their origin point (0, 0) at the top left corner. Now, with isometric tilemaps, there is no top left corner anymore. The tilemap itself is rotated by 45 degrees, which makes the topmost tile the point of origin. Figure 11–14 illustrates this well. Tiles towards the bottom right have increasing X coordinates while Tiles towards the bottom left have increasing Y coordinates. The bottommost tile then has the coordinates 29, 29 in a map consisting of 30x30 tiles.

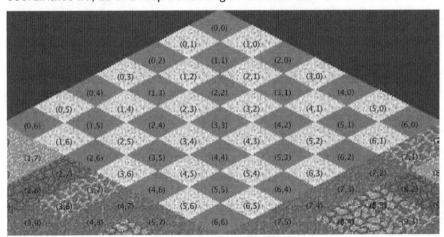

Figure 11–14. *The coordinate system of an isometric tilemap.*

This may seem strange at first, but if you lean your head a bit to the right, you may notice that the tile coordinates follow the exact same order as in orthogonal tilemaps, except that the whole map is rotated by 45 degrees.

You can now straighten your head again, because I need you to focus on the modified tilePosFromLocation method, which calculates the touched tile coordinates from a touch location on the screen. As Listing 11–2 shows, it's a wee bit more complex than the orthogonal counterpart.

Listing 11–2. *Calculating the Tile Coordinates from a Touch Location*

```
-(CGPoint) tilePosFromLocation:(CGPoint)location tileMap:(CCTMXTiledMap*)tileMap
{
        // Tilemap position must be subtracted, in case the tilemap position is
                                                                    scrolling
        CGPoint pos = ccpSub(location, tileMap.position);

        float halfMapWidth = tileMap.mapSize.width * 0.5f;
        float mapHeight = tileMap.mapSize.height;
        float tileWidth = tileMap.tileSize.width;
        float tileHeight = tileMap.tileSize.height;

        CGPoint tilePosDiv = CGPointMake(pos.x / tileWidth, pos.y / tileHeight);
        float inverseTileY = mapHeight - tilePosDiv.y;

        // Cast to int makes sure that result is in whole numbers
        float posX = (int)(inverseTileY + tilePosDiv.x - halfMapWidth);
        float posY = (int)(inverseTileY - tilePosDiv.x + halfMapWidth);

        // make sure coordinates are within isomap bounds
        posX = MAX(0, posX);
        posX = MIN(tileMap.mapSize.width - 1, posX);
        posY = MAX(0, posY);
        posY = MIN(tileMap.mapSize.height - 1, posY);

        return CGPointMake(posX, posY);
}
```

Subtracting the tilemap position to take scrolling of the tilemap into account is the same as in the orthogonal version of this method. Next I create a number of variables just to make the code a bit more readable and have less to type. I divided the map size width by half, then I create a CGPoint tilePosDiv, which is the pixel location within the tilemap divided by the tilemap's width and height, and an inverseTileY variable, which is simply the inverse of the tilemap's Y coordinates. This is necessary because the tilemap Y coordinates count from top down whereas screen Y coordinates count from bottom up.

Now I get to actually calculating the X, Y coordinates of the touched tile. Since the isometric tilemap is rotated by exactly 45 degrees, a rather simple calculation can be used. By relying on the fact that the map is rotated by 45 degrees, only the sign of the calculation needs to be changed to get the X and Y coordinates respectively.

The calculation starts with the inverse Y coordinate, which will be in the range of 0 to 29 for a 30x30 tilemap. For the X tile coordinates, because they extend to the right, the result of the screen X coordinate divided by the tile width is added and then half the map's width is subtracted, which is 15 in the case of a 30x30 tilemap. The same is done for the Y coordinate, except that Y tile coordinates extend to the left and thus we subtract tilePosDiv.x and then add half the map's width. Adding and subtracting half the map's width is shorthand for rotating the tilemap because we know that the point of origin (0, 0) of the isometric tilemap is at the center of the tilemap, or half the tilemap's width.

> **NOTE:** I'll spare you the details of the mathematical concepts behind this calculation, since you can apply the code as is and don't need to change anything. If you are interested in understanding the intricate details of isometric projection and the mathematics behind it, I recommend reading the excellently illustrated article by Herbert Glarner at www.gandraxa.com/isometric_projection.aspx.

By applying the Objective-C MIN and MAX macros, I ensure that the returned tile coordinate is within the bounds of the tilemap. In other words, it will return coordinates from (0, 0) to (29, 29) for the 30x30 tilemap used by the isometric Tilemap projects.

Scrolling the Isometric Tilemap

With the tilePosFromLocation method updated to work with isometric tilemaps, the *Tilemap06* project continues by implementing isometric tilemap scrolling, using the tile coordinates returned from the tilePosFromLocation method. Just as in the orthogonal tilemap project, this is done using the centerTileMapOnTileCoord method, shown in Listing 11–3.

Listing 11–3. *Scrolling the Screen to Center on a Specific Tile Coordinate*

```
-(void) centerTileMapOnTileCoord:(CGPoint)tilePos tileMap:(CCTMXTiledMap*)tileMap
{
        // center tilemap on the given tile pos
        CGSize screenSize = [[CCDirector sharedDirector] winSize];
        CGPoint screenCenter = CGPointMake(screenSize.width * 0.5f,
                                                        screenSize.height * 0.5f);

        // get the ground layer
        CCTMXLayer* layer = [tileMap layerNamed:@"Ground"];
        NSAssert(layer != nil, @"Ground layer not found!");

        // internally tile Y coordinates are off by 1
        tilePos.y -= 1;

        // get the pixel coordinates for a tile at these coordinates
        CGPoint scrollPosition = [layer positionAt:tilePos];

        // negate the position to account for scrolling
        scrollPosition = ccpMult(scrollPosition, -1);

        // add offset to screen center
        scrollPosition = ccpAdd(scrollPosition, screenCenter);
```

```
                // move the tilemap
                CCAction* move = [CCMoveTo actionWithDuration:0.2f position:scrollPosition];
                [tileMap stopAllActions];
                [tileMap runAction:move];
}
```

First, the screen center position is determined as before. Then I want to use the convenience method of the layer, positionAt, which returns a screen position for a tile coordinate. To do so, I get the Ground layer and assert that it exists. It doesn't matter which layer you use, as long as all layers use same size tiles.

Before calling the positionAt method, I have to subtract 1 from the tile Y coordinate to fix a persistent offset problem. Seasoned programmers may be worried that using a tile Y coordinate of 0 and subtracting 1 from it could lead to an invalid index and thus a disastrous crash. But in this case the positionAt method doesn't use the tile coordinates as indices, and it works with any tile coordinate, even negative ones.

The positionAt method returns the pixel position of the given tile coordinate within the tilemap and stores it in the scrollPosition variable. This method isn't specific to isometric tilemaps; it works for all tilemap types: orthogonal, isometric, and hexagonal. Internally, cocos2d checks which type of tilemap is currently being used and then uses the appropriate calculation, since they differ in profound ways. If you are interested in the specific implementation of each of these calculations, take a look at the methods positionForOrthoAt, positionForIsoAt, and positionForHexAt in the *CCTMXLayer.m* implementation file.

Because the tilemap may be scrolling, in which case it will have a negative position, the scrollPosition is multiplied by -1, negating it. After that I just add the screenCenter position to it and I know where to scroll to. The move action is the same as before and moves the tilemap so that the touched tile is centered on screen.

This World Deserves a Better End

Due to the diamond-shaped nature of isometric tilemaps, it's inevitable that the scrolling tilemap will reveal parts outside of the tilemap, as shown in Figure 11–15. Indeed, the tilePosFromLocation method ensures that the returned tile coordinate is always within bounds, so you can use that safely even if the player touches outside the tilemap. But if you don't want the player to see the end of your isometric tilemap world, you'll have to use a trick.

Figure 11–15. *It's the end of the world as we know it (and it feels wrong).*

Open up Tiled and load the *isometric.tmx* file from the *Tilemap06* project's resource folder. What you want to do is to add a border around the existing map and fill it with tiles that give the impression of an impassable area. In Tiled, use **Map ➤ Resize Map…** to bring up the Resize dialog shown in Figure 11–16. You need to add 10 tiles to each side of this tilemap to completely fill the border. Depending on the tile size, you will have to experiment to find the minimum number of tiles that need to be appended. In this case, enter 50 as the new width and height and also enter 10 in the offset boxes. This makes the tilemap 20x20 tiles larger and also moves everything you've edited previously to the center, so that you end up with a border of 10 tiles on each side.

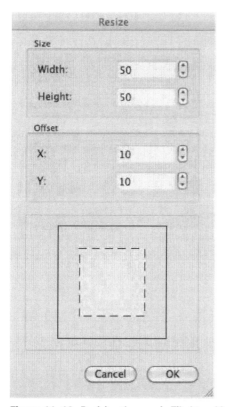

Figure 11–16. *Resizing the map in Tiled to add a border.*

You can now fill this border area to give the impression of an area of the map that is simply impassable. It helps to choose a darker ground tile to hint to the player that this area can't be entered, and of course you should add impenetrable objects onto the Objects layer and around the border of the playable area. Your result should look something like Figure 11–17. I saved my version into the resources folder of the *Tilemap07* project and named it *isometric-with-border.tmx*.

Figure 11–17. *A convincing impassable map border area*

> **NOTE:** The impassable area in Figure 11–17 does look quite repetitive and boring. You may be tempted to add more detail to that area but that is a double-edged sword. On one side, more details and variations within the impassable area will make it look better. On the other, it can also fool the player into thinking about, and even worse, spending time trying to reach that one spot in the impassable area that looks like it could be visited. The player might assume it's a secret area and he simply has to figure out how to get there. If you have a player thinking like this, it's bad for your game. You don't want to tempt the player into trying things that are absolutely impossible to achieve. It just wastes his time and it ends in frustration.

The *Tilemap07* project also implements the code that prevents you from scrolling outside the playable area by defining the inner tile coordinates of the playable area. I added two CGPoint variables, playableAreaMin and playableAreaMax, to the TileMapLayer class:

```
@interface TileMapLayer : CCLayer
{
        CGPoint playableAreaMin, playableAreaMax;
}
```

The playable area variables are initialized with a border size of 10 tiles in the init method of the class:

```
const int borderSize = 10;
playableAreaMin = CGPointMake(borderSize, borderSize);
playableAreaMax = CGPointMake(tileMap.mapSize.width - 1 - borderSize,
                                        tileMap.mapSize.height - 1 - borderSize);
```

The playable area is defined as anything within the bounds of the tile coordinates (10, 10) to (39, 39). All tiles outside this area should be considered not part of the playfield. All that remains is to update the tilePosFromLocation method by replacing the MIN/MAX lines to implement this rule of the playable area. Instead of keeping the tile coordinates within the bounds of the whole tilemap, you now want to keep it within the bounds of the playable area, as such:

```
posX = MAX(playableAreaMin.x, posX);
posX = MIN(playableAreaMax.x, posX);
posY = MAX(playableAreaMin.y, posY);
posY = MIN(playableAreaMax.y, posY);
```

If you try this out, you'll see that only the tiles within the playable area can be centered on screen. What's more, clicks outside the playable area are not just ignored; the tilemap scrolls as close as possible to the tile you clicked on. This way you don't destroy the player's impression of a world that seemingly extends far beyond what the player can see.

Adding a Movable Player Character

By adding a player character moving about the tilemap world, you get closer to an actual isometric game. In this case I chose the *ninja.png* as the player character and added it to the *Tilemap08* project. The player is a class derived from CCSprite, aptly named Player. Listing 11–4 shows the header file.

Listing 11–4. *The Player Class Interface*

```
#import <Foundation/Foundation.h>
#import "cocos2d.h"

@interface Player : CCSprite
{
}

+(id) player;

@end
```

The +(id) player method in Listing 11–5 is the static autorelease initialize, which also initializes the sprite with the *ninja.png* file.

Listing 11–5. *The Player Class Implementation*

```
#import "Player.h"

@implementation Player

+(id) player
{
        return [[[self alloc] initWithFile:@"ninja.png"] autorelease];
}

@end
```

You then create the player in the TileMapLayer class's init method:

```
CGSize screenSize = [[CCDirector sharedDirector] winSize];

// Create the player and add it
player = [Player player];
player.position = CGPointMake(screenSize.width / 2, screenSize.height / 2);

// approximately position player's texture to best match the tile center position
player.anchorPoint = CGPointMake(0.3f, 0.1f);
[self addChild:player];
```

The player's position is set to the center of the screen on purpose. Since you already have a method that allows you to center a specific tile on the screen, centering the player sprite on the screen as well makes it behave as if it were moving across the tilemap, when in fact it always remains at the same position. You don't have to move the player sprite at all!

The player's anchorPoint is offset a little from its default of (0.5f, 0.5f) to (0.3f, 0.1f) to approximately center the sprite's feet on the center position of the tile. Otherwise it might look wrong because all other game objects like trees and cacti have their roots, literally speaking, at the center of the tile. So it's only natural to try to place the player's feet at that position as well.

If you try this now, even though the player sprite never moves, it looks as if the player is walking about the tilemap world. Perfect!

Well, not quite. If you move over mountains and walls and trees and buildings, the player sprite is always drawn in front of them.

Enabling the Player to Move Behind Tiles

To allow the player to be partially hidden by object tiles in front of him, such as buildings, walls, trees, and whatnot, you have to change his vertexZ value as he moves around on the map. At the start of this chapter, when you created the Objects layer in Tiled, you gave it a property named cc_vertexz and set it to automatic. This instructed cocos2d to assign consecutive vertexZ values to the tiles in that layer. Figure 11–18 shows you which vertexZ values the tiles are assigned in a tilemap that's 50x50 tiles in size. This is different from the tile indices shown in Figure 11–14 because the vertexZ values increase in both X and Y directions. You could say that vertexZ values decrease with each horizontal row of the tilemap.

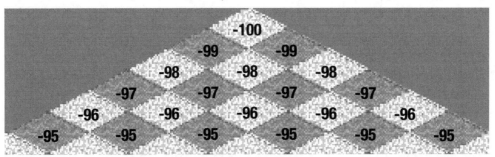

Figure 11–18. *The vertexZ values of tiles in the 50x50 tilemap*

This is reflected in code by the updateVertexZ method added to the Player class:

```
-(void) updateVertexZ:(CGPoint)tilePos tileMap:(CCTMXTiledMap*)tileMap
{
        float lowestZ = -(tileMap.mapSize.width + tileMap.mapSize.height);
        float currentZ = tilePos.x + tilePos.y;
        self.vertexZ = lowestZ + currentZ - 1;
}
```

The lowest vertexZ value is simply the sum of the map size width and height in the negative. Likewise, you can get the difference of any tile coordinate in the tilemap to the lowest vertexZ value, which is the tile at position 0, 0. It's the sum of the X and Z coordinates of that position. For example, the tile at position 2, 2 is 2 + 2 = 4 less than the lowest vertexZ value. If you add the two, you get -100 + 4 = -96. Since the player sprite is added to the TileMapLayer after the tilemap, it will render on top of tiles with the same vertexZ value. Because of this I also subtract 1 so that the end result is a vertexZ value of -97 if the player is standing on the tile coordinate 2, 2.

To make this code work you also have to define the updateVertexZ method in the Player class's interface:

```
@interface Player : CCSprite
{
}

+(id) player;
-(void) updateVertexZ:(CGPoint)tilePos tileMap:(CCTMXTiledMap*)tileMap;
@end
```

And then you should call the updateVertexZ method every time the tilemap is moved, which is done in the ccTouchesBegan method of the TileMapLayer class:

```
-(void) ccTouchesBegan:(NSSet *)touches withEvent:(UIEvent *)event
{
        CCNode* node = [self getChildByTag:TileMapNode];
        NSAssert([node isKindOfClass:[CCTMXTiledMap class]], @"not a CCTMXTiledMap");
        CCTMXTiledMap* tileMap = (CCTMXTiledMap*)node;

        CGPoint touchLocation = [self locationFromTouches:touches];
        CGPoint tilePos = [self tilePosFromLocation:touchLocation tileMap:tileMap];

        [self centerTileMapOnTileCoord:tilePos tileMap:tileMap];

        // fix the player's Z position
        [player updateVertexZ:tilePos tileMap:tileMap];
}
```

If you try this out now, you'll see that the ninja player will hide behind walls, trees, and other large objects, like a good ninja does.

Moving the Player, Tile by Tile

So far, the player (actually, the screen) moves faster the further away from the center the screen is touched. The player also moves across the tiles freely, but he really should be moving from tile to tile in only four directions. The *Tilemap09* project changes the control mechanism to one that allows you to move the player in one of the four allowed directions as long as you keep a finger on the screen. The move direction depends on where you touch the screen relative to the player.

This requires some additions to the TileMapLayer interface, shown in Listing 11–6.

Listing 11–6. *The TileMapLayer Class Interface*

```
typedef enum
{
        MoveDirectionNone = 0,
        MoveDirectionUpperLeft,
        MoveDirectionLowerLeft,
        MoveDirectionUpperRight,
        MoveDirectionLowerRight,

        MAX_MoveDirections,
} EMoveDirection;
```

```
@interface TileMapLayer : CCLayer
{
        CGPoint playableAreaMin, playableAreaMax;

        Player* player;

        CGPoint screenCenter;
        CGRect upperLeft, lowerLeft, upperRight, lowerRight;
        CGPoint moveOffsets[MAX_MoveDirections];
        EMoveDirection currentMoveDirection;
}
```

The EMoveDirection enum is later used to determine in which direction the player intends to walk, with MoveDirectionNone signaling no movement. Let's look at changes in the implementation of the TileMapLayer class's init method in Listing 11–7.

Listing 11–7. *Initializing the Player's Movement Directions*

```
// divide the screen into 4 areas
screenCenter = CGPointMake(screenSize.width / 2, screenSize.height / 2);
upperLeft = CGRectMake(0, screenCenter.y, screenCenter.x, screenCenter.y);
lowerLeft = CGRectMake(0, 0, screenCenter.x, screenCenter.y);
upperRight = CGRectMake(screenCenter.x, screenCenter.y, screenCenter.x,
                                                        screenCenter.y);
lowerRight = CGRectMake(screenCenter.x, 0, screenCenter.x, screenCenter.y);

moveOffsets[MoveDirectionNone] = CGPointZero;
moveOffsets[MoveDirectionUpperLeft] = CGPointMake(-1, 0);
moveOffsets[MoveDirectionLowerLeft] = CGPointMake(0, 1);
moveOffsets[MoveDirectionUpperRight] = CGPointMake(0, -1);
moveOffsets[MoveDirectionLowerRight] = CGPointMake(1, 0);

currentMoveDirection = MoveDirectionNone;

// continuously check for walking
[self scheduleUpdate];
```

The four CGRect variables, upperLeft, lowerLeft, upperRight, and lowerRight, divide the screen into four quadrants, each of which is the touch area to move the player in the desired direction. Thus a touch in the lower right area of the screen will move the player to the right and down along the tilemap.

The moveOffsets array contains a CGPoint for each move direction that, when added to the current tile coordinate, will return the next tile coordinate in that direction. The currentMoveDirection variable simply holds which direction the player is moving toward, and you need a scheduleUpdate to continuously check if the player still wants to move.

The ccTouchesBegan method (Listing 11–8) has changed to simply check which quadrant of the screen received the touch, and then sets the currentMoveDirection. The newly added ccTouchesEnded method sets the currentMoveDirection back to MoveDirectionNone.

Listing 11–8. *Moving the Player Based on Touch Location*

```
-(void) ccTouchesBegan:(NSSet *)touches withEvent:(UIEvent *)event

{
        // get the position in tile coordinates from the touch location
        CGPoint touchLocation = [self locationFromTouches:touches];

        // check where the touch was and set the move direction accordingly
        if (CGRectContainsPoint(upperLeft, touchLocation))
        {
                currentMoveDirection = MoveDirectionUpperLeft;
        }
        else if (CGRectContainsPoint(lowerLeft, touchLocation))
        {
                currentMoveDirection = MoveDirectionLowerLeft;
        }
        else if (CGRectContainsPoint(upperRight, touchLocation))
        {
                currentMoveDirection = MoveDirectionUpperRight;
        }
        else if (CGRectContainsPoint(lowerRight, touchLocation))
        {
                currentMoveDirection = MoveDirectionLowerRight;
        }
}

-(void) ccTouchesEnded:(NSSet *)touches withEvent:(UIEvent *)event
{
        currentMoveDirection = MoveDirectionNone;
}
```

The gist of the work has now been moved to the update method, which is scheduled to be called every frame:

```
-(void) update:(ccTime)delta
{
        CCNode* node = [self getChildByTag:TileMapNode];
        NSAssert([node isKindOfClass:[CCTMXTiledMap class]], @"not a CCTMXTiledMap");
        CCTMXTiledMap* tileMap = (CCTMXTiledMap*)node;

        // if the tilemap is currently being moved, wait until it's done moving
        if ([tileMap numberOfRunningActions] == 0)
        {
                if (currentMoveDirection != MoveDirectionNone)
                {
                        CGPoint tilePos = [self tilePosFromLocation:screenCenter
                                                                tileMap:tileMap];

                        CGPoint offset = moveOffsets[currentMoveDirection];
                        tilePos = CGPointMake(tilePos.x + offset.x, tilePos.y +
                                                                offset.y);
                        tilePos = [self ensureTilePosIsWithinBounds:tilePos];

                        [self centerTileMapOnTileCoord:tilePos tileMap:tileMap];
                }
        }
```

```
            // continuously fix the player's Z position
            CGPoint tilePos = [self floatingTilePosFromLocation:screenCenter
                                                          tileMap:tileMap];
            [player updateVertexZ:tilePos tileMap:tileMap];
}
```

The tilemap has a running action only when it is moving, so I give it a new move action only if it has no move action currently running and the currentMoveDirection isn't MoveDirectionNone. The tilePosFromLocation is no longer retrieved from the screen touch location, but instead the screenCenter position is used. Since the player is always centered on the screen, this is a convenient shortcut to the tile coordinate at the center of the screen.

The moveOffsets array returns a CGPoint that is added to tilePos to get the new tile coordinate we intend to move to. Because this can be outside the playable area, the new tile coordinate is run through the ensureTilePosIsWithinBounds method. It's the same code we used before to keep the tile coordinate within the playable area, but refactored into a separate method to avoid duplicating this code. Lastly, the centerTileMapOnTileCoord method is called to move and center the screen on the desired tile coordinate, which also adds the move action.

With the player now moving across the tilemap tile by tile, we can keep updating the player's vertexZ value. Previously, the vertexZ value was set to the target tile coordinate immediately, which caused the player to be drawn below all object tiles he was moving over. By continuously updating the vertexZ value as the player moves across the tilemap, his z position is now more accurate and removes any overlap glitches from the previous *Tilemap08* project.

Stop Player on Collisions

Lastly, we don't want the player to walk over walls and mountains. He may be a ninja, but he's not *that* good. To solve that problem, add a new Layer in Tiled via **Layer ➤ Add Tile Layer…** and name it Collisions, then move the Opacity slider just above the Layers list to about the middle. Now pick a tile from the tileset whose color is a strong contrast to the tilemap, because we'll use it to draw collision areas over the tilemap and they should be easily recognizable despite having a low opacity.

I chose one of the purple tiles. Right-click the tile of your choice and select **Tile Properties…** from the context menu. Note that this command has no equivalent in the Tiled menu; Tile Properties can only be accessed by right-clicking a tile. In the Tile Properties dialog shown in Figure 11–19, add a property named blocks_movement and set the value to 1. Actually, I'm going to ignore the value in code, it's only important that the blocks_movement value exists.

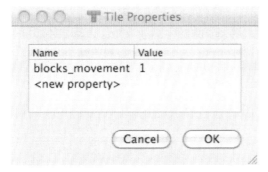

Figure 11–19. *Add a blocks_movement Tile Property.*

With the Collisions layer selected, draw on the tilemap with the tile that has the blocks_movement property set. Place a tile everywhere you don't want the player to move onto, for example walls, mountains, houses, and so on.

The tilemap *isometric-with-border.tmx* in the *Tilemap10* project is already prepared with a collision layer. The collision layer is only for checking if a tile can be moved on and should not be displayed in the game, so the first thing you do in the init method of the TileMapLayer class is to set this layer invisible (see Listing 11–9).

Listing 11–9. *Hiding the Collisions Layer*

```
CCTMXTiledMap* tileMap = [CCTMXTiledMap tiledMapWithTMXFile:

@"isometric-with-border.tmx"];
[self addChild:tileMap z:-1 tag:TileMapNode];

CCTMXLayer* layer = [tileMap layerNamed:@"Collisions"];
layer.visible = NO;
```

To check if a certain tile coordinate is blocked, I've added the isTilePosBlocked method to the *Tilemap10* project, as shown in Listing 11–10.

Listing 11–10. *Determine if a Tile Is Blocked*

```
-(bool) isTilePosBlocked:(CGPoint)tilePos tileMap:(CCTMXTiledMap*)tileMap
{
        CCTMXLayer* layer = [tileMap layerNamed:@"Collisions"];
        NSAssert(layer != nil, @"Collisions layer not found!");

        bool isBlocked = NO;
        unsigned int tileGID = [layer tileGIDAt:tilePos];
        if (tileGID > 0)
        {
                NSDictionary* tileProperties = [tileMap propertiesForGID:tileGID];
                id blocks_movement = [tileProperties objectForKey:@"blocks_movement"];
                isBlocked = (blocks_movement != nil);
        }

        return isBlocked;
}
```

The code first tries to get a tile at the given tile coordinate from the Collisions layer. If there is no tile there, the `tileGID` will be 0 and we can safely assume that this tile is not blocked. But if there is a valid `tileGID` at the `tilePos` coordinate, the `tileMap` is queried for the properties of the tile, which returns an `NSDictionary` object. If the dictionary's `objectForKey` method returns a valid object for the key named `blocks_movement`, the tile is blocked.

The place to check for collision is in the `update` method, as shown in Listing 11–11.

Listing 11–11. *Checking for Collision in the* update *Method*

```
-(void) update:(ccTime)delta
{
    ...

    // if the tilemap is currently being moved, wait until it's done moving
    if ([tileMap numberOfRunningActions] == 0)
    {
        if (currentMoveDirection != MoveDirectionNone)
        {
            CGPoint tilePos = [self tilePosFromLocation:screenCenter
                                                tileMap:tileMap];

            CGPoint offset = moveOffsets[currentMoveDirection];
            tilePos = CGPointMake(tilePos.x + offset.x, tilePos.y +
                                                            offset.y);
            tilePos = [self ensureTilePosIsWithinBounds:tilePos];

            if ([self isTilePosBlocked:tilePos tileMap:tileMap] == NO)
            {
                [self centerTileMapOnTileCoord:tilePos tileMap:tileMap];
            }
        }
    }

    ...
}
```

Before moving the tilemap, the `isTilePosBlocked` method is called to see if the player can actually move there. If the destination tile coordinate is not blocked, he will move, otherwise he won't.

Adding More Content to the Game

So far, we have a game where you guide a character through an isometric tilemap world. Hiding behind trees and avoiding collisions are just the foundation for a game set in this world. What if you want to add more actors to the world, whether enemies or non-player characters (NPCs)?

In principle, you animate them just like you'd move the player, except that the player is centered on screen whereas NPCs can be anywhere on the tilemap. Still, you only need to determine which direction the NPC should walk toward, and then move him like the layer is moved in the `centerTileMapOnTileCoord` method. The only difference is that the actions are run on the NPC and the directions need to be reversed, since you aren't moving the layer, the NPC is moving on the layer.

As soon as you have NPCs wandering around, the next step is to ask how you can get them to move from A to B while avoiding obstacles and finding the shortest route. The answer to that is the A* pathfinding algorithm, which is an industry standard and has been adapted and tweaked for many situations. Tile-based games are ideal candidates for this particular pathfinding algorithm, since actor positions are usually restricted to the tile coordinates. For an in-depth introduction to the A* pathfinding algorithm, and honestly to a lot of game programming topics in general, you must visit Amit's A* pages at `http://theory.stanford.edu/~amitp/GameProgramming/`.

And you'll want to visit Amit's Game Programming Information pages. He links to articles concerning artificial intelligence and tile-based games, including procedural world generation. A lot of the articles may seem dated but, in fact, most of them are timeless and are still valuable sources of information. Check them out at `http://www-cs-students.stanford.edu/~amitp/gameprog.html`.

Conclusion

In this chapter you've learned what's special about isometric tilemaps, how isometric tiles are designed and how to create a tilemap with a perceived depth. You learned how to create and improve such an isometric tilemap with Tiled by adding an impassable border and preventing collisions.

You also learned the techniques necessary to set up a tilemap for use with cocos2d, and how to setup cocos2d itself with 2D projection and a depth buffer for correct rendering of overlapping tiles and sprites.

Finally, we added a player whose sprite is correctly clipped depending on whether it is in front or behind tiles. You can also move the player around tile by tile by tapping and holding the screen relative to the player sprite to make him go in that direction. That he will do unless the direction is blocked by a mountain, wall, or any other movement-blocking tile that you set in Tiled.

So far, we've worked with games that needed to be controlled and animated in discrete steps. You were responsible for implementing all of the actor's movement and rotation as well as checking for collisions. In the next two chapters I'll introduce you to physics engines, which allow you to lean back as you watch your game's objects bounce around and collide with each other all by themselves. If this is the first time you've worked with a physics engine, it will be a magical experience. Hold onto your hat!

Chapter **12**

Physics Engines

Physics engines are what drive popular iOS games like Angry Birds, Stick Golf, Jelly Car, and Stair Dismount. They allow you to create a world that feels more dynamic and lifelike.

Cocos2d is distributed with two physics engines: Box2D and Chipmunk. Both are designed to work only in two dimensions, so they're a perfect fit for cocos2d.

In this chapter, you'll learn the basics of both physics engines, and along the way you'll probably come to appreciate one more than the other. I'll briefly explain the differences between the two physics engines, but for the most part it's a choice based on personal preference.

If you've never worked with a physics engine before, I'll also give you a quick introduction to their basic concepts and key elements.

Basic Concepts of Physics Engines

A physics engine can be seen as an animation system for game objects. Of course, it's up to the game developer to connect and synchronize game objects like sprites with the physics objects, called *rigid bodies*. They are called that because physics engines animate them as if they were stiff, nondeformable objects. This simplification allows physics engines to calculate a large number of bodies.

There are generally two types of bodies: *dynamic* (moving) and *static* (immovable) objects. The differentiation is important because static bodies never move—and should never be moved—and the physics engine can rely on certain optimizations based on the fact that static bodies never collide with each other.

Dynamic bodies, on the other hand, collide with each other and with static bodies. They also have at least three defining parameters in addition to their position and rotation. One is *density* or *mass*—in other words, a measure of how heavy an object is. Then there is *friction*—how resistant or slippery the dynamic body is with respect to moving over surfaces. Finally, there is *restitution*, which determines the bounciness of the object. While impossible in the real world, physics engines can create dynamic bodies that will never lose momentum as they bounce, or even gain speed every time they bounce off of some other body.

Both dynamic and static bodies have one or more shapes that determine the area the body encompasses. Most often the shape is a circle or a rectangle, but it can also be a polygon, a number of vertices forming any complex shape, or merely a straight line. The shape(s) of a body determine where other bodies and their shapes collide. And in turn, each collision generates *contact points*—the points where the two bodies' shapes intersect. These contact points can be used to play particle effects or add scratch marks at exactly the places where the bodies have collided.

Dynamic bodies are animated by the physics engine through applying forces, impulses, and torque instead of setting their position and rotation directly. Modifying position and rotation directly is advised against, because physics engines make certain predictions that no longer hold true if you manually reposition bodies.

Finally, bodies can be connected together by using a selection of *joints*, which limit the movement of connected bodies in various ways. Some joints may have motors, which for example can act as the drive wheel of a car or as friction for the joint, so that the joint tries to snap back to its original position.

Limitations of Physics Engines

Physics engines have their limits. They have to take shortcuts because the real world is prohibitively complex to simulate. The use of rigid bodies is such an example. In some extreme cases, physics engines may not be able to catch every collision—for example, when bodies are moving very fast, in which case they can tunnel through each other. While this has been proven to happen in quantum physics, real-world objects that we can actually see with our own eyes have yet to show that effect.

Rigid bodies can sometimes penetrate each other and get stuck, especially if they are constrained by joints. This can lead to undesirable trembling motions of the bodies as they struggle to move apart while keeping their joint constraints satisfied.

And of course there can be game play issues. With rigid bodies, you never know what will happen given enough players interacting with them. Eventually some players may manage to block themselves and trap themselves in a dead-end situation, or they may figure out how to exploit the physics simulation to be able to move to areas they shouldn't be able to reach.

The Showdown: Box2D vs. Chipmunk

Cocos2d is distributed with two physics engines: Box2D and Chipmunk. How should you choose between them?

In a lot of cases this boils down to a matter of taste. Most developers argue along the lines of the programming language in which the physics engines are implemented: Box2D is written entirely in C++ while Chipmunk is written in C.

You may favor Box2D over Chipmunk simply because of its C++ interface. Being written in C++ has the added advantage that it integrates better with the likewise object-oriented Objective-C language. You may also appreciate that Box2D uses fully written-out words throughout, as opposed to the many one-letter abbreviations common in Chipmunk. In addition, Box2D makes use of operator overloading so that you can, for example, add two vectors simply by writing the following:

```
b2Vec2 newVec = vec1 + vec2;
```

There are a few features that Box2D has that Chipmunk doesn't offer. For example, it has a solution for fast-moving objects (bullets) that solves the tunneling problem I mentioned earlier.

If you're not very familiar with C++, you may find the steep learning curve of the C++ language daunting. To that end, the Chipmunk physics engine may be more welcoming to you if you're more familiar with C language syntax or prefer a lightweight implementation of a physics engine that is easier to pick up and learn. Its being part of the cocos2d distribution for many months longer than Box2D has also spawned more tutorials and forum posts about Chipmunk, although Box2D tutorials are catching on.

One warning ahead of time: Chipmunk uses *C structures*, which expose internal fields. If you're experimenting and don't know what certain fields are used for, and they're not documented, that means you should not change them—as they are only used internally.

There is also the popular Chipmunk *SpaceManager*, which adds an easy-to-use Objective-C interface to Chipmunk. SpaceManager also makes it easy to attach cocos2d sprites to bodies and adds debug drawing, among other things. You can download Chipmunk SpaceManager here: `http://code.google.com/p/chipmunk-spacemanager`.

In terms of functionality, you can safely choose either engine. Unless your game relies on one particular feature that one physics engine has and the other doesn't, you can use either one to great effect. Especially if you have no familiarity with either physics engine, feel free to choose the one that appeals to you more based on the language and coding style.

I will now introduce you to the basics of both physics engines for the rest of this chapter, so that you can decide for yourself which one appeals to you more. In the next chapter, you'll learn how to build a playable pinball game with bumpers, flippers, and lanes built with Box2D and the VertexHelper tool.

Box2D

The Box2D physics engine is written in C++. It was developed by Erin Catto, who has given presentations about physics simulations at every Game Developers Conference (GDC) since 2005. It was his GDC 2006 presentation that eventually lead to the public release of Box2D in September 2007. It has been in active development ever since.

Due to its popularity, the Box2D physics engine is distributed with cocos2d. You can create a new project using Box2D by choosing the cocos2d Box2D application template from Xcode's **File → New Project** dialog. This project template adds the necessary Box2D source files to the project and provides a test project in which you can add boxes that bounce off each other, as shown in Figure 12–1. They also fall according to gravity, depending on how you're holding your device.

Figure 12–1. *The PhysicsBox2D example project*

CAUTION: Because the Box2D physics engine is written in C++, you have to use the file extension *.mm* instead of *.m* for all your project's implementation files. This tells Xcode to treat the implementation file's source code as either Objective-C++ or C++ code. With the *.m file* extension, Xcode will compile the code as Objective-C and C code, and won't understand Box2D's C++ code, which will result in numerous compile errors for every line of code that uses or makes a reference to Box2D. So if you're getting a lot of errors, check that your implementation files all end in *.mm*, and if not, rename them.

Documentation for Box2D is available in two places. First, you can read the Box2D manual online at `www.box2d.org/manual.html`, which introduces you to common concepts and shows example code. The Box2D API reference is distributed with Box2D itself, which you can download here: `http://code.google.com/p/box2d`. You can also find the Box2D API reference in the Box2D version distributed with the book's source code. The API reference is in the folder */Physics Engine Libraries/Box2D_v2.1.2/Box2D/Documentation/API*—to view it, locate and open the file *index.html* in that folder.

If you like Box2D, you should also consider donating to the project; you can do so via the **Donate** button on its home page: `www.box2d.org`.

The World According to Box2D

Because the example project provided by cocos2d is quite complex, I decided to break it down into smaller pieces and re-create the example project step by step, but not without adding some extras and variations.

Listing 12–1 shows the *HelloWorldScene* header file from the *PhysicsBox2D01* project.

Listing 12–1. *The Box2D Hello World Interface*

```
#import "cocos2d.h"
#import "Box2D.h"
#import "GLES-Render.h"

enum
{
        kTagBatchNode,
};

@interface HelloWorld : CCLayer
{
        b2World* world;
}

+(id) scene;

@end
```

It's fairly standard, except that it includes the *Box2D.h* header file and adds a member variable of type b2World. This is the physics world—think of it as the container class that will store and update all physics bodies.

The Box2D world is initialized by creating a new b2World object in the HelloWorldScene's init method, as shown in Listing 12–2.

Listing 12–2. *Initializing the Box2D World*

```
b2Vec2 gravity = b2Vec2(0.0f, -10.0f);
bool allowBodiesToSleep = true;
world = new b2World(gravity, allowBodiesToSleep);
```

Remember that Box2D is written in C++. To create a pointer from one of Box2D's classes, you have to add the new keyword in front of the class's name. If Box2D were written in Objective-C, the equivalent line might look like this:

```
world = [[b2World alloc] initWithGravity:gravity allowSleep:allowBodiesToSleep];
```

In other words, the new keyword in C++ is equivalent to the alloc keyword in Objective-C. That of course means you also have to deallocate the Box2D world. In C++ this is done using the delete keyword:

```
-(void) dealloc
{
        delete world;
        [super dealloc];
}
```

The Box2D world in Listing 12–2 is initialized with an initial gravity vector and a flag that determines if the dynamic bodies are allowed to fall asleep.

Sleeping bodies? It's a trick that allows the physics simulation to quickly skip over objects that do not need processing. A dynamic body goes to sleep when the forces applied to it have been below a threshold for a certain amount of time. In other words, if the dynamic body is moving and rotating very slowly or not at all, the physics engine will flag it as sleeping and won't apply forces to it anymore—that is, unless an impulse or force applied to the body is strong enough to make the body move or rotate again. This trick allows the physics engine to save time by not processing the bodies that are at rest. Unless all of your game's dynamic bodies are in constant motion, you should enable this feature by setting the allowBodiesToSleep variable to true, as in Listing 12–2.

The gravity passed to Box2D is a b2Vec2 struct type. It's essentially the same as a CGPoint, as it stores x and y float values. In this case, and fortunately for us in the real world too, gravity is a constant force. The 0, –10 vector is constantly applied to all dynamic bodies, making them fall down, which in this case means toward the bottom of the screen.

Restricting Movement to the Screen

World setup, check. What next? Well, we should limit the movement of the Box2D bodies to within the visible screen area. For that, we'll need a static body. The simplest way to create a static body is by using the world's CreateBody method and an empty body definition:

```
// Define the static container body, which will provide the collisions at screen borders
b2BodyDef containerBodyDef;
b2Body* containerBody = world->CreateBody(&containerBodyDef);
```

Bodies are always created through the world's CreateBody method. This ensures that the body's memory is correctly allocated and freed. The b2BodyDef is a struct that holds all the data needed to create a body, such as position and the body type. By default, an empty body definition creates a static body at position 0, 0.

> **NOTE:** The &containerBodyDef variable is passed with a leading & (ampersand) character to the CreateBody method. That's C++ for "Give me the memory address of containerBodyDef." If you look at the definition of the CreateBody method, it requires a pointer passed to it: b2World::CreateBody(const b2BodyDef *def);. Since pointers store a memory address, you can make a pointer out of a nonpointer variable by prefixing it with the ampersand character.

The body itself won't do anything. To make it enclose the screen area, you'll have to create a shape with four sides:

```
// Create the screen box sides by using a polygon assigning each side individually
b2PolygonShape screenBoxShape;
int density = 0;

// Bottom
screenBoxShape.SetAsEdge(lowerLeftCorner, lowerRightCorner);
containerBody->CreateFixture(&screenBoxShape, density);
```

```
// Top
screenBoxShape.SetAsEdge(upperLeftCorner, upperRightCorner);
containerBody->CreateFixture(&screenBoxShape, density);

// Left side
screenBoxShape.SetAsEdge(upperLeftCorner, lowerLeftCorner);
containerBody->CreateFixture(&screenBoxShape, density);

// Right side
screenBoxShape.SetAsEdge(upperRightCorner, lowerRightCorner);
containerBody->CreateFixture(&screenBoxShape, density);
```

You may notice the missing declarations for the corner variable names. I'll get to them in a moment. First I'd like you to focus on how the b2PolygonShape screenBoxShape variable is reused. Each SetAsEdge method call is followed by a call to containerBody->CreateFixture(), which uses the -> operator because containerBody is a C++ pointer, and passes &screenBoxShape. Since Box2D makes a copy of screenBoxShape, you can safely reuse the same shape to create all four sides enclosing the screen area without modifying or overriding the previous lines. Since the body is a static body, density doesn't matter, and is set to 0.

> **NOTE:** The b2PolygonShape class has a SetAsBox method that looks as it might make the definition of the screen area easier by simply providing the screen's width and height. However, that would make the inside of the body a solid object, and any dynamic body added to the screen would actually be contained inside the solid shape. This would make the dynamic bodies try to move away from the collision, possibly at rapid speeds. The sides need to be created separately in order to make only the sides of the screen solid.

Now we'll move on to the missing variable declarations. Notice that the screen width and height is divided by a PTM_RATIO constant to convert them from pixels to meters:

```
// For the ground body we'll need these values
CGSize screenSize = [CCDirector sharedDirector].winSize;
float widthInMeters = screenSize.width / PTM_RATIO;
float heightInMeters = screenSize.height / PTM_RATIO;
b2Vec2 lowerLeftCorner = b2Vec2(0, 0);
b2Vec2 lowerRightCorner = b2Vec2(widthInMeters, 0);
b2Vec2 upperLeftCorner = b2Vec2(0, heightInMeters);

b2Vec2 upperRightCorner = b2Vec2(widthInMeters, heightInMeters);
```

Why meters, and what is PTM_RATIO? Box2D is optimized to work best with dimensions in the range of 0.1 to 10. It is tuned for the metric system, so all distances are considered to be meters, all masses are in kilograms, and time is measured in—quite oddly—seconds. If you're not familiar with the meters, kilograms, and seconds (MKS) system, don't worry—you don't have to meticulously convert yards into meters and pounds into kilograms. The conversion to meters is just a way to keep the distance values for Box2D in the desirable range of 0.1 to 10, and the masses used by bodies do not resemble real-world masses anyway. The masses of bodies will often need to be tweaked by feel rather than by using realistic weights.

You should try to keep the dimensions of objects in your world as close to 1 meter as much as possible. That is not to say that you can't have objects that are smaller than 0.1 meters or larger than 10 meters, but you may run into glitches and strange behavior if you create relatively small or large bodies.

The PTM_RATIO is defined like this:

```
#define PTM_RATIO 32
```

It is used to define that 32 pixels on the screen equal 1 meter in Box2D. A box-shaped body that's 32 pixels wide and high will be 1 meter wide and high. A body that's 4×4 pixels in size will be 0.125×0.125 meters in Box2D, while a relatively huge object of 256×256 pixels will be 8×8 meters in Box2D. The PTM_RATIO allows you to scale the size of Box2D objects down to the dimensions within which Box2D works best, and a PTM_RATIO of 32 is a good compromise for a screen area that may be as large as 1024×768 pixels on the iPad.

Converting Points

Note that the b2Vec2 struct is different from CGPoint, which means you cannot use a CGPoint where a b2Vec2 is required, and vice versa. In addition, Box2D points need to be converted to meters and back to pixels. To avoid making any mistakes, such as forgetting to convert from or to meters, or simply making a typo and using the x coordinate twice, it's highly recommended to wrap this repetitive code into convenience methods like these:

```
-(b2Vec2) toMeters:(CGPoint)point
{
        return b2Vec2(point.x / PTM_RATIO, point.y / PTM_RATIO);
}

-(CGPoint) toPixels:(b2Vec2)vec
{
        return ccpMult(CGPointMake(vec.x, vec.y), PTM_RATIO);
}
```

This allows you to write the following code to easily convert between CGPoint and pixels to b2Vec2 and meters:

```
CGPoint point = CGPointMake(100, 100);
b2Vec2 vec = b2Vec2(200, 200);

CGPoint pointFromVec;
pointFromVec = [self toPixels:vec];

b2Vec2 vecFromPoint;
vecFromPoint = [self toMeters:point];
```

Adding Boxes to the Box2D World

With a static body containing the objects within screen boundaries, all that's missing is something to be kept within the screen boundaries. How about little boxes, then?

I've added David Gervais' orthogonal tileset image *dg_grounds32.png* to the *Resources* folder of the *PhysicsBox2D01* project. The tiles are 32×32 pixels, so they'll make perfect 1×1-meter boxes. Listing 12–3 is the code in the init method that adds the texture and creates a couple boxes. It also schedules the update method, which is needed to update the box sprite positions, and it enables touch so that the user can tap the screen to create a new box.

Listing 12–3. *Adding an Initial Set of Boxes*

```
// Use the orthogonal tileset for the little boxes
CCSpriteBatchNode* batch = [CCSpriteBatchNode batchNodeWithFile:@"dg_grounds32.png"
                                                        capacity:150];
[self addChild:batch z:0 tag:kTagBatchNode];

// Add a few objects initially
for (int i = 0; i < 11; i++)
{
        [self addNewSpriteAt:CGPointMake(screenSize.width / 2, screenSize.height / 2)];
}

[self scheduleUpdate];
self.isTouchEnabled = YES;
```

The addNewSpriteAt method shown in Listing 12–4 is part of the cocos2d Box2D application template project, but slightly modified to make use of all the tiles in the tileset.

Listing 12–4. *Adding a New Dynamic Body with a Sprite*

```
-(void) addNewSpriteAt:(CGPoint)pos
{
        CCSpriteBatchNode* batch = (CCSpriteBatchNode*)[self
                                                getChildByTag:kTagBatchNode];

        int idx = CCRANDOM_0_1() * TILESET_COLUMNS;
        int idy = CCRANDOM_0_1() * TILESET_ROWS;
        CGRect tileRect = CGRectMake(TILESIZE * idx, TILESIZE * idy, TILESIZE,
TILESIZE);
        CCSprite* sprite = [CCSprite spriteWithBatchNode:batch rect:tileRect];
        sprite.position = pos;
        [batch addChild:sprite];

        // Create a body definition and set it to be a dynamic body
        b2BodyDef bodyDef;
        bodyDef.type = b2_dynamicBody;
        bodyDef.position = [self toMeters:pos];
        bodyDef.userData = sprite;
        b2Body* body = world->CreateBody(&bodyDef);
```

```
        // Define a box shape and assign it to the body fixture
        b2PolygonShape dynamicBox;
        float tileInMeters = TILESIZE / PTM_RATIO;
        dynamicBox.SetAsBox(tileInMeters * 0.5f, tileInMeters * 0.5f);

        b2FixtureDef fixtureDef;
        fixtureDef.shape = &dynamicBox;
        fixtureDef.density = 0.3f;
        fixtureDef.friction = 0.5f;
        fixtureDef.restitution = 0.6f;
        body->CreateFixture(&fixtureDef);
}
```

First, a sprite is created from the CCSpriteBatchNode by using CCSprite's
spriteWithBatchNode initializer and supplying a CGRect that is 32×32 pixels in size, to
randomly pick one of the tileset's tiles as the sprite's image.

Then a body is created, but this time the b2BodyDef type property is set to
b2_dynamicBody, which makes it a dynamic body that can move around and collide with
other dynamic bodies. The previously created sprite is assigned to the userData
property. Later on, when you are iterating over the bodies in the world, this allows you to
quickly access the body's sprite.

The body's shape is a b2PolygonShape set to a box shape that is half a meter in size. The
SetAsBox method creates a box shape that is twice the given width and height, so the
coordinates need to be divided by 2—or, as in this case, multiplied by 0.5f to create a
box shape whose sides are 1 meter wide and high.

The dynamic body also needs a fixture that contains the body's essential parameters—
first and foremost the shape, but also density, friction, and restitution—which influence
how the body moves and bounces around in the world. Consider the fixture to be a set
of data used by bodies.

Connecting Sprites with Bodies

The box sprites won't follow their physics bodies automatically, and the bodies won't do
anything unless you regularly call the Step method of the Box2D world. You then have to
update the sprite positions by taking the body position and angle and assigning it to the
sprite. This is done in the update method shown in Listing 12–5.

Listing 12–5. *Updating Each Body's Sprite Position and Rotation*

```
-(void) update:(ccTime)delta
{
        // Advance the physics world by one step, using fixed time steps
        float timeStep = 0.03f;
        int32 velocityIterations = 8;
        int32 positionIterations = 1;
        world->Step(timeStep, velocityIterations, positionIterations);

        for (b2Body* body = world->GetBodyList(); body != nil; body = body->GetNext())
        {
                CCSprite* sprite = (CCSprite*)body->GetUserData();
                if (sprite!= NULL)
```

```
        {
                sprite.position = [self toPixels:body->GetPosition()];
                float angle = body->GetAngle();
                sprite.rotation = CC_RADIANS_TO_DEGREES(angle) * -1;
        }
    }
}
```

The Box2D world is animated by regularly calling the Step method. It takes three parameters. The first is timeStep, which tells Box2D how much time has passed since the last step. It directly affects the distance that objects will move in this step. For games it is not recommended to pass the delta time as timeStep, because the delta time fluctuates, and so the speed of the physics bodies will not be constant. This effect rears its ugly head when the device may be taking a tenth of a second to do background processing, like sending or receiving an e-mail in the background. This can make all physics objects move large distances in the next frame. In a game, you'd rather have the game stop for a tenth of a second and then carry on where you left off. Without a fixed time step, the physics engine would try to cope with a short interruption by moving all objects based on the time difference. If the time difference is large, the objects will move a lot more in a single frame, and that can lead to them suddenly moving a large distance.

The second and third parameters to the Step method are the number of iterations. They determine the accuracy of the physics simulation, and also the time it takes to calculate the movement of the bodies. It's a trade-off between speed and accuracy. In the case of position iterations, you can safely err on the side of speed and only require a single iteration—more position accuracy is not normally needed in games. Velocity is more important, however; a good starting point for velocity iterations is eight. More than ten velocity iterations have no discernable effect in games, but just one to four iterations won't be enough to get a stable simulation. The fewer the velocity iterations, the more bumpily and restlessly the objects will behave. I encourage you to experiment with these values.

After the world has advanced one step, the for loop iterates over all of the world's bodies using the world->GetBodyList and body->GetNext methods. For each body, its user data is returned and cast to a CCSprite pointer. If it exists, the body's position is converted to pixels and assigned to the sprite's position so that the sprite moves along with the body. Likewise, the body's angle is obtained; because that measurement is in radians, it's converted to degrees using cocos2d's CC_RADIANS_TO_DEGREES method and multiplied by –1 to rotate the sprites in the same direction as the body.

Collision Detection

Box2D has a b2ContactListener class, which you are supposed to subclass if you want to receive collision callbacks. The following code refers to the *PhysicsBox2D02* project.

Create a new class in Xcode and name it ContactListener. Then rename the implementation file to *ContactListener.mm* so it has the file extension *.mm*. Then you will be able to use both C++ and Objective-C code in the same file. Listing 12–6 shows the ContactListener header file.

Listing 12–6. *The ContactListener Class's Interface*

```
#import "Box2D.h"

class ContactListener : public b2ContactListener
{
private:
        void BeginContact(b2Contact* contact);
        void EndContact(b2Contact* contact);
};
```

It's a C++ class, so the class definition is a little different. Note the trailing semicolon after the last bracket. It's a common error to forget that semicolon. The BeginContact and EndContact methods are defined by Box2D and get called whenever there is a collision between two bodies.

In the implementation, I merely change the sprite's colors to magenta while the two bodies are in contact, and set it back to white when they are no longer in contact, as shown in Listing 12–7.

Listing 12–7. *Checking for the Beginning and Ending of Collisions*

```
#import "ContactListener.h"
#import "cocos2d.h"

void ContactListener::BeginContact(b2Contact* contact)
{
        b2Body* bodyA = contact->GetFixtureA()->GetBody();
        b2Body* bodyB = contact->GetFixtureB()->GetBody();
        CCSprite* spriteA = (CCSprite*)bodyA->GetUserData();
        CCSprite* spriteB = (CCSprite*)bodyB->GetUserData();

        if (spriteA != NULL && spriteB != NULL)
        {
                spriteA.color = ccMAGENTA;
                spriteB.color = ccMAGENTA;
        }
}

void ContactListener::EndContact(b2Contact* contact)
{
        b2Body* bodyA = contact->GetFixtureA()->GetBody();
        b2Body* bodyB = contact->GetFixtureB()->GetBody();
        CCSprite* spriteA = (CCSprite*)bodyA->GetUserData();
        CCSprite* spriteB = (CCSprite*)bodyB->GetUserData();

        if (spriteA != NULL && spriteB != NULL)
        {
                spriteA.color = ccWHITE;
                spriteB.color = ccWHITE;
        }
}
```

b2Contact contains all the contact information, including two sets of everything suffixed with A and B. These are the two contacting bodies; no differentiation is made as to which is colliding with the other—they are both simply colliding with each other. If, for example, you have an enemy colliding with a player's bullet, you would want to damage the enemy, not the bullet. It is up to you to determine which is which. Also keep in mind that the contact methods may be called multiple times per frame, once for each contact pair.

It's a bit convoluted to get to the sprite from the contact through the fixture to the body, and then get the user data from that. The Box2D API reference certainly helps you find your way through the hierarchy, and with a little experience this will become second nature.

To actually get the ContactListener connected with Box2D, you have to add it to the world. In HelloWorldScene, import the *ContactListener.h* header file and add a ContactListener* contactListener to the class as a member variable:

```
#import "cocos2d.h"
#import "Box2D.h"
#import "GLES-Render.h"

#import "ContactListener.h"

...

@interface HelloWorld : CCLayer
{
        b2World* world;
        ContactListener* contactListener;
}

...

@end
```

In the init method of HelloWorldScene, you can then create a new ContactListener instance and set it as the contact listener for the world:

```
contactListener = new ContactListener();
world->SetContactListener(contactListener);
```

What remains is to delete the contactListener in the dealloc method to free its memory:

```
-(void) dealloc
{
        delete contactListener;
        delete world;

        [super dealloc];
}
```

Now the boxes in the *PhysicsBox2D02* project will be tinted purple whenever they touch other boxes.

Joint Venture

With joints, you can connect bodies together. The type of joint determines which way the connected bodies are connected. In this example method, I create four bodies total. Three are dynamic bodies connected to each other using a *revolute joint*, which keeps the bodies at the same distance but allows them to rotate 360 degrees around each other. If you find it hard to imagine how these objects might behave, you should try them out in the *PhysicsBox2D02* project. In this case, working code can explain it better than words or a static image could. The fourth body is a static body to which one of the dynamic bodies is also attached using a revolute joint.

```
-(void) addSomeJoinedBodies:(CGPoint)pos
{
        // Create a body definition and set it to be a dynamic body
        b2BodyDef bodyDef;
        bodyDef.type = b2_dynamicBody;

        // Position must be converted to meters
        bodyDef.position = [self toMeters:pos];
        bodyDef.position = bodyDef.position + b2Vec2(-1, -1);
        bodyDef.userData = [self addRandomSpriteAt:pos];
        b2Body* bodyA = world->CreateBody(&bodyDef);
        [self bodyCreateFixture:bodyA];

        bodyDef.position = [self toMeters:pos];
        bodyDef.userData = [self addRandomSpriteAt:pos];
        b2Body* bodyB = world->CreateBody(&bodyDef);
        [self bodyCreateFixture:bodyB];

        bodyDef.position = [self toMeters:pos];
        bodyDef.position = bodyDef.position + b2Vec2(1, 1);
        bodyDef.userData = [self addRandomSpriteAt:pos];
        b2Body* bodyC = world->CreateBody(&bodyDef);
        [self bodyCreateFixture:bodyC];

        // Create the revolute joints
        b2RevoluteJointDef jointDef;
        jointDef.Initialize(bodyA, bodyB, bodyB->GetWorldCenter());
        bodyA->GetWorld()->CreateJoint(&jointDef);

        jointDef.Initialize(bodyB, bodyC, bodyC->GetWorldCenter());
        bodyA->GetWorld()->CreateJoint(&jointDef);

        // Create an invisible static body and attach body A to it
        bodyDef.type = b2_staticBody;
        bodyDef.position = [self toMeters:pos];
        b2Body* staticBody = world->CreateBody(&bodyDef);

        jointDef.Initialize(staticBody, bodyA, bodyA->GetWorldCenter());
        bodyA->GetWorld()->CreateJoint(&jointDef);
}
```

b2BodyDef is reused for all bodies, only the position is modified for each body and a random CCSprite is created and assigned as userData. The addRandomSpriteAt method contains the code that creates a sprite from the CCSpriteBatchNode, as discussed earlier. Since in the addSomeJoinedBodies method there are now several sprites needed, it made sense to refactor the creation of a sprite into the method addRandomSpriteAt.

b2RevoluteJointDef is filled with data by using the Initialize method providing two bodies to connect to each other and a coordinate where the joint is located. By using one body's GetWorldCenter coordinate, that body will be centered on the joint and only allowed to rotate around itself.

The joint is created by the CreateJoint method of the b2World class. Even though the HelloWorldScene class in the *PhysicsBox2D02* project has a b2World member variable, I wanted to illustrate that you can also get the world through any body—it doesn't matter which one—by using the body's GetWorld method. This is good to know, because in the ContactListener discussed earlier, you do not have a b2World member variable, so you'll have to get the b2World pointer through one of the contact bodies.

Chipmunk

The Chipmunk physics engine was developed by Scott Lembcke of Howling Moon Software. Chipmunk was actually inspired by an early version of Box2D, before it was a full-fledged physics engine. You can download Chipmunk from its Google Code site. If you like Chipmunk, you should also consider donating to the project, which you can do via the **Donate** button from the same site: http://code.google.com/p/chipmunk-physics. The Chipmunk documentation is located on Scott's home page, at http://files.slembcke.net/chipmunk/release/ChipmunkLatest-Docs. And if you need help, you can find that in the Chipmunk forums: www.slembcke.net/forums.

Objectified Chipmunk

There are actually two Objective-C wrappers available for Chipmunk, and more are being worked on. I don't discuss them in this book, but you should be aware of them and try them out.

Scott's Objective-C wrapper is part of the Chipmunk distribution, but only works in the iPhone Simulator. To be able to deploy it to the iPhone, you have to buy his Chipmunk Objective-C wrapper on the Howling Moon Software web site, at http://howlingmoonsoftware.com/objectiveChipmunk.php.

It's always best to try before you buy, so you can follow this tutorial on how to use the Objective-C wrapper for the iPhone Simulator: http://files.slembcke.net/chipmunk/tutorials/SimpleObjectiveChipmunk.

The alternative is Chipmunk SpaceManager, written by Robert Blackwood, which comes with a free Objective-C wrapper for Chipmunk. However, its main purpose is to make integration of Chipmunk with cocos2d easier. If you would like to try out Chipmunk SpaceManager, you can download it from the following link, where you can also donate to the project should you like it: http://code.google.com/p/chipmunk-spacemanager.

The SpaceManager API reference can be found on Robert's home page at www.mobile-bros.com/spacemanager/docs.

Both the Chipmunk and SpaceManager distributions, including their respective documentation files, are also in this chapter's source code folder, in the *Physics Engine Libraries* subfolder.

Chipmunks in Space

For the Chipmunk tutorial, I'll be building the same project as before. I'll start with the *PhysicsChipmunk01* project and the initial setup of the Chipmunk physics engine. Listing 12–8 shows the HelloWorldScene header file:

Listing 12–8. *The Chipmunk HelloWorld Interface*

```
#import "cocos2d.h"
#import "chipmunk.h"

enum
{
        kTagBatchNode = 1,
};

@interface HelloWorld : CCLayer
{
        cpSpace* space;
}

+(id) scene;

@end
```

Nothing unusual here, except for the cpSpace member variable. Instead of *world*, Chipmunk calls its world a *space*. It's a different terminology for the same thing. The Chipmunk space contains all the rigid bodies.

Chipmunk is initialized in HelloWorldScene's init method as follows:

```
cpInitChipmunk();

space = cpSpaceNew();
space->iterations = 8;
space->gravity = CGPointMake(0, -100);
```

The very first thing you must do before using any Chipmunk methods is to call cpInitChipmunk. After that you can create the space with cpSpaceNew and set the number of iterations—in this case eight. This is the same iteration count we used for velocity iterations in the Box2D example's update method. Chipmunk knows only one type of iteration—the elasticIterations field is deprecated and should no longer be used. I mention this in case you are already familiar with Chipmunk. You may get away with fewer than eight iterations if your game does not allow objects to stack; otherwise, you may find that stacked objects never get to rest and keep jittering and sliding for a long period of time.

Notice how Chipmunk can use the same CGPoint structure used in the iPhone SDK. Chipmunk internally uses a structure called cpVect, but in cocos2d you can use both interchangeably. I use a CGPoint to set the gravity to –100, which means downward acceleration that is roughly the same as that used in the Box2D project.

Of course, the space also needs to be released in the dealloc method; this is done by calling cpSpaceFree and passing the space as parameter:

```
-(void) dealloc
{
        cpSpaceFree(space);
        [super dealloc];
}
```

Boxing-In the Boxes

To keep all the boxes within the boundaries of the screen, you need to create a static body whose shape defines the screen area. First, the variables for the screen's corners are defined:

```
// For the ground body we'll need these values
CGSize screenSize = [CCDirector sharedDirector].winSize;
CGPoint lowerLeftCorner = CGPointMake(0, 0);
CGPoint lowerRightCorner = CGPointMake(screenSize.width, 0);
CGPoint upperLeftCorner = CGPointMake(0, screenSize.height);
CGPoint upperRightCorner = CGPointMake(screenSize.width, screenSize.height);
```

Contrary to Box2D, you do not have to take any pixel-to-meter ratio into account. You can use the screen size in pixels as it is to define the corner points, and to work with Chipmunk bodies in general.

Next you'll create the static body by using the cpBodyNew and passing INFINITY for both parameters, which makes the body a static body. Those parameters are mass and inertia, and with them being set to the INFINITY value, this body isn't going to go anywhere.

```
// Create the static body that keeps objects within the screen area
float mass = INFINITY;
float inertia = INFINITY;
cpBody* staticBody = cpBodyNew(mass, inertia);
```

> **NOTE:** Mass and inertia in Chipmunk are comparable to density and friction in Box2D. The difference between inertia and friction is that the former determines the resistance of a body to start moving, while the latter determines how much motion a body loses when it is in contact with other bodies.

Next, you'll define the shape that goes with the body and makes up the screen borders, as shown in Listing 12–9.

Listing 12–9. *Creating the Screen Border Collisions*

```
cpShape* shape;
float elasticity = 1.0f;
float friction = 1.0f;
float radius = 0.0f;

// Bottom
shape = cpSegmentShapeNew(staticBody, lowerLeftCorner, lowerRightCorner, radius);
shape->e = elasticity;
shape->u = friction;
cpSpaceAddStaticShape(space, shape);

// Top
shape = cpSegmentShapeNew(staticBody, upperLeftCorner, upperRightCorner, radius);
shape->e = elasticity;
shape->u = friction;
cpSpaceAddStaticShape(space, shape);

// Left side
shape = cpSegmentShapeNew(staticBody, lowerLeftCorner, upperLeftCorner, radius);
shape->e = elasticity;
shape->u = friction;
cpSpaceAddStaticShape(space, shape);

// Right side
shape = cpSegmentShapeNew(staticBody, lowerRightCorner, upperRightCorner, radius);
shape->e = elasticity;
shape->u = friction;
cpSpaceAddStaticShape(space, shape);
```

The cpSegmentShapeNew method is used to create four new line segments to define the sides of the screen area. The shape variable is reused for convenience, but it requires you to set *elasticity* (which is the same as restitution) and friction after each call to cpSegmentShapeNew. Then each shape is added to the space as a static shape via the cpSpaceAddStaticShape method.

> **NOTE:** In Chipmunk you will have to work with one-letter fields like e and u regularly. Personally, I find that this makes it hard to pick up Chipmunk because you don't immediately grasp the meaning of these fields and you have to refer to the Chipmunk documentation more often than necessary.

Adding Ticky-Tacky Little Boxes

To add boxes to the world, I used the same code in the init method of HelloWorldScene as in the Box2D example. Refer to Listing 12–3 if you'd like to refresh your memory.

I'll go straight to creating the dynamic body for new boxes, which is what the addNewSpriteAt method does (Listing 12–10).

Listing 12–10. *Adding a Body with a Sprite, Chipmunk Style*

```
-(void) addNewSpriteAt:(CGPoint)pos
{
        float mass = 0.5f;
        float moment = cpMomentForBox(mass, TILESIZE, TILESIZE);
        cpBody* body = cpBodyNew(mass, moment);

        body->p = pos;
        cpSpaceAddBody(space, body);

        float halfTileSize = TILESIZE * 0.5f;
        int numVertices = 4;
        CGPoint vertices[] =
        {
                CGPointMake(-halfTileSize, -halfTileSize),
                CGPointMake(-halfTileSize, halfTileSize),
                CGPointMake(halfTileSize, halfTileSize),
                CGPointMake(halfTileSize, -halfTileSize),
        };

        CGPoint offset = CGPointZero;
        float elasticity = 0.3f;
        float friction = 0.7f;

        cpShape* shape = cpPolyShapeNew(body, numVertices, vertices, offset);
        shape->e = elasticity;
        shape->u = friction;
        shape->data = [self addRandomSpriteAt:pos];
        cpSpaceAddShape(space, shape);
}
```

The dynamic body for the box is created with the cpBodyNew method with the given mass and a *moment of inertia*. The moment of inertia determines the resistance of a body to move, and it's calculated by the helper method cpMomentForBox, which takes the body's mass and the size of the box—in this case TILESIZE—which makes it a 32×32-pixel box.

The body's position, p, is then updated and the body added to the space via the cpSpaceAddBody method. Note that contrary to Box2D, you do not have to convert pixels to meters; you can work with pixel coordinates directly.

Then a list of vertices are created, which will become the corners of the box shape. Because the corner positions are positioned relative to the center of the box we're creating, they are all half a tile's size away from the center. Otherwise, the box shape would be twice as big as the tile.

The cpPolyShapeNew method then takes the body as input, the vertices array and the number of vertices in the array, as well as an optional offset, which is set to CGPointZero in this case. Out comes a new cpShape pointer for the box shape. The shape's elasticity and friction are set to values that give a similar behavior to the Box2D boxes, and after the sprite is set as user data to the data field, the shape is added to the space via cpSpaceAddShape.

The addRandomSpriteAt method in Listing 12–11 simply creates the CCSprite object that goes along with the new dynamic body.

Listing 12–11. *Creating New Box Objects with Random Images*

```
-(CCSprite*) addRandomSpriteAt:(CGPoint)pos
{
        CCSpriteBatchNode* batch = (CCSpriteBatchNode*)[self
                                              getChildByTag:kTagBatchNode];

        int idx = CCRANDOM_0_1() * TILESET_COLUMNS;
        int idy = CCRANDOM_0_1() * TILESET_ROWS;
                CGRect tileRect = CGRectMake(TILESIZE * idx, TILESIZE * idy, TILESIZE,
                                                                    TILESIZE);
        CCSprite* sprite = [CCSprite spriteWithBatchNode:batch rect:tileRect];
        sprite.position = pos;
        [batch addChild:sprite];

        return sprite;
}
```

Updating the Boxes' Sprites

Just like with Box2D you have to update the sprite's position and rotation to be in line with their dynamic body's position and rotation every frame. Again, this is done in the update method:

```
-(void) update:(ccTime)delta
{
        float timeStep = 0.03f;
        cpSpaceStep(space, timeStep);

        // Call forEachShape C method to update sprite positions
        cpSpaceHashEach(space->activeShapes, &forEachShape, nil);
        cpSpaceHashEach(space->staticShapes, &forEachShape, nil);
}
```

Just as with Box2D, you have to advance the physics simulation using a step method. In this case, it's cpSpaceStep, which takes the space and a timeStep as input. A fixed time step works best, and just like in Box2D, it's highly recommended to use a fixed time step as opposed to passing the delta time. As long as the frame rate doesn't fluctuate heavily (it really shouldn't anyway), using a fixed-time-step approach works very well.

The cpSpaceHashEach method calls the C method forEachShape for, well, each of the shapes. Or, more accurately, the cpSpaceHashEach method calls forEachShape for each active shape (dynamic body), and then for each static shape (static body). With the third parameter, you can pass an arbitrary pointer as a parameter to the forEachShape method, but because it's not needed in this case, it is set to nil. And even though this example project doesn't have static shapes with sprites assigned to them, it nevertheless calls the method for static shapes, just in case you want to be adding some static shapes with a sprite.

The forEachShape method is a callback method that's written in C. In the example project, you can find it at the top of the *HelloWorldScene.m* file, outside the @implementation. Although it's not strictly necessary to place the method outside the @implementation, it signals that this method isn't part of the HelloWorldScene class. The method is defined as static, which effectively makes it a global method, as Listing 12–12 shows.

Listing 12–12. *Updating a Body Sprite's Position and Rotation*

```
// C method that updates sprite position and rotation:
static void forEachShape(void* shapePointer, void* data)
{
        cpShape* shape = (cpShape*)shapePointer;
        CCSprite* sprite = (CCSprite*)shape->data;
        if (sprite != nil)
        {
                cpBody* body = shape->body;
                sprite.position = body->p;
                sprite.rotation = CC_RADIANS_TO_DEGREES(body->a) * -1;
        }
}
```

The signature for methods passed to cpSpaceHashEach is strictly defined; the method must take two parameters, and both are void pointers. The second parameter would be the data pointer passed as third parameter to cpSpaceHashEach. For both shapePointer and data pointer, you have to know what kind of object they're pointing to; otherwise, disaster will strike in the form of EXC_BAD_ACCESS.

In this case, I know that shapePointer is going to point to a cpShape struct, so I can safely cast it and then access the shape's data field to get its CCSprite pointer. If the sprite is a valid pointer, I can get the body from the shape and use that to set the position and rotation of the sprite to that of the body. As with Box2D before, the rotation has to be converted from radians to degrees first, and multiplied by –1 to correct the direction of the rotation.

A Chipmunk Collision Course

Collisions in Chipmunk are also handled by C callback methods. In the *PhysicsChipmunk02* project, I've added the contactBegin and contactEnd static methods (in Listing 12–13), which do exactly the same as their Box2D counterparts: change the color of boxes that are in contact to magenta.

Listing 12–13. *Collision Callbacks a la Chipmunk*

```
static int contactBegin(cpArbiter* arbiter, struct cpSpace* space, void* data)
{
        bool processCollision = YES;

        cpShape* shapeA;
        cpShape* shapeB;
        cpArbiterGetShapes(arbiter, &shapeA, &shapeB);

        CCSprite* spriteA = (CCSprite*)shapeA->data;
        CCSprite* spriteB = (CCSprite*)shapeB->data;
        if (spriteA != nil && spriteB != nil)
        {
                spriteA.color = ccMAGENTA;
                spriteB.color = ccMAGENTA;
```

```
        }

        return processCollision;
}

static void contactEnd(cpArbiter* arbiter, cpSpace* space, void* data)
{
        cpShape* shapeA;
        cpShape* shapeB;
        cpArbiterGetShapes(arbiter, &shapeA, &shapeB);

        CCSprite* spriteA = (CCSprite*)shapeA->data;
        CCSprite* spriteB = (CCSprite*)shapeB->data;
        if (spriteA != nil && spriteB != nil)
        {
                spriteA.color = ccWHITE;
                spriteB.color = ccWHITE;
        }
}
```

The contactBegin method should return YES if the collision should be processed normally. By returning NO or 0 from this method, you can also ignore collisions. In order to get to the sprites, you first have to get the shapes from the cpArbiter, which just like b2Contact holds the contact information. Via the cpArbiterGetShapes method and passing two shapes as out parameters, you get the colliding shapes from which you can then retrieve the individual CCSprite pointers. If they are both valid, their color can be changed.

As with Box2D, these callbacks don't get called by themselves. In the HelloWorldScene init method, right after the space is created, you must add the collision handlers using the cpSpaceAddCollisionHandler method:

```
unsigned int defaultCollisionType = 0;
cpSpaceAddCollisionHandler(space, defaultCollisionType, defaultCollisionType,
                                    &contactBegin, NULL, NULL,
                                             &contactEnd, NULL);
```

The default collision type for shapes is 0, and because I don't care about filtering collisions, both collision type parameters are set to 0. You can assign each body's shape an integer value to its collision_type property and then add collision handlers that are only called if bodies of matching collision types collide. This is called *filtering collisions*, and is described in the Chipmunk manual, at http://files.slembcke.net/chipmunk/release/ChipmunkLatest-Docs/#cpShape.

The next four parameters are pointers to C callback methods for the four collision stages: *begin*, *pre-solve*, *post-solve*, and *separation* (the same as the EndContact event in Box2D). These serve the same purpose as the corresponding callbacks in Box2D. Most of the time you'll only be interested in the begin and separation events.

I pass NULL for pre-solve and post-solve, as I'm not interested in handling these. You can use these methods to influence the collision or to retrieve the collision force in the post-solve step. The final parameter is an arbitrary data pointer you can pass on to the callback methods if you need it. I don't, so I set it to NULL as well.

With that, you have a working collision callback mechanism.

Joints for Chipmunks

The Chipmunk example project also needs its own implementation of
addSomeJoinedBodies. The setup is more verbose than for Box2D, as shown in Listing
12–14. You'll recognize most of the code as setting up static and dynamic bodies—if
you find that code familiar, feel free to skip to the end where the joints are created.

Listing 12–14. *Creating Three Bodies Connected with Joints*

```
-(void) addSomeJoinedBodies:(CGPoint)pos
{
        float mass = 1.0f;
        float moment = cpMomentForBox(mass, TILESIZE, TILESIZE);

        float halfTileSize = TILESIZE * 0.5f;
        int numVertices = 4;
        CGPoint vertices[] =
        {
                CGPointMake(-halfTileSize, -halfTileSize),
                CGPointMake(-halfTileSize, halfTileSize),
                CGPointMake(halfTileSize, halfTileSize),
                CGPointMake(halfTileSize, -halfTileSize),
        };

        // Create a static body
        cpBody* staticBody = cpBodyNew(INFINITY, INFINITY);
        staticBody->p = pos;

        CGPoint offset = CGPointZero;
        cpShape* shape = cpPolyShapeNew(staticBody, numVertices, vertices, offset);
        cpSpaceAddStaticShape(space, shape);

        // Create three new dynamic bodies
        float posOffset = 1.4f;
        pos.x += TILESIZE * posOffset;
        cpBody* bodyA = cpBodyNew(mass, moment);
        bodyA->p = pos;
        cpSpaceAddBody(space, bodyA);

        shape = cpPolyShapeNew(bodyA, numVertices, vertices, offset);
        shape->data = [self addRandomSpriteAt:pos];
        cpSpaceAddShape(space, shape);

        pos.x += TILESIZE * posOffset;
        cpBody* bodyB = cpBodyNew(mass, moment);
        bodyB->p = pos;
        cpSpaceAddBody(space, bodyB);

        shape = cpPolyShapeNew(bodyB, numVertices, vertices, offset);
        shape->data = [self addRandomSpriteAt:pos];
        cpSpaceAddShape(space, shape);

        pos.x += TILESIZE * posOffset;
        cpBody* bodyC = cpBodyNew(mass, moment);
```

```
        bodyC->p = pos;
        cpSpaceAddBody(space, bodyC);

        shape = cpPolyShapeNew(bodyC, numVertices, vertices, offset);
        shape->data = [self addRandomSpriteAt:pos];
        cpSpaceAddShape(space, shape);

        // Create the joints and add the constraints to the space
        cpConstraint* constraint1 = cpPivotJointNew(staticBody, bodyA, staticBody->p);
        cpConstraint* constraint2 = cpPivotJointNew(bodyA, bodyB, bodyA->p);
        cpConstraint* constraint3 = cpPivotJointNew(bodyB, bodyC, bodyB->p);

        cpSpaceAddConstraint(space, constraint1);
        cpSpaceAddConstraint(space, constraint2);
        cpSpaceAddConstraint(space, constraint3);
}
```

In this example I'm creating a pivot joint with cpPivotJointNew, which is the same as the b2RevoluteJoint used in the Box2D example. Each joint is created with the two bodies that should be connected to each other, and one of the bodies' center position as the anchor point. The cpPivotJointNew method returns a cpConstraint pointer, which you'll have to add to the space using the cpSpaceAddConstraint method.

Conclusion

In this chapter you learned the basics of the two physics engines distributed with cocos2d: Box2D and Chipmunk. You now have two working examples of these physics engines at your disposal, which should help you decide which one you'd like to use.

You learned how to set up a screen area that contains all the little boxes created from a tilemap as dynamic bodies. You now also know the basics of detecting collisions and how to create joints to connect bodies together in both physics engines.

In the next chapter you'll be making a game that uses the Box2D physics engine.

Chapter 13

Pinball Game

I'd like to put the Box2D physics engine to good use, so in this chapter you'll be making an actual pinball game. Pinball tables are all about using our physical world and turning that into a fun experience. With a physics engine, however, you're not just limited to real-world physics.

Some elements of the pinball table, such as bumpers and balls, can be created by simply choosing the right balance of friction, restitution, and density. Others need joints to work—a revolute joint for the flippers and a prismatic joint for the plunger. And of course you'll need lots of static shapes that define the collision polygons of the table.

Since it would be impractical to define collision polygons in source code, at least for the level of detail necessary to build a believable pinball table, I'll introduce another useful tool: VertexHelper. With that, you can create collision polygons by simply drawing the vertices one after the other.

At the end of this chapter you'll have a fully playable pinball game, as depicted in Figure 13–1.

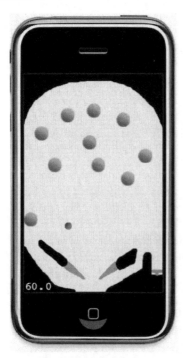

Figure 13–1. *The pinball table built in this chapter*

Shapes: Convex and Counterclockwise

Let's start with the requirements of collision polygons. The first thing you need to be aware of when defining collision polygons for Box2D and Chipmunk is that these engines expect the collision polygons to have the following properties:

- Vertices defined in a counterclockwise fashion
- Polygons as convex shapes

A *convex* shape is a shape where you can draw a straight line between any two points without the line ever leaving the shape. This is opposed to *concave* shapes, where a straight line between two points can be drawn such that the line is not entirely contained within the shape. See Figure 13–2 for an illustration of the difference between convex and concave shapes.

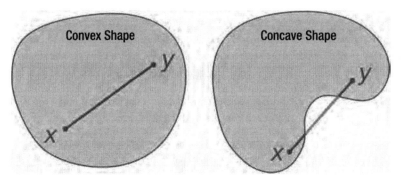

Figure 13-2. *Convex and concave shapes*

Defining the vertices of a convex shape in a counterclockwise fashion can be illustrated by drawing a convex shape in your mind. You place one vertex anywhere, and then go left to place another. Then go down and to the right, and you will have drawn a rectangle in a counterclockwise fashion. Or place another vertex, and then go right, up, and then left, and you will have drawn a counterclockwise shape. It doesn't matter where you start with the first vertex, but it's very important to follow the counterclockwise orientation of vertices.

> **TIP:** How do you know if you made a mistake and accidentally created a clockwise-oriented or concave collision shape? Well, every physics engine reacts differently. Some will tell you up-front by throwing an error. But in the case of Box2D, if a moving body hits a collision shape that is not well formed, the moving body will simply stop moving when it gets close to that shape. If you ever see that effect happening in your Box2D game, check the nearby collision polygons.

Working with VertexHelper

Armed with the knowledge about properly defining collision polygons, it's time to check out the VertexHelper tool. The VertexHelper source code is shared on GitHub at `http://github.com/jfahrenkrug/VertexHelper`.

Click the **Download Source** button on the web site, save the file somewhere on your computer, and extract it. Then open the *VertexHelper.xcodeproj* file in Xcode, and build and run it. In its main window, VertexHelper will then ask you to drop the sprite image underneath the bull's eye image. Follow that order, and drag and drop the *tablebottom.png* file from the *PhysicsBox2D03* project onto VertexHelper.

VertexHelper will show the dropped image, and you can drag and move it around. With the **Zoom In** and **Zoom Out** buttons you can increase and decrease the size of the image. You should position and zoom the image in such a way that you can comfortably define the edge vertices for the collision polygons, so zoom in at least two or three times.

Next, you should set up the image and output properties at the bottom, otherwise VertexHelper will not allow you to add vertices. For **Rows/Cols**, enter **1** into both boxes because you're not using a tiled image—it's just one big tile as far as VertexHelper is concerned. The option to edit multiple parts of an image is only useful if you have a Texture Atlas in which the images are evenly spaced and all the same size. However, since you'll likely be using Zwoptex to create your Texture Atlas, you should and probably will have to edit the vertices for each image individually.

Set the **Type** to **Box2D** and the **Style** to **Initialization**, and change the **Name** to vertices— although that name is my personal preference and it's really up to you. Then you can click the **Edit Mode** check box to start editing vertices, which you can do by clicking in the image and placing a new vertex for each click.

> **CAUTION:** Keep in mind that VertexHelper has its rough edges. Once you start adding vertices, you cannot undo, delete, or move them. So every click has to be right on target. If you make a mistake, you'll have to go to **File ➤ New** to create a new window, and then drag and drop the image onto VertexHelper again to start over.
>
> It's also possible to create red oval shapes instead of vertices by clicking and dragging. This may either be a bug or a hidden feature—in either case, you don't want the oval shapes for the pinball game, so avoid clicking and dragging. Also, don't click the **Scan** button. VertexHelper will then automatically create a convex shape around the image (which can be quite useful in some cases, but for the pinball game the automatically generated shapes cannot be used).

Remember to create vertices in a counterclockwise fashion, and to create convex shapes at all times. With the *tablebottom.png* file you cannot create the collision polygon in one go, because that would create a concave shape. Instead, as you can see in Figure 13–3, you can define several shapes one after the other.

VertexHelper is really designed to create one shape per image, but you can also define several shapes in one go by remembering which shapes you created and how many points you defined for each shape. Once you copy the initialization text, you can then split it apart into several initialization lines—one for each shape containing only the points defined for that shape. In Figure 13–3, for example, the first shape is the rightmost one, which contains four points. So you would copy the initialization text, delete all but the first four points, and change the num variable from 26 to 4. The next shape has six points, and so uses the fifth through tenth point with num set to 6. In this way, you can create multiple shapes for a single image by splitting up the generated text once you're done defining the shapes in VertexHelper. Just be careful to properly adjust the number of vertices, otherwise Box2D might crash.

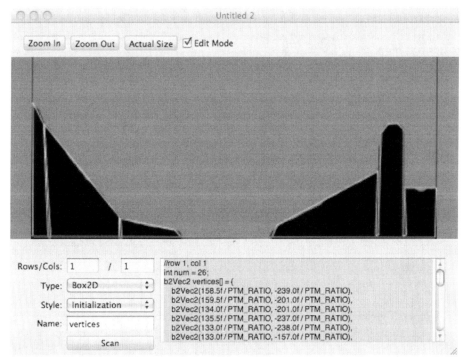

Figure 13–3. *Editing collision shapes in VertexHelper*

All of the collision polygons for the pinball game have been created using VertexHelper. You can continue to define the collision polygons for the remaining images, namely *flipper-left.png*, *flipper-right.png*, *plunger.png*, and *tabletop.png*. Only the ball and bumper shapes use Box2D's internal b2CircleShape.

> **NOTE:** You'll notice that the vertices don't perfectly overlap each other. They don't have to. As long as the gaps and grooves are noticeably smaller than the ball itself, they won't have a noticeable effect on the physics simulation of the pinball table.

Creating the Pinball Table

With the collision polygons defined in VertexHelper, you need to copy the generated text from VertexHelper and paste it into your source code. In the case of the *PhysicsBox2D03* project, I've created a TableSetup class that contains all the collision shapes for the static bodies of the pinball table.

> **NOTE:** Keep in mind that because I'm using Box2D for this project, every class's implementation file must use the *.mm* extension to avoid compiler errors.

There are several methods to set up the vertices for the pinball table's collision shapes, but I don't want to bore you with dozens of lines of repetitive code, so let's just take a look at one of these methods, called createLanes:

```
-(void) createLanes
{
        // right lane
        {
                // row 1, col 1
                int num = 5;
                b2Vec2 vertices[] = {
                        b2Vec2(100.9f / PTM_RATIO, -143.9f / PTM_RATIO),
                        b2Vec2(91.4f / PTM_RATIO, -145.0f / PTM_RATIO),
                        b2Vec2(58.2f / PTM_RATIO, -164.4f / PTM_RATIO),
                        b2Vec2(76.3f / PTM_RATIO, -185.5f / PTM_RATIO),
                        b2Vec2(92.1f / PTM_RATIO, -176.1f / PTM_RATIO),
                };
                [self createStaticBodyWithVertices:vertices numVertices:num];
        }
        // left lane
        {
                // row 1, col 1
                int num = 5;
                b2Vec2 vertices[] = {
                        b2Vec2(-65.6f / PTM_RATIO, -165.1f / PTM_RATIO),
                        b2Vec2(-119.3f / PTM_RATIO, -125.2f / PTM_RATIO),
                        b2Vec2(-126.7f / PTM_RATIO, -128.3f / PTM_RATIO),
                        b2Vec2(-126.7f / PTM_RATIO, -136.1f / PTM_RATIO),
                        b2Vec2(-83.3f / PTM_RATIO, -175.6f / PTM_RATIO)
                };
                [self createStaticBodyWithVertices:vertices numVertices:num];
        }
}
```

This is basically the text generated by VertexHelper that you can copy and paste into your code. The generated code contains all of the vertices making up the collision shape in a format specific to Box2D. The vertices array is then passed on to the createStaticBodyWithVertices method. Each collision shape definition is enclosed in an extra pair of brackets, right underneath the comments right lane and left lane. Each pair of brackets defines a new scope for variables, and variables declared inside the brackets are not accessible outside the brackets. You know this already from if, while, for, and other language constructs that use brackets to define their scope. You can also use the brackets without any keyword to define a new scope. In this particular case, VertexHelper allows you to use the same variable names, such and num and vertices, within the same method without the compiler complaining about the redeclaration of an existing variable. This allows you to paste the code generated by VertexHelper without having to modify it, and without having to add a new method for each added shape. After all, you may have to go back to VertexHelper several times to change some of the shapes, so replacing any generated block of code should be as straightforward as possible.

The method `createStaticBodyWithVertices` actually creates the static body using the vertices as its collision shape:

```
-(void) createStaticBodyWithVertices:(b2Vec2[])vertices numVertices:(int)numVertices
{
        b2BodyDef bodyDef;
        bodyDef.position = [Helper toMeters:[Helper screenCenter]];

        b2PolygonShape shape;
        shape.Set(vertices, numVertices);

        b2FixtureDef fixtureDef;
        fixtureDef.shape = &shape;
        fixtureDef.density = 1.0f;
        fixtureDef.friction = 0.2f;
        fixtureDef.restitution = 0.1f;

        b2Body* body = world_->CreateBody(&bodyDef);
        body->CreateFixture(&fixtureDef);
}
```

The `b2PolygonShape` uses the vertices by calling the `shape.Set(vertices, numVertices)` method to construct the static body's collision shape. The `b2FixtureDef` parameters are set to reasonable values for wall shapes—mostly, you don't want them to have a high restitution because they're supposed to be hard surfaces.

The `b2BodyDef` position is set to the center of the screen. For this pinball table, the background images are created as 320×480 images and then added to a Zwoptex Texture Atlas. This way you save texture memory; also, placing the image at the center of the screen always positions it correctly (except on the iPad, of course, which would require an additional set of 1024×768 images not used by this example). The `screenCenter` position is obtained through the `Helper` class, which contains static helper methods, all of which I've discussed before.

The `world_` member variable is a temporary variable for initialization holding the `b2World` pointer, as shown in Listing 13–1.

Listing 13–1. *The TableSetup Class's Header File*

```
#import <Foundation/Foundation.h>
#import "cocos2d.h"
#import "Box2D.h"

@interface TableSetup : CCNode
{
        b2World* world_;
}

+(id) setupTableWithWorld:(b2World*)world;

@end
```

Not too scary. So let's turn our attention to the initialization of the `TableSetup` class right away in Listing 13–2.

Listing 13–2. *Initialization of the TableSetup Class*

```
-(id) initTableWithWorld:(b2World*)world
{
        if ((self = [super init]))
        {
                // weak reference to world for convenience
                world_ = world;

                CCSpriteBatchNode* batch =
                                [CCSpriteBatchNode batchNodeWithFile:@"table.png"];
                [self addChild:batch];

                CCSprite* tableTop =
                                [CCSprite spriteWithSpriteFrameName:@"tabletop.png"];
                tableTop.position = [Helper screenCenter];
                [batch addChild:tableTop];

                CCSprite* tableBottom =
                                [CCSprite spriteWithSpriteFrameName:@"tablebottom.png"];
                tableBottom.position = [Helper screenCenter];
                [batch addChild:tableBottom];

                // create the static bodies
                [self createTableTopBody];
                [self createTableBottomLeftBody];
                [self createTableBottomRightBody];
                [self createLanes];

                // world is no longer needed after init:
                 world_ = NULL;
        }

        return self;
}

+(id) setupTableWithWorld:(b2World*)world
{
        return [[[self alloc] initTableWithWorld:world] autorelease];
}
```

The static autorelease initializer `setupTableWithWorld` takes a `b2World` pointer, allocates the memory, and calls `initTableWithWorld`. This in turn stores the world pointer in the `world_` member variable, but only during initialization, for just as long as it's needed. Using the `world_` member variable in this case is merely a matter of convenience, as opposed to having to pass the `b2World` pointer to each method in the `TableSetup` class. The whole purpose of this class is just to set up the table. Note that the `world_` pointer is set to `NULL` as opposed to `nil` because it's a C++ pointer. Technically they're the same thing, but using `NULL` signals that this is a pointer to a class, which is not derived from `NSObject`. It's not even strictly necessary to assign `NULL`, but it's useful in that it also signals that you're done using the `world_` pointer for this particular class.

The init method creates a `CCSpriteBatchNode` for the table's static background elements, and creates the `tableTop` and `tableBottom` sprites, which are centered on the screen. The various `create` methods then set up the static bodies for the pinball table, using the collision shapes defined using VertexHelper.

The `TableSetup` class is initialized by the `PinballTable` class, which is very similar to the `HelloWorldScene` class of the Box2D project from Chapter 12. Its interface is shown in Listing 13–3.

Listing 13–3. *PinballTable's Header File*

```
#import "cocos2d.h"
#import "Box2D.h"
#import "GLES-Render.h"

#import "ContactListener.h"

enum
{
        kTagBatchNode,
};

@interface PinballTable : CCLayer
{
        b2World* world;
        ContactListener* contactListener;

        GLESDebugDraw* debugDraw;
}

+(PinballTable*) sharedTable;

// returns a scene that contains HelloWorld as the only child
+(id) scene;

-(CCSpriteBatchNode*) getSpriteBatch;

@end
```

It contains references to the `ContactListener` and `GLESDebugDraw` classes. The latter I'll get to shortly; the `ContactListener` class will play a role when you're adding the pinball game's plunger. For now, let's look at the initialization of the `PinballTable` class in Listing 13–4.

Listing 13–4. *Initializing the Pinball Table*

```
-(id) init
{
        if ((self = [super init]))
        {
                pinballTableInstance = self;

                [self initBox2dWorld];
                [self enableBox2dDebugDrawing];

                // preload the sprite frames from the Texture Atlas
                [[CCSpriteFrameCache sharedSpriteFrameCache]
                                        addSpriteFramesWithFile:@"table.plist"];
```

```
            // a bright background is desirable for this pinball table
            CCColorLayer* colorLayer =
                        [CCColorLayer layerWithColor:ccc4(222, 222, 222, 255)];
            [self addChild:colorLayer z:-3];

            // batch node for all dynamic elements
            CCSpriteBatchNode* batch =
                    [CCSpriteBatchNode batchNodeWithFile:@"table.png" capacity:100];
            [self addChild:batch z:-2 tag:kTagBatchNode];

            // set up static elements
            TableSetup* tableSetup = [TableSetup setupTableWithWorld:world];
            [self addChild:tableSetup z:-1];

            [self scheduleUpdate];
        }
        return self;
}
```

The initialization of the Box2D physics engine is moved to a separate `initBox2dWorld`. The setup is essentially the same as in the last chapter, with one exception: the static screen boundary shape that keeps dynamic objects inside the screen area defines no bottom shape, allowing dynamic bodies to fall outside the screen through the bottom. We'll need that for the ball to be able to roll into the table's drain.

The `CCSpriteFrameCache` initializes the Texture Atlas used by the game by loading the *tables.plist* file. There's also a `CCColorLayer` added to replace the default black background with a light-gray one, because the table's static elements are drawn in black as well. There's also a `CCSpriteBatchNode` set up for the dynamic bodies we'll be adding later on. Through use of the singleton pattern and the `pinballTableInstance` static variable, the dynamic bodies get access to that sprite batch.

Then the `TableSetup` class is created and added as child. If you run this project now, you'll see . . . a pinball table. Great. But how do you know that the collision shapes are properly placed and used?

Box2D Debug Drawing

This is where the `GLESDebugDraw` class comes in handy. It's also the reason why in Listing 13–4 all child objects are added using a negative z-order. Remember that any drawing done by OpenGL ES code in a node's `draw` method is drawn at a z-order of 0. If you want the OpenGL ES drawings to actually be drawn over other nodes, those nodes need to have a negative z order.

Let's first look at the `enableBox2dDebugDrawing` method of the `PinballTable` class:

```
-(void) enableBox2dDebugDrawing
{
        debugDraw = new GLESDebugDraw(PTM_RATIO);
        world->SetDebugDraw(debugDraw);

        uint32 flags = b2DebugDraw::e_shapeBit;
        debugDraw->SetFlags(flags);
}
```

An instance of the GLESDebugDraw class is created, using the pixel-to-meter ratio defined by PTM_RATIO, and then stored in the PinballTable member variable debugDraw. The debugDraw instance is then passed to the Box2D world via the SetDebugDraw method. You can define what to draw by adding the bits defined in b2DebugDraw, the e_shapeBit being the most important because it draws the collision shapes of all bodies.

That alone isn't enough—you also have to override the draw method of the PinballTable class and call the debugDraw->DrawDebugData() method to actually draw the debug info. Since you don't want the end user to see the debug info, the draw method is enclosed in an #ifdef DEBUG...#endif statement:

```
#ifdef DEBUG
-(void) draw
{
        glDisable(GL_TEXTURE_2D);
        glDisableClientState(GL_COLOR_ARRAY);
        glDisableClientState(GL_TEXTURE_COORD_ARRAY);

        world->DrawDebugData();

        // restore default GL states
        glEnable(GL_TEXTURE_2D);
        glEnableClientState(GL_COLOR_ARRAY);
        glEnableClientState(GL_TEXTURE_COORD_ARRAY);
}
#endif
```

To render the debug info correctly, some of the OpenGL ES states need to be disabled. You don't have to concern yourself with that, but if you're interested in learning more, a good starting point is the OpenGL ES 1.1 reference: www.khronos.org/opengles/sdk/1.1/docs/man.

> **NOTE:** Cocos2d currently uses OpenGL ES 1.1 internally, with support for OpenGL ES 2.0 code being specified in the development roadmap as an upcoming feature for cocos2d version 1.x. This means that games written with cocos2d currently can't take advantage of new iPhone 3GS, iPad, and iPhone 4 graphics features. Unfortunately, you can't mix OpenGL ES 1.1 code with OpenGL ES 2.0 code; these two versions are incompatible with each other. There's no way to just add optional OpenGL ES 2.0 code on your own without extensive modifications to the cocos2d graphics engine.

Adding Dynamic Elements

So far, the pinball table has nothing going for it. Nothing moves, and there's obviously nothing to bounce off of. But before we add a ball and bumpers, and later flippers and plungers, I'd like to introduce the BodyNode class, which makes it a little more comfortable to work with dynamic bodies and cocos2d sprites in unison.

The BodyNode Class

The idea behind the BodyNode class is that you want to use a self-contained object for all of your dynamic classes. So far, we simply added the CCSprite to a body's userData field. But suppose you want to actually interact with the class represented by that sprite—for example, during one of the ContactListener methods. You couldn't, because all you got was the CCSprite object.

To solve this problem, I created the class BodyNode in the *PhysicsBox2D04* project. BodyNode is derived from CCNode and contains both the body and the sprite as member variables. The reference to the body is for convenient access to it by child classes. The BodyNode class also contains a CCSprite pointer so that the class can still be displayed on the screen in the update method of the PinballTable class. With all dynamic bodies being derived from the BodyNode class, you have a common class to work with, which you can then further probe for its type—for example, by using the isKindOfClass method that all classes derive from NSObject support.

In addition, the BodyNode class header file includes commonly used headers such as *Box2d.h* and *Helper.h* (see Listing 13–5).

Listing 13–5. *The BodyNode Header File*

```
#import <Foundation/Foundation.h>
#import "cocos2d.h"
#import "Box2D.h"
#import "Helper.h"
#import "Constants.h"
#import "PinballTable.h"

@interface BodyNode : CCNode
{
        b2Body* body;
        CCSprite* sprite;
}

@property (readonly, nonatomic) b2Body* body;
@property (readonly, nonatomic) CCSprite* sprite;

-(void) createBodyInWorld:(b2World*)world bodyDef:(b2BodyDef*)bodyDef
fixtureDef:(b2FixtureDef*)fixtureDef spriteFrameName:(NSString*)spriteFrameName;

-(void) removeSprite;
-(void) removeBody;

@end
```

The BodyNode also provides properties for its two members, body and sprite, so that they can be conveniently accessed. The method createBodyInWorld is used by classes deriving from BodyNode to initialize the rigid body using the supplied b2BodyDef and b2FixtureDef, as well as the accompanying CCSprite, which is created by the name of the sprite frame from a common Texture Atlas. Listing 13–6 shows the implementation.

Listing 13–6. *The BodyNode Class Implementation*

```objc
#import "BodyNode.h"

@implementation BodyNode

@synthesize body;
@synthesize sprite;

-(void) createBodyInWorld:(b2World*)world bodyDef:(b2BodyDef*)bodyDef
                                     fixtureDef:(b2FixtureDef*)fixtureDef
                                     spriteFrameName:(NSString*)spriteFrameName
{
        NSAssert(world != NULL, @"world is null!");
        NSAssert(bodyDef != NULL, @"bodyDef is null!");
        NSAssert(spriteFrameName != nil, @"spriteFrameName is nil!");

        [self removeSprite];
        [self removeBody];

        CCSpriteBatchNode* batch = [[PinballTable sharedTable] getSpriteBatch];
        sprite = [CCSprite spriteWithSpriteFrameName:spriteFrameName];
        [batch addChild:sprite];

        body = world->CreateBody(bodyDef);
        body->SetUserData(self);

        if (fixtureDef != NULL)
        {
                body->CreateFixture(fixtureDef);
        }
}

-(void) removeSprite
{
        CCSpriteBatchNode* batch = [[PinballTable sharedTable] getSpriteBatch];
        if (sprite != nil && [batch.children containsObject:sprite])
        {
                [batch.children removeObject:sprite];
                sprite = nil;
        }
}

-(void) removeBody
{
        if (body != NULL)
        {
                body->GetWorld()->DestroyBody(body);
                body = NULL;
        }
}

-(void) dealloc
{
        [self removeSprite];
        [self removeBody];

        [super dealloc];
}

@end
```

On first look, BodyNode simply calls the world's CreateBody method and the body's CreateFixture method when appropriate. The body is of course stored in the body member variable. But the key point to take away here is actually that the BodyNode manages object allocation and deallocation for you, for both the sprite and the body. It creates the sprite from the same Texture Atlas and puts it in a common sprite batch. Likewise, via the call to body->SetUserData(self), it assigns the current BodyNode instance as the user data pointer to the body.

Also, if a class derived from BodyNode goes out of scope—for example, if you remove it as a child from its cocos2d parent node—then BodyNode will take care of destroying the Box2D body for you, as well as removing the sprite from the CCSpriteBatchNode. This also makes the createBodyInWorld method reentrant. If you want to change the existing body, simply call the method again with other parameters and it will destroy the old body and sprite and create new ones.

The classes derived from BodyNode now only have to concern themselves with setting the b2BodyDef and b2FixtureDef fields appropriately, and supplying the correct name for the desired sprite frame.

The update method in the PinballTable class has also been rewritten to account for the user data change from CCSprite to BodyNode:

```
-(void) update:(ccTime)delta
{
        float timeStep = 0.03f;
        int32 velocityIterations = 8;
        int32 positionIterations = 1;
        world->Step(timeStep, velocityIterations, positionIterations);

        for (b2Body* body = world->GetBodyList(); body != nil; body = body->GetNext())
        {
                BodyNode* bodyNode = (BodyNode*)body->GetUserData();
                if (bodyNode != NULL && bodyNode.sprite != nil)
                {
                        bodyNode.sprite.position = [Helper toPixels:body->GetPosition()];
                        float angle = body->GetAngle();
                        bodyNode.sprite.rotation = -(CC_RADIANS_TO_DEGREES(angle));
                }
        }
}
```

The user data pointer is now a BodyNode object and no longer a CCSprite. The sprite is now accessed through the bodyNode.sprite property.

> **TIP:** The CCNode class also has a userData property, which you can use in the same way as b2Body's userData field.

The Ball

Can you imagine a pinball game without a pinball? I can't, so let's add one and have a look at its implementation. The aptly named `Ball` class is derived from `BodyNode`, and also implements the `CCTargetedTouchDelegate` protocol for experimentation purposes (see Listing 13–7).

Listing 13–7. *The Ball Class's Interface*

```
#import "BodyNode.h"

@interface Ball : BodyNode <CCTargetedTouchDelegate>
{
        bool moveToFinger;
        CGPoint fingerLocation;
}

+(id) ballWithWorld:(b2World*)world;

@end
```

There's the usual static initializer `ballWithWorld`, which takes a `b2World` pointer as input. Then we have the member variable `moveToFinger`, which determines whether the ball should move toward the touch location, and the `fingerLocation` `CGPoint` variable, which specifies the actual location of the finger. We can use those to have a little fun with the ball as long as the pinball game doesn't contain other interactive elements. Take a look at the `Ball` initialization and `dealloc` methods in Listing 13–8.

Listing 13–8. *The init and dealloc Methods of the Ball Class*

```
-(id) initWithWorld:(b2World*)world
{
        if ((self = [super init]))
        {
                [self createBallInWorld:world];
                [[CCTouchDispatcher sharedDispatcher] addTargetedDelegate:self
                                                 priority:0 swallowsTouches:NO];
                [self scheduleUpdate];
        }
        return self;
}

+(id) ballWithWorld:(b2World*)world
{
        return [[[self alloc] initWithWorld:world] autorelease];
}

-(void) dealloc
{
        [[CCTouchDispatcher sharedDispatcher] removeDelegate:self];
        [super dealloc];
}
```

Creating the Ball (Again)

The initialization and `dealloc` methods are fairly self explanatory, so let's jump right into the `createBallInWorld` method in Listing 13–9, which initializes the ball and sets all of its parameters. It also positions the ball just above the insertion point where the plunger will eventually be placed.

Listing 13–9. *Creating a Pinball*

```
-(void) createBallInWorld:(b2World*)world
{
        CGSize screenSize = [[CCDirector sharedDirector] winSize];
        float randomOffset = CCRANDOM_0_1() * 10.0f - 5.0f;
        CGPoint startPos = CGPointMake(screenSize.width - 15 + randomOffset, 80);

        b2BodyDef bodyDef;
        bodyDef.type = b2_dynamicBody;
        bodyDef.position = [Helper toMeters:startPos];
        bodyDef.angularDamping = 0.9f;

        NSString* spriteFrameName = @"ball.png";
        CCSprite* tempSprite = [CCSprite spriteWithSpriteFrameName:spriteFrameName];

        b2CircleShape shape;
        float radiusInMeters = (tempSprite.contentSize.width / PTM_RATIO) * 0.5f;
        shape.m_radius = radiusInMeters;

        b2FixtureDef fixtureDef;
        fixtureDef.shape = &shape;
        fixtureDef.density = 0.8f;
        fixtureDef.friction = 0.7f;
        fixtureDef.restitution = 0.3f;

        [super createBodyInWorld:world bodyDef:&bodyDef fixtureDef:&fixtureDef
                                                spriteFrameName:spriteFrameName];

        sprite.color = ccRED;
}
```

Let me just point out the curiosities in this method that I haven't discussed so far. The `b2BodyDef` field `angularDamping` is set to `0.9f`, which makes the ball's angular motion more resistant to change. This allows the ball to slide over a surface without rolling too much, which is standard behavior for heavy pinballs made of metal.

Since the radius of the `b2CircleShape` should depend on the size of the image, I created a temporary sprite. This sprite's image width is divided by the pixel-to-meter ratio and then multiplied by 0.5f because we're defining the circle shape by its radius, not its diameter.

`b2FixtureDef` uses values for density, friction, and restitution that I found to resemble a pinball without spending too much time tweaking them. Tweaking physics values is usually a very labor-intensive aspect that requires careful consideration of each change. It's also frequently underestimated by both designers and programmers alike. You'll notice that this example pinball game, while it does a fairly good job of simulating a pinball game, would still require a lot of tweaking and fine-tuning for everything to feel just right.

At the end, the super method createBodyInWorld is called, passing bodyDef, fixtureDef, and spriteFrameName to create both body and sprite. The super class in this case is of course the BodyNode class. And after this call, you can then use the body and sprite member variables because they're now initialized. For example, in this case I set the ball's color to red.

The createBallInWorld method is actually called every time the ball falls into the drain and has left the table, just so that it's set back to its initial position. You can also set a body's position directly by using the following:

```
body->SetTransform(newPosition);
```

However, the disadvantage to that approach is that it only changes the position—not the body's current angular and positional velocities. So it's very convenient to be able to call createBodyInWorld again, which then takes care of removing any existing bodies from the world, and any existing sprite from the sprite batch before creating a new body and sprite.

To actually make the ball appear on the pinball table, you'll also have to add it to the scene. This is done in the init method of the TableSetup class, like so:

```
Ball* ball = [Ball ballWithWorld:world];
[self addChild:ball z:-1];
```

Forcing the Ball to Move

So far, the ball is just dropping down, and that's it. We need a way, at least temporary, to control the ball. The ball class implements the CCTargetedTouchDelegate and has registered itself to receive touches. Let's check what the touch delegate methods do:

```
-(BOOL) ccTouchBegan:(UITouch *)touch withEvent:(UIEvent *)event
{
        moveToFinger = YES;
        fingerLocation = [Helper locationFromTouch:touch];
        return YES;
}

-(void) ccTouchMoved:(UITouch *)touch withEvent:(UIEvent *)event
{
        fingerLocation = [Helper locationFromTouch:touch];
}

-(void) ccTouchEnded:(UITouch *)touch withEvent:(UIEvent *)event
{
        moveToFinger = NO;
}
```

These methods specify that while a finger is touching the screen, the ball moves toward the finger; and while the finger is moving, the fingerLocation is constantly updated.

Next, let's take a quick look at the `update` method:

```
-(void) update:(ccTime)delta
{
        if (moveToFinger == YES)
        {
                [self applyForceTowardsFinger];
        }

        if (sprite.position.y < -(sprite.contentSize.height * 10))
        {
                // create a new ball and remove the old one
                [self createBallInWorld:body->GetWorld()];
        }
}
```

I'll get to the `applyForceTowardsFinger` method next. But while we're here, notice how we check to see if the ball has gone down the drain. The sprite's y position is compared with the sprite image's height multiplied by 10. Why the multiplication? That's just to give the impression that it takes a short moment for the ball to roll back before it reappears. If the ball has fallen far enough, the `createBallInWorld` method is called again and the fun begins anew.

Now let's have a look at the `applyForceTowardsFinger` method, which makes the ball accelerate toward the finger, in Listing 13–10.

Listing 13–10. *Accelerating the Ball Toward the Touch Location*

```
-(void) applyForceTowardsFinger
{
        b2Vec2 bodyPos = body->GetWorldCenter();
        b2Vec2 fingerPos = [Helper toMeters:fingerLocation];

        b2Vec2 bodyToFinger = fingerPos - bodyPos;
        bodyToFinger.Normalize();

        b2Vec2 force = 2.0f * bodyToFinger;
        body->ApplyForce(force, body->GetWorldCenter());
}
```

We have the two positions of the body and the finger, and then we subtract the finger from the body. The `b2Vec2` struct makes use of a technique called *operator overloading*, which makes it possible to subtract, add, or multiply two or more `b2Vec2` structs with each other. Operator overloading is a feature of the C++ language; it's not available in Objective-C—so you can't subtract, add, or multiply `CGPoint` variables this way.

The `bodyToFinger` vector is pointing from the body to the finger. When `Normalize` is called on the `bodyToFinger` vector, it's turned into a *unit vector*. A unit vector is a vector of length 1—or one unit. This allows you to multiply it with a fixed factor, in this case doubling its length, to create a constant force vector pointing in the direction of the finger. You can then use the `ApplyForce` method of the body to apply this as an external force to the body's center. You could also use a position other than the center; however, in that case the body would start spinning.

The end result of this is that the ball accelerates toward the point on the screen that your finger is touching. The ball will usually overshoot, slow down, and return. A little bit like the gravitational pull the sun exerts on our planets. However, as someone interested in astronomy, I do have to correct myself. Gravity is a force that falls off by the square of the distance between two objects pulling on each other through gravity. So if you want a more realistic simulation of gravity in your game, simply replace the applyForceTowardsFinger code with that in Listing 13–11.

Listing 13–11. *Simulating Gravitational Pull*

```
b2Vec2 bodyPos = body->GetWorldCenter();
b2Vec2 fingerPos = [Helper toMeters:fingerLocation];
float distance = bodyToFinger.Normalize();

// "real" gravity falls off by the square over distance
 float distanceSquared = distance * distance;
b2Vec2 force = ((1.0f / distanceSquared) * 20.0f) * bodyToFinger;
body->ApplyForce(force, body->GetWorldCenter());
```

The multiplication by 20.0f in this case is a magic number. It's just there to make the gravitational pull noticeable enough. Now the ball will speed up more the closer it gets to your finger, and will barely move if you touch the screen relatively far away from the ball.

While the applyForceTowardsFinger code only serves as a temporary control mechanism, you can use the gravity code in Listing 13–11 to create magnetic objects on your pinball table.

The Bumpers

Now that you have a ball that you can move with your finger, let's make things a little bit more interesting by introducing bumpers to the game. What are bumpers? They're the round, mushroom-shaped objects that will force the ball away when the ball touches them.

Listing 13–12 shows the interface of the Bumper class:

Listing 13–12. *The Bumper Class's Interface*

```
#import "BodyNode.h"

@interface Bumper : BodyNode
{
}

+(id) bumperWithWorld:(b2World*)world position:(CGPoint)pos;
@end
```

Of course, the Bumper class is derived from BodyNode. The initialization looks very much like Listing 13–9, in which the ball was initialized, so I'll just focus on the important part in Listing 13–13.

Listing 13–13. *Initializing the Bumper with High Restitution*

```
-(id) initWithWorld:(b2World*)world position:(CGPoint)pos
{
        if ((self = [super init]))
        {
                ...

                b2FixtureDef fixtureDef;
                fixtureDef.shape = &circleShape;
                fixtureDef.density = 1.0f;
                fixtureDef.friction = 0.8f;

                // restitution > 1 makes objects bounce off faster than they hit
                fixtureDef.restitution = 1.5f;

                [super createBodyInWorld:world bodyDef:&bodyDef fixtureDef:&fixtureDef
                                                spriteFrameName:spriteFrameName];
                sprite.color = ccORANGE;
        }
        return self;
}
```

The only key ingredient for the Bumper class is to set its restitution parameter to above 1.0f—in this case it's set to 1.5f. This gives any rigid body touching the surface of the bumper an impulse that is 50 percent higher than the force with which the bumper was hit. The result is something that's not possible in the real world: an increased velocity after hitting a surface. Of course, in this case it's very desirable because we save ourselves a lot of headaches in implementing the bumper's logic. Box2D does it for you.

What's left is to add some bumpers by putting the following lines in the init method of the TableSetup class. Feel free to reposition the bumpers as you desire:

```
// add some bumpers
[self addBumperAt:CGPointMake(150, 330)];
[self addBumperAt:CGPointMake(100, 390)];
[self addBumperAt:CGPointMake(230, 380)];
[self addBumperAt:CGPointMake(40, 350)];
[self addBumperAt:CGPointMake(280, 300)];
[self addBumperAt:CGPointMake(70, 280)];
[self addBumperAt:CGPointMake(240, 250)];
[self addBumperAt:CGPointMake(170, 280)];
[self addBumperAt:CGPointMake(160, 400)];
[self addBumperAt:CGPointMake(15, 160)];
```

Have a look now and try out how the bumpers feel in the *PhysicsBox2D03* project—pretty close to actual pinball bumpers, I think.

The Plunger

I hate to take control away from you, but for now I have to. We're adding the plunger now, and being able to control the ball with your fingers might get in the way. So go into the Ball class's update method and comment out the call to applyForceTowardsFinger:

```
if (moveToFinger == YES)
```

```
{
        // disabled: not needed right now
        // [self applyForceTowardsFinger];
}
```

Now you can add the `Plunger` class, which I've already done in the *PhysicsBox2D05* project. Listing13–14 shows the `Plunger` class's interface, which is also derived from `BodyNode`:

Listing 13–14. *The Plunger's Header File*

```
#import "BodyNode.h"

@interface Plunger : BodyNode
{
        b2PrismaticJoint* joint;
        bool doPlunge;
        ccTime plungeTime;
}

@property (nonatomic) bool doPlunge;

+(id) plungerWithWorld:(b2World*)world;

@end
```

It has a member variable for `b2PrismaticJoint`, which it's going to use to propel itself upward. A prismatic joint allows only one axis of movement—a telescope bar is a good example of a prismatic joint. You can only move the smaller pipe inside the larger pipe in one direction.

Initializing the plunger is also straightforward, as Listing 13–15 shows. The position needs a little tweaking, and I set its friction and density to extreme values so that the ball doesn't bounce on it, to ensure a smooth launch. The plunger's shape was created by using VertexHelper.

Listing 13–15. *Initializing the Plunger*

```
-(id) initWithWorld:(b2World*)world
{
        if ((self = [super init]))
        {
                CGSize screenSize = [[CCDirector sharedDirector] winSize];
                CGPoint plungerPos = CGPointMake(screenSize.width - 13, 32);

                b2BodyDef bodyDef;
                bodyDef.type = b2_dynamicBody;
                bodyDef.position = [Helper toMeters:plungerPos];

                b2PolygonShape shape;
                int num = 4;
                b2Vec2 vertices[] = {
                        b2Vec2(10.5f / PTM_RATIO, 10.6f / PTM_RATIO),
                        b2Vec2(11.8f / PTM_RATIO, 18.1f / PTM_RATIO),
                        b2Vec2(-11.9f / PTM_RATIO, 18.3f / PTM_RATIO),
                        b2Vec2(-10.5f / PTM_RATIO, 10.8f / PTM_RATIO)
                };
```

```
            shape.Set(vertices, num);

            b2FixtureDef fixtureDef;
            fixtureDef.shape = &shape;
            fixtureDef.density = 1.0f;
            fixtureDef.friction = 0.99f;
            fixtureDef.restitution = 0.01f;

            [super createBodyInWorld:world bodyDef:&bodyDef fixtureDef:&fixtureDef
                                          spriteFrameName:@"plunger.png"];
            sprite.position = plungerPos;

            [self attachPlunger];

            [self scheduleUpdate];
    }
    return self;
}
```

More interesting is the call to `attachPlunger` and the actual creation of the prismatic joint in this method, as shown in Listing 13–16.

Listing 13–16. *Creating the Plunger's Prismatic Joint*

```
-(void) attachPlunger
{
        // create an invisible static body to attach joint to
        b2BodyDef bodyDef;
        bodyDef.position = body->GetWorldCenter();
        b2Body* staticBody = body->GetWorld()->CreateBody(&bodyDef);

        // create a prismatic joint to make plunger go up/down
        b2PrismaticJointDef jointDef;
        b2Vec2 worldAxis(0.0f, 1.0f);
        jointDef.Initialize(staticBody, body, body->GetWorldCenter(), worldAxis);
        jointDef.lowerTranslation = 0.0f;
        jointDef.upperTranslation = 0.75f;
        jointDef.enableLimit = true;
        jointDef.maxMotorForce = 60.0f;
        jointDef.motorSpeed = 20.0f;
        jointDef.enableMotor = false;

        joint = (b2PrismaticJoint*)body->GetWorld()->CreateJoint(&jointDef);
}
```

First, a static body is created at the same location as the plunger's dynamic body. The `staticBody` will hold the plunger in place.

The `worldAxis` restricts the prismatic joint's movement to the y axis (i.e., up and down). The `worldAxis` is expressed as a normal vector with values from 0.0f to 1.0f; when the y axis is set to 1.0f, the `worldAxis` becomes parallel to the y axis. If you were to set both x and y axis to 0.5f, the `worldAxis` would be a 45 degree angle. `b2PrismaticJointDef` is initialized with the `staticBody` and the world center position of the plunger's dynamic body. As anchor point for the joint the `worldAxis` is used, which restricts motion of the prismatic joint along the y axis

Now follows a set of parameters. The lower and upper translations define how far along the axis the plunger is allowed to move. In this case, it is allowed to move 0.75f meters upward, which is exactly 24 pixels. The enableLimit field is set to true so that this movement limit is actually adhered to by the connected bodies. Since the static body won't move, the plunger will move the full extent. If both were dynamic bodies, both bodies would be able to move, which would be undesirable in this case.

Next, I set maxMotorForce to 60 (the unit in this case is Newton-meters, which is a unit of torque). In Chipmunk this is called the body's *moment*. The maxMotorForce value limits the torque, or energy, of the joint's movement. The motorSpeed then determines how quickly, if at all, this maxMotorForce is reached. I determined both values merely by trial and error until it felt about right. The ball is now catapulted up and around with just about the right speed. The motor is initially disabled because I only want the plunger to go off when there's a ball touching it.

The joint is then created using the world's CreateJoint method and stored in the joint member variable. Since CreateJoint returns a b2Joint pointer, it has to be cast to a b2PrismaticJoint pointer before assignment.

Notice that it is not necessary to destroy the joint that the Plunger class is keeping as a member variable. The joint is automatically destroyed when either body it is attached to is destroyed, and in this case the BodyNode's dealloc method destroys the body.

Launching the Ball on Contact

The actual launch of the ball is done automatically, to illustrate the use of the ContactListener class. In the BeginContact method, the code in Listing 13–17 changes the plunger's doPlunge property to YES, which we'll use to detect when to launch the plunger upward.

Listing 13–17. *Determining When to Launch the Plunger*

```
void ContactListener::BeginContact(b2Contact* contact)
{
        b2Body* bodyA = contact->GetFixtureA()->GetBody();
        b2Body* bodyB = contact->GetFixtureB()->GetBody();
        BodyNode* bodyNodeA = (BodyNode*)bodyA->GetUserData();
        BodyNode* bodyNodeB = (BodyNode*)bodyB->GetUserData();

        if ([bodyNodeA isKindOfClass:[Plunger class]] &&
                                        [bodyNodeB isKindOfClass:[Ball class]])
        {
                Plunger* plunger = (Plunger*)bodyNodeA;
                plunger.doPlunge = YES;
        }
        else if ([bodyNodeB isKindOfClass:[Plunger class]] &&
                                        [bodyNodeA isKindOfClass:[Ball class]])
        {
                Plunger* plunger = (Plunger*)bodyNodeB;
                plunger.doPlunge = YES;
        }
}
```

Since both the plunger and ball can be either body A or B, we have to check for both cases. We only want to set the plunger's doPlunge property if the plunger is in contact with the ball and not any other body. Since we're storing BodyNode instances in the userData field of the body, it makes it easy to simply check for the BodyNode class by using the isKindOfClass method.

Now what happens when doPlunge is set to YES? For one, the plunger's update method repeatedly checks whether doPlunge is set to YES, and if so, it then sets doPlunge back to NO and starts the joint's motor. Another selector is scheduled to stop the motor of the joint so that gravity can take over and allow the plunger to come down again after a short period of time:

```
-(void) update:(ccTime)delta
{
        if (doPlunge == YES)
        {
                doPlunge = NO;
                joint->EnableMotor(YES);

                // schedule motor to come back
                [self unschedule:_cmd];
                [self schedule:@selector(endPlunge:) interval:0.5f];
        }
}
```

The endPlunge method simply unschedules itself and disables the joint's motor:

```
-(void) endPlunge:(ccTime)delta
{
        [self unschedule:_cmd];
        joint->EnableMotor(NO);
}
```

Like all the other table elements, the plunger is created and added in the init method of the TableSetup class:

```
Plunger* plunger = [Plunger plungerWithWorld:world];
[self addChild:plunger z:-2];
```

The Flippers

The final ingredients are the flippers, with which you'll control the action. The two flippers are going to be controlled by touching the screen on either the left or right side, as Listing 13–18 shows.

Listing 13–18. *The Flipper Interface*

```
#import "BodyNode.h"

typedef enum
{
        FlipperLeft,
        FlipperRight,
} EFlipperType;
```

```
@interface Flipper : BodyNode <CCTargetedTouchDelegate>
{
        EFlipperType type;
        b2RevoluteJoint* joint;
        float totalTime;
}

+(id) flipperWithWorld:(b2World*)world flipperType:(EFlipperType)flipperType;

@end
```

Each flipper is anchored using a b2RevoluteJoint. Take a look at the flipper
initWithWorld method in Listing 13–19 to see how the flippers are created.

Listing 13–19. *Creating a Flipper*

```
-(id) initWithWorld:(b2World*)world flipperType:(EFlipperType)flipperType
{
        if ((self = [super init]))
        {
                type = flipperType;

                CGSize screenSize = [[CCDirector sharedDirector] winSize];
                CGPoint flipperPos = CGPointMake(screenSize.width / 2 - 48, 55);
                if (type == FlipperRight)
                {
                        flipperPos = CGPointMake(screenSize.width / 2 + 40, 55);
                }

                // create a body definition, it's a static body (bumpers don't move)
                b2BodyDef bodyDef;
                bodyDef.type = b2_dynamicBody;
                bodyDef.position = [Helper toMeters:flipperPos];

                // define the dynamic body fixture
                b2FixtureDef fixtureDef;
                fixtureDef.density = 1.0f;
                fixtureDef.friction = 0.99f;
                fixtureDef.restitution = 0.1f;

                b2PolygonShape shape;
                b2Vec2 revolutePoint;
                b2Vec2 revolutePointOffset = b2Vec2(0.5f, 0.0f);

                if (type == FlipperLeft)
                {
                        int numVertices = 4;
                        b2Vec2 vertices[] = {
                                b2Vec2(-20.5f / PTM_RATIO, -1.7f / PTM_RATIO),
                                b2Vec2(25.0f / PTM_RATIO, -25.5f / PTM_RATIO),
                                b2Vec2(29.5f / PTM_RATIO, -23.7f / PTM_RATIO),
                                b2Vec2(-10.2f / PTM_RATIO, 12.5f / PTM_RATIO)
                        };

                        shape.Set(vertices, numVertices);
                        revolutePoint = bodyDef.position - revolutePointOffset;
                }
                else
```

```
                {
                        int numVertices = 4;
                        b2Vec2 vertices[] = {
                                b2Vec2(11.0f / PTM_RATIO, 12.5f / PTM_RATIO),
                                b2Vec2(-29.5f / PTM_RATIO, -23.5f / PTM_RATIO),
                                b2Vec2(-23.2f / PTM_RATIO, -25.5f / PTM_RATIO),
                                b2Vec2(19.7f / PTM_RATIO, -1.7f / PTM_RATIO)
                        };

                        shape.Set(vertices, numVertices);
                        revolutePoint = bodyDef.position + revolutePointOffset;
                }

                fixtureDef.shape = &shape;

                [super createBodyInWorld:world bodyDef:&bodyDef fixtureDef:&fixtureDef
                                            spriteFrameName:@"flipper-left.png"];

                if (type == FlipperRight)
                {
                        sprite.flipX = YES;
                }

                [self attachFlipperAt:revolutePoint];

                [[CCTouchDispatcher sharedDispatcher] addTargetedDelegate:self
                                            priority:0 swallowsTouches:NO];
        }
        return self;
}
```

I took the left flipper as my reference, so if `flipperType` is set to `FlipperRight`, I simply change the right flipper's position and later flip the sprite. The same distinction is made in the `attachFlipperAt` method, which creates the joints (see Listing 13–20), in order to change the orientation and upper limit of the rotation. There's a `revolutePoint` variable passed to this method, which determines the point of rotation for each flipper, since it isn't supposed to rotate around its center.

Listing 13–20. *Creating the Flipper Revolute Joint*

```
-(void) attachFlipperAt:(b2Vec2)pos
{
        // create an invisible static body to attach to
        b2BodyDef bodyDef;
        bodyDef.position = pos;
        b2Body* staticBody = body->GetWorld()->CreateBody(&bodyDef);

        b2RevoluteJointDef jointDef;
        jointDef.Initialize(staticBody, body, staticBody->GetWorldCenter());
        jointDef.lowerAngle = 0.0f;
        jointDef.upperAngle = CC_DEGREES_TO_RADIANS(70);
        jointDef.enableLimit = true;
        jointDef.maxMotorTorque = 30.0f;
        jointDef.motorSpeed = -20.0f;
        jointDef.enableMotor = true;

        if (type == FlipperRight)
```

```
        {
                jointDef.motorSpeed *= -1;
                jointDef.lowerAngle = -jointDef.upperAngle;
                jointDef.upperAngle = 0.0f;
        }

        joint = (b2RevoluteJoint*)body->GetWorld()->CreateJoint(&jointDef);
}
```

The static body is created to attach the flipper to an unmovable body, to keep it in place. b2RevoluteJointDef uses lowerAngle and upperAngle as the rotation limits, which are in radians. I'll set the upperAngle to 70 degrees and convert it to radians with the CC_DEGREES_TO_RADIANS macro provided by cocos2d.

The revolute joint also has maxMotorTorque and motorSpeed fields, which are used to define the speed and immediacy of the movement of the flippers. However, in this case the motor is enabled all the time. While the flippers are down, the motor forces them down so that they don't bounce when the ball hits them.

In the ccTouchBegan method, the location of the touch is obtained, which is validated with the isTouchForMe method before actually reversing the motor.

```
-(BOOL) ccTouchBegan:(UITouch *)touch withEvent:(UIEvent *)event
{
        BOOL touchHandled = NO;

        CGPoint location = [Helper locationFromTouch:touch];
        if ([self isTouchForMe:location])
        {
                touchHandled = YES;
                [self reverseMotor];
        }

        return touchHandled;
}

-(void) ccTouchEnded:(UITouch *)touch withEvent:(UIEvent *)event
{
        CGPoint location = [Helper locationFromTouch:touch];
        if ([self isTouchForMe:location])
        {
                [self reverseMotor];
        }
}
```

isTouchForMe implements the check to figure out on which side of the screen the touch was, and whether the current instance of the class is the correct flipper to respond to this touch.

```
-(bool) isTouchForMe:(CGPoint)location
{
        if (type == FlipperLeft && location.x < [Helper screenCenter].x)
        {
                return YES;
        }
        else if (type == FlipperRight && location.x > [Helper screenCenter].x)
        {
```

```
        return YES;
    }

    return NO;
}
```

Reversing the motor then simply allows the flipper to spring up, and to spring back down again when the touch ends.

```
-(void) reverseMotor
{
    joint->SetMotorSpeed(joint->GetMotorSpeed() * -1);
}
```

The rest is just physics. If the ball is on the flipper and you touch the screen on the correct side, the flipper will be accelerated upward, pushing the ball with it. Depending on where on the flipper the ball lands, it will be propelled more or less straight upward.

Conclusion

In this chapter you learned how to use the VertexHelper tool to define the collision shapes for the bodies used in the pinball game. With just the ball in place, I illustrated how you can simulate acceleration toward a point, including how to model the effects of gravity or magnetism more or less realistically.

I hope this chapter gave you an impression of how much fun physics can be, regardless of what you may have experienced in physics class. But then again, you didn't build pinball machines in physics class—or did you?

If you'd like to go beyond this example—for example, using more joints or taking more control of the collision process—I'd like to refer you to the Box2D manual, at www.box2d.org/manual.html.

On the other hand, if you need more information about individual classes and structs, you should look at the Box2D API reference. It's not available online, but it is provided in the *Documentation* folder of the Box2D download, which you can obtain here: http://code.google.com/p/box2d.

To get help with Box2D, you can check out the official Box2D forums, at www.box2d.org/forum/index.php, and the Physics subsection of the cocos2d forums, at www.cocos2d-iphone.org/forum/forum/7.

Chapter 14

Game Center

Game Center is Apple's social network solution. It enables you to authenticate players, store their scores and display leaderboards, and track and display their achievement progress. Furthermore, players can invite friends to play or choose to quickly find a match to play a game with anyone.

In this chapter I'll not only introduce you to Game Center and the Game Kit API, but also the basics of online multiplayer programming, and of course, how to use Game Center together with cocos2d.

Since a lot of Apple's examples are intentionally incomplete, I'll be developing a GameKitHelper class in this chapter. This class will remove some of the complexities of Game Center programming from you. It will make it easier for you to use Game Kit and Game Center features, and it will allow you to easily reuse the same code for other games.

To configure your application for use with Game Center, you are going to use iTunes Connect. The information on the iTunes Connect web site is considered Apple confidential information, so I can't discuss it in this book. However, I will point you to Apple's excellent documentation for each step—and quite frankly, setting up leaderboards and achievements on iTunes Connect is possibly the easiest aspect of Game Center.

Enabling Game Center

Game Center is the service that manages and stores player accounts, each player's friend lists, leaderboards, and achievements. This information is stored online on Apple's servers, and accessed either by your game or the Game Center app that is installed on all devices running iOS 4.1 or above.

> **NOTE:** Game Center is only available on devices running iOS 4.1 and above, and is not available on first-generation devices or the iPhone 3G. Game Center currently runs on iPod touch second, third, and fourth generations, iPhone 3GS and iPhone 4, and iPad, as long as they have iOS 4.1 or higher installed. The easiest way for a user to check if their device supports Game Center is to locate the Game Center app on the device. If it exists, the device is ready for Game Center; otherwise, it is not. If the Game Center app is not available but the device is eligible for upgrading to iOS 4.1, Game Center support will become available after upgrading the device's operating system via iTunes.
>
> If you don't have access to a Game Center–enabled device, worry not. You can program and test Game Center features using the iPhone/iPad Simulator. With the exception of matchmaking, all Game Center features can be tested in the simulator.

On the other side, the Game Kit API is what you use to program Game Center features. Game Kit provides programmatic access to the data stored on the Game Center servers, and is able to show built-in leaderboards, achievements, and matchmaking screens. But Game Kit also provides features besides Game Center—for example, peer-to-peer networking via Bluetooth and voice chat. These are the only two Game Kit features already available on devices running iOS 3.0 or higher.

The final ingredient in this mix is iTunes Connect. You set up your game's leaderboards and achievements through the iTunes Connect web site. But most importantly, it allows you to enable Game Center for your game in the first place. I'll start with that step first, so you can and should do this before you have even created an Xcode project for your game.

Your starting point for learning more about Game Center and the steps involved in creating a game that uses Game Center is at Apple's Getting Started with Game Center web site: `http://developer.apple.com/devcenter/ios/gamecenter`.

For a high-level overview of Game Center, I recommend reading the Getting Started with Game Center document: `http://developer.apple.com/ios/download.action?path=/ios/getting_started_with_ios_4.1/gettingstartedwithgamecenter.pdf`.

Creating Your App in iTunes Connect

The very first step is to log in with your Apple ID on the iTunes Connect web site: `https://itunesconnect.apple.com`.

Then you want to add a new application, even if it doesn't exist yet. For most fields that iTunes Connect asks you to fill out, you can enter bogus information. There are only two settings that you have to get right. The first is, obviously, to enable Game Center when iTunes Connect asks you whether the new application should support Game Center.

The other is to enter a Bundle ID (also referred to as Bundle Identifier) that matches the one used in the Xcode project. Since you don't have an Xcode project yet, you are free to choose any Bundle ID you want. Apple recommends using reverse domain names for Bundle IDs with the app's name appended at the end. The catch is that the Bundle ID needs to be unique across all App Store apps, and there are tens of thousands of them.

For the book's example, I've chosen `com.learn-cocos2d` to be the app's Bundle ID. Since this Bundle ID is now taken by me, you will have to use your own Bundle ID. If you want, you can simply suffix it with a string of your choosing, or choose an entirely new string. Just remember to use your Bundle ID whenever I refer to the `com.learn-cocos2d` Bundle ID.

For a detailed description of how to create a new app and how to set up Game Center for an app on iTunes Connect, please refer to Apple's iTunes Connect Developer Guide: `https://itunesconnect.apple.com/docs/iTunesConnect_DeveloperGuide.pdf`.

Specifically, the section labeled Game Center explains in great detail how to manage the Game Center features on iTunes Connect.

Setting Up Leaderboards and Achievements

For the most part, after enabling Game Center for an app, what you'll be doing on iTunes Connect is setting up one or more leaderboards, which will hold your player's scores or times, as well as setting up a number of achievements that players can unlock while playing your game.

To access the Game Center leaderboards and achievements, you refer to them by ID. For leaderboards, you should note the leaderboard category ID strings, and for achievements the achievement ID strings, to be able to query and update the correct leaderboards and achievements.

For the purpose of this chapter, I have set up one leaderboard with a score format of Elapsed Time and a leaderboard category ID of `Playtime`. For achievements I've entered one achievement, with an achievement ID of `PlayedForTenSeconds`, that grants the player 5 achievement points.

Feel free to set up additional leaderboards and achievements, but keep in mind that the example code in this chapter relies on at least one leaderboard with a category ID of `Playtime` and one achievement with an achievement ID of `PlayedForTenSeconds` to exist.

Creating a Cocos2d Xcode Project

Now it is time to create the actual Xcode project. You can start the project from any cocos2d template—for example, the cocos2d HelloWorld application template. You can also use an existing project.

There's but one caveat: the cocos2d version should be at least v0.99.5 beta 3. You can determine which version of cocos2d your project is using in three ways. First, if your project is built and you run it, one of the first lines in the debugger console will read something like this:

```
2010-10-07 15:33:58.363 Tilemap[1046:207] cocos2d: cocos2d v0.99.5-beta3
```

Or, you can use the global method `cocos2dVersion` to print it out yourself—for example, using CCLOG in this way:

```
CCLOG(@"%@", cocos2dVersion());
```

The final option is to simply look it up. In your project, in the group containing the cocos2d sources, locate the file *cocos2d.m* and open it. It contains the version string in plain text:

```
static NSString *version = @"cocos2d v0.99.5-beta3";
```

I decided to continue working with the tilemap projects, so I was facing the problem of having to upgrade cocos2d from a previous version to v0.99.5 beta 3. Many developers have faced and will continue to face this issue, and it's not a simple or straightforward task. In fact, if you rely on the cocos2d templates to create cocos2d projects for you, the current version of the cocos2d code will be copied into your project. You can't upgrade that code by simply copying over the new code because you don't know which source code files might have been added, renamed, relocated, or removed entirely from the cocos2d distribution.

The easiest way to upgrade cocos2d is actually to create a new project from a cocos2d template that uses the latest cocos2d version, and then read all your source files and resources to this new project. That way, at least you can be sure that whatever errors appear are either caused by incompatibilities introduced by the latest cocos2d version, or by missing source code or resource files.

> **TIP:** If you grow tired of this tedious upgrade process, I've written a tutorial and Xcode project that only adds references to the *cocos2d-ios* source code project. This allows you to up- or downgrade the *cocos2d-ios* project at any time with relatively little fuss. You can find the tutorial and the Xcode project on my web site: `www.learn-cocos2d.com/knowledge-base/tutorial-professional-cocos2d-xcode-project-template`.

The requirement to use at least v0.99.5 beta 3 of cocos2d is because this version added a `RootViewController` object. Thus far, cocos2d has never used a `UIViewController` because it never needed one, but Game Center does need a `UIViewController` to be able to show its built-in UIKit user interface. To avoid a plethora of issues that occurred when developers started adding `UIViewControllers` to support Game Center in their cocos2d projects, the implementation of the `RootViewController` was a welcome addition to cocos2d. The `GameKitHelper` class will make use of it.

Configuring the Xcode Project

The first thing you should do now is enter the Bundle ID you've entered for your app in iTunes Connect. Remember that while I'm using `com.learn-cocos2d` as the Bundle ID for the example projects, you can't use the same because it's already taken now, and Bundle IDs must be unique.

Locate the file *Info.plist* in your project's *Resources* folder and select it. You can then edit it in the Property List editor, as shown in Figure 14–1. You will want to set the `Bundle identifier` key to have the same value as your app's Bundle ID. In my case that will be `com.learn-cocos2d`, and in your case it will be whatever string you chose as the app's Bundle ID.

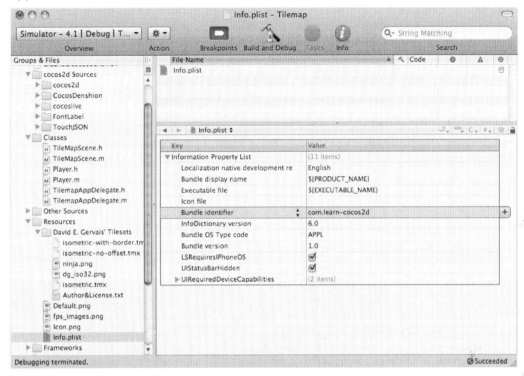

Figure 14–1. *The Bundle identifier key must match your app's Bundle ID.*

There are actually two ways to use Game Kit, and Game Center for that matter. One is to require it, which means your app will only run on devices that support Game Center and are running iOS 4.1 or higher. However, for the examples I've written, I did not make Game Center a requirement because it's relatively easy to check if Game Center is available, and then not use it if it isn't. This allows your game to be run on older devices, just without all the Game Center features.

But if you do want to require Game Kit and Game Center to be present, you can set this in your app's *Info.plist* `UIRequiredDeviceCapabilities` list. By adding another key named `gamekit` with a Boolean value and checking the check box, as shown in Figure 14–2, you can tell iTunes and potential users that your app requires Game Kit and thus requires iOS 4.1 or higher.

You can learn more about iTunes requirements and the `UIRequiredDeviceCapabilities` key in Apple's Build Time Configuration documentation:
`http://developer.apple.com/library/ios/#documentation/iPhone/Conceptual/iPhoneO SProgrammingGuide/BuildTimeConfiguration/BuildTimeConfiguration.html`

CAUTION: If you add the `gamekit` key but later decide you don't want to make Game Kit a requirement, make sure you remove the `gamekit` entry. If you simply uncheck the `gamekit` check box, it actually tells iTunes that your app is not available on devices that do support Game Center. That's exactly the opposite of what you might expect. To actually make Game Kit an optional requirement, you'll have to remove the `gamekit` entry altogether.

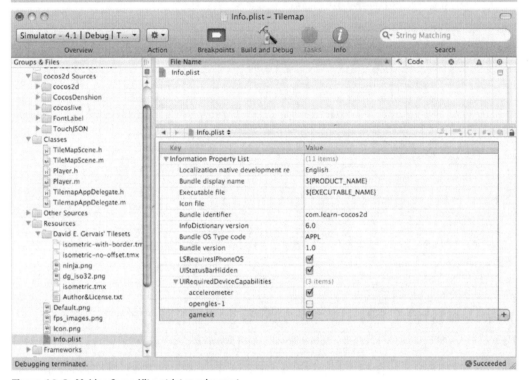

Figure 14–2. *Making Game Kit a strict requirement*

Next, you need to add the Game Kit framework to your Xcode project—more specifically, to every target in your project. Locate the **Targets** group in the **Groups & Files** pane, and look for the bull's eye icon. In my test project there's only one target, called Tilemap, which you can either double-click or right-click, and then select **Get Info** to open the target's **Info** dialog.

On the **General** tab, in the lower half, is the list of linked libraries that are used by this target. To add another library, click the + button below the **Linked Libraries** list. You'll see another list pop up like the one in Figure 14–3. You may need to unfold the category labeled **Device – iOS 4.1 SDK**, and then locate the *GameKit.framework* entry and click the **Add** button.

GameKit.framework will be added to the **Linked Libraries** list. By default, new libraries are added as **Required**. See the second column in the **Linked Libraries** list, labeled **Type**. The setting **Required** means that your app will only work on devices where the GameKit.framework library is available. If that is what you want, and you've added the gamekit key to *Info.plist*, you can leave it at that. Otherwise, change the setting to read **Weak** in order to be able to run the app even on devices that don't have Game Center available. We can account for that with a relatively simple check in code, and then disable any Game Kit features in case a device doesn't support Game Kit.

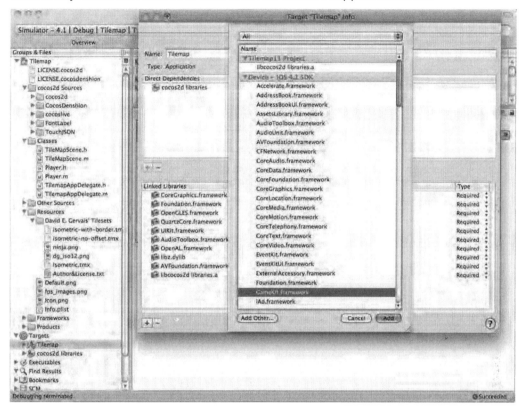

Figure 14–3. *Adding GameKit.framework*

Finally, you will want the *GameKit.h* header file to be available in all of your project's source files. Instead of adding it to each and every source file, you should add it to your project's *Prefix.pch* file. This is the precompiled header that contains header files from external frameworks to allow the project to compile faster. But it also has the added benefit that every header file added to the prefix header will make its definitions available to every source code file in the current project.

The prefix header file is always prefixed with the project's name. So, for example, in the case of the tilemap project, the file name is *Tilemap_Prefix.pch* and the file can be found in the Other Sources group. Open the one in your project and add the GameKit header to it, as shown in Listing 14–1.

Listing 14–1. *Adding the GameKit Header to Your Project's Prefix Header*

```
#ifdef __OBJC__
        #import <Foundation/Foundation.h>
        #import <UIKit/UIKit.h>

        #import <GameKit/GameKit.h>
#endif
```

That's it, your app is set up for use with Game Center.

Summary

To summarize, enabling Game Center for your app requires the following steps:

1. Create a new app in iTunes Connect:

    a. Specify a Bundle ID for the new app.

    b. Enable Game Center for this app.

2. Set up your initial leaderboards and achievements in iTunes Connect:

    a. Note the leaderboard category IDs and achievement IDs. (Note that you will likely continue to edit and add leaderboards and achievements throughout the development of your game.)

3. Create or upgrade the Xcode project:

    a. Make sure to use cocos2d v0.99.5 beta 3 or higher.

4. Edit *Info.plist*:

    a. Enter the app's Bundle ID in the **Bundle identifier** field.

    b. Optionally require Game Kit by adding a Boolean value labeled `gamekit` to the `UIRequiredDeviceCapabilities` list.

5. Add the necessary Game Kit references:

    a. Add the GameKit.framework linked library to each target. Change its **Type** from **Required** to **Weak** if Game Kit support is optional.

    b. Add `#import <GameKit/GameKit.h>` to your project's prefix header file.

Before you proceed, make sure you have followed each step. You can always go back and make the necessary changes later on. However, if you don't do all of these steps at the beginning, chances are that you will get errors or something won't work, but the associated error message won't necessarily point you to a mistake or oversight concerning one of these steps.

Common causes for Game Center to not work properly are a mismatch between the Bundle ID in the project's *Info.plist* file and the Bundle ID set up for your app in iTunes Connect. Also, using cocos2d v0.99.5 beta 3 or above is an essential requirement for Game Center.

Game Kit Programming

Before I get into programming Game Center with the Game Kit API, I'd like to mention the two important resources on Apple's developer web site.

There is the Game Kit Programming Guide, which provides a high-level, task-based overview of Game Kit and Game Center concepts: http://developer.apple.com/library/ios/#documentation/NetworkingInternet/Conceptual/GameKit_Guide/Introduction/Introduction.html.

For in-depth detailed information about the Game Center classes and protocols, you can refer to the Game Kit Framework Reference: http://developer.apple.com/library/ios/#documentation/GameKit/Reference/GameKit_Collection/_index.html.

The GameKitHelper Delegate

I mentioned earlier in this chapter that I will use a GameKitHelper class to provide easier access to Game Kit and Game Center features. Since connecting to an online server causes responses to be delayed by several milliseconds, if not seconds, it's a good idea to have a central class manage all Game Center–related features. All of the Game Center examples are based on the isometric game developed in Chapter 11. You'll find the following example code in the *Tilemap11* project.

One of your game's classes can then use this functionality and register itself as a GameKitHelper delegate to get notified of events as they occur. To do that, the delegate must implement the GameKitHelper @protocol that is defined in the *GameKitHelper.h* header file (Listing 14–2). Only classes implementing this protocol can be assigned to the GameKitHelper delegate property to receive the protocol messages. The protocol is simply a list of method definitions that a class using the protocol must implement. If any of the methods in the protocol aren't implemented, the compiler will let you know about that.

Listing 14–2. *The GameKitHelper Header File*

```
#import "cocos2d.h"
#import <GameKit/GameKit.h>

@protocol GameKitHelperProtocol
-(void) onLocalPlayerAuthenticationChanged;
-(void) onFriendListReceived:(NSArray*)friends;
-(void) onPlayerInfoReceived:(NSArray*)players;
@end

@interface GameKitHelper : NSObject
{
        id<GameKitHelperProtocol> delegate;
        bool isGameCenterAvailable;
        NSError* lastError;
}

@property (nonatomic, retain) id<GameKitHelperProtocol> delegate;
@property (nonatomic, readonly) bool isGameCenterAvailable;
```

```
@property (nonatomic, readonly) NSError* lastError;

+(GameKitHelper*) sharedGameKitHelper;

// Player authentication, info
-(void) authenticateLocalPlayer;
-(void) getLocalPlayerFriends;
-(void) getPlayerInfo:(NSArray*)players;
@end
```

For your convenience, the GameKitHelper class also stores the last error in its lastError property. This allows you to check if any error occurred, and if so, what kind of error, without actually receiving the Game Center messages directly. The GameKitHelper class is a singleton, which was described in Chapter 3, so I'll leave the singleton-specific code out of the discussion.

The remaining properties and methods will be discussed shortly. For now, let's have a look how the TileMapLayer class is extended so that it can function as the delegate for GameKitHelper. The essential changes to the header file are importing *GameKitHelper.h* and specifying that TileMapLayer implements GameKitHelperProtocol:

```
#import "GameKitHelper.h"

@interface TileMapLayer : CCLayer <GameKitHelperProtocol>
{
        ...
}
```

Then you can set the TileMapLayer class to be the delegate of the GameKitHelper class, in the init method:

```
GameKitHelper* gkHelper = [GameKitHelper sharedGameKitHelper];
gkHelper.delegate = self;
[gkHelper authenticateLocalPlayer];
```

Note that you are responsible for setting the GameKitHelper delegate back to nil when appropriate—for example, shortly before changing scenes. Because GameKitHelper retains the delegate, it will not be released from memory, even if it otherwise would (e.g., during a scene change). That would not only keep the delegate itself in memory but all of its member variables as well, including all of its children if it's a CCNode class.

Checking for Game Center Availability

The GameKitHelper class starts by checking for Game Center availability right in its init method (Listing 14–3). It only needs to do that once because the conditions never change while the app is running.

Listing 14–3. *Testing for Game Center Availability*

```
// Test for Game Center availability
Class gameKitLocalPlayerClass = NSClassFromString(@"GKLocalPlayer");
bool isLocalPlayerAvailable = (gameKitLocalPlayerClass != nil);

// Test if device is running iOS 4.1 or higher
NSString* reqSysVer = @"4.1";
```

```
NSString* currSysVer = [[UIDevice currentDevice] systemVersion];
bool isOSVer41 = ([currSysVer compare:reqSysVer
                              options:NSNumericSearch] != NSOrderedAscending);

isGameCenterAvailable = (isLocalPlayerAvailable && isOSVer41);
```

The first test is simply to check if a specific Game Center class is available. In this case, the Objective-C runtime method NSClassFromString is used to get one of the Game Center classes by name. If this call returns nil, you can be certain that Game Center is unavailable.

But it's not quite that simple. Because Game Center was already partially available in beta versions prior to iOS 4.1, you also need to check if the device is running at least iOS 4.1. This is done by comparing the reqSysVer string with the systemVersion string.

Once both checks are made, the results are combined using the && (and) operator, so that both must be true for isGameCenterAvailable to become true. The isGameCenterAvailable variable is used to safeguard all calls to Game Center functionality within the GameKitHelper class. This avoids accidentally calling Game Center functionality when it is not available, which would crash the application.

Note that this is how Apple recommends to check for Game Center availability. You should not try any other methods—for example, determining the type of device your game is running on. While certain devices are excluded from using Game Center, this is already accounted for with the preceding check.

Authenticating the Local Player

The local player is a fundamental concept to Game Center programming. It refers to the player account that is signed into the device. This is important to know because only the local player can send scores to leaderboards and report achievement progress to the Game Center service. The very first thing a Game Center application needs to do is authenticate the local player. If that fails, you cannot use most of the Game Center services, and in fact Apple recommends not using any Game Center functionality unless there is an authenticated local player.

In the GameKitHelper init method, the registerForLocalPlayerAuthChange method is called so that GameKitHelper receives events concerning authentication changes for the local player. This is the only Game Center notification that is sent through NSNotificationCenter. You register a selector to receive the message, as shown in Listing 14–4.

Listing 14–4. *Registering for Local Player Authentication Changes*

```
-(void) registerForLocalPlayerAuthChange
{
        if (isGameCenterAvailable == NO)
                return;

        NSNotificationCenter* nc = [NSNotificationCenter defaultCenter];
        [nc addObserver:self
                selector:@selector(onLocalPlayerAuthenticationChanged)
```

```
                     name:GKPlayerAuthenticationDidChangeNotificationName
                     object:nil];
}
```

As you can see, `isGameCenterAvailable` is used here to skip the rest of the method in case Game Center isn't available. You'll notice other methods doing the exact same thing, and I'll refrain from repeating this in the book's code.

The actual method being called by `NSNotificationCenter` simply forwards the message to the delegate:

```
-(void) onLocalPlayerAuthenticationChanged
{
        [delegate onLocalPlayerAuthenticationChanged];
}
```

> **NOTE:** The local player's signed-in status may actually change while the game is in the background and the user runs the Game Center app and signs out. This is due to the multitasking nature of iOS 4.0 and above. Essentially, your game must be prepared to handle the local player logging out and some other player signing in at any time during game play. Typically, you should end the current game session and return to a safe place—for example, the main menu. But you should consider saving the current state of the game for each local player as they sign out, so that when a particular local player signs back in, the game continues exactly where that player left the game.

The actual authentication is performed by the `authenticateLocalPlayer` method, in Listing 14–5.

Listing 14–5. *Authenticating the Local Player*

```
-(void) authenticateLocalPlayer
{
        GKLocalPlayer* localPlayer = [GKLocalPlayer localPlayer];
        if (localPlayer.authenticated == NO)
        {
                [localPlayer authenticateWithCompletionHandler:^(NSError* error)
                {
                        [self setLastError:error];
                }];
        }
}
```

At first glance, that's relatively straightforward. The `localPlayer` object is obtained, and if it's not authenticated, the `authenticateWithCompletionHandler` method is called. And the `NSError` object returned by the method is set to the `lastError` and . . . hey, wait a second. That's all part of the method's parameter?

Yes. These inline methods are called *block objects*. I'll tell you more about them in the next section. For now, you only need to know that the block object is a C-style method that's passed as a parameter to the `authenticateWithCompletionHandler` method. It's run only after the authentication request has returned from the server.

If you call the authenticateLocalPlayer method, your game will display the Game Center sign-in dialog, shown in Figure 14–4. If you have an Apple ID, you can sign in with your Apple ID and password. Or you can choose to create a new account.

Figure 14–4. *Game Center sign-in dialog*

But there's a third possibility—if Game Center detects that there's already a signed-in player on this device, it will simply greet you with a "welcome back" message. How do you sign out in that case? This is done through the Game Center app, which also exists on the iPhone/iPad Simulator for that very reason. If you run the Game Center app, select the first tab that reads either **Me** or **Sandbox**, and then click the label at the bottom that starts with **Account:**, and you'll get a pop-up dialog that allows you to view your account or sign out. After signing out through the Game Center app, the next time you run your app and it's going through the player authentication process, the sign-in dialog in Figure 14–4 will be shown again.

> **NOTE:** If the [GKLocalPlayer localPlayer].underage property is set after the local player was authenticated, some Game Center features are disabled. You can also refer to the underage property if your game should disable optional features that are not suitable for underage players.

Now, about error handling, you'll notice that GameKitHelper uses the setLastError method wherever there's an error object returned. This allows the delegate class to check if any error occurred through the lastError property. If it is nil, then there was no error.

However, only the last error object is kept around, and the next method returning an NSError object will replace the previous error, so it is crucial to check for the lastError property right away if error handling is important in that particular case. In some cases, you can safely ignore errors. They might only lead to temporary problems, like an empty friends list. Regardless, the setLastError message copies the new error after releasing the old one, and then prints out diagnostic information so that you can always keep an eye on the kinds of errors that occur during development:

```
-(void) setLastError:(NSError*)error
{
        [lastError release];
        lastError = [error copy];

        if (lastError != nil)
                NSLog(@"GameKitHelper ERROR: %@", [[lastError userInfo] description]);
}
```

If you receive an error and would like to know more about it, you can refer to Apple's
Game Kit Constants Reference, which describes the error constants defined in the
GameKit/GKError.h header file. You can find the Constants Reference here:
`http://developer.apple.com/library/ios/#documentation/GameKit/Reference/GameKit`
`_ConstantsRef/Reference/reference.html`.

After the local player has successfully signed in, you can access his friend list,
leaderboards, and achievements. But before I get to that, let's sidestep for a moment
and review the important aspects of block objects.

Block Objects

The inline method shown in Listing 14–5 is called a block object. You might have heard
of *closures* from other languages, or *anonymous functions*, which are essentially the
same concept. Block objects (known less accurately as *blocks*) are the way Objective-C
declares a method that can be implemented within another method and even assigned
to variables or passed as parameters. Refer to Apple's Blocks Programming Topics
documentation if you are interested in the details of block objects:
`http://developer.apple.com/library/mac/#documentation/Cocoa/Conceptual/Blocks/A`
`rticles/00_Introduction.html`.

I'll cut out the actual block object from Listing 14–5 to discuss it separately:

```
^(NSError* error)
{
        [self setLastError:error];
}
```

It looks like a method, except it has no name and it begins with a caret symbol (^). The
NSError pointer is the only variable passed to it, but there can be multiple variables
delimited by commas, as in this example:

```
^(NSArray* scores, NSError* error)
{
        [self setLastError:error];
        [delegate onScoresReceived:scores];
}
```

If that reminds you of a C method's parameters, you are correct. If you will, you can
consider a block to be a C method whose name is ^ and can be passed to one of the
many Game Kit methods taking block objects as parameters.

There are two technicalities I'd like to point out. First, local variables can be accessed in a block. But they can't normally be modified, unless they are prefixed with the __block keyword. Consider this code snippet:

```
__block bool success = NO;
[localPlayer authenticateWithCompletionHandler:^(NSError* error)
{
        success = (error == nil);
        lastError = error;
}];
```

With blocks, it is only legal to modify a local variable declared outside the block's scope if the variable is declared with the __block keyword. In this case, the success variable is declared locally outside the block, but is modified within the block, so it must be prefixed with the __block keyword. On the other hand, the lastError variable is a member variable of the class. Member variables can be modified within blocks without the use of the __block keyword.

Also, in the case of Game Kit, you'll be frequently passing block objects to Game Kit methods, but the block objects won't be run until a later time. You are probably used to code being executed in sequence, but in Game Kit programming it is not! The block passed to a Game Kit method is only called when the call completes a round trip to and from the Game Center server. That takes time because data needs to be transmitted to the Game Center servers and processed, and then a result needs to be returned to the device. Only then does the block object gets executed.

Let's take an example. You may find yourself tempted to write something like this:

```
__block bool success = NO;

[localPlayer authenticateWithCompletionHandler:^(NSError* error)
{
        success = (error == nil);
}];

if (success)
        NSLog(@"Local player logged in!");
else
        NSLog(@"Local player NOT logged in!");
```

However, this example will always report that the player is not logged in. Why? Well, the execution path is such that the authenticateWithCompletionHandler will take your block as a parameter and store it while it sends a request to the server and waits for the response to come back. However, the execution continues right away after the authenticateWithCompletionHandler method, and that's where the success variable decides which log statement to print. The problem is, the success variable is still set to NO because the block hasn't been executed yet.

Several milliseconds later, the server responds to the authentication and that triggers the completion handler—the block object—to be run. If it returns without error, the success variable is set to YES. But alas, your logging code has already been run, so the assignment has no effect.

Note that this is not a problem of block objects in general; there are methods that immediately, or even repeatedly, run a block right away before returning back to you. But in the case of almost all Game Kit methods, the block objects are used exclusively as pieces of code that will be run whenever the Game Center server has responded to a particular request. In other words, the block objects used by Game Kit are run asynchronously after an unspecified delay (and possibly not at all if the connection is interrupted).

Receiving the Local Player's Friend List

When the local player signs in or out, the onLocalPlayerAuthenticationChanged method is received and forwarded to the delegate. The delegate in these examples is the TileMapLayer class, which implements this method to ask for the local player's friend list in Listing 14–6.

Listing 14–6. *Asking for the List of Friends*

```
-(void) onLocalPlayerAuthenticationChanged
{
        GKLocalPlayer* localPlayer = [GKLocalPlayer localPlayer];
        if (localPlayer.authenticated)
        {
                GameKitHelper* gkHelper = [GameKitHelper sharedGameKitHelper];
                [gkHelper getLocalPlayerFriends];
        }
}
```

It checks if the local player is authenticated, and if so, it calls the getLocalPlayerFriends method of the GameKitHelper class right away. Let's take a look at that in Listing 14–7.

Listing 14–7. *GameKitHelper Requesting the Friends List*

```
-(void) getLocalPlayerFriends
{
        GKLocalPlayer* localPlayer = [GKLocalPlayer localPlayer];
        if (localPlayer.authenticated)
        {
                [localPlayer loadFriendsWithCompletionHandler:
                ^(NSArray* friends, NSError* error)
                {
                        [self setLastError:error];
                        [delegate onFriendListReceived:friends];
                }];
        }
}
```

Because the getLocalPlayerFriends method doesn't know when it's called or by whom, it plays things safe by checking again that the local player is actually authenticated. Then it calls the GKLocalPlayer class's loadFriendsWithCompletionHandler method, for which you'll supply another block object that is run when the server returns a list of player identifiers as strings. Unsurprisingly, this list of identifiers is stored in the friends array.

Once the call to loadFriendsWithCompletionHandler has succeeded, you can access the current player identifiers of the local player's friends through the GKLocalPlayer class:

```
NSArray* friends = [GKLocalPlayer localPlayer].friends;
```

Note that the friends array can be nil or not contain all friends. In the delegate that receives the onFriendsListReceived message, and in all other GameKitHelper delegate methods for that matter, you should check if the received parameter is nil before working with it. If it is nil, you can refer to the lastError property of the GameKitHelper class to get more information about the error for debugging, logging, or possibly presenting it to the user when it makes sense to do so.

The delegate method onFriendsListReceived simply passes the player identifiers back to GameKitHelper, requesting more info about the player identifiers in the friends list:

```
-(void) onFriendListReceived:(NSArray*)friends
{
        GameKitHelper* gkHelper = [GameKitHelper sharedGameKitHelper];
        [gkHelper getPlayerInfo:friends];
}
```

That's straightforward, so let's turn our attention back to the GameKitHelper class's getPlayerInfo method. If the playerList array contains at least one entry, it will call the loadPlayersForIdentifiers static method of the GKPlayer class, as shown in Listing 14–8.

Listing 14–8. *Requesting Players from a List of Player Identifiers*

```
-(void) getPlayerInfo:(NSArray*)playerList
{
        if ([playerList count] > 0)
        {
                // Get detailed information about a list of players
                [GKPlayer loadPlayersForIdentifiers:playerList withCompletionHandler:
                ^(NSArray* players, NSError* error)
                {
                        [self setLastError:error];
                        [delegate onPlayerInfoReceived:players];
                }];
        }
}
```

Again, a block object is used to handle the returned results from the server. And as always, the lastError property is updated before calling the delegate's onPlayerInfoReceived method. The players array should now contain a list of GKPlayer class instances, which the delegate then simply prints to the debugger console in the absence of a proper friend list user interface:

```
-(void) onPlayerInfoReceived:(NSArray*)players
{
        for (GKPlayer* gkPlayer in players)
        {
                CCLOG(@"PlayerID: %@, Alias: %@", gkPlayer.playerID, gkPlayer.alias);
        }
}
```

The `GKPlayer` class has only three properties: the player identifier, an alias, and the `isFriend` flag, which is `true` for all the players in this particular case. The alias is simply the player's nickname.

Leaderboards

In the *Tilemap12* project, I added functionality for posting and retrieving leaderboard scores. I hooked into the `onPlayerInfoReceived` method in the `TileMapLayer` class to submit a dummy score to Game Center, under the `Playtime` category:

```
-(void) onPlayerInfoReceived:(NSArray*)players
{
        GameKitHelper* gkHelper = [GameKitHelper sharedGameKitHelper];
        [gkHelper submitScore:1234 category:@"Playtime"];
}
```

The `submitScore` method shown in Listing 14–9 is implemented in `GameKitHelper` and calls the `onScoresSubmitted` message back to the delegate. Since there's no return parameter to pass on, it simply reports through the `success` value if the score was transmitted without an error.

Listing 14–9. *Submitting a Score to a Leaderboard*

```
-(void) submitScore:(int64_t)score category:(NSString*)category
{
        GKScore* gkScore = [[[GKScore alloc] initWithCategory:category] autorelease];
        gkScore.value = score;
        [gkScore reportScoreWithCompletionHandler:^(NSError* error)
        {
                [self setLastError:error];

                bool success = (error == nil);
                [delegate onScoresSubmitted:success];
        }];
}
```

The score value is of type `int64_t`, which is the same as `long long`. It's a 64-bit value, so it can store an incredibly large number—one with 19 digits. That allows for over 4 billion times greater values than a regular 32-bit integer can represent!

A temporary `GKScore` object is created and sent the autorelease message, so you don't need to worry about releasing it. It's initialized with a leaderboard category identifier, which you define in iTunes Connect. In this case, the category ID is `Playtime`. The `GKScore` object also gets the score assigned, and then its `reportScoreWithCompletionHandler` method is called, which will transmit the score to the Game Center server and to the correct leaderboard.

The delegate receives the `onScoresSubmitted` message, and subsequently calls the `retrieveTopTenAllTimeGlobalScores` method to get the top ten scores:

```
-(void) onScoresSubmitted:(bool)success
{
        if (success)
        {
```

```
                    GameKitHelper* gkHelper = [GameKitHelper sharedGameKitHelper];
                    [gkHelper retrieveTopTenAllTimeGlobalScores];
          }
}
```

The GameKitHelper class's retrieveTopTenAllTimeGlobalScores simply wraps the call to retrieveScoresForPlayers and feeds it with preconfigured parameters:

```
-(void) retrieveTopTenAllTimeGlobalScores
{
          [self retrieveScoresForPlayers:nil category:nil range:NSMakeRange(1, 10)
                                    playerScope:GKLeaderboardPlayerScopeGlobal
                                    timeScope:GKLeaderboardTimeScopeAllTime];
}
```

Feel free to add more wrapper methods for retrieving scores as you see fit, depending on your game's needs. Since there are a variety of ways to retrieve leaderboard scores and several filters to reduce the number of scores retrieved, it makes sense to use wrapper methods to reduce the potential for human error. Listing 14–10 shows the retrieveScoresForPlayers method in full.

Listing 14–10. *Retrieving a List of Scores from a Leaderboard*

```
-(void) retrieveScoresForPlayers:(NSArray*)players category:(NSString*)category
                                    range:(NSRange)range
                                    playerScope:(GKLeaderboardPlayerScope)playerScope
                                    timeScope:(GKLeaderboardTimeScope)timeScope
{
          GKLeaderboard* leaderboard = nil;
          if ([players count] > 0)
          {
                    leaderboard = [[[GKLeaderboard alloc] initWithPlayerIDs:players]
                                                                          autorelease];
          }
          else
          {
                    leaderboard = [[[GKLeaderboard alloc] init] autorelease];
                    leaderboard.playerScope = playerScope;
          }

          if (leaderboard != nil)
          {
                    leaderboard.timeScope = timeScope;
                    leaderboard.category = category;
                    leaderboard.range = range;

                    [leaderboard loadScoresWithCompletionHandler:
                    ^(NSArray* scores, NSError* error)
                    {
                              [self setLastError:error];
                              [delegate onScoresReceived:scores];
                    }];
          }
}
```

First, a GKLeaderboard object is initialized. Depending on whether the players array contains any players, the leaderboard may be initialized with a list of player identifiers to retrieve only scores for those players. Otherwise, the playerScope variable is used, which can be set to either GKLeaderboardPlayerScopeGlobal or GKLeaderboardPlayerScoreFriendsOnly to retrieve only friends' scores.

Then the leaderboard scope is further reduced by the timeScope parameter, which allows you to obtain the all-time high scores (GKLeaderboardTimeScopeAllTime), only those from the past week (GKLeaderboardTimeScopeWeek), or only today's scores (GKLeaderboardTimeScopeToday).

Of course, you also have to specify the category ID for the leaderboard; otherwise, GKLeaderboard wouldn't know which leaderboard to retrieve the scores from. Finally, an NSRange parameter allows you to refine the score positions you'd like to retrieve. In this example, a range of 1 to 10 indicates that the top ten scores should be retrieved.

Make sure that you limit the score retrieval using all these parameters (especially the NSRange parameter) to reasonably small chunks of data. While you could, it's not recommended to retrieve all the scores of a leaderboard. If your game is played online a lot and a lot of scores are submitted, you might be loading hundreds of thousands—if not millions or billions—of scores from the Game Center servers. That would cause a significant delay when retrieving scores.

With the leaderboard object set up properly, the loadScoresWithCompletionHandler method takes over and asks the server for the scores. When the scores are received, it calls the delegate method with onScoresReceived, passing on the array of scores. The array contains objects of class GKScore sorted by leaderboard rank. The GKScore objects provide you with all the information you need, including the playerID, the date the score was posted, and its rank, value, and formattedValue, which you should use to display the score to the user.

Fortunately for us, Apple provides a default leaderboard user interface. Instead of using the scores I just retrieved, I'm going to ignore them and use the onScoresReceived delegate method to bring up the built-in leaderboard view:

```
-(void) onScoresReceived:(NSArray*)scores
{
        GameKitHelper* gkHelper = [GameKitHelper sharedGameKitHelper];
        [gkHelper showLeaderboard];
}
```

Game Kit has a GKLeaderboardViewController class, which is used to display the Game Center leaderboard user interface, as shown in Listing 14–11.

Listing 14–11. *Showing the Leaderboard User Interface*

```
-(void) showLeaderboard
{
        GKLeaderboardViewController* leaderboardVC =
                        [[[GKLeaderboardViewController alloc] init] autorelease];
        if (leaderboardVC != nil)
        {
                leaderboardVC.leaderboardDelegate = self;
                [self presentViewController:leaderboardVC];
        }
}
```

The leaderboardDelegate is set to self, which means the GameKitHelper class must implement the GKLeaderboardViewControllerDelegate protocol. The first step is to add this protocol to the class's interface, like so:

```
@interface GameKitHelper : NSObject <GKLeaderboardViewControllerDelegate>
```

Then you must implement the leaderboardViewControllerDidFinish method, which is used to simply dismiss the view and to forward the event to the delegate:

```
-(void) leaderboardViewControllerDidFinish:(GKLeaderboardViewController*)viewController
{
        [self dismissModalViewController];
        [delegate onLeaderboardViewDismissed];
}
```

Now there's a bit of behind-the-scenes magic going on. I've added a few helper methods to GameKitHelper that deal specifically with presenting and dismissing the various Game Kit view controllers making use of cocos2d's root view controller. If you remember, cocos2d creates a root view controller in version 0.99.5 beta 3 and higher, and this controller will be used to display the Game Center views. Those methods are shown in Listing 14–12.

Listing 14–12. *Using Cocos2d's Root View Controller to Present and Dismiss Game Kit Views*

```
-(UIViewController*) getRootViewController
{
        return [UIApplication sharedApplication].keyWindow.rootViewController;
}

-(void) presentViewController:(UIViewController*)vc
{
        UIViewController* rootVC = [self getRootViewController];
        [rootVC presentModalViewController:vc animated:YES];
}

-(void) dismissModalViewController
{
        UIViewController* rootVC = [self getRootViewController];
        [rootVC dismissModalViewControllerAnimated:YES];
}
```

The rootViewController is a UIWindow property, and the main window used by cocos2d is the keyWindow property of the UIApplication class. There's only one catch: the current cocos2d project templates do not assign the new root view controller to the UIWindow's property, so normally it's unavailable unless you expose it in the AppDelegate class itself. But there's a better way to make the rootViewController accessible to all classes without requiring to import the AppDelegate class. You'll have to open the project's AppDelegate class and add the following line in the applicationDidFinishLaunching method, just above the call to [window makeKeyAndVisible]:

```
window.rootViewController = viewController;
[window makeKeyAndVisible];
```

After you've done this, the cocos2d rootViewController is accessible from anywhere through the keyWindow.rootViewController property.

The GKLeaderboardViewController will load the scores it needs automatically and present you with a view like the one in Figure 14–5.

Figure 14–5. *The Game Kit leaderboard view*

NOTE: The built-in Game Kit views are presented in portrait mode. If your game uses a landscape orientation, the default views may not be ideal, as players will have to rotate their devices to view leaderboards, achievements, friends, and matchmaking views. In this case you might have to consider writing your own user interface to display Game Center information.

Achievements

In the *Tilemap13* project, instead of showing the leaderboard, I'm calling the GameKitHelper showAchievements method in the onScoresReceived method to bring up the Achievements view (Listing 14–13).

Listing 14–13. *Showing the Achievements View*

```
-(void) showAchievements
{
        GKAchievementViewController* achievementsVC =
                                [[[GKAchievementViewController alloc] init] autorelease];
```

```
        if (achievementsVC != nil)
        {
                achievementsVC.achievementDelegate = self;
                [self presentViewController:achievementsVC];
        }
}
```

This is very similar to showing the leaderboard view in Listing 14–11. Once more, the GameKitHelper class also has to implement the proper protocol, named GKAchievementViewControllerDelegate:

```
@interface GameKitHelper : NSObject <GKLeaderboardViewControllerDelegate,
                                        GKAchievementViewControllerDelegate>
```

The protocol requires the GameKitHelper class to implement the achievementViewControllerDidFinish method, which is also strikingly similar to the one used by the leaderboard view controller:

```
-(void) achievementViewControllerDidFinish:(GKAchievementViewController*)viewControl
{
        [self dismissModalViewController];
        [delegate onAchievementsViewDismissed];
}
```

You can see an example of the achievements view in Figure 14–6, in which one achievement is already unlocked.

Figure 14–6. *The Game Kit achievements view*

So what else can you do with achievements?

Obviously, you'll want to determine whether an achievement has been unlocked, and actually you'll want to report all the progress a player makes toward completing an achievement. For example, if the achievement's goal is to eat 476 bananas, then you would report the progress to Game Center every time the player eats a banana. In this example project, I'm simply checking for time elapsed, and then I report progress on the PlayedForTenSeconds achievement. This is done in the TileMapLayer's update method, shown in Listing 14–14.

Listing 14–14. *Determining Achievement Progress*

```
-(void) update:(ccTime)delta
{
        totalTime += delta;
        if (totalTime > 1.0f)
        {
                totalTime = 0.0f;

                NSString* playedTenSeconds = @"PlayedForTenSeconds";
                GameKitHelper* gkHelper = [GameKitHelper sharedGameKitHelper];
                GKAchievement* achievement =
                                        [gkHelper getAchievementByID:playedTenSeconds];
                if (achievement.completed == NO)
                {
                        float percent = achievement.percentComplete + 10;
                        [gkHelper reportAchievementWithID:playedTenSeconds
                                                        percentComplete:percent];
                }
        }

        ...
}
```

Every time a second has passed, the achievement with the identifier PlayedForTenSeconds is obtained through GameKitHelper. If the achievement isn't completed yet, then its percentComplete property is increased by 10 percent and the progress is reported through GameKitHelper's reportAchievementWithID method (Listing 14–15).

Listing 14–15. *Reporting Achievement Progress*

```
-(void) reportAchievementWithID:(NSString*)identifier percentComplete:(float)percent
{
        GKAchievement* achievement = [self getAchievementByID:identifier];
        if (achievement != nil && achievement.percentComplete < percent)
        {
                achievement.percentComplete = percent;
                [achievement reportAchievementWithCompletionHandler:
                ^(NSError* error)
                {
                        [self setLastError:error];
                        [delegate onAchievementReported:achievement];
                }];
        }
}
```

To avoid unnecessary calls to the Game Center server, the achievement's `percentComplete` property is verified to actually be smaller than the percent parameter. Game Center does not allow achievement progress to be reduced, and thus will ignore such a report. But if you can avoid actually reporting this to the Game Center server in the first place, you avoid an unnecessary data transfer. With the limited bandwidth available on mobile devices, every bit of data not transmitted is a good thing.

> **NOTE:** Reporting an achievement's progress may fail for a number of reasons—for example, the device might have lost its Internet connection. Be prepared to save any achievements that couldn't be transmitted. Then retry submitting them periodically or when the player logs in the next time. Fortunately, the final `GameKitHelper` class contains additional code to cache achievements that failed transmission to the Game Center server. You'll find the final version of the `GameKitHelper` class in the code folder for this chapter.

This still leaves the question open: where do the achievements come from in the first place? They are loaded as soon as the local player signs in. To make this possible, I extended the block object used in `authenticateWithCompletionHandler` to call the `loadAchievements` method if there wasn't an error:

```
[localPlayer authenticateWithCompletionHandler:^(NSError* error)
{
        [self setLastError:error];

        if (error == nil)
        {
                [self loadAchievements];
        }
}];
```

The `loadAchievements` method uses the GKAchievement class's `loadAchievementsWithCompletionHandler` method to retrieve the local player's achievements from Game Center (Listing 14–16).

Listing 14–16. *Loading the Local Player's Achievements*

```
-(void) loadAchievements
{
        [GKAchievement loadAchievementsWithCompletionHandler:
        ^(NSArray* loadedAchievements, NSError* error)
        {
                [self setLastError:error];

                if (achievements == nil)
                {
                        achievements = [[NSMutableDictionary alloc] init];
                }
                else
                {
                        [achievements removeAllObjects];
                }

                for (GKAchievement* achievement in loadedAchievements)
```

```
                    {
                            [achievements setObject:achievement
                                           forKey:achievement.identifier];
                    }

                    [delegate onAchievementsLoaded:achievements];
            }];
}
```

Inside the block object, the `achievements` member variable is either allocated or has all objects removed from it. This allows you to call the `loadAchievements` method at a later time to refresh the list of achievements. The returned array `loadedAchievements` contains a number of `GKAchievement` instances, which are then transferred to the `achievements` `NSMutableDictionary` simply for ease of access. The `NSDictionary` class allows you to retrieve an achievement by its string identifier directly, instead of having to iterate over the array and comparing each achievement's identifier along the way. You can see this in the `getAchievementByID` method in Listing 14–17.

Listing 14–17. *Getting and Optionally Creating an Achievement*

```
-(GKAchievement*) getAchievementByID:(NSString*)identifier
{
        GKAchievement* achievement = [achievements objectForKey:identifier];

        if (achievement == nil)
        {
                // Create a new achievement object
                achievement = [[[GKAchievement alloc] initWithIdentifier:identifier]
                                                                     autorelease];
                [achievements setObject:achievement forKey:achievement.identifier];
        }

        return [[achievement retain] autorelease];
}
```

This is where you need to be careful. The `getAchievementByID` method creates a new achievement if it can't find one with the given identifier, assuming that this achievement's progress has never been reported to Game Center before. Only achievements that have been reported to Game Center at least once are obtained through the `loadAchievements` method in Listing 14–16. For any other achievement, you'll have to create it first. So `getAchievementsByID` will always return a valid achievement object, but you'll only notice whether that achievement is really set up for your game when you try to report its progress to Game Center.

One curiosity here may be that the achievement returned gets a retain method and an autorelease method. This is to ensure that, in case the achievements dictionary is cleared by a call to `loadAchievements`, any achievement returned through `getAchievementsByID` remains valid. But the idea is to let `GameKitHelper` manage the achievements, so any other code shouldn't store achievement objects, but just obtain them through `GameKitHelper` whenever they are needed.

You can also clear the local player's achievement progress. This should be done with great care, and not without asking the player's permission. On the other hand, during development, the resetAchievements method in Listing 14–18 comes in handy.

Listing 14–18. *Resetting Achievement Progress*

```
-(void) resetAchievements
{
        [achievements removeAllObjects];

        [GKAchievement resetAchievementsWithCompletionHandler:
        ^(NSError* error)
        {
                [self setLastError:error];
                bool success = (error == nil);
                [delegate onResetAchievements:success];
        }];
}
```

Matchmaking

Moving on to the *Tilemap14* project, we enter the realm of matchmaking—connecting players and inviting friends to play a game match together, that is. To start hosting a game and to bring up the corresponding matchmaking view, I've added a call to GameKitHelper's showMatchmakerWithRequest method after the local player has been authenticated, as shown in Listing 14–19.

Listing 14–19. *Preparing to Show the Host Game Screen*

```
-(void) onLocalPlayerAuthenticationChanged
{
        GKLocalPlayer* localPlayer = [GKLocalPlayer localPlayer];
        if (localPlayer.authenticated)
        {
                GKMatchRequest* request = [[[GKMatchRequest alloc] init] autorelease];
                request.minPlayers = 2;
                request.maxPlayers = 4;

                GameKitHelper* gkHelper = [GameKitHelper sharedGameKitHelper];
                [gkHelper showMatchmakerWithRequest:request];
        }
}
```

A GKMatchRequest instance is created and its minPlayers and maxPlayers properties are initialized, indicating that the match should have at least two and at most four players. Every match must allow for two players, obviously, and a peer-to-peer match can be played with up to four players. *Peer-to-peer networking* means that all devices are connected with each other, and can send data to and receive it from all other devices. This is opposed to a server/client architecture, where all players connect to a single server and send and receive only to and from this server. In peer-to-peer networks, the amount of traffic generated grows exponentially, so most peer-to-peer multiplayer games are strictly limited to a very low number of allowed players.

> **NOTE:** Game Center can connect up to 16 players, but only if you have a hosted server application to manage all matches using a client/server architecture. That requires a huge amount of work and know-how to set up and use properly, so I'll leave it out of this discussion and focus only on peer-to-peer networking.

The showMatchmakerWithRequest method is implemented in a strikingly similar way to the code that brings up the leaderboard and achievement views, as Listing 14–20 shows.

Listing 14–20. *Showing the Host Game Screen*

```
-(void) showMatchmakerWithRequest:(GKMatchRequest*)request
{
        GKMatchmakerViewController* hostVC = [[[GKMatchmakerViewController alloc]
                                        initWithMatchRequest:request] autorelease];
        if (hostVC != nil)
        {
                hostVC.matchmakerDelegate = self;
                [self presentViewController:hostVC];
        }
}
```

Figure 14–7 shows an example matchmaking view, waiting for you to invite a friend to your match. You can also wait until Game Center finds an automatically matched player for your game, but since you're currently developing the game, it's rather unlikely that anyone but you will be currently playing it.

If you followed the leaderboard and achievement view examples, you'll know that each required the GameKitHelper class to implement a protocol, and with matchmaking it's no different. I also added GKMatchDelegate because we're going to need it soon.

```
@interface GameKitHelper : NSObject <GKLeaderboardViewControllerDelegate,
                                GKAchievementViewControllerDelegate,
                                GKMatchmakerViewControllerDelegate,
                                        GKMatchDelegate>
```

The GKMatchmakerViewControllerDelegate protocol requires three methods to be implemented: one for the player pressing the Cancel button, one for failing with an error, and one for finding a suitable match. The latter deserves a mention:

```
-(void) matchmakerViewController:(GKMatchmakerViewController*)viewController
                        didFindMatch:(GKMatch*)match
{
        [self dismissModalViewController];
        [self setCurrentMatch:match];
        [delegate onMatchFound:match];
}
```

Figure 14–7. *The host game matchmaking view*

If a match was found, this match is set as the current match, and the delegate's onMatchFound method is called to inform it about the newly found match.

Instead of hosting a match, you can also instruct Game Center to try to automatically find a match for you, as shown in Listing 14–21. If successful, the delegate receives the same onMatchFound message.

Listing 14–21. *Searching for an Existing Match*

```
-(void) findMatchForRequest:(GKMatchRequest*)request
{
        GKMatchMaker* matchmaker = [GKMatchMaker sharedMatchmaker];
        [matchmaker findMatchForRequest:request withCompletionHandler:
        ^(GKMatch* match, NSError* error)
        {
                [self setLastError:error];

                if (match != nil)
                {
                        [self setCurrentMatch:match];
                        [delegate onMatchFound:match];
                }
        }];
}
```

While Game Center is searching for a match, you should give the user visual feedback, like an animated progress indicator, because finding a match can take several seconds or even minutes. That's where the CCProgressTimer class comes in handy, which I discussed in Chapter 5. You should also give your user a means to cancel the matchmaking process, and if she does so, you should call the cancelMatchmakingRequest method:

```
-(void) cancelMatchmakingRequest
{
        [[GKMatchmaker sharedMatchmaker] cancel];
}
```

At this point, the match has been created, but all the players might not yet be connected to the match. As players join the game, the match:didChangeState method of the GKMatchDelegate protocol is called for each player connecting or disconnecting. Only when the expectedPlayerCount of the match has been counted down to 0 by the Game Kit framework should you start the match. The GKMatch object updates the expectedPlayerCount property automatically, as Listing 14–22 shows.

Listing 14–22. *Waiting for All Players Before Starting the Match*

```
-(void) match:(GKMatch*)match player:(NSString*)playerID
                               didChangeState:(GKPlayerConnectionState)state
{
        switch (state)
        {
                case GKPlayerStateConnected:
                        [delegate onPlayerConnected:playerID];
                        break;
                case GKPlayerStateDisconnected:
                        [delegate onPlayerDisconnected:playerID];
                        break;
        }

        if (matchStarted == NO && match.expectedPlayerCount == 0)
        {
                matchStarted = YES;
                [delegate onStartMatch];
        }
}
```

If at any time during your game a player drops out and the expectedPlayerCount property becomes greater than 0, you can call addPlayersToMatch to fill up the now empty space with a new player, as in Listing 14–23 (assuming that your game supports players joining a match in progress). Since there's no guarantee that a player will actually be found, you should not interrupt the game while GKMatchmaker is looking for a new player.

Listing 14–23. *Adding Players to an Existing Match*

```
-(void) addPlayersToMatch:(GKMatchRequest*)request
{
        if (currentMatch == nil)
                return;

        [[GKMatchmaker sharedMatchmaker] addPlayersToMatch:currentMatch
                                matchRequest:request completionHandler:
        ^(NSError* error)
        {
```

```
        [self setLastError:error];

        bool success = (error == nil);
        [delegate onPlayersAddedToMatch:success];
    }];
}
```

Once all players are connected and the match has officially started, you can start sending and subsequently receiving data. The easiest way to do so is to send data to all players, as shown in Listing 14–24.

Listing 14–24. *Sending and Receiving Data*

```
-(void) sendDataToAllPlayers:(void*)data length:(NSUInteger)length
{
        NSError* error = nil;
        NSData* packet = [NSData dataWithBytes:data length:length];
        [currentMatch sendDataToAllPlayers:packet
                               withDataMode:GKMatchSendDataUnreliable error:&error];
        [self setLastError:error];
}

-(void) match:(GKMatch*)match didReceiveData:(NSData*)data
fromPlayer:(NSString*)playerID
{
        [delegate onReceivedData:data fromPlayer:playerID];
}
```

The sendDataToAllPlayers method takes a void pointer as input, and wraps it into an NSData object. You can send any data as long as you provide the correct length of that data. Typically, networked programs send structs like CGPoint (or any custom struct) to make this process easier, since you can then use sizeof(myPoint) to get the length (size in bytes) of such a data structure. Also, to speed up transmission, most data is sent unreliably. Data that is sent frequently can especially be sent unreliably because if a packet ever gets lost, the clients simply have to wait for the next packet to arrive. If you do need every packet to arrive—for example, because it contains crucial information that is only sent once, then you should set the data mode to GKMatchSendDataReliable. This instructs GameKit to simply transmit the packet again if it could not be delivered. Since GameKit has to receive a return packet from clients to acknowledge that they received the packet, this adds additional traffic.

What data you should send and how often you should send it depend entirely on the game itself. The ground rule is to send as little as you can, as rarely as possible. For example, instead of transmitting each player's position every frame, you should send a packet for each movement action, because the movement in the tilemap game is always 32 pixels in one direction and done by a CCMoveAction. So it's sufficient to send when the move should start and in which direction it should be, which saves a lot of traffic compared to sending each player's position every frame.

Conclusion

I hope this chapter and the provided `GameKitHelper` class help you get comfortable with Game Center programming. Sure, network programming is no easy task, but I've laid a lot of the groundwork for you, and even block objects are no longer foreign territory for you. In particular, the checklist of tasks to enable Game Center support for your game should help you avoid a lot of the initial pitfalls faced by developers.

Over the course of this chapter, you've become comfortable using the leaderboard and achievement features of Game Center. Those alone bring your game to a new level. And with the user interface provided by Game Center, you don't even have to write your own user interface to display leaderboards and achievements.

I then introduced you to the matchmaking features of Game Center, which allow you to invite friends to join your game, find random players on the Internet, and allow them to send and receive data.

With this chapter, I already departed a little from pure cocos2d programming; in fact, you can apply what you just learned about Game Center to any iOS game engine. In the next chapter, I'll depart even further from cocos2d game engine programming. I'll show you where to go from here, where to find help, and where all the useful resources are. What's more, I'll delve into marketing, public relations, and publishers. Understanding these topics can help you sell more units and connect with more developers and fans.

Chapter 15

Out of the Ordinary

This final chapter contains no source code. I'm not even going to talk much about cocos2d. Instead, I'd like to focus on where you can go after you've read this book—for example, to ask questions and to learn more. But you should also investigate which technologies may be useful to implement in your game, such as advertising, analytics, one of the many social networking libraries, and even server technology used in persistent world games.

Everything you ever wanted to know is probably somewhere on the Internet. It may simply be hiding. If you want to know where to find art, audio, and freelancers, I'll provide good starting points. And I'll continue to provide more information and links on my blog, so be sure to visit my web site, at www.learn-cocos2d.com.

I'm also giving you a glimpse into marketing and public relations in this final chapter. Those are topics that are often asked about, full of mystery and misunderstandings. They include working with a publisher and how you can benefit from such a relationship, and also how to market your game and yourself. For an independent developer it's very important to be recognized by the community as an aspiring, enthusiastic game developer and to connect with the community. All of your social networking efforts will then help you to promote your game simply by being able to reach out to more like-minded people. If you can build a network of followers, the success of your game will follow. A lot of people get that mixed up and think it's the other way round. It's not.

You'll also learn about the reference games and apps made available with cocos2d. They'll give you a good impression of what's possible with the cocos2d game engine, and also what you can achieve as an independent developer. One of the most exciting learning tools is other people's source code, so I've included a list of commercial cocos2d source code projects that are on sale for exactly this reason.

Most of all, "out of the ordinary" should be the guiding principle for whatever you do. Create something that's different, and don't be afraid to be different.

Useful Technologies

Every platform has a number of peripheral technologies that are helpful if not essential, at least in some cases and for some developers. On the iOS platform, this includes the ever-growing list of social networking platforms to choose from, besides Apple's Game Center. Then there's server development kits that you might need for developing persistent games that ought to connect to your own server, be it to find and run matches of more than four players, or simply to save characters, progress, settings, and worlds online.

And sometimes regarded dubiously, providing ads in games can create an additional revenue stream, especially for free games and lite versions. Often in conjunction with ads you can also investigate if it would help your game to add analytics and metrics, in order to find out where players fail most often, what buttons they click the most and how frequently they play individual game modes. This can help you tweak your game to be more fun for more players.

Social Networks

Besides Apple's Game Center technology, there are a number of different social networking platforms. All are more or less similar in that they allow players to connect, post high scores, earn achievements, and do many other things, including posting game events to Twitter and Facebook—and all of them are free for both players and developers!

Since their feature sets are constantly evolving and the market for social networks is booming, the final decision is up to you. I'll list the big players here and mention some of their outstanding features.

> **NOTE:** Most of the social networking SDKs already include support for connecting your users with Twitter and Facebook, so you don't need to learn and implement the separately available Facebook and Twitter APIs. If all you need is access to Twitter, you should have a look at the excellent MGTwitterEngine API from Matt Gemmell, at `http://mattgemmell.com/2008/02/22/mgtwitterengine-twitter-from-cocoa`. And if you need to integrate Facebook into your app, the official Facebook iOS SDK is located on GitHub: `http://github.com/facebook/facebook-ios-sdk`.

OpenFeint is the perceived leader of iOS social networking SDKs. It boasts Game Center compatibility and turn-based multiplayer features to stand out from the crowd. But first and foremost it's very popular, with an audience of players in the millions. Have a look at OpenFeint's developer portal: `www.openfeint.com/developers`.

Scoreloop sets itself apart from the competition by offering additional revenue streams via downloadable content, sharing virtual goods and in-game currencies. It also includes analytics to determine what your players are doing. Take a feature tour on the Scoreloop home page: www.scoreloop.com.

Agon-Online is the third big player of free, no-strings-attached social networks. The biggest plus is that it allows you to store persistent player profiles, and it gives you up to 5KB of data, and more on request. Agon-Online calls this *Cloud Storage*, and you can read more about it on their developer web site: http://developer.agon-online.com.

Geocade is another social networking platform whose primary differentiation factor is its support for location-aware gaming. Other social networks also have geolocation in their feature sets, but Geocade is worth checking out if your game calls for a social network specifically for people in the local area. However, you have to send an e-mail to request being signed up. You can do so here: http://geocade.com/publishers.html.

Plus+ is the social networking platform created by ngmoco, a big publisher of iOS games. It's currently only available to ngmoco's development partners. Ngmoco is looking for select developers to partner with; if you think you have what it takes, then you might want to apply on their developer web site: http://plusplus.com/developers.

Chillingo's Crystal is the other big iOS publisher's social networking platform. And just like with Plus+, access is not automatic—you need to request it. You can register your e-mail address on the Crystal SDK web site: www.crystalsdk.com.

Socket Server Technology

If you're looking to build a game that requires more sophisticated server-side game logic and storage than the social networking platforms are able to offer, you will have to write your own socket server. Luckily, the difficult part of writing a server/client architecture with socket connection and other networking voodoo has already been done for you.

Hosting your online games on a socket server has several advantages. For some games it's very important that players can't cheat, so running the most critical game logic isolated on the server while being able to verify the data coming from clients can prevent a lot of common cheating mechanisms. A server-based approach is also the only way to write a game that supports a lot of players at once. With peer-to-peer technology, you quickly run into scaling issues, because each device's bandwidth is rather limited, and every player in a peer-to-peer match adds computational overhead to every device connected to that match. Apple's Game Kit restricts peer-to-peer connections between devices to a maximum of four players for a reason. The server hardware is ultimately more powerful and has a higher bandwidth than any device connected to it, which allows you to host more players in the same match.

Electrotanks's Electroserver is a comprehensive server technology used by professionals worldwide. It's priced accordingly, but it does have a free version that allows for up to 25 concurrent users to be connected with the game server. If that's sufficient for you, give it a try: www.electrotank.com.

SmartFoxServer by gotoAndPlay() follows in the tracks of Electroserver. It's not as feature rich, but it's very popular among independent game developers, mostly because it has a completely free Lite version, while the Basic and Pro versions still allow up to 20 users for free. In general, the prices are more affordable by independent developers. Compare the SmartFoxServer editions on the products page: `www.smartfoxserver.com/products`.

Exit Games follows a two-pronged approach by offering a networking component called Photon and a managed service for developing persistent online games called Neutron. Neutron natively supports the development of turn-based multiplayer games, and it can suspend and resume game sessions. Photon has a free version that supports up to 50 concurrent users per app or server, and Neutron has a free trial version. Compare features and prices on the Exit Games web site: `www.exitgames.com`.

Ads and Analytics

Advertisements provide a way to generate additional revenue from apps and games. It can be very lucrative if the app is very popular, but frankly speaking, it's also easy to put off users by displaying ads, and it's much more likely to make little to no money. It's still worth experimenting with advertisements—for example, if you use them as a motivator in free versions of your app by letting your users know that the full version removes the ads—besides offering all the other cool features the players want, of course.

Regardless of whether you dislike ads or not, there's another reason to evaluate the ad space. That's because most advertising SDKs can also provide you with insightful metrics and analytics. This not only includes statistical data such as which iOS version your users have installed and which device they're using, but also custom metrics, such as which game mode is played most often and where players tend to fail more frequently. This allows you to tweak the difficulty and the user interface layout according to how the users are actually using your app.

When it comes to advertising on iOS devices, the first contender is iAd by Apple. You can get an overview of the iAd Network on Apple's advertising web site: `http://advertising.apple.com`.

Next up is clearly AdMob for App Developers. You can learn more about the iOS version of AdMob at `www.admob.com/appdevs`, while their Mobile Analytics product is hosted on this web site: `http://analytics.admob.com`.

Lastly, Flurry Analytics is the only product that focuses solely on metrics and analytics. Note that Flurry bought Pinch Media, and its products have merged into Flurry Analytics, in case you're wondering why I'm not mentioning the very popular Pinch Analytics. Begin your research into Flurry Analytics here: `www.flurry.com/product/analytics/index.html`.

Push Notification Providers

You may have heard of Apple's push notification service, but if not, you can learn more about it in Apple's Push Notification Programming Guide: `http://developer.apple.com/library/ios/#documentation/NetworkingInternet/Conceptual/RemoteNotificationsPG/Introduction/Introduction.html`.

Push notifications allow apps to broadcast messages to individual devices. If you implement one of the social networking platforms, you'll get this feature for free, and you don't need to care about the complexities of push notification programming. However, in some cases you might need to implement your own solution, and for that you need a push notification provider. That's a server that can communicate with Apple's servers and the iOS devices. You can write your own server with the free and open source apns-sharp library (see `http://code.google.com/p/apns-sharp`), or you can sign up for the Mono Push service (`www.monopush.com`) or Urban Airship (`http://urbanairship.com`).

Source Code Projects to Benefit From

Personally, I learn best by browsing through other people's code. One of the first things I did when I got cocos2d and found the documentation to be lacking was to invest in the Sapus Tongue source code project to see how cocos2d is actually being used in a game. It was very helpful for getting started quickly. The advantage of commercially sold source code compared to the open source projects is that you rarely get support for the latter and they're almost never updated, to the point that most of the open source projects you'll find are still using versions of cocos2d prior to v0.9. So I won't mention those here.

There's only one open source game that's quite up to date: the iPhone game Puff Puff from 6thMega. Puff Puff is a game about the Gulf oil spill, and was released as goodware, and 6thMega actively endorses remixes and encourages developers to contribute to the project. Some of this is in an effort to raise awareness for such environmental issues. You can download the source code and find more information on the developers page: `http://6thmega.com/developers`.

The following source code projects are all commercial offerings. I refrain from listing prices because they are subject to change.

Sapus Tongue Source Code

Sapus Tongue is a game created by the author of cocos2d for iPhone, Ricardo Quesada. The object of the game is to rotate the device to spin a monkey in order to throw it as far as possible. For over two years the Sapus Tongue source code has been frequently updated to stay current with both the development of cocos2d and the iPhone SDK, always integrating the latest features added to cocos2d. It's the most instructive source code package for learning the cocos2d game engine, and recent updates have added iAd, Game Center, and HD support.

The license allows you to use the source code in your own projects royalty-free for any purpose. However, you cannot use the supplied images and music, and you're not allowed to create a clone of the Sapus Tongue game.

You can choose from three packages. The Basic version includes no updates and no support. The Updates version adds six months of updates, while the Premium version also entitles you to receive e-mail support for six months. Update and support renewals are available separately, and the purchase of any Sapus Tongue source code version entitles you to a discount for LevelSVG.

The product page with more information, including links to the various versions of Sapus Tongue on the App Store, can be found on the Sapus Media web site: www.sapusmedia.com/sources.

LevelSVG

Also from Ricardo Quesada, LevelSVG allows you to design labyrinth and platform game levels. Scalable Vector Graphics (SVG) is an open standard that describes two-dimensional vector graphics in an XML format. It's understood by most modern browsers, and you typically design SVG files using a specialized drawing tool. In the case of LevelSVG, only the free Inkscape graphics editor is supported. You can download Inkscape here: http://inkscape.org.

The LevelSVG source code reads the SVG files produced by Inkscape and creates a level scene with collisions. Rounding off this package are a number of predefined game play elements—such as a built-in hero who can move, jump, and shoot—and a virtual joypad.

There is no licensing information for the product, but it is safe to assume that the license is similar to the one used by the Sapus Tongue source code. Customers who also bought the Sapus Tongue source code get a discount. The only version available is the Premium version, which includes six months of updates and support. License renewal is also available separately.

On the LevelSVG product page you can find screenshots of the game, an example video, the LevelSVG manual, and a link to the LevelSVG app containing mini games built with LevelSVG. Visit the LevelSVG product page here: www.sapusmedia.com/levelsvg.

The iPhone RPG Game Kit

Created by Nathanael M. Weiss, the iPhone Game Kit is also known as the iPhone RPG Kit. The game Quexlor is a role-playing hack-and-slash game following in the footsteps of Diablo, featuring a large tilemap world with multiple levels, various monsters, and plenty of items. The game kit comes with a huge amount of royalty-free graphics created by Reiner Prokein, a comprehensive Make Your Own iPhone Game e-book, and a publishing guide that explains in detail how to submit your game to the App Store. Obviously, you also get the game's excellently crafted source code, but that almost seems secondary.

There are no notable licensing restrictions. You get a 60-day money-back guarantee and free updates for life, although it does not specify whose life. Support is available through the support forum, where you can also share your work with other Game Kit customers.

You can find the link to the Quexlor game on the App Store and a whole lot more information about the iPhone Game Kit on its web site, so I suggest having a look: www.iphonegamekit.com.

Line-Drawing Game Starterkit

My Line-Drawing Game Starterkit is modeled after successful games like Flight Control and Harbor Master. If you like to create line-drawing games, this starter kit gets you going with drawing lines, moving objects along the paths, collision detection, and a clearly structured code base, including both iPhone and iPad versions.

Each purchase grants you a site license, which means your whole team is allowed to use the game's source code and assets. Since it's a starter kit, you are naturally allowed to make clones of the game. I also offer a 30-day money-back guarantee, and I'll be happy to help you learn the starter kit's source code and give directions on how to extend it.

The Line-Drawing Game Starterkit's product page contains the starter kit's feature list, links to the demo apps, a code sample, and the complete documentation: www.learn-cocos2d.com/store/line-drawing-game-starterkit.

For Your Reference

Following is a list of games and apps made with cocos2d. They should serve as shining examples of what you can do with cocos2d as well as the creativity of cocos2d developers.

Instead of providing an iTunes link to each app in the book, I decided to create a post on my blog where I host all the links to the games mentioned here, and I'll update this list to include noteworthy games released after the book has been published. You can find the list of links to these apps, including other links of interest, on the Great Apps Made With cocos2d page: www.learn-cocos2d.com/2010/10/great-apps-made-with-cocos2d.

The Elements (iPad) is a graphical representation of the periodic table of elements. The outstanding features are the plentiful photographs and smooth 360 animations that invite you to explore the elements that make up you, me, and the rest of the universe (excluding empty space, of which there's a lot I've been told). It's priced highly but worth every cent, and if you need an app that will let you brag about your new iPad, this is it!

Bloomies is a colorful gardening game, full of bees. If that doesn't sway you, maybe the idea of fostering and nurturing your own garden does. The flowers need your constant attention, and the game play is addictive, just like any Tamagotchi-style game. Oh, and it happens to be made by two former colleagues of mine. It's just a beautiful game, and so is their follow-up game, Super Blast.

StickWars is a game where you defend your castle from incoming stick figures by flicking them in the air or literally shaking them to the ground. The developer, John Hartzog, had never before worked with Objective-C or on mobile devices, but he pulled it off. StickWars remains to this date within the top 100 games, and continues to be updated even a year after the initial release.

ZombieSmash is also a castle defense game, except that this time hordes of zombies are attacking, and you get explosives, 16-ton weights, shotguns, and other cool items that make a bloody mess to fend them off. Your castle is your barn, and if you can defend it, you'll be rewarded with a slow-motion animation of the final zombie losing its, err, unlife. The outstanding feature of this game is certainly the rag doll animation system that allows zombies to walk, crawl, or otherwise try to move even if they lost some of their limbs.

Super Turbo Action Pig revives the simple game play concept of a scrolling level where your character always falls down, except when you touch the screen to boost his jetpack. The extraordinary part here is that the game's graphics are extremely well made and the overall presentation of the game, the trailer, the web site, and the humor set a great example.

Then there's Farmville—do I even have to explain what it's about? It's an incredibly successful Facebook game that has millions of players worldwide building their farms in an isometric landscape. It just goes to show how powerful cocos2d is if a company like Zynga uses it to port its most successful game to the iPhone. It's notable that Zombie Farm came out on the iPhone before Farmville, and it was also created with cocos2d.

Melvin Says There's Monsters (iPad) is a beautifully animated cartoon kid story with professional-quality voiceovers. The story is cleverly constructed and has an insightful turning point. It's a pleasure to watch even for an adult, and it also uses cocos2d's page-flip animations very effectively. If you have an iPad and kids, it's a must have!

Trainyard is an innovative puzzle game that was clearly engineered with the user in mind. It features a mode for the color-blind, is optimized to use little battery power, saves and loads the game just as the user left it, and even allows users to share puzzle solutions on the Web, using a duplicate of the game engine written in Flash. This all besides being a really innovative puzzle game where you lay tracks and combine trains to match them with colored train yards.

AbstractWar 2.0 is a dual-stick shooter featuring colorful and vibrant geometric visuals. It's obviously inspired by Geometry Wars on Xbox Live Arcade. It's an intense space-shooter with plenty of game modes. You can even play it in multiplayer mode via a Bluetooth connection, and it allows you to use your own iPod music.

Fuji Leaves is an interesting music game, where dropping balls hit leaves, and depending on speed and location of impact, a sound is played. With several balls on the screen bouncing around, you can dynamically create musical scores. It's intensely fascinating to play this game, trying to come up with interesting scores and just the right placement of leaves. Before you know it, an hour has passed.

Working with Publishers

In the early days of computer programming, developers single-handedly copied their game code onto floppy disks and shrink-wrapped it to sell it in local software and hardware stores. Those days are long gone, and with the increasing complexity of games, publishers took on the task of distributing and marketing games. This model has been the default for the past 20 years or so, but with the advent of the indie game scene in recent years, mostly driven by new technologies such as downloadable games, the Xbox Live Indie Games channel, and Apple's App Store, more and more game developers are turning to self-publishing again. So why would you want to work with a publisher these days?

The first aspect is technical support and testing. Publishers want to make sure that every game they release does not reflect badly on them, so one of their goals is to release games with as few bugs as possible and with polished game play. If you're not used to this process, which includes the scrutiny of a quality assurance team, you'll be in for a surprise, and it may not always be a pleasant one—for example, if the game's release is held back due to yet another obscure and hard to-find bug. So that's a bad thing? To the contrary, it forces you to work with an attention to details that's all too often neglected and dismissed by hobbyist developers. And in the end, you'll be rewarded with a better game. In most cases, this also translates to more favorable reviews by press and players alike, and thus more sales.

Working with an established publisher also reflects positively on you, simply because of the respected games already released by said publisher. I don't mean that in an ego-trip kind of way. You're not special because you're working with big-name publisher X—but you sure will learn a lot, and that's going to make you stand out from the crowd. The experiences working with a publisher don't just involve game programming and the things you'll pick up from technical support and the quality assurance process. You'll also sign a contract and get a glimpse at all the legalese and paperwork involved (don't worry, it's not that bad).

Signing a standard contract with a publisher is more like opening a bank account. Everything is ready-made, and you just have to fill in a few blanks. And, if you allow yourself to learn from the process, it can be very insightful to get an impression of the details that need to be specified to get everything in order from a financial and legal point of view. If the publisher has a good track record with other developers, you can feel assured that they're not going to screw you over. But you definitely need to understand the terms you're signing, because if you're used to posting your sales numbers, those may now be covered by a nondisclosure agreement you signed with the publisher.

You do give up a certain amount of freedom, and you need to be able to live with it and trust the publisher to do the best job they can for those parts you're giving up. For example, if a publisher is asking you for a change in direction about certain aspects of your game, you should seriously consider it. At least most of them know what they're talking about, and they also know what's working and what isn't (this certainly isn't the case for all of them, though). However, since games is a very subjective field, publishers do have the tendency to favor proven sets of features over other risky but innovative ones—but less so on the iOS, where publishers are more willing and able to give their developers creative freedom, if not total control over the design of the game.

In return for giving up some freedoms, they'll reward you with marketing for your game. They know the channels, and they have a direct feed to the review web sites and the press. And that's possibly another area of expertise you'll learn a lot from. The press has a certain way they like to receive and consume the information they need to write a review about your game. Your publisher knows all about it, and they'll request a few things from you that you wouldn't have considered in the first place. High-resolution artwork may be one of those things, or a one-line catchphrase that really gets players interested in your game.

If you get the chance to cooperate with a publisher, my advice is to go for it at least once, no matter how much you value your creative freedom. Afterward, you'll understand much better what you're giving up and what you're receiving in return, at least in that particular case. Whatever your experience may be, the experience alone and what you'll learn should make it worthwhile (and maybe it will be rewarding enough to do it again—but if not, you'll know why).

There are several game publishers you might want to consider contacting. Your best shot would be those who market specifically for iOS or mobile devices, and in that area two names stand out from the crowd. One is ngmoco, who published Goldfinger, We Rule, We Farm, Epic Pet Wars, and Rolando. Visit ngmoco's web site at `www.ngmoco.com`. The other is Chillingo, who has released games like Minigore, the Quest, and Knight's Rush. Their web site is `www.chillingo.com`. If you're wondering why I didn't mention Angry Birds, that's because they have a separate label for quick-and-fun games called Clickgamer. Most of their games are published through the Clickgamer label (see `www.clickgamer.com`).

Finding Freelancers

If you believe in your game and you are ready to invest money into it, you may want to get help by professional freelancers worldwide. Besides asking for jobs in the cocos2d forum itself, you can also post a job offer on one of the more popular outsourcing web sites. Likewise, you can also offer your expertise as a freelancer to employers on these sites. There are plenty of web sites offering such services, you'll even find some that can hook you up with someone close to where you live.

I'll refer you to the ones that I know work best and have a good reputation: they are eLance (`www.elance.com`) and Guru (`www.guru.com`).

They both work on the same principle. You post a job offer, which could be a small task or an entire project. Then you receive proposals from candidates, from which you can pick one or more to do the job. Once you have received, reviewed, and approved the work, the freelancers get paid. Abuse can be reported and basically locks you out of the platform, so while you need to be able to trust people you've never worked with, the risks are minimal for both parties. To start, I recommend choosing smaller tasks. Just as if you were to get into the stock market, you want to get a good feel for how this works and what can happen by starting small.

Finding Free Art and Audio

The alternative to hiring someone to do the work for you is to find the work available on the Internet (preferably free). However, be careful about anything that's "free." I'm not saying that it might have a catch, I'm warning about the common misconception that free means "can be used freely." It may not cost you anything to get an image or audio file that's free, but that doesn't tell you anything about what you're legally allowed to do with it. That's typically where a license should come into play but often doesn't. A lot of people publish their own source code, artwork, audio, and writings for free on the Internet, but forget to add a proper license file to it if the work is intended to be used by others. The problem is that by default, the author has the copyright and retains all rights to how the work can be used. If there's no explicit waiver, preferably in the form of a license, then you should not use this work (especially not in commercial products, and that includes $0.99 apps sold via the iTunes App Store).

For reference, I'd like to point you to Funplosion Labs, who has an article listing web sites where you can get free game graphics and audio. Funplosion also disclaims this with a warning about the copyright and a link to the license agreement for each web site (see `http://funplosion.com/free-assets.html`).

> **CAUTION:** Be wary of the General Public License (GPL), especially if it is used by a source code library that you want to use or integrate into a commercial app. Using GPL-licensed code in your own project requires you to open-source your own project's source code. Not just that, but anyone is subsequently given the right to use your source code, and to copy, modify, and redistribute it. Note that the Lesser General Public License (LGPL) license is not as stringent. Refer to this link for a comparison of common source code licenses: `http://developer.kde.org/documentation/licensing/licenses_summary.html`.

Finding the Tools of the Trade

Sometimes you may wish you had a tool that does just *that*, whatever *that* might be. There are times as a game developer where you need to process data, modify images, or build whole worlds—things that are tedious and error prone to do in code, or simply too time-consuming to do on your own because you'd rather focus on writing your game.

My tip is to use the Indie Game Tools web site, which collects, categorizes, and allows others to rate game design tools for independent game developers. The focus here isn't on expensive software used by professional studios, but low-cost and free solutions for about anything, from game engines to converters, from scripting languages to server technologies, from asset packages to game editors. Maintained by Robert "Robc" Charney, it's the place I go to see if there's a tool available that fits my bill. Visit the site here: `http://indiegametools.com`.

Just a minor caveat: Don't put too much weight on the ratings of individual tools. The number of ratings is very small, so there can be huge differences between similar tools, and the ratings may be biased by both unhappy users and proactive communities. You should leave your mark and add some of your own ratings so that over time the ratings become more accurate. In addition, some tools simply can't be compared by rating; they may have totally different uses, making it unfair to compare them based on their rankings on the Indie Game Tools web site.

Marketing

So, you made a game and submitted it to the App Store. Now what? How do people find your game in the first place?

The story starts at the beginning. The moment you begin working on your game should also be the starting point for your marketing efforts. Get a web site up and running, and post your development experiences and maybe some work-in-progress screenshots. That should be the first step to connect with other game developers.

In terms of the marketing and business aspects, I'd like to save you some time. The following link is to the Big List of Indie Marketing and Business Tips, and I have to say that's an understatement. You'll find most of the meaningful and intelligent articles ever written on the subject on just this one page, so be sure to check it out even if you're only mildly interested in the marketing and business aspects of indie game development. Check it out at `www.pixelprospector.com/indev/2010/08/the-big-list-of-indie-marketingand-business-tips`.

Still interested in marketing? Good, check out the free e-book Videogame Marketing and PR, written by Scott Steinberg. You can get it on the book's web site: `www.sellmorevideogames.com`.

Marketing Your Game and Your Self

If you're really not sure whether your game is going to be a success based on how much fun its going to be, one rather effective way to increase your chances is to make a game that's very presentable and colorful, and just looks like great fun in screenshots. With the low barrier to entry on mobile devices due to the low price points, a great-looking game with little in terms of play depth more often than not will outperform and outsell a complex game with multiple game modes and many hours of potential game play. It may pain some developers because it goes against everything they believe in, but it's an unavoidable fact of life. Of course, if you can combine the two and create an innovative, fun game that just looks great, the opportunities are endless.

If you browse reviews, there's one thing you should be giving a lot of attention to. The most prominently featured screenshots are always action scenes from the game, usually with a lot of things going on at the same time. This has almost become an art form; professional developers will even develop specialized tools to stage scenes where they can take the best possible action screenshots, without having to play the game and rely on luck to get it just right. Maybe you should consider that, too. So, the best artwork you can create or pay for should definitely be a priority for you, and so should making a convincing trailer for your game. Outstanding presentation is a very important buy-in to get to talking with a publisher as well.

This advice goes for your blog as well. You do have a blog, don't you? If not, start one right now! You can get a free blog on `http://wordpress.com`, and you'll learn how to work with the most popular blogging software along the way. As your blog matures, you may want to consider hosting your blog on your own server; you can do that with WordPress as well, but with a lot more options for customization through plug-ins and themes.

Your blog is an important piece for marketing yourself. The most important aspect here is that self-marketing will indirectly benefit anything you do from now on. Blogging gets you in touch with other like-minded people, who sooner or later will be willing to help you, sometimes for free. If you are really making a name for yourself in your development community, it's good news, because it could get you attention from publishers, who follow the same channels you're working in (as opposed to most of the players of your game, which you'll have to reach out to on a different level).

And since your blog should be your public face, it should be you who's talking. Don't put on a mask and try to sound like a big corporation—for example, by saying things like what you're doing is going to revolutionize the way we play games. I call that . . . a term I won't write out in this book, but I'm sure you know what I mean.

Make sure you don't come across as cocky on your blog, but likewise don't belittle yourself. You may be a beginner, but you're learning, so focus on what you've learned. The things you do learn will seem like things that millions of other developers already know, so you might wonder whether you should really blog about them. I'm familiar with these thoughts, and frankly speaking, you'll always have doubts about whether what you write is going to be of interest to others. It is, trust me. And if it isn't, no big deal. The truth is, even though there are millions of developers who may already know about what you post, there are millions more who don't, and who will be able to learn from you.

And remember to put your best skills up front and avoid blogging about your weaknesses. You may not know it all, but you can learn it. If you really want to know how multiplayer game programming can be enhanced by predicting client movements, learn about it. The web is a great resource—collect what you find, and blog about what you found and learned. Others will respect you for it. Blogging takes years of practice, so it's best to start now because it will pay off in the end—possibly in ways you can't even imagine right now.

Another important way of marketing yourself is by using Twitter. Once you have something to tell the world, you'll be happy to be able to reach out to dozens, hundreds, if not thousands of your followers at once. It's a very effective marketing tool. How to use it effectively is a matter of following simple steps. First, don't protect your tweets—it seriously limits the number of people who are going to follow you. (I certainly won't.) Then provide an interesting bio, which should include your interests, what you do, and anything else that makes you seem like an interesting person to follow. Simply using a joke, poem, or quote as your bio is a no-no. And don't forget to link to your blog! The most important thing is to tweet regularly, and tweet about things others might find interesting. Tweeting only about yourself and your products (or just retweeting other's posts) isn't going to convince many people to follow you.

Public Relations and Press Releases

If you work alone and you don't want to cooperate with a publisher, hiring a public relations (PR) firm or agent to give yourself and your game a better chance in the market may be a wise decision. But it could also be downright stupid and pointless. In the latter case, it's usually not the fault of whoever is doing the PR, it's a matter of understanding the benefits of PR—what it takes to make it work effectively—and assessing whether it's worth spending thousands of dollars on.

As an independent developer, you are likely to have a very limited budget. Even entry-level prices for PR agents are going to make your jaw drop to the floor. If that's the case, walk away and get back to working on your game. Your gut reaction is correct.

Now, if you already have a game out there and it's presentable, and you've earned not just money but also some influence with the people around you, things may be a little different. Perhaps you have some money to spare, you've learned a lot from your first game, your second one is even better, and you already have players waiting for it to come out. Can you give it a boost with the help of professional PR? In this case it's more likely.

If you take on the help of a PR agent, you should definitely try to find one who has a track record of working for the game industry—preferably with independent game developers and the mobile games niche. They're not easy to find, so ask around. Using a PR agent who isn't into game development is a waste of time and money—you need to have PR with the ability to reach out to your game's target audience. But most of all, the deciding factor should really be your game.

If you know you have something special, and testers tell you so, and the game just looks gorgeous, then investing a few thousand dollars in PR might be a good choice. PR wants game reviewers to write about your game and game development sites to take notice of your special abilities. If these aren't clearly visible, professional PR won't be able to make a big difference. PR works best if you can provide gorgeous screenshots and an intriguing, funny, and captivating trailer movie.

How do you know if your game is something special? By asking the people who wouldn't hesitate to tell you what they don't like. Family and friends are typically too kind to provide the sometimes harsh criticism needed to improve a game. You should ask on forums for private beta testers and provide them with an appetizer, which could be a screenshot or a description of your game's special features, so that they'll be more interested to try out your game. How you deal with criticism and feature requests, and generally how you interact with your testers, is also a matter of PR. Dealing with user feedback, and specifically criticism, is a vital skill you should hone as early as possible.

But who's to say you can't try for yourself first? There are press release services specifically for independent developers, and they cost a fraction of what a professional PR agent would charge you. And writing a press release isn't that hard if you follow the rules. The following press release services tap into exactly the right channels for game players and developers. The hottest candidates are the Indie Press Release Service, at `www.gamerelease.net`, and the Game Press Release Submission Service at Mitorah Games, at `www.mitorahgames.com/Submit-Game-Press-Release.html`.

Unsurprisingly, both services are run by independent developers themselves. Specifically, Juuso Hietalahti created the Indie Press Release Service and also runs the very insightful `www.gameproducer.net` blog. This blog is especially interesting if you want to learn more about production and marketing aspects.

You should also consider the Games Press web site, which is frequented by game journalists worldwide (see `www.gamespress.com/about_howtosubmit.asp`).

Where to Find Help

Whether you are facing a technical problem that you can't solve on your own or need more people to work on your game, there are places where you can get help. In addition, if you're looking for art, audio, or tools, I know just the places where you can find what you're looking for, or at least where you can begin your search.

One important tip: If you get stuck and you don't know what else to try, it can help to just write down what the problem is, what you're trying to achieve, and what you've done so far. Most of the time it frees your mind to think of things you haven't tried yet, and more often than not it leads to a solution. If not, you now have a summary that you can post to a forum or Q&A site, which will help you get a good answer more quickly. The art of asking questions is all about making it easy for others to answer them.

Cocos2d Home Page

This may seem obvious, but if you have a question related to cocos2d, you should stop by and join the cocos2d community in the forum: `http://cocos2d-iphone.org/forum`.

In the cocos2d forum you can ask about anything related to cocos2d. It has subforums for hot topics like audio programming, physics engines, social networks, and ads, as well as a general forum for Objective-C and iPhone SDK–related questions. For the most part, the cocos2d community is friendly and very helpful, and a lot of great example code and development stories have been shared on the forum.

Before asking questions, be sure to search both the forum and the official cocos2d documentation wiki: `http://cocos2d-iphone.org/wiki/doku.php`.

In addition, you can announce your newly released game in the cocos2d games forum. Don't forget to also add it to the list of games made with cocos2d. You can do this on the cocos2d Games page: `www.cocos2d-iphone.org/games`.

Stack Exchange Network

Forums are a great way for communities to interact with each other. But as such, they tend to get a little chatty, and searching for a specific answer can be cumbersome because the forum's content isn't strictly limited to solving problems.

That's exactly where Q&A web sites like Stack Exchange shine. You go in, ask a particular question, and get answers. Since the focus is on Q&A, it's easier to find existing answers. And if you really like a question or answer, you can vote it up so it will be listed higher on search results.

I'm regularly amazed by the show of expertise from contributors on the Stack Exchange network. This is in part thanks to the built-in badge and points system, making it very rewarding to both ask interesting questions and write thoughtful, in-depth answers. The Stack Exchange network is comprised of several free Q&A web sites, the most popular and my personal favorite being `http://stackoverflow.com`, which is about programming questions in general.

You won't find as many questions about cocos2d on Stack Overflow as you will on the official cocos2d forum, but the questions on Stack Overflow are good ones, and almost all of them get good answers. There's a bit of confusion about the use of search tags on the site, with both cocos2d and cocos2d-iphone used to tag questions regarding the iPhone version of cocos2d. This can be attributed to the success of cocos2d for iPhone, in that it has become synonymous with the name cocos2d itself. Use these two links to find all the cocos2d for iPhone–related questions on Stack Overflow:

- `http://stackoverflow.com/questions/tagged/cocos2d`
- `http://stackoverflow.com/questions/tagged/cocos2d-iphone`

Stack Exchange is expanding as a Q&A web sites network. One of the latest additions is the Game Development Q&A web site. On this site you can ask general game programming questions and about anything game development–related in general, including design, marketing, and sales. Check out the Game Development Stack Exchange site at `http://gamedev.stackexchange.com`.

Tutorials and FAQs

There are plenty of tutorials for cocos2d on the Web, but one tutorial writer clearly stands out from the crowd: Ray Wenderlich. He has written over a dozen cocos2d tutorials and published them on his web site, at `www.raywenderlich.com/tag/cocos2d`. Besides cocos2d tutorials, on this site you'll also find other highly interesting iPhone

SDK–related tips and tricks. In at least one particular case this is also helpful for cocos2d developers, where Ray explains how to save and load your app's data. This can be applied to saving and loading games as well (see `www.raywenderlich.com/1914/how-to-save-your-app-data-with-nscoding-and-nsfilemanager`).

Then there's the wonderful Coconut College. It provides entry-level tutorials and a hand-holding approach. The web site's clean and professional design is both inviting and to the point. The author goes by the nickname cjl and calls himself the Dean of Coconut College, but otherwise keeps a very low profile. Check out Coconut College at `www.coconutcollege.net`, and if you do want to reach out to the author, you can try his cocos2d forum profile: `www.cocos2d-iphone.org/forum/profile/49`.

The knowledge base on my Learn & Master cocos2d web site (`www.learn-cocos2d.com/knowledge-base`) hosts my own tutorials and FAQs. Currently I offer an Xcode tutorial, which allows you to keep the cocos2d files separate, in order to be able to update cocos2d more easily. Another tutorial is about Hiero, the bitmap font editor, and includes a number of FAQs. This site is also where I blog about topics and post links of general interest to cocos2d developers.

Famous Last Words

When I started the Learn & Master cocos2d web site in May 2010, my goal was to provide much-needed detailed documentation for the cocos2d game engine in the form of tutorials and FAQs. I had been working with cocos2d since May 2009, and it hurt me to see that one year had passed and developers were still struggling with the same concepts, simply because the documentation did not get the same dedicated effort that was put into the game engine itself.

Within a month after the Learn & Master cocos2d web site went live, I was given the chance to write this book you're holding in your hands. I poured a lot of time and effort into it—over four months working on it full time, writing code, and learning a lot more about cocos2d than I already knew. My goal was to write a book that was unlike other game development book by taking notice of what cocos2d developers are asking and what they are having problems with. It's up to you to decide whether I've succeeded.

Looking back, I have to say the book is now basically the print version of what I had in mind for the Learn & Master cocos2d web site, although it came together in a much shorter time frame. I hope you have enjoyed reading this book as much as I did writing it. Thank you for reading!

Conclusion

I hope you enjoyed learning about some of the surrounding technologies that may be useful for creating your game, including where to get help and where to find royalty-free game art and audio.

As mentioned in this chapter, marketing and public relations will definitely need to be on your table if you want to actually earn a living from making games. I've only scratched the surface of those here, but it should help you get started.

Finally, remember to buy and use other cocos2d games in order to learn from them. As a game developer, you need to be constantly playing new games to feed your creativity with new ideas, and you also need to learn what players are saying about other developers' games. Improving your knowledge of how games are made is just as important—purchasing one or several commercial cocos2d source code projects is certainly going to be a wise investment.

This book ends here, but your journey has just begun. I'm sure you'll still have lots of questions, and for that reason I've created a Questions & Answers page on my web site: `www.learn-cocos2d.com/questions-and-answers`. Feel free to stop by and ask me anything about cocos2d, the book, my Starterkit, marketing, publishers, Xcode, Objective-C, or anything else related to game development. I'm looking forward to hear from you, and I'll be happy to answer your questions . . . all of them.

Index

B

Printed by Publishers' Graphics LLC USA
DBT131201.20.07.24